LANGUAGES

of the State

Narrating Native Histories

BRET GUSTAFSON

NEW LANGUAGES *of the State*

*Indigenous Resurgence and the
Politics of Knowledge in Bolivia*

Duke University Press
Durham and London
2009

© 2009 Duke University Press

All rights reserved

Printed in the United States of America on acid-free paper ∞

Designed by Heather Hensley

Typeset in Monotype Bembo by Keystone Typesetting, Inc.

Library of Congress Cataloging-in-Publication Data appear on the last printed page of this book.

For my father Ralph,

and for *Yari*,

who both gave without

asking in return.

Contents

About the Series

Narrating Native Histories aims to foster a rethinking of the ethical, methodological, and conceptual frameworks within which we locate our work on Native histories and cultures. We seek to create a space for effective and ongoing conversations between North and South, Natives and non-Natives, academics and activists, throughout the Americas and the Pacific region. We are committed to complicating and transgressing the disciplinary and epistemological boundaries of established academic discourses on Native peoples.

This series encourages symmetrical, horizontal, collaborative, and auto-ethnographies; work that recognizes Native intellectuals, cultural interpreters, and alternative knowledge producers within broader academic and intellectual worlds; projects that decolonize the relationship between orality and textuality; narratives that productively work the tensions between the norms of Native cultures and the requirements for evidence in academic circles; and analyses that contribute to an understanding of Native peoples' relationships with nation-states, including histories of expropriation and exclusion as well as projects for autonomy and sovereignty.

New Languages of the State is an exemplary ethnography of indigenous activism in Latin America. Bret Gustafson insightfully probes the discourses of indigenous activists and of the Bolivian state that underpin bilingual education efforts in lowland Bolivia. Moving deftly from macro-political analysis to pan-Guarani organizers' use of interculturalist educational philosophies, between activist and government interpretations of interculturalism, and from the texts of official documents to the practice of local activists, Gustafson traces the movement from interculturalism to decolonization under the Evo Morales government. Motivated first and foremost by a deep solidarity with the Guaraní educational cause, *New Languages* is at once the product of collaboration between anthropologist and social movement, and an attempt at a reasoned critique of indigenous efforts.

Acknowledgments

I have followed bilingual intercultural education and indigenous resurgence in Bolivia since 1992 through several years of extended residence and field-work and frequent return visits. This book draws on this experience—in part collaborative work, in part anthropological study. Over these fifteen years, I worked primarily with an indigenous movement, the Assembly of the Guarani People (APG). I also did short-term teaching and research with development agencies, state offices, and other indigenous organizations. I therefore write from the position of academic anthropology and from a stance of critical engagement with indigenous movements and their state and development network allies. In this book, I negotiate this position by attempting to objectively portray facts, words, and events tied to the politics of knowledge and indigenous movements, and by making clear—without, I hope, undue self-absorption—my own sympathies and biases. I apologize in advance to those *compañeros* and interlocutors under scrutiny, but I turn the ethnographic light on people of all sorts, indigenous, criollo, gringo, and otherwise, hoping for a fair portrayal and, in a small way, the decolonization of our discipline. I hope this book will document a crucial segment of Bolivian indigenous history and the country's pursuit for a distinct social, cultural, and economic order. If it provides a source of reflection for future research, activism, and change, all the better.

The impetus behind this book dates to my undergraduate studies at Tulane University. R. McKenna Brown, Linda Curcio-Nagy, Judith Maxwell, and Maureen Shea encouraged engaged research and a fascination with Latin American social movements. They started me on a journey that began in Guatemala and ended in Bolivia. After my first stint in Bolivia (1992–94), my graduate studies at Harvard and continued fieldwork benefited from the support of David Maybury-Lewis, Sally Falk Moore, and Kay Warren. Begoña Aretxaga, Steve Caton, William Fisher, Kenneth George, Michael Herzfeld, Ted Macdonald, Ben Penglase, María Clemencia Ramirez, Sarah

Robinson, Mary Steedly, and Stanley Tambiah also shaped my thinking. Along the way, I owe thanks to others who read chapters or gave critiques or encouragement: Lesley Bartlett, Carol Benson and her colleagues at the Center for the Study of Bilingualism at Stockholm University, Manuel Contreras, Jason Cross, James Dunkerley, Arturo Escobar, María Elena García, Lesley Gill, Daniel Goldstein, Merilee Grindle, David Guss, Charles Hale, Kevin Healy, Jean Jackson, Joshua Kirshner, Erick Langer, Brooke Larson, Aurolyn Luykx, Walter Mignolo, Elizabeth Monasterios, Harry Patrinos, Joanne Rappaport, Helena Reutersward, Javier Sanjinés, Marcia Stephenson, Kay Warren, and mi querida Bolivian cultural interpreter—on-demand, Claret Vargas. Joanne Rappaport provided crucial support and inspiration. Catalina Laserna and her students generously commented on the entire manuscript. Fellow students of Guarani country—Jordi Benería, Isabelle Combés, Kathleen Lowrey, and Nancy Postero—shared experiences that nourished this work. In Cambridge, Wren Fournier and Pam Summa gave writing advice. At Washington University in St. Louis, Richard Smith, John Bowen, Geoff Childs, Mabel Moraña, Jim Wertsch, and the Department of Anthropology offered support during the final writing. Andrea Cuff provided research assistance. Grants from Harvard University, Washington University in St. Louis, the National Science Foundation, and Fulbright-IIE supported this work at various points. Work with and for UNICEF-Bolivia, the Bolivian Ministry of Education, and PROEIB-Andes funded collaborations with the Guarani and with Andean bilingual education activists. Julia Paley, whose work in Chile influenced my own, was a generous reader of the manuscript. I thank her and an anonymous reviewer for their insights. Finally, I thank Valerie Milholland, my editor at Duke, for her energetic support, and the editors of the Narrating Native Histories series. I am honored to have been included in this initiative. G. Neal McTighe and Petra Dreiser were skilled, patient, and thorough editors whom I thank for guiding me and the text to its final form.

In Bolivia many people offered knowledge and friendship over the years. These include Xavier Albó, Amalia Anaya, Lucia D'Emilio, Fernando Garcés, Carmen Lucas, Antonieta Medeiros, Sonia Noriega, Fernando Prada, and Carmen "Beba" de Urioste. My Aymara teacher Vitaliano Huanca and the linguists Felix Layme and Pedro Apala helped me find my way to the Guarani. Celia Miranda began teaching me Guarani. The Jesuit expert on Guarani Bartomeu Meliá and the Franciscan Father Ivan Nasini gave encouragement in Camiri. I owe a special thanks to Luis Enrique López and Mónica Sahonero, much-cherished supporters over many years. In La Paz, Tomás Robles and his wife Nora Mengoa continue to provide a surrogate family during my travels. Tomás and Nora deserve much of the credit for the story told here.

The Guarani and their non-Guarani allies also opened their lives to me. I hope this text does justice to them. In Camiri, the APG and the Mboarakuaa Guasu (Guarani Education Council) were key supporters. The captaincy of Alto y Bajo Izozog in Santa Cruz and La Brecha, the Council of Captains of Chuquisaca at Monteagudo, and the captaincy of APG-Itïka at Entre Ríos were also welcoming. Guarani value generosity and deplore stingy people who are *jäkatëi*, of a "useless head." While my continuous taking of knowledge threatened to place me in the latter category, I thank the generosity of many who asked nothing in return. These include Elsa Aireyu, Herlan Aireyu, Eriberto "Pachin" Aireyu, Rogelio Aireyu, Vicenta Abapori, Valentín Abayu, Bonifacio Barrientos, José Barrientos, Enrique Camargo, Edgar and Sergio Chávez, Fanor Chávez, Silvia Chumiray, Guido Chumiray, Julio Chumiray, Mateo Chumiray, Miguel Cuellar, Calixto Guachama, Marcelino Ibañez, Arukayu Katuire, Geromo Katuire, Mbarandai Machirope, Marcia Mandepora, Ceferino Manuel, Sabino Manuel, Darío Ñanduresa, Valentín Ñanduresa, Boni Rivero, Marcelino Robles, Felipe Román, Rubena Velásquez, Ismael Velásquez, José Domingo Véliz, and Angel Yandura. The faculty of Camiri's teacher training institute, INSPOC, karai and Guarani alike, always provided warm welcomes and *despedidas*. Clemente Baure, UNICEF's Guarani driver in Camiri, was a storyteller, companion, and invaluable source of intellectual and practical assistance. Lucy Gutiérrez, an Isoceña Guarani, and Paolo Malfatti, her Italian husband, put me up and put up with me in Camiri in 1998. Lucy, deeply knowledgeable in her language, also worked with me in Guarani text production, and I learned much from her. Thanks also to the Sisters of the Presentation at Entre Ríos in O'Connor Province. Led in 1993 by the hearty Iowan Maura "Hermana Maura" McCarthy, they, Renán Sánchez, and Noé Cesar Quisberth facilitated my work and contributed much to the Guarani movement.

In the midst of drought and scarcity, my hosts in the village of Itavera demonstrated that they were true *mborerekua iya*, masters of generosity. This text is a feeble gesture of reciprocity, and I hope that in some way the work we carried out has contributed to their lives. I thank them all and apologize to those who tired of my queries. Save that of Airase, real names are not used here out of respect for their privacy.

Many people central to this story have passed on, and I offer a modest tribute here. David Maybury-Lewis, whose support of indigenous rights inspired my early interest in anthropology, passed away as this book went to the publisher. While anthropology has changed between our generations, I learned a great deal about South American ethnology from David. He and his wife Pia were a much-loved outpost of humor and warmth during graduate school. In graduate school, I also learned much from my friend and fellow student Julie Goldman as she battled the cancer that took her life. Her acerbic critique of power's dehumanizing effects and her insights on neo-liberalism drawn from work with Chilean fruit packers shaped this work. In Guarani country, the *capitanes* Mateo Chumiray and Rogelio Aireyu, always dropping pithy bits of wisdom and ribald humor for the young gringo, are also gone now. They were of the old leaders, true knowledge masters, and I thank them. In Itavera the elder grandmother I call Yari, who speaks at various points herein, also passed away in 2003. She chided me saying, "I do not need people crying over me when I am gone." At the risk of annoying her, I remember her for the words she shared. In the summer of 2006 Itavera also lost Airase, my host there whose story I tell in chapter 3. My wife and I arrived ten days after he died, to cry alongside his keening wife, daughters, sons, and relatives. His machete, axe, and hoe, his tobacco and coca bags, his water bottle, his hat, and his knife in its leather sheath, objects ingrained in my memory of his generosity, were laid carefully over his grave inside his house. He often told me, "They will remember what I did for this community!" and perhaps this book will help make that true. As I finished it, we also lost my own father, suddenly, tragically, and too soon to make sense. He would be glad to see it done. To my wife Patty, my mother Judith, my brother Kurt, and my children, thank you for your love and patience.

Acronyms

EDUCATION POLICIES AND INSTITUTIONS

EIB   Educación Intercultural Bilingüe
(Bilingual Intercultural Education)
(state policy, 1994–present)

PEIB   Project on Bilingual Intercultural Education
(pilot phase, 1989–94)

ETARE   Equipo Técnico de Apoyo a la Reforma Educativa
(Technical Support Team for Educational Reform)

INSPOC   Instituto Normal Superior Pluriétnico del Oriente y
Chaco Boliviano
(Pluriethnic Superior Teachers' Institute of the Bolivian
East and Chaco)

MEC-D   Ministerio de Educación, Cultura, y Deportes
(Ministry of Education, Culture, and Sport)

MECS   Ministerio de Educación y Culturas
(Ministry of Education and Cultures) (after 2005)

PGFD   Programa Guaraní de Formación Docente
(Guarani Teacher Training Program)
(after 2000: INSPOCB)

SIL   Summer Institute of Linguistics / Wycliffe Bible
Translators

NGOS, AID AGENCIES, BANKS

APCOB   Apoyo para el Campesino-Indígena del Oriente
Boliviano
(Aid for the Peasant-Indian of the Bolivian East)

CIPCA   Comisión de Investigación y Promoción del
Campesinado
(Commission for the Investigation and Promotion
of the Peasantry)

DANIDA   Danish International Development Agency

GTZ   German Technical Aid Agency

IADB	Inter-American Development Bank
SIDA	Swedish International Development Agency
TEKO-Guaraní	Taller de Educación y Comunicación Guarani (Workshop for Guarani Education and Communication)
UNICEF	United Nations Infant and Children's Educational Fund
UNESCO	United Nations Education, Science and Culture Organization

MAJOR POLITICAL PARTIES

ADN	Acción Democrática Nacionalista (Nationalist Democratic Action) (right)
MAS	Movimiento al Socialismo (Movement to Socialism) (left/indigenist)
MBL	Movimiento Bolivia Libre (Free Bolivia Movement) (center left)
MIR	Movimiento Izquierdista Revolucionario (Leftist Revolutionary Movement) (right)
MNR	Movimiento Nacionalista Revolucionario (Nationalist Revolutionary Movement) (right)
PODEMOS	Poder Democrático Social (Social Democratic Power) (right)

On Languages and Labels

The Guarani people and language in Bolivia are often called Chiriguano in academic literature. The term *Chiriguano* originated in colonial myth, and I see no reason to replicate it for academic purposes. Guarani call themselves Guarani. They call their language Guarani (*guaraní*), "our language" (*ñandeñee*) or "mbɨa language" (*mbɨa iñee*). I use the alphabet approved by the Assembly of Guarani People in 1989 and spelling conventions adopted in 1997. There are three dialect regions (Ava, ɨsoso, Simba) and some spelling debates. I use the unified form as a nod to the unity of the Guarani. Bolivian Guarani is closely related to indigenous Mbya, Chiripá, and the Guarani languages of Paraguay, Argentina, and Brazil. It is also related to Paraguayan *yopará*, or Guarani criollo, the most widely spoken of these languages. The orthographic unification of these languages is under discussion, but it has yet to become reality.

The pronunciation of Guarani vowels *a*, *e*, *i*, *o*, and *u* is like that in Spanish. The high central vowel *y*, written "ɨ" ("y" in Paraguay) is a bit tighter and higher than the "oo" sound in *soot*. All vowels occur in nasal forms, written "ä," "ë," "ï," "ö," "ü," and "ɨ̈." For example, *tëta* (house, community, nation), is pronounced "tenta"; and *tüpa* (god, deity), is pronounced "toompa." The *j* is like Spanish *j* (written "h" in Paraguay): *jëe* (sweet or tasty). The *y* is similar to the Spanish *y* or *ñ* when nasalized (written "j" in Paraguay): *yemboe* or *ñemboe*, (school learning, knowledge).

Though perhaps tiresome for readers, I include Guarani and Spanish words and texts to highlight aural, aesthetic, and semantic textures of linguistic difference that are locally significant. Words frequently repeated are used without translation. For example, *arakuaa*, Guarani knowledge; *yemboe*, school knowledge; *capitán* captain; and *kereɨmba*, warrior. I indicate word origins by language with Q (Quechua), A (Aymara), S (Spanish), or G (Guarani). A glossary follows chapter seven.

Labels are contentious things. I use *Guarani country*, much as I would

Indian country in the United States, to refer to southeastern Bolivia, home to the Guarani (see map on page 2). This area does not constitute an official or monoethnic territory, but a multiethnic mosaic shaped by Guarani history and language. Non-Guarani Bolivians also live here. Guarani see this entire region as their main field of action, and the transformation of their subordinate space therein defines their political agenda.

I use labels for people that reflect the shifting positioning of the story. When writing in and about Guarani country, I use *karai* for non-Guarani, Spanish-speaking Bolivians, whites, mestizos, or Europeans, as the Guarani do. It is not pejorative. Karai who speak Guarani use the term *karai*. Those who do not speak Guarani call themselves *cristianos* (Christians), *blancos* (whites), *hispanos* (Spanish-speaking), *mestizos* (mixed), or more often use regional labels of geographic origin like *chapaco, camba, chaqueño, valluno,* and so on. In eastern Bolivia, Guarani, karai, and regionalist labels are distinguished from *kolla,* which refers to Andean Bolivians of indigenous and nonindigenous descent.

When writing in and from the Andes I refer to nonindigenous Bolivians as *criollos* (Aymara and Quechua call them *q'ara*). Criollos sometimes call themselves white, *hispano, mestizo,* or *kolla.* I use the terms *indigenous, people, Indian, indio, indígena, pueblo originario,* and *native* to refer to Amerindian Bolivians. My usage is certainly not pejorative, though I indicate when these appellations may reflect locally charged meanings.

ETHNOGRAPHIC ARTICULATIONS
IN AN AGE OF PACHAKUTI

> There are two modes of language use in the schools: (1) Monolingual: in Spanish with the secondary study of a national indigenous language [*lengua nacional originaria*]; (2) Bilingual: in a national indigenous language as the first language and Spanish as the second language.
> —*Bolivian Education Reform Law #1565, July 7, 1994*

In 1994, amid rising indigenous mobilization and a government turn toward free-market policies, the Bolivian congress signed a national education reform into law. The reform proposed to restructure Bolivian schooling in tandem with a wider process of neoliberal structural adjustment.[1] The plan included a controversial component called bilingual intercultural education (EIB, from the Spanish *educación intercultural bilingüe*) that promoted the introduction of indigenous languages alongside Spanish in public elementary schools in indigenous regions. That children should study in their own language—pedagogical common sense and a human right enshrined in global charters—does not make for a radical idea. Yet in Bolivia EIB constituted a radical departure from the longer history of forced *castellanización*, the Spanishization of indigenous peoples that characterized Bolivian public schooling as it expanded following the 1952 revolution. EIB echoed the government's turn toward so-called interculturalism, a new buzzword that found some support among neoliberal reformers who saw the recognition of cultural pluralism as a way to talk about citizen difference while dismantling structures of politics that arose from the class-centered paradigms of centralized corporatist rule. Also a demand of indigenous movements who were pursuing distinctly non-neoliberal visions of collective rights, EIB came into being as a paradoxical—and conflictive—convergence between free-market

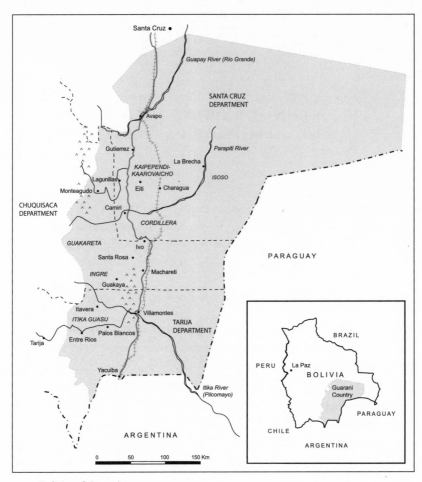

MAP Bolivia and Guarani country

reformism and indigenous struggles for territory and equality. Between the emerging language of neoliberal governance and the literal and symbolic languages of indigenous struggle, EIB unsettled long-standing ideas about relations among schooling, power, and indigeneity in the country, bringing a new politics of knowledge to the center of struggles over the state itself.

Over the next ten years EIB was implemented to different degrees and effects across indigenous regions of the country, including the territory of the Guarani people whose story is the focus of this book. EIB sparked conflicts from village schools to government offices and was alternately embraced and distrusted by indigenous organizations, foreign donors, school-reform proponents, nonindigenous school teachers, and nonindigenous Bolivians. Detractors saw it as ethnic fundamentalism or foolish romanticism. Critics—including some indigenous people—viewed it as a neoliberal plot to control indigenous people through new forms of exclusion. Yet EIB also flourished in many regions, unsettling racist paradigms of schooling and creating new political languages, actors, and platforms for movement expansion. Through the upheavals of the early 2000s and to the present moment, as an indigenous-led national-popular regime confronts new forms of racism and reaction among a conservative elite minority, EIB in various forms has remained at the center of indigenous platforms to decolonize schooling and the state. Securing the right to know and speak in different ways—with corresponding rights to reorder and rethink relations of power—remains an unresolved battle tied to the changing foundations of the Bolivian state.

As in many other countries targeted by structural adjustment during the 1990s, education reform came to Bolivia as a component of hybrid development prescriptions tied to foreign aid. These contradictorily promoted a limited state role in primary schooling in the name of poverty reduction and social inclusion while pushing market policies that exacerbated inequality and exclusion. Bolivia thus experienced a global development trend shared with other countries. Yet Bolivia is also a unique case that shaped education reform in particular ways. Transnational intellectual networks allied with assertive indigenous political and intellectual movements across the Andes were largely behind the push for EIB, making it, at least in part, its own hybrid regional project. On the other hand, the limited acquiescence to EIB by neoliberal ideologues can be explained in part by their attempts to undercut teachers unions in Bolivia, which rank among the most militant in Latin America. Pulled between the symbols of class struggle and corporatist rule, the indigenous push for decolonization, and attempts to impose new standardizing knowledges amenable to market-oriented rule, EIB brings into relief quandaries faced by many countries, "dealing with the colonial legacy on one hand whilst simultaneously engaging with the demands posed by rapid globalization on the other" (Crossley and Tikly 2004:151).

Many top-down studies of international education reform, research often allied with the interests of elites themselves, depart from an acritical, pro-reformist perspective, focusing on successful strategies for implementing reforms or measures of evaluation. Others, usually from the bottom up, broadly attack school reform (and EIB) as an extension of neoliberalism, dismissing it as a privatizing and Westernizing conspiracy to rule teachers, Indians, or both.[2] Both perspectives are limited by an institution-centered approach that highlights surface forms (policies, statistics, textbooks, or classrooms) while detaching multilayered reform politics from the heterogeneous social fields in which it comes to ground. I came to education as an ethnographer of the state, development, and social movements and thus approach school reform and EIB much like the Guarani did—as an emergent field of encounter and conflict that articulated with their particular histories in ways often radically distinct from other indigenous movements and the lives of Bolivian political elites. I thus tell several stories about schooling and EIB, programs at once tied to a decadent hegemonic project, engaging the sympathies of progressive nonindigenous elites and intellectuals, sparking the fascination of foreign donors, and serving as a flashpoint and platform for popular and indigenous movement agendas.

My questions fall into two areas. First, I explore how school reform played out as a struggle over the (de)legitimation of inequality amid shifting strategies of elite rule and contested narratives of the past and future trajectories of the Bolivian nation-state. This entails asking how schooling is linked to the meaning and practice of authority and citizenship rights; how reformists and their opponents contest control over the production of legitimate knowledge as an individual and collective vehicle of self-transformation and sociopolitical change; and how school reform contributed to the transformation of the symbolic, institutional, and territorial forms of the state. These questions are familiar to students of education politics who seek to understand how schooling—beyond the walls of classrooms and schools— articulates with contests over sovereignty, territory, and authority, in short, with the nature of the state itself.[3]

Second, building on the visions of indigenous movements, I ask in a related way how EIB in particular articulated with indigenous and non-indigenous alliances seeking to dismantle the coloniality of power in Bolivia.[4] The coloniality of power operates through racialized discourses about knowledges, languages, and their human bearers inherited from Bolivia's colonial past and institutionalized in juridical, territorial, administrative, and political forms. Coloniality also operates in quotidian and formal discourses about schooling and in day-to-day ways of speaking about peoples' (unequal) rights to speak and claim full humanity and a place in Bolivian society. This is, to be sure, also a question of inequality and the state. Yet phrasing the question in terms of coloniality draws attention to epistemic and linguistic inequality as core components of political and economic inequality.[5] State technocrats, at least until Evo Morales's election in 2005, rarely used the word *decolonize* to talk about state change and bilingual education, although indigenous intellectuals and leaders certainly did. In dialogue with this longer history of indigenous movement struggle, I thus consider what decolonization might mean in Bolivia and Latin America, whether and how EIB plays a role therein, and what implications these schooling politics might have in relation to wider Andean indigenous movement proposals to create a "plurinational state." Some background on this book and the wider context of schooling and movement politics will help further elucidate the significance of these questions.

BETWEEN NEOLIBERAL UTOPIA AND ANDEAN PACHAKUTI

I arrived in Bolivia for the first time in January of 1992, the five hundredth year of what many indigenous people call the European invasion. I hoped to witness a dramatic indigenous resurgence, imagining that the arrival of this historic date might spark a millenarian rupture with the past. Instead I found Bolivia in a frenzy of free-market reformism. Development banks based in the United States, led by the International Monetary Fund (IMF) were pursuing their own utopian rupture, assisting Bolivian elites as they turned away from state-led corporatism toward market liberalization. Launched in 1985, the neoliberal turn promoted a managerial, individually oriented form of market-friendly governance in the name of growth. Neoliberal technocrats, backed by American economists like Jeffrey Sachs, introduced a new language of authority in which state-led development and narratives of nationalism, anti-imperialism, and social liberation were out. The message that poverty reduction would come from free markets, individualist striving, efficiency, decentralization, and competition was in.

By 1992 neoliberalism's effects were already becoming clear. Downsizing and privatization had pared down the state apparatus. Hyperinflation had been stamped out, a success touted by reformists. Yet government cutbacks had also led to the massive dislocation of workers. Discontent spread among labor, teachers', and miners' unions. People decried the "damned laws" of decree 21060, the legal charter of structural adjustment. There were frequent protest marches in the streets of La Paz, and I often heard the hollow pop of police tear-gas canisters alternating with the boom of giant roman candles and dynamite, the preferred noisemakers of popular movements. The invisible hand of the market, were it to work at all, still depended on the heavy hand of the state.

Market liberalization also depended on infusions of welfare, both to those suffering the effects of reform and to the state itself. To this end, a flood of foreign aid arrived with projects to fill in the gaps in social services, stave off protest, and ensure the running of the government.[6] With one of the lowest per capita gross domestic products (GDPs) in Latin America and a picturesque population of colorfully dressed yet extremely poor indigenous people, Bolivia attracted development projects and nongovernment organizations (NGOs) that embraced interculturalism as a new way of talking about poverty and exclusion. Many in the state-dependent middle class faced a crisis of employment and recast themselves as development consultants, competing for jobs in NGOs and aid projects. By the early 1990s Bolivia had become an aid-dependent state, with donors from Swiss to Swedes and Americans to Japanese arriving to help the poor, pursue good governance, or promote social inclusion. Everything from latrines to garbage trucks and schoolbooks were stamped with the seal of a foreign country or aid agency. The liberalizing rhetoric ignored this contradiction between market freedom and aid dependence. State sovereignty was an illusion.

Yet beyond the flurry of structural adjustments and foreign aid, other histories were unfolding. Bolivia's indigenous and popular movements possessed deep reserves of collective memory imbued with an intensely felt sense of their own unfinished transformative agendas. Neoliberalism had weakened organized labor. Yet indigenous movements, as I detail in the chapters that follow, had expanded through the 1980s, merging ethnocultural claims with narratives of class struggle, the defense of national sovereignty, and demands for the decolonization of the state. Aymara and Quechua peoples of the Andes have traditionally been the main protagonists of indigenous-peasant struggles, yet newly assertive indigenous movements also arose in eastern Bolivia, including the Assembly of Guarani People (APG, from Asamblea del Pueblo Guaraní). By 1992, with indigenous peoples at the fore, Bolivian social movements were pursuing new strategies to re-articulate their own visions of state transformation.

While Ecuador, the southern highlands of Peru, and southern Mexico also have significant indigenous populations, Bolivia, like Guatemala, has a solid indigenous majority (around 60 percent). Quechua, Aymara, Guarani, and thirty other native peoples disproportionately suffer poverty, racism, and political marginality, a pattern shared across Latin America.[7] Though indigenous peoples have organized politically since before the arrival of the first Spaniard, since the 1950s their identity as indigenous peoples was framed primarily through the language of class (as a rural peasantry) and the structures of corporatist representation (as peasant unions subordinate to elite-led parties). Yet by the 1990s indigenous people *as indigenous peoples* had moved to the fore: Latin America was witnessing what the anthropologist Xavier Albó (1991) called the "return of the Indian."

The state and donor embrace of interculturalism formed a response to this resurgent indigeneity. Interculturalism took off in 1993 with the election of the free-market reformer President Gonzalo "Goni" Sánchez de Lozada and his running mate, the Aymara Victor Hugo Cárdenas (Albó 1994; Van Cott 2000). As with multiculturalism in Europe and America, official understandings of interculturalism in Latin America offered a way of talking about inclusion while *not* talking about racism, epistemic alterity, or class inequality. Members of the neoliberal elite like Goni invoked interculturalism to suggest that market-led growth was compatible with the recognition of Bolivia's mostly indigenous poor as bearers of distinct cultural traditions. Yet this tentative acknowledgment of ethnic collectivities (Aymara, Guarani, Quechua, etc.) did not embrace robust indigenous claims. It was a limited interculturalism congruent with the decentralizing logic of reform and attempts to channel indigenous movements into forms amenable to the market turn (Gustafson 2002). Indigenous and popular movement understandings of interculturalism differed from this official vision. As events played out over the years, it was clear that the latter could not easily absorb the former.

One of my memorable moments in 1992 occurred on October 12, Columbus Day. There was a massive indigenous gathering in La Paz that coincided with similar events across the Americas. Thousands of Aymara and Quechua and contingents of Guarani and eastern Bolivian indigenous peoples gathered in La Paz's San Francisco Plaza and called for a *pachakuti* that would overturn the existing order of things.[8] Their goal was to launch an Assembly of Nationalities that would unify indigenous and popular organizations. I asked two Aymara men in the crowd if I could take their picture (see figure 1). One wore dark Ray-Bans and an Andean *chullu* stocking cap. He held a *wiphala*, the flag symbolizing Andean plurinational indigeneity. The other wore a fedora and held a cardboard sign with a poster tacked to it, reading:

WANTED: CHRISTOPHER COLUMBUS.
Great thief. Genocidist. Racist.
Initiator of the destruction of cultures.
Rapist, torturer and oppressor of the
originary nations and the instigator of the
Great Lie!

What strikes me looking back is how the two not only denounced the criminal violence of colonialism but also an underlying epistemic crime: the *Great Lie*. One might interpret this Great Lie in many ways—as the scientific lie of biological racism, the religious lie that cast indigenous spirituality as superstition, the lies of experts who called indigenous languages inferior dialects, the lies of anthropologists who denied indigenous coevalness, and so on. Against these lies the pair claimed a modest right to know and speak as equals in their own lands, while invoking a long historical memory that transcended the reformist boom of the moment.[9] As I argue below, indigenous resurgence thus conceived is more than a struggle for *inclusion* in the existing state; rather, it constitutes a historical project that seeks to rearrange relations and symbols of legitimacy, territory, and authority through the *transformation of* the Bolivian nation-state. The triumphalist claims of neoliberal interculturalism were thin layers of recent date that barely masked this deeper rethinking of Bolivia's past and future.

Even so, the pachakuti did not happen. Fractured by divisions among organizations, struggling with clientelistic links to dominant parties, and confronting the effects of neoliberal restructuring, social movements failed to unify in 1992. The breakdown of the Assembly of Nationalities proffered a useful reminder that indigenous peoples do not share homogeneous identities and interests as ethnic groups. Despite the apparent diffusion of a broad

FIGURE 1 The Great Lie. Aymara protestors on Columbus Day, La Paz, Bolivia, October 11, 1992.

indigenous political consciousness, the emergence of sustained multiethnic or pan-indigenous movements relied on organizational foundations not present, at least for the moment.

I had come to appreciate diversity within the wider category of "indigenous" in other contexts as well. I originally went to Bolivia to study the Festival of Gran Poder, a magnificent spectacle associated with the urban Aymara of La Paz. I was looking for indigenous cultural resistance and found it, in a way, dancing and drinking with Aymara merchants. Yet these Aymara shared a sense of identity and ways of engaging power that differed from "those of the wiphala," the peasant-indigenous movements denouncing the lies of Christopher Columbus. Though tied to rural communities through networks of kin, contraband, and ritual, middle-class Aymara carried fat wads of dollars, drove SUVs, discussed the virtues and defects of Brazilian and Chinese appliances, and spent weekends until dawn in beer and Johnnie Walker–fueled parties. Though embracing my efforts to practice Aymara with them, they demonstrated by consumption that they were definitely not like other indigenous "peasants." Displays of wealth and baroque cultural performance were a testament to their relative success in the struggle against racism. Yet they also demonstrated how terms like *indio, indígena*, Aymara, or Guarani mask complex social realities. Understanding the contested place of bilingual education and trajectories of indigenous mobilization requires keeping these complexities in mind.

I had also studied with Mayan activists in Guatemala during the late 1980s, where indigenous struggles revolved separately and together around issues of land and language. I hoped to find these kinds of movements in Bolivia, so I steered away from the dancing merchants and began making inquiries into the field of indigenous education, an arena that might link urban indigenous intellectuals to rural indigenous communities. Rather acritically, and with a dose of essentialism, I imagined that the defense of indigenous language and culture through bilingual schooling might contribute both to indigenous political mobilizing and to social liberation, a nod to my reading of the liberation theologist Paulo Freire. I had not worked through the problems of this theory of collective action and the notion that schooling might make one free. Yet, unburdened by details, I asked my Aymara teacher Vitaliano Huanca about bilingual education, and he set me off on a series of contacts that eventually led me to the Guarani.

Vitaliano had introduced me to EIB activists who suggested that the Guarani might be an interesting case to explore. In mid-1992 I met Guido Chumiray, a leader of the Assembly of Guarani People (APG), and Tomás Robles, a Peruvian advisor of the movement. Guido and Tomás had come to La Paz for a conference on bilingual education, and I sought them out to volunteer my unsolicited assistance. Guido was a seasoned leader and founder of the APG who had once served on the executive committee of the national indigenous-peasant union, the Confederación Sindical Única de Trabajadores Campesinos de Bolivia (CSUTCB). Tomás, I later learned, had taken an interest in culture as an analytical category after a decade of Marxist-inspired work supporting Aymara struggles in Peru. The APG was a hybrid organization situated in the paradoxical space between the boom in development aid to native peoples (on which it depended) and the political visions of the indigenous resurgence described above. A prime example of this hybridity was the APG embrace of EIB. It was then a "project" funded by UNICEF and in its third year of pilot work in the Aymara, Quechua, and Guarani regions.[10] Yet I listened excitedly as they explained how EIB also formed a core component of the Guarani political movement. After a series of conversations, they decided an anthropologist might be of some use. Tomás arranged for UNICEF to pay me $250 a month to join them.

My Aymara studies lagged, and I began reading the handful of books available on the Guarani. With the help of Celia Miranda, a Guarani student in La Paz, I started studying the language. In November I took the two-day bus ride down from La Paz to tropical Santa Cruz. There I hopped a small plane to the provincial town of Camiri. Far from the Andes, this was an entirely new world of indigenous politics. Despite the paradox of aid dependence and state tutelage, EIB in Guarani country was shaped by Guarani languages of struggle and a discourse of popular liberation. It seemed to fit my vision of indigenous resurgence perfectly, and I worked on and off with the Guarani over the following fourteen years.

This book draws on the Guarani experience to trace two decades of indigenous resurgence and education politics in Bolivia. Unlike traditional anthropological fieldwork, which usually bases itself in a particular community for a year or two, this study moves across time and space, weaving together two interconnected processes. The first is the state turn toward neoliberal interculturalism as expressed in the national education reform and in bilingual interculturalism as a model of public schooling for indigenous Bolivians. The second is the resurgence of indigenous movements as expressed through the case of the Guarani and examined here in relation to other indigenous and nonindigenous movements and to non-Indian society. Methodologically, one ethnographic anchor lies in Guarani country, where the story unfolds through a discussion of Guarani history, life, language, and the movement's embrace of EIB. Guarani leaders and communities and their allies and opponents are the main characters in Guarani country. A second ethnographic anchor lies in La Paz, Bolivia's capital city, where school reform and state power are conceptually and institutionally centered. Foreign aid personnel, academics, bureaucrats, movement leaders, and teachers are the main characters there. My peripheral role in both sites is used to shed light on the dilemmas of engaged anthropology seeking to make itself useful for projects of change.

INDIGENOUS MOVEMENTS AND REFORMIST NETWORKS

The Guarani political federation, the Assembly of Guarani People (APG), was founded in 1987. The APG is a member of CIDOB, the Indigenous Confederation of Eastern Bolivia and a participant in COICA, a transnational confederation of indigenous organizations of the Amazon Basin (Coordinadora de las Organizaciones Indígenas de la Cuenca Amazónica). The Guarani have become significant national players despite their relatively small population of sixty thousand as compared to the 1.6 million Aymara and 3.2 million Quechua of the Andean highlands. They also occupy a crucial geopolitical position in eastern Bolivia, making them the flashpoint of state attempts to co-opt eastern Bolivian indigenous movements and pit them against Andean movements. They are also situated in a geopolitical tug of war between nationalist and regionalist agendas unfolding in battles over the gas reserves beneath their lands. From 1988 through the early 2000s, the Guarani were at the vanguard of bilingual intercultural education in Bolivia, which explains in part their wider national role and visibility and the expansion and growing autonomy of their movement today.

The bulk of the Guarani population lives in rural farming communities, working in small-scale agriculture and livestock raising. What land is held provides mostly for semisubsistence farming, and Guarani also work for local *karai* (non-Guarani) farms or migrate seasonally to Santa Cruz. Those who no longer have access to land generally migrate to the urban peripheries of large cities, seek informal jobs in provincial towns like Camiri, or find periodic labor on road projects or gas exploration crews. After fifteen years of educational struggle, the Guarani teaching class has become a significant economic and political player in the region (it was nonexistent when I began work there in 1992). A handful of Guarani work in NGOs, and many aspire to university study.

The APG is led by a council of "captains" elected yearly by representatives of twenty-four subregional territories called "zones" or "captaincies." Beneath the umbrella of the APG, each of these zones has its own, somewhat autonomous nuclei of leadership networks. These include, for example,

Kaipependɨ-Kaarovaicho, the home of the scribe Elsa, introduced in chapter 2; Ɨtɨka Guasu, or Grand Ɨtɨka, described in chapter 3; and Ɨsoso, a captaincy that often acts independently of the wider APG. Beyond the traditional Guarani areas, many Guarani have migrated to urban Santa Cruz, creating new organizational structures that also participate in the wider APG.[11] Guarani zones are neither ethnically homogenous nor spatially contiguous, but are intermingled with karai, non-Guarani people, towns, and ranches. In Guarani country, my fieldwork unfolded primarily across two expressions of the movement—the APG leadership and bilingual education activist networks centered in the town of Camiri, where many captaincies frequently came together, and rural communities in the region called Ɨtɨka Guasu. I am familiar with most of Guarani country and draw on this knowledge to contextualize events, actors, and processes linked to bilingual education. Despite internal heterogeneity, the Guarani and the APG are unified as a language community and a political entity that comes together at key times of conflict. EIB was imagined as a project for the entire Guarani nation, and I emphasize this vision herein.

The other mooring is the Bolivian educational field at the national level. I refer to a segment of this field as the reformist network, people and agencies defined by their support for the education reform. Reform was hammered out through agreements between donors and elites and packaged in a complex plan funded with loans from the World Bank (over $200 million) and the Inter-American Development Bank (IADB) ($80 million). UNICEF and bilateral donors (Sweden, Germany, Denmark, and the Netherlands) added US$38.8 million through the late 1990s (IADB 1994; World Bank 1998a). The reformists, Bolivian and foreign, worked primarily out of La Paz, where most of my encounters with them took place. Reformists included politicians, experts, World Bank, IADB, or European aid agency employees, indigenous and nonindigenous academics and leaders, NGO personnel, and the state bureaucratic staff charged with implementation. This constituted a socially and ideologically heterogeneous group. Some reformists leaned leftward toward the language of indigenous rights, against neoliberalism, and in defense of a social-democratic state. Others leaned rightward, speaking the language of official interculturalism while embracing the free market and managerial discourses then dominant among the ruling elite. Reformists, known locally as *los de la reforma*, were financed by foreign banks and donors, structurally aligned against teachers' unions, and in tactically shifting relations with indigenous movements, the public, and political parties.

Bilingual education was a subcomponent of the wider education reform aimed at indigenous peoples. It depended on targeted aid from UNICEF, Sweden, Denmark, and Germany. Nonetheless, it was touted by the government as their flagship project that set Bolivia apart from education reform elsewhere, with interculturalism and participation promoted as discursive pillars of legitimacy central to the wider agenda of state change. Some reformists supported EIB, but many did not. For instance, most of the elite pundit and political class spoke positively of education reform while questioning EIB, as did some *técnicos* within the education reform itself. I thus use the phrases *EIB activists* or *EIB networks* to refer to those within and outside of the reformist networks who supported bilingual intercultural education. EIB activists (among whom I include myself) also formed a heterogeneous transnational network that crossed lines of state, donor, NGO, and movement fields of practice. Some EIB activists followed a grass-roots vision of indigenous movements as part of a broader popular and nationalist agenda. Some were curricular experts who spoke mostly of pedagogical quality or economic rationality. Others espoused a romantic or essentialist defense of indigenous cultural and linguistic preservation. Despite the government opening to interculturalism, EIB began to lose official support toward the end of the neoliberal era (1999–2003). Yet EIB activists, like indigenous movements, were around before education reform and persist amid the current political crises. After the election of Evo Morales in 2005, a new network of public university intellectuals, school teachers, and EIB activists came in with new energy. At this writing, EIB activists continue to work from within and beyond the state as the slow transformation of schooling continues.

Many in the United States react to mention of bilingual education with suspicion (it's coddling the immigrants!) or romanticism (it will help save language and culture!). Replacing *immigrant* with *indigenous*, many non-indigenous Bolivians react similarly. Yet the political location and historical meaning of bilingual education—and of native languages and peoples in Latin America—differ from those of immigrants. There are also some significant distinctions between North and South American native language education processes. EIB in Bolivia proposed that speakers of indigenous languages (*lenguas originarias*) be schooled through the eighth grade in their mother tongue (*lengua materna*, L1) and in Spanish, the second language (*segunda lengua*, L2). In the initial cycle (years 1–3), the native language would receive equal or more attention than Spanish. Afterward, literacy and numeracy skills in L1 are transferred to L2 and the relationship becomes a 50/50 distribution. The ideal product is a citizen-subject literate, numerate, and orally proficient in both languages. Indigenous organizations obtained official acknowledgment in the 1994 law that EIB was a project of language "maintenance and development," not a project of assimilation to Spanish. Indigenous peoples, distinct from immigrants, and like Native Americans elsewhere, also base their demands in international covenants like International Labor Organization Convention 169 (which guarantees indigenous rights to language and education administration). Yet because it is not formally contained in a reservation system, is associated with large majorities rather than minorities, and because indigenous languages are quite audible in the public sphere, EIB in Bolivia generates a different political reaction among nonindigenous peoples than native schooling might in the United States. Whereas most non-Indians in the United States remain ignorant of Native American language and education issues—and certainly do not fear the idea of native languages being taught in schools—many non-indigenous Bolivians see in EIB the legitimation of an opaque, threatening space of communication in "native tongues" that may not be safely contained in schools. It was always incredible to me—though I learned to understand it—how EIB intensified latent fears about indigenous subversion, the breakdown of hierarchies, and the disruption of deeply felt understandings of linguistic, political, and epistemic orders. It is this deeper political sensitivity that activists like the Guarani had to negotiate and that distinguishes EIB in much of the Andes from its parallels in the North.

In negotiating these sensibilities, some outsiders (like me) often cited ILO 169 in defense of EIB. Yet most nonindigenous EIB activists—and often indigenous leaders themselves—relied in public on technical and economic, rather than political, justifications. By any measure, those who speak indigenous languages attain less schooling and are poorer. A well-documented correspondence between illiteracy, indigeneity, and poverty exists across Latin America (Hall and Patrinos 2005). Bilingual pedagogies are effective if implemented well, and EIB demonstrably lowers dropout rates and improves

	1846	1900	1950	1976	1992	2001
Population	1,378,896	1,816,271	3,019,031	4,613,486	6,420,792	8,274,325
% Indigenous	80	56.63	63	54	58 (d)	62 (e)
% Quechua	–	–	36.5	39.7	34	20
% Aymara	–	–	24.5	28.8	23.5	13
% Other indigenous	–	–	–	–	0.5	1
% Monolingual indigenous	–	–	54.7	21.2	12.6	n.a.
% Monolingual Spanish	–	–	–	–	42 (c)	n.a.
% criollo-mestizo	20 (a)	42.64 (b)	36	33	–	50.05
Literacy (%) female/male	7	20	31	63.2	72/88	81/93
Poverty (%) Nonindigenous/ indigenous	–	–	–	–	57/75	53/74 (f)

TABLE I Indigeneity, multilingualism, literacy, and poverty in Bolivia, 1846–2001. *Sources*: 1846, 1900 and 1950: de Mesa et al. (1997); 1976 and 1992: Albó (1995). 2001: www.ine.gov.bo and Ministerio de Educación (2004). Poverty rates from Hall and Patrinos (2005). (a) "criollos" (b) Includes 30.81% "mestizo" and 11.83% "white." (c) "monolingual Spanish." (d) Based on self-reported knowledge of an indigenous language. (e) Based on self-identification of propulation fifteen years and older. (f) 2002 figures.

test scores, promising better-quality schooling. Thus EIB could be defended as a technical solution to indigenous poverty and exclusion, especially in regions with high indigenous monolingualism. Because indigenous girls and women are less likely to speak Spanish, EIB, some also argued, favors women and girls. For these reasons, beyond the decolonizing agenda of indigenous movements, a certain kind of EIB could be embraced even by hard-nosed technocrats who sounded like progressives supporting poverty reduction, social inclusion, gender equality, and educational quality. This technical stance came with political risks, yet indigenous EIB activists learned to speak of the process in different registers, for different audiences, providing for the paradoxical articulation between quite divergent understandings of EIB in practice.[12]

Against both technical and political arguments, skeptics voiced ignorance about native languages being dialects unsuited for modern life or suggested that EIB would keep indigenous peoples from learning Spanish and thus from "progressing." Some indigenous parents expressed similar fears for different reasons. Yet statistics show that with or without EIB, the trajectory of history is erasing indigenous languages (Albó 1995; see table 1). Spanish is privileged in all realms and threatened in none. EIB was not a radical ethnicist plan, nor an exclusive turn to indigenous monolingualism, but in fact a modest shift in a deeper history of Andean nation-building long defined by assimilationist language policies (Mannheim 1989).

COLONIALITY, INEQUALITY, AND SCHOOLING

After an initial visit to Camiri in November of 1992, I returned to La Paz to move my bookshelf, frying pan, desk, books, and mattress back east for an extended stay. I gave notice to my criolla landlady in La Paz, telling her I was off to the Chaco to work on bilingual education with indigenous peoples (*los pueblos indígenas*). She grimaced at the thought, but smiled charitably and said, "How nice, they are educating the little Indians" (Que bién que están educando a los indiecitos). She gasped with dismay when I visited her again in early 1994. The Zapatista movement in southern Mexico had exploded. "My God," she said commenting on the news, "have you seen? They've got a *guerra de indios* [Indian war]!" Bolivia's own upheavals of the early 2000s were still far off, yet this imagined specter of "Indian war" was always an unspoken fear of criollo Bolivians. Criollos like my otherwise kindhearted landlady understood themselves as the public "we," the real citizens and civil(ized) society who confronted an indio other, a threat to order and authority. This language derived from colonial schisms of race and class rooted in popular imaginaries and state institutions. The criollo "we" in charge of the state alternately saw Indians as childlike inferiors (indiecitos) needing control through education or as threatening savages (guerra de indios) needing control through violence. Most of this criollo "we" had difficulty seeing indios, especially those who spoke languages other than Spanish, as political or social equals. Though violence against indios had long been licensed by criollo society as sometimes necessary and thus legitimate, education was more polemical. Some of the criollo "we" saw schools as a way to domesticate the savage within the child. To be educated in this way was not seen as a means to equality but to create an *indio educado*, obedient and respectful of authority.[13] Others feared schools would create rebellious Indians. As a counterpart to the familiar "the only good Indian is a dead Indian," a Bolivian saying maintains "indio letrado, indio alzado" (a lettered Indian is a rebellious Indian). Indigenous schooling through most of Bolivia's past thus oscillated between hardening boundaries of exclusion and imposing violent processes of subordinate inclusion. From the perspective of the dominant criollo "we," schooling was never about producing pluralist models of citizenship, much less social or juridical equality.

These views echo broader Latin American understandings of citizenship and knowledge tied to the coloniality of power. Spanish literacy was a marker of the racial, spatial, and political boundary between the white, male, urban *letrado* (literate citizen subject) and the dark-skinned, feminized rural indio (Indian peasant), a racially inferior object, neither lettered, propertied, nor possessed of citizenship (Rama 1996). The boundary-making work of literacy is evidenced in these terms. *Indio* represented rural, backward, dark, and inferior. *Letrado* represented urban, modern, white, and superior. Within the patriarchal and racist order dominated by the letrados, debate on whether the education of the Indian was desirable or viable revolved around the child-savage axis throughout Latin American history, and in many ways it still does. Too little education, elites hypothesize, and the animalistic savage might lash out. Too much education, and the childlike Other might upset the social and racial order. Violence and schooling thus constituted two sides of colonial rule.

Through the colonial lens it was assumed that one could not be both indio and letrado. Spanish literacy was offered to native peoples to make them *cristianos*, reorienting indigenous loyalties and epistemes toward the church-state administrative, linguistic, and territorial project (see Mignolo 1995). Limited indigenous literacy proved instrumental for indirect rule and strategically accentuated differentiation within indigenous communities. Yet when indigenous access to literacy expanded beyond colonial control, indigenous schooling demands, invariably linked to territorial struggles, met with violence.[14] With the rise of modern liberal nation building, the meanings of schooling maintained these archaic, colonial senses of education as a process of racial and cognitive evolution away from Indianness that never fully allowed for equal status. Schools were seen to move indios on a track between savagery (darkness) and civility (whiteness). Between was a gradated scale of *mestizaje* (cultural and racial mixing) along which one could be placed based on a combination of education level, wealth, and bodily appearance. Yet indigenous and mestizo subjects, even if literate, were always racially marked and thus ever "behind" and "below" the European endpoint. Schooling thus reaffirmed boundaries even as it promised their transgression (Cadena 2000). Put another way, the state promised citizenship if indigenous peoples gave up their customs, lands, and language. Yet it continually moved the boundaries of real citizenship out of reach through this story of mestizaje as incomplete evolution (Luykx 1999; García Linera 2003). Could EIB transform these colonial ideas?

Beyond this coloniality of power embedded in schooling, Bolivian education has another historical dimension tied to the languages of social rights, class struggle, nationalism, and equality. Since the turn of the twentieth century, and in Bolivia especially after 1952, mass schooling formed part of centralized nation-building projects and the debate on development in Latin America. Education was enshrined in constitutions as the "highest function" of what was called the "teacher state" (*estado docente*), a state with moral and legal obligations to educate its citizens.[15] Backed by national teachers' unions—and despite the racism that lies within its form—Bolivian public education was framed by social movements as a politically and economically democratizing institution of nation building. Schools became vehicles for transforming structural inequalities and answering the collective aspirations of the *pueblo*, the people. After 1952 this axis of school history as it related to the idea of the state played out in a tug of war between teacher-led discourse on revolutionary and popular education and elite attempts to contain schooling in idioms of growth, order, and progress.

STUDYING STATES, MOVEMENTS, AND SCHOOLS

To assess the meaning of EIB—and to understand how it intersected with ongoing processes of state-building and movement praxis—requires juggling these two axes of schooling history: one tied to the colonial legacy and the contested status of indigenous bodies, tongues, and knowledges; the other to the conflict over schooling as an instrument of nation building that pits state-centric visions of popular struggle against exclusionary and market-oriented agendas for governance. Methodologically, dealing with state reform and indigenous resurgence while engaging this deeper history of coloniality and nation building calls for a multiscalar processual ethnography focused on articulations across time and space, rather than on the observation of insti-tutionally or spatially contained events and subjects. An ethnography of development and education means going beyond the discursive and institu-tional boundaries of the aid project or the classroom. It means transcending dyadic models of state-movement opposition to consider how these bound-aries are blurred or hardened in shifting political practices. This admittedly dizzying multisitedness gains empirical coherence through its focus on the Guarani and EIB. Conceptual coherence comes from my concerns with the historical axes of inequality and legitimacy (the battle over the state) and of epistemic-linguistic alterity (the coloniality of power). These questions intersect four areas of related research: the ethnography of neoliberal gov-ernmentality and the state; indigenous movements and interculturalism; indigenous knowledge and schooling; and the ethnography of translocal, multiscalar, networked processes.

Ethnographers of neoliberalism have used Michel Foucault's understand-ing of power and the concept of governmentality to understand new forms of rule associated with the spread of development knowledge like that im-plemented in Bolivia during the 1990s (see Ferguson 1990; Escobar 1995; D. Nelson 1999; Paley 2001; Sawyer 2004; Ong 2006; and Li 2007). Govern-mentality, or the "conduct of conduct," refers to a form of power that circulates through the inculcation of discourses and routines aimed at pro-moting individualizing autonomous self-regulation (rather than centralized state control or corporatist representation). This is reinforced through the bureaucratization of knowledge and the narrowing of authority over claims to truth. Authoritative institutions (or experts) measure, validate, and assess subjects to determine their place and utility in the social order. Apparatuses of security back this knowledge-power regime (Foucault 1991). Western education systems are quintessential apparatuses of governmentality that op-erate through the individualizing problematization of the self and this total-izing bureaucratization of authoritative knowledge.[16] Subjects are imagined —and ideally come to see themselves—as needing improvement, hygiene, discipline, self-control, and the like to be realized through classroom in-culcation of autonomy and docility in the name of self-realization. School-ing affirms bureaucratic hierarchies and control by defining valid knowledge and useful bodies. Accepting the necessary good of schooling means accept-ing this modality of individualizing and totalizing power.

This modality of power is visible in Bolivian reform and schooling prac-tice. I consider (especially in chapters 3 and 7) how this reading of schooling as governmentality might lead one to dismiss the possibility that EIB as a schooling project could offer anything epistemically alternative. Schooling of any sort bureaucratizes knowledge, orality, and textuality, offering disci-pline, not freedom (Hunter 1996). It is with absolute critical clarity about this that some traditionalist Guarani reject all schooling, bilingual or other-wise. Public debate in the wake of the Movimiento al Socialismo (MAS) victory of 2005 is also reconsidering how and if decolonization requires a more radical rethinking of schooling to confront these individualizing effects (Prada 2007a).

I sympathize with this critical view of schooling, but the notion that projects like education reform and EIB are always and everywhere an expres-sion of neoliberal governmentality leads to a pessimistic view of all knowl-edge politics. It also unselfconsciously contributes to an antistate and de-politicizing sensibility amenable to neoliberalism itself. It fails to see the multiple layers of real political struggle over the state as an open-ended possibility, choosing instead to assume that effects are already achieved. The Foucauldian reading also proves insufficient for taking seriously the multiple forms of embodied subjectivity that emerge in and around schooling prac-tices, as well as through other experiences and rationalities. It further fails to recognize the incapacity of state institutions to effectively generate docile, manageable subjects. With well over 70 percent of Bolivia living in the informal economy and with average levels of schooling that hover around five years, the apparatuses for imposing the conduct of conduct simply do not exist in Bolivia (hence neoliberal anxiety for modernizing schools). Bolivians' rich traditions of protest are a testament to this ultimate incom-pleteness of disciplinary projects of rule.

As Tania Murray Li (2007) suggests, discourses of governmentality are reflected in intentions of rule, but ethnographies of rule must go beyond institutional and project boundaries to examine articulatory processes that link and oppose expert and indigenous or local knowledges and contradictions between lived experience and official discourse that generate not docility, but active resistance (see Moore 2005; Escobar 2005). In addition, policy shifts like education reform as often concern the rearrangement of political and economic relations (such as marginalizing teachers or redistributing state capital as patronage) as they do achieving their stated goals (quality schooling or useful human capital) (Moore 1973, 1987). As such, using *governmentality*—and even the scare word *neoliberalism*—requires paying close attention to how new tactics are mediated by class, gender, and race; absorbed into prior and ongoing histories of rule; disrupted by violence (or fears thereof); and redirected through alternative epistemic and linguistic forms that also circulate through daily life and political practice. As Mitchell Dean points out (2001:44), neoliberalism as a rationality of power is always "articulated with [other] rationalities and forces that seek in some manner to affect [its] employment."

These redirections become most visible in social movement practice, including in the cautious embrace and resignification of interculturalism, a second area of anthropological debate. Proponents of Latin American interculturalism have argued that the focus on "inter-" distinguishes a view of dialogue and exchange across cultural boundaries, away from the American and European "multi-," which highlights tolerance between distinct yet separate groups (López 2005). Yet in practice interculturalism means many things. Official interculturalism sought to objectify culture as an individual trait while managing difference, with minor exceptions, through standardized templates of rule. Some have argued that this interculturalism in the neoliberal mode promised recognition of sorts, but not redistribution (toward material equality) (Hale 2002). Yet interculturalism—even in its official form—was as anxiety producing when voiced by elites as it was a useful tool of power, since even recognition unsettled dominant understandings of elite privilege. For movements, interculturalism proved multivariate. It seemed like a way to make modest affirmative action–type claims on jobs for indigenous people in some cases, while legitimating calls for radical structural or epistemic upheaval in others. As such it is useful to distinguish these grassroots interculturalisms as transformative and creative projects from official or managerial visions of interculturalism (Escobar 2001; Rappaport 2005).

Whether and how EIB worked as an official or grass-roots intercultural project is a point of contention.

The answer to this question lies both in the internal characteristics of EIB and in its articulations with other phenomena across temporal and scalar conjunctures of state and movement processes. As with governmentality, ethnographic critiques of interculturalism as official discourse risk losing sight of what social movements and state elites are actually doing in practice. Bolivians are not dupes of official policy and proudly sustain a deeply counterhegemonic subjectivity for which I use the awkward translation "contestative" (for *contestataria*). In the Andes this is said to stem from the violences of colonialism that generate epistemic resistance, such as the *janiwa!* (no!) said to lie at the core of Aymara consciousness (Sanjinés 2004). Yet beyond resistance, indigenous and other movements engage in their own projects for reconstituting the state from the ground up. As I argue throughout, the Guarani pursued interculturalism as they saw it, seeking to "walk and speak out loud among the karai," a goal that had multiple political facets. Interculturalism had unsettled meanings well into the 2000s, pushed into new debates by the MAS project of decolonization, pulled back into an older mestizaje discourse by regional elites, and molded with the language of class and popular struggle by factions of the Guarani. Juxtaposing the multiplicity of practice with official discourse yields a more complex reading of interculturalism and movements.

Governmentality and interculturalism intersect with a third thematic area, that of indigenous knowledge and its relation to schooling. EIB and indigenous movements are often read through a dialectic that pits Western against indigenous knowledges, and indigenous languages are understood as the authentic vehicle of the latter.[17] Many studies of indigenous knowledge and formal schooling reify this dichotomy. Schooling is seen as a place in which one can receive more or less of either indigenous or Western knowledge. I consider this view in relation to curricular and textbook development and classroom practice (chapters 2, 4, and 5). However, I do not propose to resolve this debate here (much less propose how one might "indigenize" a curriculum). I am more interested in the production and deployment of indigenous knowledge not as a symbolic or textual corpus, but as a hybrid, networked form of sociopolitical and cultural practice that articulates with other forms of knowledge production and practices. This leads me to emphasize struggles over epistemic (i.e., political) authority and legitimacy, rather than debates over purism, identity, authenticity, or essentialism. I consider this through my own attempts to curricularize indigenous knowledge in confrontation with indigenous knowledge practices in chapter 2, and through discussion of public Guarani historical commemorations and the hunger strike of 1998 in chapter 6. Both as hybridized networked practice and as a locally rooted form of sociality and exchange, indigenous knowledge articulates with other rationalities and relations. It is not useful to contain it as a static philosophical, cognitive, or ideological corpus.

Discourses of rule, interculturalism, and indigenous knowledge practices are interconnected, translated, detached, and deployed through articulation and networks, two words I repeat often. In vogue in social analysis, the terms also form part of on-the-ground struggle and of self-reflective analysis in Bolivia. As with *decolonization*, drawing distinctions between local and academic uses of these terms offers a fruitful way to think about social movement practice as generative of its own theories. On the analytical level, I borrow Anna Tsing's (2005) understanding of transnational processes as contingent articulations. In Tsing's usage, notions of overwhelming forces like neoliberal governmentality often assume the durability of projects of rule that are in fact ephemeral hegemonies that fall into rapid disintegration (as we saw in Bolivia in 2003). As Tsing argues, state elites, regional social movements, and transnational actors seek to articulate and connect across difference by strategically translating points of common interest (or silencing points of contention). These articulations create networked relations, channels, and practices that may persist at one moment in time, only to delink and reconfigure in a different way later.[18] This draws attention to the terms and conditions of interconnection, the prospects that these contingent articulations may or may not generate durable transformations, and the possibility that what we observe is inherently unstable, ephemeral, and fragmented.

While not an altogether satisfying way to think about the reality of power, violence, capital, and the state, articulations and networks are useful for grappling with the shifting strategies of movements and the fickle tactics of transnational aid and state actors in unstable settings like Bolivia. Understanding articulation in this sense constitutes a means of considering how moments of transformative potential arise and disappear, creating moments at which social movements (and state actors) must hone their capacity to read and act in shifting locations. The lexicon of movements like that of the Guarani and even that of the criollo elite illustrate the dynamics of articulation in practice. Movements speak of articulating (*articular*) across lines of difference, as in alliances between mestizo peasants, urban progressives, and indigenous peoples. Conservative editorialists speak of the need for the state or army to disarticulate (*desarticular*) and deactivate (*desactivar*) these threats to order, terms that come close to equating mobilization with criminality, as bands and gangs are also "disarticulated" by police. In circles of reflection indigenous leaders speak of articulating with various others (actors, processes, events) to seek a repositioning (*reposicionamiento*) and a change of the configuration (*configuración*) of power at regional and national levels. This is not simply resistance, but articulations (*articulaciones*) of networks (*redes*) that bring NGOs, state actors and institutions, and movements of various sorts into temporary alignment and exchange (of bodies, resources, symbols, legitimacy, etc.).

Governmentality, interculturalism, and indigenous knowledge politics all in some ways constitute a series of contingent networked articulations—wagers made by various players—that play out as durable projects until they exhaust their productive potential or until temporal moments shift and the conditions of articulation disintegrate. EIB articulated with an elite strategy of reform for a time, but it rapidly began to disarticulate when elites came to see it as a threat. EIB held organizing potential for Guarani for a time, until it was absorbed into state processes and the locus of knowledge production shifted. Understanding movements, I posit, means understanding these translocal articulations and the possibilities for creating durable change that they generate or close across different interlocking social fields.

THE STRUCTURE OF THE BOOK

This book is divided into three parts: initial resurgence (1980s to 1994); indigenous and state engagements with EIB (1994 to 1998); and movement redirections of struggle (1998 to 2006). The chapters shift between sites, actors, times, and places. To facilitate the reading of proximity and distance across articulated fields, I have written interludes between the chapters that help the reader traverse and connect places and historical moments. My methods are specified along the way, but I introduce them briefly here along with the structure of the book.[19]

Part 1, "Resurgent Knowledge," addresses the historical context and early moments of Guarani political mobilization and schooling in southeastern Bolivia. The three chapters contained therein draw on fieldwork and collaboration between 1992 and 1994, combined with historical interviews and secondary research carried out in later years. Chapter 1 traces histories of Guarani schooling as frontier mission practice juxtaposed with nation-building processes and indigenous resistance at the state's Andean center. The chapter is anchored in the Kuruyuki massacre of 1892, an event central to Guarani schooling narratives today. The chapter also considers the disparate effects of the 1952 revolution in the Andes and in Guarani regions to highlight the uneven effects of nation building that shape different indigenous responses to EIB and schooling regimes today.

The interlude "To Camiri" describes a typical arrival to Guarani country and sets the stage for chapter 2, on the Guarani intellectuals I call the "scribes." The scribes wrote schoolbooks for Guarani schools. I examine them and the effects of their creative and political work in relation to the regional expansion of the Guarani movement. I focus in particular on one scribe, Elsa Aireyu, whose experience highlights how EIB destabilized gendered and raced categories of inequality while affirming both a sense of collective ethnolinguistic and territorial unity and emergent class divisions within the Guarani.

Setting the stage for chapter 3, the interlude "To Itavera" traverses the social and geographic distance between Camiri and the small Guarani village of Itavera where I gathered ethnographic knowledge to contribute to textbook production in 1993 and 1994. The chapter considers EIB in relation to pan-Guarani organizing and to local understandings of schooling and knowledge. It is rooted in the experience of a new Guarani teacher named Ernesto "Tüi" José and the village captain, Airase. My own travails illustrate dilemmas of ethnography as collaboration and indigenous knowledge as school text.

Part 2, "Transnational Articulations" shifts scale and perspective, moving from Guarani country to the reformist networks in La Paz. It focuses on the rise and insertion of EIB and interculturalism into state practice. The interlude "To La Paz, via Thailand," illustrates one kind of articulation, a research project that tied global discourses on education to places like Itavera. Chapter 4 traces the national emergence of bilingual education as an indigenous demand marked by meanings of social liberation and indigenous self-determination. I illustrate how this vision underwent containment in articulation with market-oriented education reform.

A cabinet meeting in 1994, described in the interlude "Bolivia or Yugoslavia?" takes us into realms of state power as EIB was passed into law. Chapter 5 argues that official interculturalism spoke the language of neoliberal governmentality yet relied on the mobilization of racialized forms of class exclusion and corporatist logics of rule that it claimed to transform. These contradictions, and the outsider status of EIB, are illustrated through one of the reform's long-standing criolla proponents and EIB activists, the former education minister Amalia Anaya.

Part 3 is titled "Return to Struggle." Drawing on fieldwork between 1997 and 2006, this section illustrates the rearticulation of movements as neoliberalism began to crumble. The interlude, "La Indiada, como para Dar Miedo" ("The Indian hordes gathered in a way that struck fear in you"), sets the stage for understanding the distance between central regime processes and Guarani country and the rising karai fears about Guarani activism.

Chapter 6 analyzes two events: the Kuruyuki commemoration of 1998 and a Guarani hunger strike that year. I juxtapose classroom practice with these events to show how EIB and indigenous knowledge constituted platforms for the production of "insurgent citizenship" (Holston 1999) outside schools more than within. These events also show how Guarani constructed meanings of EIB that transcended the intentions of official education reform: creating contestative teaching subjects and enacting a particular kind of interculturalism in multiethnic public spaces.

The interlude "Interculturalism to Decolonization" moves back from Guarani country to the Andes, describing an army assault at the Aymara bilingual intercultural teacher training school at Warisata that sparked the social conflagration of October 2003. In the context of the collapse of neoliberalism and the rise of Evo Morales and the MAS, chapter 7 examines the current situation and future trajectory of bilingual education. I consider the shift from interculturalism to decolonization as official discourse and the violent reaction of the regionalist right, now moving beyond neoliberal interculturalism to pursue its own form of sovereign control over schools, land, and territory against the supposed nationalist and indigenist threat.

DILEMMAS OF ENGAGEMENT

Anthropologists who work for a long time in a place engage their hosts in ways that go beyond "pure" research to forms of collaborative engagement. This may stem from genuine solidarity or from the self-interested defense of a research agenda. However, in my case collaborative engagement and solidarity led to research, rather than the other way around. This exchange made later research rewarding and, I venture, less colonial than traditional fieldwork. Yet engagement generates dilemmas as well. Most Guarani in leadership circles knew that I supported EIB. I was acknowledged as an ally of the APG and of the Guarani. Yet some Guarani worried that I was policing their support of bilingual education. Others did not differentiate between what I and other karai did: taking something to get rich off Guarani. I had tense (or no) relations with karai who opposed EIB and Guarani mobilization.

My knowledge of the Guarani language also generated dilemmas. As my fluency improved, most took it as a sign of respect and dedication. Speaking Guarani was associated with having a deep connection to place and people. Yet again, some saw my interest in the language, affirmed by the fact that I ultimately left the region, as evidence that I had something to gain. This is, relatively speaking, true. As I discuss in chapter 3, while the books and documents I wrote with the Guarani were my way of returning knowledge, this work did not validate my presence for all Guarani.

A changing professional life also challenged fieldwork relations and collaborative engagement. In the early years I often spent weeks on end fishing and chewing coca with Guarani; I was rarely hurried. With graduate school and academic employment, I returned in ever shorter visits. I made great efforts to take the long trip to Itavera, even if only for a few days. Yet dropping in was not taken as a sign of sacrifice and sentiment (as I saw it), but as a sign of extractive interest and the avoidance of meaningful sociality and exchange. E-mail and easier access to towns like Camiri sustained relations with Guarani leadership circles, but some leaders questioned the fact that I had not stayed. In 2005 a Guarani leader known for his hard-edged manner acknowledged my collaboration but suggested that to make it authentic I would have to return, stay, and die in Guarani country. He told me that I had left parts of my soul there. "You will not die in peace [if you don't come back]," he told me one night over coca and boxed wine. "When you are on your deathbed you'll be calling out Itɨka, Itavera, Tëtaguasu, Kamii, Isoso," places that had captured a bit of my being, bits that would have to be gathered up before I could go into that good night. It was an intense, if chilling, acknowledgment of a longer relationship, as well as a moral critique. Against anthropologists' celebratory claims of having "engaged" people, from Guarani eyes, had I really *engaged* them, I would have stayed forever. I may not—for the moment—be able to live up to these expectations; nor do I plan to die in Guarani country. Yet I hope this book plays a role in the ongoing exchange of knowledge and sociality, and that it ultimately supports the Guarani movement in ways that go beyond an anthropological trafficking in indigenous histories.

Part One RESURGENT KNOWLEDGE

Chapter One

SOLDIERS, PRIESTS, AND SCHOOLS

State Building in the Andes and the Guarani Frontier

In January of 1892, Guarani warriors from a dozen villages in the heart of Guarani country struck back against the colonizers.[1] Guarani captains, including the famous Guɨrakota, rallied loosely confederated villages against outposts of the karai state, burning ranches, sugar mills, and isolated cattle posts in the bush. Reaching a scale not seen since the Guakaya valley wars of 1874, the Guarani mobilization of 1892 was the last of the *guerras de indios* against the colonial order. Karai settlers lived in fear of such outbreaks, not so much because of the possibility of their success, but because they were symptoms of deeper disorder and subversion—they were signs of autonomous Guarani action outside the control of frontier state and mission institutions. Though much of Guarani country was by then under the ostensible control of the colonial state,[2] this insurgency emerged in the last semi-autonomous Guarani redoubt in the Ivo region, an area facing the final thrust of karai settlers eager to occupy farmlands on the Bolivian frontier (see map on page 2).

To the Guarani, the karai, Spanish-speaking whites and mestizos, were invaders. To the karai, the Guarani were savages, made useful only by way of the domestication of the whip on the hacienda, or if kept docile under the tutelage of the Franciscan fathers in the missions. Otherwise they represented obstacles to progress that required elimination. Against these "savages," the karai called themselves *nacionales* (no longer Spaniards, but subjects identified with the Bolivian nation-state) or *cristianos* (Christians, loyal to the epistemic and political authority of the Catholic Church), the latter of which is still used today.

Guarani and karai had been engaged in intermittent warfare and exchange for over three hundred years, a period in which the Guarani had often held their own, if not thrived. Yet, as elsewhere in the Americas, the period of global economic expansion in the late nineteenth century boosted state efforts to pacify the frontier. Backed by a wealthier state with new military technology, frontier karai were now on the offensive. Cattle farms and sugar-cane fields that supplied markets in Andean cities were displacing Guarani corn. The Guarani freedom to make and break alliances eroded as their independent land base shrank. Overt armed resistance to the karai invasion was rare (Langer 1994a, b). Most Guarani were surrounded and reduced (*reducidos*) to dependence on Franciscan missions or to violent subjugation as laborers on karai haciendas. The Bolivian nation-state was superimposed on them in the form of provincial governors, missions, forts, ranches, towns, Catholicism, and the Spanish language. A colonial social, cultural, and political fabric had woven itself into—and in some spaces silenced—Guarani lives, languages, and spaces. The wars of 1892 were the last gasp of armed Guarani resistance to the expanding colonial state.

Guarani war leaders had for some time been quietly mobilizing around a young itinerant shaman called Apiaguaiki Tüpa.[3] It was a hefty name. *Apiaguaiki* had disputed meanings, to which I return below. Yet *tüpa* is the Guarani word for beings or objects of supernatural power, the same word that Jesuits and Franciscans took to refer to the Christian God (Shapiro 1987). A person called Tüpa was in effect an elevation of a more mundane figure, the *ipaye*, a curer or shaman. Ipayes were bastions of counterhegemonic knowledge that undermined the claims of priests, who considered them agents of the devil. Under certain conditions, leaders with ipaye qualities were transformed into tüpa, roughly "person-deity" or "prophet." The tüpaist movements that followed constituted large-scale epistemic, political, and military challenges to colonial authority. Tüpaist movements appeared periodically throughout the colonial period. Like messianic movements elsewhere, they relied on local forms of knowledge while mimicking or appropriating symbols of colonial authority (Saignes 1990). These subversive epistemes and practices were invariably met with excesses of colonial violence that pursued order through terror.

The young prophet Apiaguaiki Tüpa was even more unsettling because of his traveling companion, an older literate mission Guarani named Juan

Ayemotï. Ayemotï, or, I-Have-Made-Myself-White, learned Spanish and rudimentary literacy under Franciscan tutelage at the Santa Rosa mission. Yet the putative convert Ayemotï left the mission to follow Apiaguaiki, reportedly after watching the prophet cure sick Guarani right under the priest's nose. In the months before the uprising, the pair had become regional news of some concern. In late 1891 the *Star of the East*, a provincial newspaper in Santa Cruz, two hundred miles north, printed reports of the curious duo. The scribe Ayemotï was said to be a "savage of some age," traveling around the region with a Guarani claiming to be a prophet (Sanabria Fernández 1972:127). Wielding the subversive knowledge of a Guarani tüpa and ipaye was one thing. Yet now bolstered with the control of the karai language and script in the tongue and hands of a supposed Guarani neophyte, the tüpa proved doubly subversive. Literacy was supposed to transform savages into governable subjects, if not citizens. Yet here it threatened to operate outside the sovereign control of the church and state. By virtue of their mere existence the pair deeply undermined the colonial dependence on a clear boundary between Guaraniness and the literacy-mediated legitimacy of colonial religio-political authority.

Angélico Martarelli, an Italian Franciscan stationed at the Santa Rosa mission, was also concerned. Apiaguaiki Tüpa was calling himself a son of God and gathering followers near Kuruyuki, scarcely ten miles from his mission gates. Guarani were coming to Kuruyuki from throughout the region to see and hear the prophet, further unsettling frontier spatial orders as they left ranches and villages thought under firm karai control. Furthermore, Ayemotï had been a charge of Martarelli himself. His own "son," as it were, had now turned away from his authority and back toward "savagery." Frontier karai and politicians frequently attacked the church for monopolizing Guarani labor or failing to civilize the indigenous population fast enough, and Ayemotï's reconversion would give fuel to these critics. Martarelli did not hesitate to call for Bolivian militia reinforcements from Monteagudo. Even local karai settlers, themselves no friend of the mission, quickly became nervous and sought refuge there as tension increased. As Martarelli wrote in a later account: "Fanaticism took control of their [Guarani] spirits at the news of the appearance of the Tunpa [Tüpa], and a multitude of savages gathered at Guruyuqui [*sic*. Kuruyuki], whose number was calculated around 5,000, apt for war, without counting women and children. . . . This unusual movement of Indians toward Curuyuqui naturally generated in the Missionary Fathers and Christians of the region the suspicion of some insurrection that was being planned there" (Martarelli 1918:8–9). Whether an insurrection was really planned remains unknown. Sometime in December of 1891, the tüpa, by way of Ayemotï, had sent a letter to Martarelli and his fellow father Romualdo D'Ambroggi. They asked to be left in peace, because

> the rage [that the tüpa] has for the *caraises* [karai] is because they have been evil to us, but not the fathers who always give food and services in the communities and who do not let the *carai* [karai] finish us all off as they want. None of ours complain about the fathers, nor does the *tunpa* [tüpa] complain; he says nothing against You, only of those who have taken land from the people and killed for the joy of killing and robbed our things. (qtd. in Sanabria Fernández 1972:225–27)[4]

Bolstered by the troops from Monteagudo, Martarelli then arranged a parley with the tüpa. The latter argued that his only activities as an ipaye were praying for rain, which Martarelli interpreted as stalling for time.[5] The historian Hernando Sanabria Fernández imagines that Ayemotï translated these words to Spanish for the benefit of the karai soldiers, even though the tüpa reportedly spoke a bit of Spanish himself, learned from labor as a houseboy on a karai hacienda. Forced to speak in the outsider's tongue in their own land, the Guarani found that bilingualism, like power, was one-sided. Nonetheless, both parties agreed to meet again on January 4, 1892.

Before this meeting, the assault broke out, yet only after the karai murder of a Guarani woman. During the New Year festivities, a frontier official raped and murdered the woman at Ñuumbïte, the karai settlement near the mission. As word spread, the war captains allied with the prophet launched attacks in the early days of January. The *insurrectos*, as these rebel Guarani were called, eventually massed at Ivo and laid siege to the Santa Rosa mission. With the help of mission Guarani and frontier militiamen, the army detachment repelled the assault. The insurrectos retreated and dug in at Kuruyukï. Bolivian reinforcements from Santa Cruz arrived on January 27. Again assisted by mission Guarani, the Bolivians counterattacked on January 28, the infamous date of what is now called the Massacre of Kuruyukï.

In writing of the violence later, Martarelli wrote of his terror on hearing the cacophony of Guarani flutes and drums and seeing smoke rising from burning settlements. Yet like most colonial violence, the killing and terror was unilateral. According to the military report, eight hundred Guarani men and boys were slaughtered, with only four Bolivian soldiers lost (Sanabria Fernández 1972). Martarelli celebrated the victory of the "nationals" over the "rebels." Yet he noted the "valor demonstrated by the savages" and recognized the massacre for what it was: "The clear reality of the tragic spectacle was the horrendous devastation [estrago] that the hailstorm of fire from the rifles had done to the enemy [Guarani] lines; the trenches were full of cadavers" (1918:28).

Bolivian troops and militiamen eager for the spoils of war and the security of order pacified the region through overkill. The troops hunted down Guarani in villages that had reportedly answered the tüpa's call, killing almost two thousand more Guarani men and boys in the following weeks. Insurgent Guarani communities saw their lands and bodies divided up among karai, in what was in effect an ethnic cleansing operation aimed at land and labor seizure. Soldiers carefully tabulated the captured Guarani children and women and noted their distribution as slave labor and war booty to "good Catholic families" in the cities of Sucre, Santa Cruz, and Tarija (Sanabria Fernández 1972:230; see also Pifarré 1989:385–87; Albó 1990:21–22).

Apiaguaiki Tüpa and Ayemotï escaped the battle and sought refuge in the bush. Ayemotï wandered for two weeks with the war leader Guïrakota, until both eventually surrendered near Ivo at Łäkaroïsa, Cold Creek. Bolivian troops took the two to Monteagudo for military trial. Perhaps as a sign of a nervous frontier or as a further staging of absolute control, the two were whipped "to learn of the general plans of the rebels." The military report added that no information was gained. The report then states dryly that Guïrakota and the "camba [injun] Aimonte [Ayemotï] who served as treasurer and principal chief of the Tumpa [Tüpa]" were executed by a firing squad. In Sanabria's account, perhaps embellished, Ayemotï died at "the roar of the guns" invoking the name of "his" tüpa, "after saying something in his native language" (Sanabria Fernández 1972:213). Six hundred hacienda Guarani laborers from the nearby Ingre valley were paraded past the bodies.

Apiaguaiki Tüpa escaped into the Taremakua hills where Guarani warriors of legend had also sought refuge. A few weeks later, a Guarani leader lured him down with promises of shelter, only to hand him over to the soldiers. At Monteagudo, he was also subjected to "various tortures" and "passed before arms" on March 29. Some accounts suggest that he was impaled (sodomized) on a long pike before being killed. This emasculation is echoed in one version of the name by which he is remembered today, Japia oeki, the castrated one.[6] The tüpa's body was displayed for twenty-four hours in the plaza of Monteagudo and then quartered and burned (Sanabria Fernández 1972). The scorched-earth spectacle and terror of ethnic cleansing was now coupled with a performance that sought to conjure the unquestioned sovereignty of the karai state. Unruly bodies and tongues, as well as claims to epistemic and territorial authority, were silenced, destroyed, and dispersed. The subversion of colonial order had been brought to a halt.

At least for a moment. One hundred years later, the story of the Massacre of Kuruyuki provided an allegory for the resurgence of a different kind of Guarani struggle. In 1987, with the help of NGOs tied to the Catholic Church, Guarani community leaders reemerged to create the Assembly of Guarani People (APG). On the centennial of Kuruyuki (which coincided, randomly, with the 1992 quincentennial), the APG staged a march through the region that culminated near the battlefield at Ivo. Guarani leaders again questioned the racial and political order. Yet by the late 1990s their way of speaking was in part situated in the language of NGO development projects, the intercultural reforms of the state, and global visions of indigenous rights, much like that of other such movements in Latin America (Yashar 2005). The Guarani were not armed. Many were bilingual speakers of Spanish and Guarani. Not a few had converted to Catholicism or Protestantism. Still playing flutes and drums, most wore clothes like those of the rural karai, replacing long, flowing hair with cowboy or baseball hats. Other than their features, woven shoulder bags, and the proud use of their language, little distinguished them from rural peasants.

The gathering at the battlefield inaugurated a massive bilingual literacy campaign for adult Guarani. On one level the literacy campaign represented the expanding apparatus of global development aid. The Guarani attracted funding from sources like UNICEF, UNESCO, and the World Bank because of their status as poor and marginal communities blessed with the exotic allure of indigenous identity and a colorful narrative of heroic struggle. Guarani played this role astutely, gently acknowledging that the karai still feared Guarani mobilization and suggesting that their embrace of education was good for the region. Guarani leaders assured the multiethnic audience at

Kuruyuki (which included then Bolivian president Jaime Paz Zamora) that education was their instrument of struggle. "We will fight no more with arrows and clubs," said the old leader Mateo Chumiray; "now we will fight with pencils and notebooks" (Chumiray 1992).

Yet among Guarani leadership circles the literacy campaign was not just about development, but about political resurgence. Though accepting schooling as a legitimate instrument, Chumiray denounced the violence suffered by the Guarani ancestors at the hands of the karai state, the slavery still practiced on karai haciendas, and the poverty resulting from land dispossession. This was the talk about education and citizenship that made karai nervous. The leaders named the campaign Tataendi for the embers fanned back to life in Guarani fire pits each morning. They said that an eternal flame of sorts—Guarani language, culture, and history—was being rekindled from beneath the ashes and violence of colonialism (APG 1992; Ventiades and Jauregui 1994; Yandura 1996).

SITUATING HISTORIES

The Kuruyuki narrative and the contemporary uses made of it by the Guarani are useful for contextualizing understandings of EIB and schooling today. Across this history of colonial terror and modern resurgence, the tensions between literacy and violence as referential metaphors and practices of both emancipatory struggle and governmental control remain central to the relationship between indigenous peoples and the Bolivian state. Schooling and violence are still competing frames that shape the ways people talk—and worry—about interethnic relations, differences, and futures. The longer history of colonial expansion and its transnational foundations of epistemic, linguistic, religious, and political power also have echoes in contemporary development politics. Without exaggerating the significance of Kuruyuki— which, it should be clear, constitutes a dense and problematic narrative—I return in chapter 6 to consider how Kuruyuki and EIB continue to serve as an emergent language of the state that seeks to transcend the coloniality of power inherited from the past.

Yet the Kuruyuki story is also useful because of how it links the Guarani to a wider national history. Even if partly apocryphal, the historical factuality of Apiaguaiki Tüpa and the colonial terror faced by the Guarani (including the quartering and burning of the rebel hero) link the Guarani to the similar histories of Andean and other lowland peoples. The near-mythic sublima-tion of figures like Apiaguaiki Tüpa is tactical. It links the Guarani and their hero to histories like that of the Aymara martyrs Tupak Katari and Bartolina Sisa (who met similarly gruesome ends). Popular Bolivian nationalism, as much as local indigenous struggle, is invoked through Kuruyuki. Kuruyuki thus helps me, and by extension, the reader, to root the histories that follow in a historical space centered on Guarani lives and lands and to look outward from there, while simultaneously mooring these histories to patterns of colo-nial and republican nation building situated at the center of the Andean state.

The rest of this chapter returns to the years before and after Kuruyuki to trace these different yet parallel histories linking Andean state formation with Guarani lives on the frontier. I focus on state and nonstate education apparatuses as these arise in tension with indigenous modes of resistance and accommodation. The story of Andean, and especially Aymara, education and struggle is fairly well known (Choque Canqui 1992; Luykx 1999; Lar-son 2003; Gotkowitz 2007). I retrace key points of this Andean history here, tacking back and forth with Guarani schooling and struggle on the frontier. I draw on the work of historians and oral histories I collected over the years. I attempt to show how the Aymara and Guarani represent cases that illustrate both the wider unity of indigenous experience and the "historico-structural heterogeneity of transnationalized state spaces" (Mignolo 2005:48). This opens up multiple lenses through which to interpret contemporary change, both unified in relation to regimes of power like neoliberalism, the state, and the aid-funded education-reform project and also mediated and complicated by the particularities of local histories of language, knowledge, and struggle.

Race and Nation in the Andes

Several decades before Kuruyuki, during the 1820s, Bolivian state institu-tions reemerged in the aftermath of the independence wars against Spain. Indigenous peoples had participated in these battles, but the shift from col-ony to republic did little to change the colonial structure of rule. Criollo elites struggled among themselves over control and the construction of the state. Ideas of liberal citizenship were spreading, but the rulers of the nascent state felt disinclined to distribute liberty, equality, and fraternity so quickly. Their debates centered around the meaning of a supposedly modern nation and around the place of Indians therein. Initially, citizenship juridically legitimated gender, class, and racial inequality, limiting this status to white, literate, property-owning men. The poor and the illiterate, as well as women, Indians, mestizos, and Afro-Bolivians, were all excluded. Since literacy was understood as Spanish literacy, native languages were similarly marked as ill-suited for equality. Education became the domain of a patriarchal ruling class. On the one hand, it served as a boundary-maintenance instrument. On the other, it constituted a mode of producing knowledges of rule, less for the control of subjects—still largely governed by violence—than for the formation of a ruling class. Early state efforts thus sought to train criollo men in the administrative and technical skills needed to manage the state and to extract resources, principally mineral ones. Institutes of mining and public administration were established by the early presidents Antonio José de Sucre (1825–38) and Andrés de Santa Cruz (1829–39). In the wake of the silver boom of the 1860s, the state formalized "public" schooling through the Statute on Public Instruction (1874). That same year another law ordered the dissolution of indigenous-held collective lands. One sought to improve the education of the male criollo "public," the other to transform Andean indigenous communities into landless laborers. In 1892, the year of the Kuruyuki massacre, the state again expanded its efforts to modernize schooling for urban whites in La Paz (Langer and Jackson 1990:20; Martinez 1999). Geographically and socially restricted, schooling mirrored the fledgling state, centered as it was around the urban ruling class and a colonial model of resource extraction and exclusionary citizenship.

Indigenous peoples, like women and Afro-Bolivians, were excluded from rights as equals within this state schooling project despite their inclusion as laboring subjects. The literacy that did emerge in indigenous communities was tied to the catechistic and administrative work of the Catholic Church (Arnold and Yapita 2006). Selective violence interspersed with softer techniques of secular and religious administrative control continued as the preferred form for controlling indigenous land, labor, and knowledge. Criollo elites opposed efforts by indigenous peoples to gain access to literacy to defend their lands in court, as well as suggestions that indigenous peoples should be included in mass public schooling. Elite dependence on native labor distinguished the country from neighboring Argentina and Chile, whose genocidal violence against indigenous peoples in the late nineteenth century paved the way for European immigration. Unlike Bolivia, those countries by this time already merged projects of mass schooling with nation and citizen formation in an explicit way through the creation of the "teacher state" (*estado docente*) (Nuñez 2005).

Bolivian criollos feared that expanding literacy for indigenous peoples would undermine a state that depended economically and ideologically on their legal subjugation. The positivist racism of the time further led to questions about whether indios were suited for modernity at all. The liberal turn of the early twentieth century thus led to debates about education not for mass citizenship, but to pursue linguistic homogeneity and so-called racial improvement to make indigenous peoples less different, though not equal, subjects of a modern nation (Unzueta 2000). These debates were rooted in biological understandings of race in which language was (mis)understood as a physiological phenomenon biologically linked to geography and culture. Whether and how the Indian might be "improved" thus depended on whether indigenous languages were vehicles for, or obstacles to, change. Implicitly accepting that indigenous peoples could be transformed, and that native languages had no future in the nation, most intellectuals echoed Claudio Sanjinés, who wrote in 1917 that "the *castellanización* of the indigenous element constitutes a supreme necessity for the unification of the Republic" (Choque Canqui 1994:21–23). A few argued that the native languages, being a biological element, might be useful for effective education, without the pretense of making indios into criollos. The general consensus, however, was that "barbarous" tongues had no place in a modern nation (Choque Canqui 1994:21–23).

The historian Ann Zulawski (2007:21–31) points out that criollo nation builders were never in agreement over whether Indians could or should be brought into the nation as equal citizens. Another historian, Francoise Martinez (1999), suggests that three proposals shaped state approaches to the Indian in this era: get rid of the Indian (through genocide or miscegenation); isolate and separate the Indian (through the "two republics" model of Spanish colonialism); or "improve" the Indian through special education. Dependent on Indian labor yet fearful of indigenous rebellion, criollo elites leaned toward separation and improvement. Though opposed by many criollo landowners, the official strategy in the early twentieth century was to use schools and the military to supposedly improve Indians while keeping them separate as a racially distinct lower caste. Indigenous peoples would be made to speak the language of the state—not as citizens, but as subjects to be *instruido* (instructed, not empowered), *educado* (disciplined, not learned), and *gobernado* (governed, not represented) by the criollo state.[7]

To bolster their efforts, the Bolivians turned to European knowledge and experts, early international development consultants who represented the modernity of Europe as the beacon of progress to which Latin American elites aspired. French and German officers were hired to advise the Bolivian military. The French Napoleonic pattern for centralized governance (state-department-province-*cantón*) was established in Bolivia in 1826 (Slater 1995:56). The French system of centralized public schooling also provided a model for Bolivia. Hence Bolivian "normal" schools, *escuelas normales*, are sites for teacher training today, modeled after the *écoles normales* in France. A Chilean was hired in 1906 to run the education department. By 1913, the Belgian Georges Rouma ran the Office of Public Instruction. Rouma went on to spearhead the Bolivian education reform of 1917, in which the inclusion of white women constituted the major goal. He later opened and ran the first normal school for teachers in Sucre.

In racist terms, elites also hoped to model their own citizens after European bodies. For example, the liberal positivist and education minister Daniel Sánchez Bustamante traveled to France, Sweden, and Belgium on a pedagogical mission just after the turn of the century (Martinez 1999). Sánchez Bustamante was most impressed by supposed Swedish racial superiority then assumed to be somehow linked to their highly disciplined form of physical education. Subscribing to the Lamarckian notion that acquired traits could be passed to future generations, Sánchez Bustamante thought that schooling routines could generate durable racial transformations of the Bolivian Indian. In addition, as Martinez (1999) describes, the Swedes were seen as pacifists compared to the bellicose Germans. Criollo elites saw this as a bonus, hoping that schooling would subdue, not militarize, the Aymara. Sánchez Bustamante eventually hired the Belgian Rouma to implement the Swedish curriculum in Bolivian teachers' colleges.

This selective appropriation of knowledge decontextualized from its practice in one site and reassembled elsewhere reflected the universalist positivism and Eurocentrism of dominant elites as well as then dominant racist logic. Some opposition came from contrarian thinkers like Franz Tamayo. In his *Creation of the National Pedagogy* (1910), Tamayo initiated an early, if timid, defense of the Indian, calling for a pedagogy rooted in national rather than foreign models. Yet even Tamayo believed that racial engineering was necessary to prevent the degeneration of the Indian into the mestizo *cholo* (urbanized Indian), and his "national pedagogy" was derived from European philosophic origins. He saw indigenous peoples not through a critical understanding of colonial economic and political structures, but through a telluric spiritualism that sought to capture their "vital energy" and their relation to the earth and to put this essence into the service of the nation (Sanjinés 2004:61–63). In some manner, interculturalism as an icon of national particularity that makes of indigeneity a development resource—devoid of critiques of racism and structural inequality or of substantive epistemic engagement with indigenous alterity—might be read in the same way today. Radical for its time, Tamayo's critique of Eurocentric racism was nonetheless sidelined by history.

In the Aymara region, state proposals to separate and improve the Indian through special schooling faced multiple obstacles. Landowners had no interest in educated workers. The state's own infrastructural weakness further hindered the idea. More important, state efforts were overshadowed by the Aymara's own attempts to access schooling. Local demands for literacy spread through movements of the Aymara region's leaders as communities mobilized to find and support teachers. These efforts culminated in the founding of the Warisata school experiment in *educación indigenal* in 1931. It met with hacendado violence that led to its closure shortly thereafter (see Choque Canqui 1992; the interlude following chapter 6). The state's efforts to link schooling and racial control also backfired. Aymara projects to seek literacy were intimately linked to struggles to defend community lands (Mamani Capchiri 1992; Arnold and Yapita 2006). Judging by Aymara uprisings in 1921 and 1927—and 2001 and 2003—the state attempt to create docile subjects through schooling made little progress.

Mission Schooling on the Guarani Frontier

While criollo intellectual and political schisms merged with weak state capacity and Aymara protagonism to frustrate schooling projects in the Andean center, Guarani lives at the turn of the twentieth century unfolded in a quite different milieu. After the Massacre of Kuruyuki, many Guarani were dispersed into marginal lands not sought by karai, or they fled south to Argentina. Those who remained faced life as mission neophytes or hacienda peons. A number of regions maintained a semblance of autonomy under the leadership of Guarani captains. Yet this was a subservient autonomy in which captains became intermediaries and labor contractors for karai, solidifying once flexible leadership arrangements into hierarchical structures of indirect rule—the "reduction" of the Guarani appeared near completion. In 1912, the Italian missionary-ethnographer Bernardino de Nino wrote that the "Chiriguano" (Guarani) of today was not the Chiriguano of the past.

> He is not the one who fought tenaciously against the soldier of the Inca army, against the Spaniard, and even against the Bolivian soldier. This change has been demonstrated, I'll say once again, by the loss of their territory and their independence. . . . Whether through good relations or through violence, the Chiriguano have had to subject themselves to the laws of the republican Government that now exercises supreme authority over them, [carried out] in the Missions through the Fathers, in the Provinces through the subprefects, or in the counties through the *corregidores*, who generally use a [Guarani] cacique or mayor for gathering people to perform some labor of public utility. (1912:115)

On the haciendas, schooling was nonexistent. In the missions, schools inculcated new knowledge through literacy, yet often they did so against the protests of the region's settlers (who saw no good reason to school the Guarani laborer) and the resistance of Guarani parents (who recognized the catechism as subjugation). A brief excursion into mission schooling provides a useful counterpoint to state efforts in the Andes.

Franciscan mission schooling projects date to two periods: the era of Spanish colonialism (1600s–1810s) in which Jesuit, and later Franciscan, missions staffed by Spaniards spread across southern and eastern Guarani country; and the republican era (1840s–1930s), when Italian Franciscan fathers rebuilt missions destroyed during the independence wars. This latter period directly anticipated the ongoing role of the church in Guarani education and political organizing today.

Missions were instruments of evangelization, and, offering a refuge from overt violence, they represented the least bad option for native peoples. Guarani only turned to missions when they saw no alternatives and had nowhere else to flee the karai advance. Missions nonetheless formed part of the colonial project, serving as state allies or surrogates where the state was weak. With no other options, Guarani faced either mission dependence or state violence. Even so, as mission historians like Erick Langer (e.g., 1989, 1994a) and Barbara Ganson (2004) point out, neither dependence nor the threat of violence produced absolute control over Guarani. Proud Guarani were deeply resistant to evangelization. Thierry Saignes uncovered one testimonial of a Guarani elder who declared to an earnest priest in the late 1700s that his desire was to live freely and die as his ancestors had, "Because my grandfathers were not Christian and I want to go with them to hell" (Saignes 1990:84). A century later the Guarani still resisted subjugation. To cajole them to send their children to mission schools, missionary fathers offered certain freedoms and goods to adults and nonbelievers. Franciscans resigned themselves to failure of one sort (the conversion of Guarani adults) in the hopes of achieving future success of another (the "civilization" of Guarani children). Yet as with the weak Bolivian state today, which negotiated certain political openings in the present for control over future subjects, this contingent solution did not assure schooling success. As Father Martarelli complained:

> The heathen adult Chiriguanos [are] very sensual and tenacious in their customs and barbarous superstitions, [and] without a miracle of divine grace, it is not easy to reduce them to be instructed in the truths of our august religion and to leave their bad habits; to obligate them to this would be to lose the hopes of moralizing and civilizing their children and the new generation. They have not subjected themselves to live under the Government of the Missionary Fathers with the intentions of embracing Christianity and reforming their customs, but rather to obtain some temporary advantage, to preserve their lands, and to avoid losing their liberty. (1890:194–95)

For example, Guarani captains like Mandeponay, who surrendered to mission tutelage at Macharetɨ in the late 1800s, astutely avoided direct participation in the 1892 insurrection (Langer 1989). By staying out of the fight, he managed to maintain kin and alliance networks that contributed to his authority, albeit within mission walls. The old leader refused baptism while using his influence to organize Guarani labor parties who traveled to higher-paying cane plantations in Argentina to avoid the conditions on Bolivian farms. Mandeponay used the wealth earned as a labor-contractor to reproduce massive drinking events *(aretes)* and redistributive networks. In exchange for this circumscribed autonomy, the old chief agreed to let the missionary fathers school Guarani children.

Whether mission schools obtained their religious objectives in any durable way is questionable. Ayemotï's defection to the rebel cause in 1892 suggests that conversion was an additive, rather than a wholly transformative, process. Yet in the short term the Bolivian state was not deeply concerned with souls or learning. The state saw the missions as a way to keep Guarani labor under control and in its place. To stem the gradual outflow of Guarani labor (and the people's decimation through disease and poor living conditions), in 1924 the Bolivian minister of war and colonization decreed that the primary goal of the missions should be to stop the emigration of the Guarani to Argentina (qtd. in Riester 1995:263). These goals found their way into mission schooling projects, as reflected in an early bilingual primer written by Nino, *The Child* (*El nene*, 1905). Written in both Guarani and Spanish, phrases like, "It's not good that the Indians go far away, when they go away, they lose their things," sought to inculcate an immobile and docile labor force (Nino 1905:12). Yet the Guarani who had received some schooling or crafts training were usually the first to migrate (Langer 1987).

These built-in failures did not mean that schooling projects had no durable effects. Mission schooling contributed to the transformation and in many cases the erasure of distinctive Guarani markers of difference and freedom (or "savagery," as it was termed). This meant cutting the boys' long hair (called *simba* from the Quechua word for "braid"). This also meant forbidding the placement of the *tembeta*, the lip plug that men wore under their lower lip. When Guarani girls entered school, the one-piece *mandu* (or *tipoi*) worn by Guarani women was replaced with a *pollera* dress "like that worn by mestizo women" (Nino 1912:305). Boys were dressed in cotton pants and ponchos, much like the rural karai. As Martarelli wrote (qtd. in Langer 1995:66): "It is necessary that the [Indian] forgets all that had to do with their savage and superstitious state. . . . With this goal in mind, it has been determined to have school boys and girls adopt the clothing of the Christians . . . of these regions."

Guarani bodies were refashioned to become laborers and artisans whose products went to support the reproduction of the mission itself (Langer

1995:62–63). Boys were taught skills like carpentry, leatherwork, and the distilling of cane brandy. Girls were taught loom weaving and sewing. These labors formed part of the daily routine of schooling, giving form to the factory-like quality of schooling everywhere. New routines of order were imposed through the use of time and the ubiquitous school bell. Priests focused their disciplinary efforts on preaching against "vices" like witchcraft, polygamy, and sloth, all seen as the fundamental weaknesses of the otherwise proud and sturdy Guarani, yet traits that subverted colonial epistemes of religion, political authority, and economy.[8]

In public writing (and in laws about mission administration) Franciscans supported *castellanización* as a tool for pursuing these civilizing goals and for extending the national project of the state. Nino's *The Child* began with the observation that "among the necessary means for civilizing a barbarian tribe, language occupies [a central] place . . . so that the barbarians might understand those of the civilized nation" (Nino 1905:1). Cognizant of the state's impatience with what was seen as coddling savages, Franciscans struggled to defend their labors to domesticate the Guarani. It is hard to say whether the Franciscans were violent assimilators or simply echoing the perceived interests of the state. In any case, Nino was clear about the trajectory he foresaw for the language:

> The language in its most pure form cannot be found in any *pueblo* or in the Missions. In the former because they live amongst the whites and are continually emigrating to Argentina. In the Missions, [the] reason is the Spanish training that the Missionaries give to the boys and girls in the schools; in a way that, if the race doesn't disappear first, as is feared [due to the] continuous epidemics and vagrancy, the language will be lost anyway and the few books that exist will only serve as a historical monument for posterity, who will know how to recognize the merit and labor of the Missionaries who went out to spill their sweat among these [Guarani], with the only goal of civilizing them in a Christian way. (1912:77)

Another Franciscan boasted of mission achievements in this area, writing that "after overcoming so many difficulties [the school] has been able to uproot [*desterrar*] from the children the Chiriguano language and . . . the dress, substituting for it the dress and language of the country [i.e., Bolivia]" (qtd. in Langer 1994a).

Nonetheless, the Franciscans were also consummate students of Guarani. They were engaged in an intellectual battle with the Jesuits whose legacy of linguistic work on Paraguayan Guarani was constantly contrasted with their work on "our" Guarani. Hence the preference for the label *Chiriguano* to distinguish these territorial and linguistic turfs from points east. Franciscans like Doroteo Giannechini went to great lengths to write grammars, dictionaries, and sermons in Guarani. Even in the wake of Kuruyuki, Giannechini gave painstakingly handwritten sermons in Guarani at the San Francisco mission near Villamontes, a large collection of which are archived in Tarija today. Though some Franciscans were rather assimilationist, others were more inclined to isolate their wards from the karai, promoting the use of Guarani to this end (Erick Langer, personal communication, 2002).

Franciscan mission schools did not homogenize or assimilate the Guarani, but rather created new forms of differentiation. Some regions noted for the influence of the *pai* (the priests) are today marked by more loyalty (and dependence) on the Catholic Church. Other ex-mission towns are now largely Spanish-speaking. Some have entirely transformed into karai communities, a testament to the pacifying efforts that led to Guarani dispossession. Other former mission areas along the Santa Cruz–Argentina highway are still Guarani, yet they are largely bilingual and in transition to Spanish. Other regions like Isoso, Kaipependi, and much of the southern and eastern Simba areas never had missions after the independence wars. The population was subjugated on haciendas or able to carve out spaces of negotiated autonomy. Here the language remains more vibrant. It is hard to know if these differential linguistic effects have wholly resulted from mission influence or from other socioeconomic factors, since missions were located along major trade and settlement routes that also spurred Guarani displacement and linguistic assimilation through labor relations and intermarriage with karai.

Other mission legacies persist in the language and ideology of schooling. Like their Jesuit counterparts and modern Guarani activists, the Franciscans engaged in language engineering. For instance, the word *tüpa* was retranslated to "God." Priests sought to highlight the religio-political power of literacy by glossing *tupapire*, "paper," as "the skin of God" (*tüpapire*). In fact it derives from the word for parchment taken from a reed (*tupa*).[9] They also reengineered the meanings of knowledge. Most salient to the discussion that follows is the word for school learning or school knowledge, *yemboe*. The verb -*yemboe* literally means "to make oneself be made to speak." Its root is -*e*, to speak. Yemboe historically referred to Guarani ritual oratory. Ritual speech constituted a means of reproducing sociopolitical relations and communicating across the human-supernatural divide. This nonbureaucratic, decentralized knowledge and authority emerged in those who came to possess special knowledge by virtue of an inherent characteristic, an experiential practice, or a supernatural encounter. By the early twentieth century, as today, yemboe had been resignified to mean "school learning," that is, "to be made to speak." During the mission years this meant being made to speak the word of God through liturgical reading and repetition, with the entire weight of the church and state bureaucracy behind it.[10] Being made to speak thus built on the religious connotations of conversion and subjection to institutionalized power.[11]

As school knowledge inflected by the liturgical form and meaning of catechism, this kind of yemboe was understood to produce subjects temporally, morally, cognitively, and to an extent, biologically advanced in comparison to "savage" Guarani. Recall here the name of Apiaguaiki Tüpa's scribe Juan "I-Have-Made-Myself-White" Ayemotï. Ayemotï's name invoked his own passage to literacy and Christianity, a religious, linguistic, and racial conversion.[12] In contemporary times, the conversion one undergoes when "being made to speak" is primarily linguistic, though it maintains the religious undertone because a deeper sense of social and ethnic transformation is understood to accompany language change and literacy. Before the ideological turn of EIB, which began unraveling these ideas, young Guarani could be heard to say, "ayemboema aï, che campesinoäma ko che" (I have been educated, that is, I have been made to speak; I am no longer a peasant [i.e., indio]). Whether in religious or secular forms, conversion through schooling pursued subjects predisposed to be governed under new hierarchies of knowledge, territory, and sociopolitical order. Though not unique to the Franciscans, nor entirely attributable to their efforts, this view of evolutionary transformation from Indian primitiveness to Christian modernity constituted a core legacy of the religiously rooted colonial schooling project that underlay all projects of state formation in the indigenous territories of the Americas. Decolonizing this legacy remains a major challenge.

By the 1910s the military state no longer needed mission assistance, thus cementing the Guarani position as absolute noncitizens in their own lands. Powerful karai landlords pressured the state to close or "secularize" the missions, a process initiated in 1915 and completed in 1948 (Métraux 1930b; Pifarré 1989:406).[13] With this last buffer against a more savage colonialism removed, the Guarani region became a landlord-dominated backwater like the rest of eastern Bolivia in the twentieth century. Many Guarani migrated to Argentine sugar cane plantations or began an ongoing exodus north to the proletarian peripheries of Santa Cruz. Between 1933 and 1935 the Chaco War between Bolivia and Paraguay hit the region with full force, furthering displacement of Guarani. Some Guarani even faced accusations of treason because they spoke Guarani (like Paraguayan troops).[14]

Historians generally argue that the Chaco War represented a watershed leading to the creation of a national consciousness for Andean masses who fought in the war and later returned with a new sense of citizenship to question conditions of peonage in the Andes (e.g., Klein 1992). Indeed, the Chaco War was followed by rising Andean indigenous mobilization, the growth of Marxian-inspired labor movements, and the intensification of revolutionary nationalism against the mining barons. These processes culminated in the revolution of 1952, with land reform and the spread of mass public schooling transforming the Andean countryside. Guarani country continued as a marginal, feudal frontier.

Revolution in the Andes, Stasis on the Frontier

Led by middle-class reformers of the National Revolutionary Movement (MNR) party, the 1952 revolution was at its core a conservative, bourgeoisie-headed development project aimed at displacing the mining and agrarian oligarchies and implementing a corporatist model of state-led capitalism.[15] Yet miners, indigenous peoples, and workers also featured as protagonists. They succeeded in radicalizing the revolution in some regions, sparking peasant occupations of large landholdings (latifundia) and the initiation of a de facto land reform later institutionalized by the revolutionary government. Other changes came with the granting of the vote to the indigenous peasantry and the gradual expansion of mass public schooling. With land, schooling, and suffrage, Andean Indians were supposedly on their way to citizenship. Native peoples were officially relabeled as "peasants" (campesinos) to mark the end of their subjugation as indios. The nationalization of industry would liberate the nation from the tentacles of imperialism, land reform was to liberate the indio from feudalism, and education in Spanish would liberate them from their very Indianness.

The MNR regime incorporated indigenous communities into a national peasant federation (*confederación sindical campesina*) built on a pyramid of departmental, provincial, and community unions (*sindicatos*). Miners, workers, and schoolteachers were unionized in a similar form and scale. These "classes" or "sectors" were represented vis-à-vis the state by leaders who entered into *co-gobierno* (cogovernment) relationships with criollo elite political parties. Jobs and resources in and for these sectors were managed through ministries, themselves distributed (*repartido*) among party coalitions or, later, military officers. Competition for access to public goods of the state and their selective and negotiated distribution downward toward workers and peasants became the raison d'être of the party, the union, and the state system. Corporatist representation and pacts of negotiated cogovernment between the criollo parties and the laboring sectors would last for five decades, even through periods of military dictatorship, deeply imprinting the public language and practice of politics in Bolivia.

The revolution did not grant full citizenship to indigenous peoples and did not overhaul the coloniality of power. It in fact yielded another fifty years of its stability, with effects clearest in education. The 1955 Education Code expanded public schooling and rendered official castellanización for the entire country, institutionalizing a violent process of linguistic extirpation. Though promising equality through assimilation, schooling reproduced the colonial spatial and social hierarchy and the separate-and-improve logic that differentiated the rural indio from the urban citizen. The school apparatus was divided into rural and urban administrative entities with separate management structures, budgets, teaching schools, and teachers' unions. Initially, rural schools were administered by the Ministry of Peasant (i.e., Indian) affairs, while the Ministry of Education operated urban schools (Contreras and Talavera Simoni 2003). Schools in cities or towns were urban schools largely attended by mestizos or criollos. Schools in small agrarian communities (whether mestizo or indigenous) were deemed rural and attended by the poor agricultural classes. All public schools were in practice and perception inferior to private schools, where those with means educated their children. Urban whiteness thus became reified as educationally and juridically distinct from rural Indianness, while class hierarchies were reinforced through differentiated schooling structures. This ideology and structure of schooling remains largely intact today.

Nonetheless, revolutionary schooling and land reform initiated processes of class and race mobility with effects unforeseen by elites. Rural education gave indigenous peasants rudimentary skills in Spanish literacy that fed the defense of territorial and social formations and encouraged migration to urban areas (Arnold and Yapita 2006). Indigenous merchant classes of cholos—those I learned to dance with in the 1990s—grew in urban centers like La Paz and Cochabamba, upsetting the unstable colonial association between racial difference, rurality, and lower class. By the 1970s, a generation of indigenous youth with ties to both city and countryside achieved new forms of consciousness with public university study. Discourses of Indian pride bloomed among these new indigenous intellectuals. Aymara and Quechua as well as lower-middle-class mestizos of pueblos and mine centers also began to fill the ranks of the rural teachers' unions, imbuing them with a militant revolutionary discourse and, in some regions, with an implicit, if stigmatized, ethnic identity (Luykx 1999). Land reform sustained the emergence of a national peasant union that evolved into the CSUTCB (Confederación Sindical de Trabajadores Campesinos de Bolivia), a de facto Aymara-Quechua ethnic federation allied with mestizo smallholders. By 1979 the CSUTCB had become a powerful autonomous actor shaped by demands for decolonization (*descolonización*) that mobilized symbols of peasant-worker struggle and ethnolinguistic revindication (Albó 1991). Despite the attempts to fix Indians in their place, the revolution sparked direct and indirect conquests for indigenous peoples that continue to shape Bolivian politics today.

These transformations were practically nonexistent in Guarani country. The MNR party had a tenuous hold on power at the state center and little capacity to impose radical change in the peripheries. There it relied on landowner support. Thus the land reform that swept the Andes did not liberate the Guarani from peonage. In fact, it stimulated a renewed rush on Guarani lands by outsiders. In western Guarani country, organized Quechua and mestizo settlers were able to take advantage of land reform to displace the "unorganized" Guarani peons (Healy 1982). Guarani, generally landless or living on semisubsistence plots, gained little or nothing.[16] Nor did the expansion of rural schools reach across Bolivia. Schooling was nonexistent on the haciendas, where entire communities were still treated as the property of karai landlords. Some karai hacendados were barely literate themselves and also spoke Guarani, using it as a language of control, with the power to "write" and speak Spanish marking a thin line of power. Preventing Guarani access to Spanish—and what Guarani call the power to talk back—proved crucial to the maintenance of social hierarchy. As late as 1994 during a research project on educational needs, one teenager from the Ingre valley north of the Pilcomayo told us: "We only study until third grade; then the *patrón* makes us work when they see we can work like the other peons. It's true that the land is ours, but the karai still have us like tame donkeys [*burros mansos*]" (Robles, Gustafson, and Rojas 2002).

The Letter Enters with Blood

The corporatist system shifted rightward after a coup in 1964, and Bolivia entered two decades of nearly uninterrupted right-wing military dictatorship. The Cold War language of the era spoke of national security rather than national revolution. School expansion followed suit, extending the institutional reach of the state as a tool of development and control rather than of liberation. The assistance of the United States proved crucial during this period, as eastern Bolivia was seen as a great frontier of development and a breeding ground for subversion because of a weak state and grinding rural poverty. In 1965, the first regional teachers' school opened in the dusty little karai town of Charagua. In 1999, the original plaque with the two clasped hands of the U.S. Alliance for Progress (also the icon of today's USAID) still hung above the doors of the Charagua Normal School. Above the cafeteria door, ornately painted letters read in gothic script, "You must work to enjoy the bread of your labors."

In 1968, the military government passed the Organic Statute for Education (López 1994, 1996). Replacing the rhetoric of liberation, anti-imperialism, and revolution of the 1955 Education Code, national security, discipline, order, and work now framed the concept of schooling. Political winds shifted briefly back to the left during the populist interlude of General Juan José Torres (1970–71), reaffirming the revolutionary principles of education "as an instrument of liberation" against "underdevelopment, neocolonial pressures, and subjugation to foreign interests" (MEC 1970:19–22). Paulo Freire even visited Bolivia to discuss popular literacy. Yet the shift was fleeting. General Hugo Bánzer, who hailed from eastern Bolivia, led a coup against the populists in 1971 and ruled until 1978, reestablishing "bread" and "work" as slogans for patriotism (perhaps explaining the cafeteria motto at the Charagua school). Bánzer rewrote the educational code to emphasize order and development. Only in this period did schooling begin to expand for the Guarani, not as a revolutionary and indigenous awakening, but as a militarized product of counterinsurgency logic and Cold War history.

The first generations of rural teachers trained at the Charagua Normal School reflected this history. Not of indigenous roots, as in the Andes, they were karai sons and daughters of the hacienda and of the rural merchant classes. Eastern Bolivia was a stronghold of pro-military landholders, and these teachers were less inclined to see themselves as revolutionaries liberating peasants than as karai disciplining and purifying the Guarani. As one karai professor told me, "Salíamos de la Normal para castellanizar, eso era nuestra misión, a golpes si fue necesario" (We came out of [Charagua] Normal to impose Spanish, that was our mission, through beatings if necessary). The phrase, the "letter enters with blood," still heard in talk of schooling during the 1990s and 2000s, here literally described a practice.[17] Still, this did not lead to massive Guarani access to schooling. Schools were built mainly in karai towns and pueblos, and Guarani villages rarely had access to more than the *básico*, the one-room school that covered three or sometimes five years. Study beyond básico required sending children to a karai town, a privilege limited to leadership families with some extra wealth or some benefactor in the form of U.S. Protestant missionaries or Catholic priests.

During this period, the karai-dominated rural teachers' union negotiated its local power with military officers who controlled job assignments and school budgets. Teachers aligned with the left were persecuted (especially in the late 1970s and early 1980s). Yet regardless of the ideological leanings of the teacher, educational practice as remembered by karai teachers and Guarani students was mimetic of military discipline and order. "The whole district," one older karai teacher recalled, "functioned along military order." Students lined up for morning flag raisings, as they often still do, by age, gender, and height. Teachers called them to attention and put them at ease like drill sergeants. Civic acts (celebrating Independence Day, Mother's Day, the

Day of the Sea, etc.) were accompanied by military-style parades. School-teachers, many of them male and having done obligatory military service, borrowed disciplinary practices learned in the barracks. Making unruly children stand in the sun or hold bricks above their heads, beating kids on bare calves, and making them kneel on corn kernels, pebbles, or bottle caps are but a few of the repertoire I frequently heard described.

Violence and military-like practice in Bolivian schools was not limited to indigenous regions. Yet in the Guarani and other indigenous cases the violence took on extra meaning in reference to the need to control the *ava* or *camba* (derogatory, "Injun") and their subversive use of language. The vocalization of Guarani was the audible sign and symptom of a space of communication and a subjective locus opaque to most teachers and outside their control. Guarani who talked with me about their or their children's experience in school always described physical and verbal violence experienced as a punishment for speaking Guarani, even well into the 1990s. In Itavera, where I lived in 1993 and 1994, Irma, a mother of four, directly associated language use with the amount of violence suffered by her children, "The first teacher only knew Spanish. She continuously beat the children. The one that came after her knew how to speak a little bit of Guarani, she only beat the children a little bit." In Ipitacito del Monte, a larger Guarani community just off the Santa Cruz highway north of Camiri, a Guarani leader of around forty told me of his experience with karai teachers, all of whom were kin of landlords who lived in nearby Ipita.[18] The grizzled leader spoke in Guarani. Yet Spanish loanwords like *punish, control, time, recess,* and *classroom* (in italics below) outlined a disciplinary lexicon of schooling absent in the Guarani language:

> Way back when I was little, while I was a *student,* back in those *times,* everyone was pure, completely Guarani. . . . Our ancestors were speakers of pure Guarani, and so we grew up with our language. That's why I only came to know to speak a little of the language of these karai in the *school.* And in the *school,* during those *times,* they . . . they . . . *controlled* us, see? If there was someone in the *classroom,* or out there, in *recess,* if there was someone speaking Guarani, when we went back into the *class,* they *punished* us, they beat us. They even watched us in our houses, [the teachers] snuck up on [hunted] us, they watched us secretly, and if we were speaking Guarani, they would *punish* us the next day in *school.*

This linguistic extirpation reinforced a vision of schooling as labor control. Still prominent on the walls of Ipitacito's school in 1998, a mural showed a peon leading an ox cart. The caption read, "Fuerza camba, que el trabajo es árduo!" (Strength, camba, because work is hard!). The Guarani leader Darío Ñanduresa from the Isoso region said of this era, "The only thing we learned in schools was how to serve the *patrón* better." Schooling in the Guarani region when I arrived in 1992 was thus full of paradoxes. On the one hand, significant parts of the region were denied schooling beyond two or three years or schools were nonexistent. Here the Guarani language and functional illiteracy served as an ethnic and class boundary, with exclusion from Spanish and literacy aimed at maintaining Guarani subjugation. In other regions where schooling, however limited, had existed for ten or twenty years, a violent legacy of castellanización was in evidence. In such communities, bilingualism is more common, often to the detriment of Guarani (as with Ipitacito) (see figure 2). One might conclude that access to Spanish literacy nonetheless proved positive, given the alternative of exclusion. Yet those who emerged from this kind of schooling suffered a violent process that sought to break down ethnic and social loyalties while reproducing racial and class hierarchies. This alienating process did not generate equality, but created subjects who would, as later teachers, work to deculturate their own people (see Luykx 1999). The first Guarani teachers to graduate from Charagua in the 1970s illustrated this. All were said to be worse than karai when it came to beating Guarani children to make them speak Spanish.

With pedagogies aimed at discipline and the stigmatization of linguistic difference, rural schooling achieved exclusion more than education. In the mid 1990s, of forty-three thousand Guarani (an estimate lower than the sixty thousand cited by the Guarani themselves) roughly 54 percent were functionally illiterate. This figure reached 80 percent on the haciendas (CIPCA n.d.). The 1992 census tabulated levels of Guarani bilingualism that ranged from 30 to 70 percent (Albó 1995). Both were signs of the limited pedagogical effect, and perhaps the more intense ideological effect, of schools. Guarani wryly joked in their ever-present humor masking intense bitterness that they came out of schools as *ni-lingües* ("nether-lingual," as opposed to *bilingüe*, "bilingual"). In other words, they did not learn good Spanish, and they lost or learned to despise and thus not speak well their own language. They had little to show for suffering through school.

FIGURE 2   To be made to speak Spanish. Guarani schoolgirls in Ipitacito del Monte, 1998.

In addition to this exclusion combined with castellanización, processes of class mobility and union protagonism present in the Andes did not manifest here. The ethnolinguistic and class divide generated a deep schism between the Guarani and the teachers union as a political actor, while indigenous Andeans were appropriating this state-sanctioned space for new political agendas. These divergent historical experiences of schooling shaped later differences between Andean and lowland peoples' embrace of EIB. With the return of electoral democracy in 1982 and the rise of indigenous organizations, substandard education was highlighted in indigenous political tracts and reformist agendas as one factor in poverty and exclusion. Better education would be a vehicle for transforming that condition. Yet within indigenous organizations and between these and the reformist state, there were differences about how schooling (and the state) should change, what other factors were involved in reproducing inequality, and how ethnolinguistic and epistemic difference should be addressed. Against this background indigenous resurgence and neoliberal developmentalism would meet on the terrain of school change during the 1990s and 2000s.

Return to Kuruyuki

I began this chapter with the Massacre of Kuruyuki, a historical event that serves as both anchor and allegory for Guarani struggles today. Kuruyuki also became central to representations of the Guarani to non-Guarani publics and my own introduction to these Guarani histories also came by way of Kuruyuki. In the early days of February 1992, I was in La Paz, and knew nothing about bilingual education or the Guarani. The first Kuruyuki commemoration and Guarani literacy campaign had just unfolded on January 28. I was just off the plane and enthralled with Bolivia. Having come in search of social movements, I filled up my cold little La Paz apartment with newspaper clippings about conflict and injustice around the country. The mainstream press was clearly pro-government, so I started buying the one critical weekly still in print. Called *Aquí*, it was tied to the progressive wing of the Catholic Church and founded by Luis Espinal, a Jesuit priest killed by the military in 1980. That first week in February, *Aquí* ran a brief note on the Massacre of Kuruyuki. The note outlined the history of the battle, the execution of Apiaguaiki Tüpa, the emergence of the Assembly of Guarani People, and their demand for bilingual education. Like many, I was initially surprised to learn that there were Guarani in Bolivia at all. Given Bolivia's Andean-centric slot in American anthropology, Guarani were usually associated with Paraguay. As I read on, I was intrigued. The article fit my perception of indigenous mobilization: an impoverished rural people struggling against racial, cultural, and class subjugation and using education as a tool of consciousness raising. I thought it would be neat to travel to Guarani country, so I taped the article on my wall.

A little more than a year after I read the *Aquí* note, I had found my way to Guarani country. The literacy campaign was in full swing and bilingual education was growing. By then I had read other accounts of Kuruyuki published by the Jesuit scholars Xavier Albó (1990) and Francisco Pifarré (1989). I had heard Guarani leaders speak of the massacre. In day-to-day life around Guarani activists, *lo de Kuruyuki* (the Kuruyuki events) were frequently repeated in conversations about movement history that conjoined what happened in 1892 with what resurged in 1992. Yet it remained abstract, political rhetoric more than living memory. This changed out in Itavera, where I spent most of 1993. I was chatting one day with Yarɨ, the elder grandmother. Old and blind, Yarɨ generally restricted her movements to the area around her daughter's house fire where I often sat with her. She asked me about a recent trip I had made to Camiri, and I commented offhandedly that the APG was organizing an event (by now the third Kuruyukɨ commemoration of 1994). It would be held at Kuruyukɨ, the "place where they fought with karai," I said in Guarani.

"Waiiiii!" she said in a high-pitched voice, showing sympathetic anguish. My comment sparked a story, and she began to recall what she had been told of Kuruyukɨ. "There must be many bones in that place," she began. Punctuating each phrase with *ndaye*, "it is said," she looked toward me with unseeing eyes and spoke in a voice strained with age:

> There must be many bones in that place,
> the karai killed the Guarani like locusts, it is said
> the karai were killing for three days, it is said
> they killed them with the big guns,
> they were long-haired *simbas*, youngsters![19] it is said
> the dead were piled like firewood! it is said
> and our blood ran like water in the creeks.

Her metaphors rooted memories of the violence in evocative everyday images—of locusts that swarm Guarani fields, stacks of firewood piled helter-skelter behind Guarani houses, shallow streams gurgling in rivulets through sandy creek beds. She went on to recount how her grandfather and his family had fled south in the aftermath of the battle, seeking refuge along the river in land unattractive to karai. I listened, recorder running, managing a whispered *taaata* between her phrases, a way to acknowledge the weight of her words.

[The Guarani] was a stranger in a land that had always been his, shut out because he couldn't speak the language of the *patrón*.
—*Jesus Urzagasti,* En el pais del silencio

Camiri, my destination in late 1992, was once a Guarani community called Kaami, meaning "little woods." An agrarian outpost in the wake of the Massacre of Kuruyukɨ, by the early twentieth century it began an oil boom, eventually growing to a city of some thirty thousand inhabitants and calling itself the "Oil Capital of Bolivia." Though Guarani were relegated to the margins in this and other urban political and economic centers, Camiri in the 1990s became an epicenter of Guarani organizing. Though much Guarani organizing dealt with rural land, urban spaces like Camiri were also—by virtue of associations between urbanity, power, and citizenship—targets of indigenous transformative agendas. Camiri had become the main site for bilingual education and for APG activities, and it was there that I first went to find the Guarani movement.

The flight from Santa Cruz to Camiri quickly leaves behind the rich agro-industrial tropical plain and heads over the hills of Guarani country. The flight follows a range called Aguaragüe (G. once a fox), the backbone of Guarani lands. Rugged geological wrinkles running north to south fold up against the Andes on the west, where the range known as Inkawasi (Q. house of the Inca), once disputed between Guarani and Inca warriors, forms the de facto boundary of Guarani country. The hills flatten abruptly into the dry Chaco to the east, refuge and home to *chaqueño* peoples now largely disappeared. The tiny towns below bear the imprint of the colonial state: ex-missions named for Catholic saints; settlements named for karai landlords; or Spanish translations of Guarani places. Guarani toponyms persist like the language and the Guarani themselves, entangled in these historical layers.

The plane follows the highway and the railroad south toward Argentina. The train bears its own histories. Through much of the twentieth century, Guarani were packed into cattle cars and carried north or south to work on cane plantations, a history that gave the train its nickname today, the Chahuanquero, Injun-hauler.[1] At the Río Grande the railroad tracks angle eastward, and the plane follows a southerly route over the highway. At Lagunillas a road branches off toward Sucre. Che Guevara established his first guerrilla camp near there in 1966, only to meet his fate further north. The road to Sucre continues over the hairpins of Inkawasi to Monteagudo, where Apiaguaiki Tüpa and Ayemotï were also executed by the state. Along that road are the so-called Guarani slave zones, where peonage persisted into the 2000s. Beyond Camiri to the south the highway turns west to Tarija along the southern borderlands of Guarani country. These dirt roads are centuries old, representing circuits that placed the Guarani in a colonial squeeze from all sides.

During the rainy months from September to January, a green carpet of trees covers the hills. From above, it gives the impression of tropical abundance. But the region is plagued by drought and blistering heat. Guarani place names like Ivo (bubbling spring), Iupaguasu (big pond), Iäkaguasu (big creek), Iäkaroïsa (cold creek), and Ingre (stinky water) mark the concern for water. Water scarcity is exacerbated by the unequal distribution of land. Amid the valleys rain is fickle, with the distance between shriveled crop and abundant harvest sometimes being as little as a few kilometers. Guarani occupy lower-quality lands with fields carved into hollows and hillsides. Karai occupy the moist valley floors like those lining the highway, the result of a history of dispossession. By the mid 1980s, 93 percent of the cordillera's arable land was in the hands of ranchers, while the Guarani majority subsisted on the rest (Pifarré 1989:412–13).

Karai and Guarani live in close proximity, and archipelagos of Guarani lands exist in a mosaic with karai settlements. Some Guarani communities are clearly distinct, while others have karai households interspersed within.

In still others, some Guarani and karai are intermarried. Members of these mixed (G. *oyeayea*) and karai families usually occupy positions of relative power, such as merchant, teacher, cowboy, or slightly less poor cattle owner. The region is also interspersed with Quechua and Aymara settlers and merchants, Italian priests, a handful of Lebanese, Croats, and Syrians, and a dabbling of Germans and Americans—the former Nazis or their Jewish victims who arrived after the Second World War, the latter missionaries and settler adventurers. Save the Aymara and Quechua, referred to as *kollas*, all the others are karai.

For karai the region is imagined as one of centers of *cristianos* or *blancos* and peripheries of rural *cambas* (derogatory, Indians, Guarani). Karai centers extract labor, agricultural commodities, and cultural symbols from the Guarani periphery. In this spatial template, the camba subject must remain in its place and under control. Cambas may only enter karai spaces as silent laborers or spectators. In the early 1990s, karai distanced themselves from Guarani bodies and space with a lexicon of derogatory terms: *ava, camba, kuña* (woman, as "squaw"), *kunumi* (boy), *chaguanco* (cane worker), *tɨmaka* (leg), *indio, come-mote* (corn eater). These condensed rurality, manual labor, darkness, ugliness, Indianness, and the audible qualities of the Guarani language. To colonial and karai ears, speaking Guarani was useful only for dealing with laborers, or if heard elsewhere, it was like not speaking at all.

These boundaries were also gendered. Guaraniness was a space of (weaker) femininity; karainess, of (dominant) masculinity.[2] Yet karai see Guarani women and men in slightly different temporal and biological relationships to them, though both are denied full personhood. Two statues on Camiri's outskirts enshrine these meanings in stone. On one end of the town stands a large statue of a Guarani warrior in a loincloth. Karai notables built this "Homage to the Ava-Guarani Man" in the 1970s. A headband is wrapped around streaming, long hair. Muscular arms and thighs bulge as the warrior poses in a defiant bowman's stance. Exaggerated lips and nose mark a grimacing face. A tautly drawn bow aims an arrow to the north. The statue recognizes and entombs the Guarani man in the image of the violent, and extinct, warrior of the past. Today's poor Guarani farmer in sandals and well-worn clothes merits no homage or recognition. On the road out of the town to the south stands the statue's counterpart. The thirty-foot tall "Cuñatay" (G. *kuñataɨ*, young woman) is a darkly painted woman carrying a water jug on her head. A bright red, skin-tight dress stretches over robust breasts and hips. Not consigned to history like her male counterpart, this Guarani has a place in the present as a silent laborer and sexual object, a recurring character in the folkloric and erotic fantasies of karai. Yet neither she nor her male counterpart speaks, for this would only legitimate violence against them.[3]

Most travelers make the journey to Camiri by bus or truck, a laborious fourteen-to-twenty-hour trip from Santa Cruz. Before it was paved in the late 1990s, the dirt highway turned to deep mud in the rainy season. Bus breakdowns were common. If one's budget and nerves allowed, an off-duty Bolivian Air Force (FAB) pilot could be hired to fly in a rickety Cessna. This was the preferred mode of travel for state functionaries, UNICEF officers, and aid consultants, a luxury I enjoyed a handful of times. Nonetheless, flying in created a false sense of proximity between state centers and Guarani lands. The quick hop of the plane resembled the partial knowledge of agents who planned, implemented, and evaluated. It gave the impression of easy access to people and places. Yet by collapsing time and space in ways unavailable to most locals, it constituted a superficial mode of engagement that left few or skewed traces behind. The long, hot, dusty truck, train, or bus ride gave a better sense of distance and difference as one traveled from La Paz through Santa Cruz into Guarani country. Though imagined like plane flights, state and development policies more closely resembled bus rides, fragmented by the topography, translated, broken down, reworked through local voices, ignored altogether or later pulled out and dusted off for special performances when a plane arrived bearing functionaries. This was how EIB unfolded, in part through aid and state flows that dropped like parachutes, in part emerging out of entangled Guarani and karai spaces and histories.

Suddenly the Parapeti River appears below, wrapping Camiri in a wide arc. The plane dives down to the dirt airstrip. The pilot slides his window open and the loud buzz of the propellers roars in as the plane bounces to a stop. I hop off, collect my bag, and a few minutes later a taxi drops me at the APG office near Camiri's central square, a few blocks from the warrior statue. By the 2000s, the Guarani had painted their own warrior on the outside wall of the office. Theirs also had a bow, but he was shooting arrows through the barbed-wire fences of cattlemen. It was a provocative retort. "La APG," the driver informs me politely. He feigns disinterest, gazing at the Guarani milling around the office door, probably wondering what these cambas are up to.

Chapter Two

GUARANI SCRIBES

Bilingual Education as Indigenous Resurgence

I will not live to see the results of this bilingual education, but this is how we will carry our people [G. *tëta*], our nation [S. *nación*] forward. You all know that we Guarani were conquerors long ago, they say. Because of this history, [foreign donors] say, "These Guarani are really a people [S. *pueblo*]." They say, "Let's help them rise up around their language." And so they help us. No longer will the karai beat us when we speak our language out loud. Now we can speak our language loudly when we walk through the town plaza. No longer is it as it was in the past, when they heard us and said, "Aaah this is a Guarani, this is a *camba*." In those days we were ashamed to speak out loud. Now we will speak without shame, we will make our language blossom again.

—*Mateo Chumiray, Ñeerokï Guarani Language Congress, 1997*

When I arrived in Camiri in November of 1992, the Guarani were in the midst of what I call indigenous resurgence. The APG, then four years old, was electing leaders, holding regional meetings, staging marches and events, all the while pressing power holders on land rights and labor conditions. They had marched with other lowland indigenous peoples to La Paz in 1990 and had played a significant role in the lowland confederation CIDOB. The Guarani were also increasingly visible internationally, something reflected in inflows of aid. National press coverage, as evidenced in my own "discovery" of the Guarani, also increased with both laudatory and denunciatory accounts of resurgence.[1]

Resurgence revolved in part around EIB, which began in 1989 in twenty Guarani schools (around 10 percent of the Guarani territory).[2] The UNICEF-funded initiative brought resources for schooling while indirectly providing a platform for political claims and unsettling traditional class and ethnic relations. For example, since there were practically no credentialed Guarani teachers, in 1990 sixty Guarani youth received UNICEF scholarships to study at the Charagua Normal School. What had been until then the fief of provincial karai was hit with instant desegregation. It was a "camba invasion," one karai professor recalled.

Resurgence tied to EIB was also linked to the literacy campaign of 1992, remembered as the first "massive mobilization at the level of the entire Guarani people" (M. Robles, qtd. in Gustafson, Manuel, and Gutiérrez 1998:111). APG and NGO posters linked literacy to mobilization with slogans like "Yajata ko yeyora kotɨ" (We are walking toward liberation) and "Yaiko iyambae" (We will live without masters). I saw some of this mobilizing firsthand when I visited a group of young Guarani literacy campaigners training in Monteagudo in early 1993. Most of them had grown up on haciendas with only two or three years of schooling. With a bit of training they received the designation of kereɨmba (G. warriors) and were sent to teach Guarani peasants to read. At one training session I attended, an NGO worker used the Sandinista example of the Nicaraguan Revolution to equate Guarani literacy with a struggle against imperialism. It seemed a bit opaque to these hardened hacienda youth, but the message of resistance resonated as they talked of abusive "patrons." Later these and other kereɨmba told of emotional encounters between the impoverished Guarani hacienda peons and Guarani activists from other zones, as together they began speaking of a new consciousness, rights, and organization (Ventiades and Jauregui 1994; Yandura 1996).

Resurgence also became visible in cultural resilience. In February of 1993, Guarani took me to my first arete (G. ara-ete, day-exemplary), the grand harvest festival that coincides with carnival. This particular arete took place at the ex-mission of Santa Rosa, the one attacked by Apiaguaiki Tüpa's warriors in 1892. It happened to be the hometown of a young Guarani artist who was illustrating bilingual schoolbooks in Camiri a century later. Santa Rosa's large square plaza was still a grid of houses, much as Franciscans pursuing civil order had laid it out. Yet in the plaza the Guarani danced in large drunken and exuberant circles to an endless drum-and-flute melody. They greeted the return of the ancestors, shared barrels of corn beer, and celebrated the harvest. I took a break from the drinking and made my way up to the ruins of the mission itself. There I looked out toward Kuruyuki. Enamored of the narrative of resurgence, I saw the Guarani dancing on the ruins of missionization and in spite of colonialism. As leaders framed it, they were in a *tataendi*, a rekindling of life from under the ashes of history.

I went to work in this exciting setting with a group of Guarani activists I call the scribes. Initially the scribes were a small group of biliterate and bilingual Guarani charged with writing schoolbooks and implementing EIB. They came into existence in 1989 with the support of UNICEF's PEIB project. In 1994, they were transferred to La Paz when the state made EIB into a national policy. In 1999, as the market orientation of school reform took root, they were outsourced to private publishing companies. I discuss these later phases in chapters 5–7. Here I focus on the scribes and the movement in the early days of resurgence from 1987 through 1994.

INDIGENOUS SCRIBES AND MOVEMENTS

Intellectuals like the Guarani scribes hold central positions in Latin American indigenous movement politics, even though their roles may not be formalized in the term *intellectual* or in cultural or organizational categories. In the Guarani case, the scribes were a combination of grass-roots intellectual, state functionary (as schoolteacher), NGO employee, and movement leader, and they often merged these roles over time. Their authority does not necessarily draw on formal credentials (diplomas, etc.), and it is not useful to draw false distinctions between literate/oral or modern/traditional types of knowledge-bearing actors. The Guarani scribes were biliterate and engaged with schooling issues, but they also engaged with and mobilized nonschool knowledge and actors. Politically, they might be called what Antonio Gramsci called "organic intellectuals" in that they emerged out of indigenous movements and worked from subordinate positions to transform hegemonic knowledge forms and actors (Rappaport 2005:10–12; Gramsci 1971:5–14). Yet the scribes also served as translators and intermediaries operating within and outside movements to represent indigeneity for external audiences and internal constituencies, a position that at times gave them relative power and that involved the deployment of hegemonic knowledge itself (Warren and Jackson 2002).

Indigenous resurgence and the appearance of new intellectuals do not reflect stasis or a return to tradition, but index wider transformations underway in society. For example, Kay Warren (1998:48–51) describes how Mayan academics, grass-roots activists, schoolteachers, and indigenous religious authorities in Guatemala managed to mobilize new forms of "cultural capital" in the context of a wider continental resurgence of indigeneity. This cultural capital included the new symbolic value of indigenous languages, a renewed and transformed self-understanding, and knowledge of indigenous and nonindigenous cultural worlds. As cultural producers with access to media (various print media, radio, and eventually, the Internet) and resources (NGO or state teaching jobs), they took privileged positions in expressions of indigenous resurgence. An objective for students of social movements, Warren suggests, is to consider what indigenous intellectuals' work might tell us both about processes of transformation underway and about how intellectuals "structure the production and circulation of the political vision that is crucial to their movement" (1998:49).

Since these visions invariably invoke particularity as a way to formulate political demands, many view indigenous intellectuals as entrepreneurs who foment intolerance based on inauthentic or illegitimate identity or interest claims. It would be naïve to say that such "entrepreneurs" do not exist. Yet this view itself expresses interested intolerance tinged with colonial understandings of indigeneity and does not satisfactorily describe the heterogeneity of indigenous intellectual practices in Latin America. Indigenous leaders have long been positioned in between their own cultural and linguistic milieus and nonindigenous actors, movements, and parties. For tactical reasons and practical fact, they operate through nonindigenous knowledges imposed and appropriated in the struggle against colonialism that are engaged in dialogue (and often unequal) exchange with their own knowledges, language, and experiences. As Joanne Rappaport (1998, 2005) and Jean Jackson (1995) suggest based on work with Nasa and Tukano intellectuals in Colombia, school-oriented knowledge production as a component of indigenous political mobilization emerges through webs of relationships that bring together indigenous and nonindigenous activists and collaborators, academics, grass-roots leaders, religious agents, state bureaucrats, and so forth. Rather than constituting a field of purist ethnic ideology, this "fertile ground for the construction of a native political ideology" is characterized more by intercultural engagement than by stances of epistemic incommensurability and intolerance (Rappaport 2005:15; Arnold and Yapita 2006).

As I show here, Guarani scribes reflected these wider Latin American patterns. In this chapter I trace their experiences to consider two levels of EIB as indigenous resurgence in practice. At one level I look at EIB as a school-oriented knowledge-producing practice emergent through new textual forms and destined for circulation through schooling. At another level, I show how EIB was a socially and politically situated network of practice that sought to transform the geopolitics of epistemic authority, as expressed both in the lives of the scribes and in the wider social and political effects of their work in the context of Guarani mobilizing. These levels are intertwined through transformations in peoples' lives, textualizing practices, and state spaces. As a whole, this chapter provides a view of EIB and early intercultural-ism in talk and practice. I begin with the scribes themselves.

Guarani Scribes and Their Allies

The Guarani scribes began as a group of ten to fifteen textbook writers who over the years moved between writing schoolbooks, teaching in rural schools or in the state education administration, working for NGOs, and—for men—exercising formal leadership positions in the APG.[3] While the core group of actual text writers stayed small, the social category of bilingual and biliterate Guarani that I call scribes blossomed as the ranks of Guarani schoolteachers grew. By the mid 2000s they numbered in the hundreds.

The early group I knew best in the 1990s included three women, Elsa Aireyu, Rubena Velásquez, and Silvia Chumira (all schoolteachers); three men, Enrique Camargo, Romero Sánchez, and Edmundo Anca (all with only a primary education); and one Guarani-speaking karai teacher named José Barrientos. Elsa, Rubena, and Silvia were three of the fewer than a dozen Guarani speakers then credentialed as rural schoolteachers. As women and Guarani they were exceptions to two patterns: that of wider Guarani exclusion from postsecondary schooling and that of the generally male-dominated leadership posts in the APG and the rural teachers' class. As I describe in further detail through Elsa's story below, EIB created a context in which their literacy, bilingualism, and credentials as teachers unsettled gen-der norms and racist stereotypes that crossed Guarani and karai domains, making this new social category a target of continuous opposition by EIB detractors.

The three Guarani men also unsettled norms. The men were APG political appointees whose credentials came not from schooling but from experience. They were now taking very public jobs recrafting schools. Deemed bearers of linguistic and other knowledges crucial to the EIB by the Guarani, they occupied positions once limited to credentialed teachers. Edmundo was a rural laborer and leader active in early Guarani land struggles in the 1980s, efforts for which he had spent time in jail and suffered beatings and ranchers' death threats. Though he possessed only rudimentary literacy skills, EIB sought to engage his rural leadership experience. Enrique and Romero also shared rural backgrounds, although both had received some schooling under the tutelage of American missionaries and were shaped by their experience as *creyentes* (S. believers, i.e., Protestant converts). Romero was an Isoseño, the only one on the team. As one of the few biliterate Isoseños, his presence reflected an attempt to sustain pan-Guarani linguistic unity through EIB. Yet Romero was zealous about his evangelical beliefs and met with ideological friction that compounded interdialect tensions. Symbols like the arete festival and ipaye curing were crucial to EIB, yet creyentes deemed them sinful. Enrique, though also a convert, was more self-reflective and had become more of an indigenous thinker than a zealous Christian.[4] With the peasant, the preacher, and the modern-day Ayemotï now working on schoolbooks, an unprecedented articulation of social positions and practices was coming together around formal schooling.

José, the only karai on the team, was a schoolteacher who had learned Guarani from laborers on his family farm. He literally embodied interculturalism, since his presence deflected criticisms that EIB constituted a particularistic ethnic project. Yet José was also atypical in his sympathy for the Guarani and their language. He later faced death threats as well—a rancher's pistol once placed on his forehead—accused of betraying his identity to ally with Guarani and stir them up through EIB. Though seen by detractors as opportunistic, he continues as a key reference point in Guarani language and schooling debates. As social actors the scribes were thus, like EIB itself, unsettling epistemic, linguistic, and political orders by virtue of their very existence.

I spent much time with the scribes in Camiri at the NGO TEKO-Guarani (Taller de Educación y Comunicación), in their homes, or at social gatherings and APG meetings. Their work was energized by discoveries, discussions about their language, and debates on the past, the present, and the future of the Guarani. Though seemingly mundane, their schoolbook work took wider significance as EIB expanded and their ideas circulated through movement practice, reverberating in the dynamics of schooling and power in the region and across the country.

On a typical day the scribes worked around a table piled with books and papers. They designed outlines based on curricular objectives and wrote out texts by hand in Guarani. Given limited practical experience in writing the language, this proved a tedious task. There were almost word-by-word debates on how to spell or determine word and affix boundaries. Translations across languages and epistemes spurred both frustration and good-humored joking that ranged from sexual innuendo and arguments about the putative cannibalism of ancestral Guarani in discussions of body parts to self-deprecating critiques tied to the perceived limitations of Guarani in some schooling domains. They cut and pasted bits of paper with text onto model pages and passed these to an artist for illustration. An NGO staffer transferred text and images to one of the early box-shaped Macintosh computers. These proofs were then returned for editing and classroom testing. UNICEF monies from Sweden facilitated publication, and the Bolivian government offered its imprimatur through the Ministry of Education. These activities are familiar in settings of indigenous linguistic and education activism.[5]

The production of schoolbooks reflected an amalgam of inputs. On the one hand, EIB emerged against a legacy of translation, the historically dominant paradigm for thinking about education in indigenous languages. Some of the scribes had worked with the Summer Institute of Linguistics (SIL) or with Catholic priests, both of them concerned with translating biblical texts and concepts into Guarani. Translation work had provided useful writing skills, yet translation situated Guarani language and literacy as bridges to karai knowledge, rather than as platforms for autonomous creation. Similarly, as translators, indigenous writers had no autonomous epistemic authority, and as a paradigm for working in Guarani literacy, translation pushed EIB toward superficial change.[6] Some outside experts and donors contributed to the view that saw EIB as a way of accessing something currently unavailable, such as Spanish literacy or modern pedagogical theory. Guarani shaped by the translation paradigm thus tended to ask, "What do you want me to translate?" and reached for schoolbooks at hand.

Translation practice nonetheless acknowledged that valuable outsider knowledge *did exist*, knowledge that Guarani *wanted* to access. It also offered a safe way to start changing education that paralleled an emergent creative vision based on Guarani rethinkings of schooling. This creative view held that *both* languages and cultures (Guarani and Spanish) constituted sources of valid knowledge, and that epistemic authority should be balanced between Guarani and others. This amplified the space of articulation with nonliterate Guarani, now seen as legitimate sources of knowledge. It also made for a step toward the inversion of a colonial model in which nonschooled indigenous peoples represented the antithesis of literate subjects. Creativity was not about preserving tradition, but about critically resignifying schooling practice. Always complementary, translation and autonomous creativity were political indicators that reflected relative degrees of distance between EIB, local movement process, and epistemic authority: more translation meant more distance and less power; more creative autonomy locally grounded engagement and authority.

Either way, Guarani text writers embraced other forms of writing. Close at hand were photocopies of the Franciscans' early works on Guarani, including Doroteo Giannecchini's *Chiriguano-Spanish Dictionary* (Romano and Cattunar 1916) and Bernadino de Nino's (1912) *Chiriguano Ethnography*. Guarani texts from Paraguay supplied ideas for neologisms. The scribes borrowed from technical documents on EIB projects like *The Natural Sciences in Bilingual Education* (Dietschy-Scheiterle 1989) that emerged from a German-funded EIB project in Peru; from books on *Culture, Language, and Education* published by UNESCO; and the GTZ-published *Reading Books for Children of Vernacular Languages: An Experience in the Peruvian Altiplano* (Chatry-Komarek 1986). The Jesuit-written trilogy published by CIPCA also served as a key reference: Francisco Pifarré's *Guarani-Chiriguano: History of a People* (1989); Xavier Albó's *The Community Today* (1990); and Bartomeu Meliá's *Our Culture* (1988).

The scribes' work also entered into a dialogue with outsiders who might be called collaborators (following Rappaport 2005). Some of these were long-term interlocutors like the Italian NGO director Father Pietro. Another, my friend Tomás, was a Peruvian sociologist who worked with the scribes for over a decade. Mónica, a Bolivian pedagogue, was a curricular advisor who stayed for several years. Rufino Chuquimamani, a Peruvian Quechua, was hired by UNICEF to share experiences gained from his work in EIB in Puno and Cuzco, Peru (see López and Jung 1988). Short-term experts in mathematics flew in for stints. Classroom evaluators came from Germany. Linguistic gurus like the Jesuit father Bartomeu Meliá visited from Paraguay. I found myself positioned in this same category of collaborator on and off for the following decade and a half.

Collaborators brought their own orientations to the process. There were expressions of a Latin American, Andean-flavored convergence of university-based intellectuals promoting popular education and indigenist cultural revitalization paradigms. There were European and American visions of academic research merged with solidarity "light" (as opposed to the rhetoric of revolution). The American sense was marked (or tainted) by blind faith in literacy and by the moralizing missionary zeal to help; and the European was nourished by a similar devotion to education energized (or skewed) by a romantic, Herderian sense of culture and language. Outsiders generally shared the position that bilingual education was pedagogically defensible (children learned better) and ideologically progressive (society would be made better). Beyond that, positions varied, often invoking, yet mostly leaving unspecified, a varied set of ideas about politics, justice, and paths to change.[7]

Collaborators claimed legitimacy through discourses of technical expertise and through solidarity voiced at meetings, workshops, or visits to Guarani schools. Yet we were products of the hierarchy we hoped to dismantle, there because donor organizations and the Guarani relied on symbols of nonindigenous academic authority, albeit for different reasons. The fact that collaborators were often gringos implicitly affirmed local racist assessments that autonomous Guarani intellectual action was biologically improbable. As I discuss in chapter 3, collaboration also risked paternalism and exploitation. Yet since we produced work that stayed there (rather than simply extracting data) and worked for and with the organization, I considered our skills a resource that could be used—or not—by the Guarani for Guarani purposes (Escobar 2001). It was a comforting if problematic self-assurance. We benefited from relatively higher pay (especially the foreign short-term consultants) and the luxury of being able to leave if conditions shifted. Scribes, on the other hand, were rooted in webs of life and power that went beyond collaborative jaunts or development experiments. An Isoseña scribe, Lucy

Gutiérrez, reminded me of this as we argued over how to write about missionaries. While I wanted to critique them harshly as colonial agents, she chided me: "You can write these things and leave. We have to stay here."

A Meeting on an Intercultural Curriculum

As scribes and collaborators came to the table to create a new kind of schooling called EIB, a transformative urge to change met with the fairly durable meanings and forms of bureaucratic schooling. Similarly, terms like *education, interculturalism,* and *bilingualism* were open for debate, something made clear in a meeting organized to discuss what an anthropologist might contribute to the process. By this time, in early 1993, the Guarani were both translating and experimenting creatively in their pursuit of EIB. For example, an early first-grade text included the image of an ipaye smoking a cigar over a child as part of a health lesson illustrating one positive way to treat illness. This constituted a radical challenge to traditional schooling ideologies. Yet the text also translated other hygiene lessons directly from Bolivian school-books. Having produced two grades of texts, by 1993 the scribes and their advisors were taking stock of what EIB was and might become. The meeting traced themes I heard often over a decade of work in EIB. They illustrate how school-talk was a way to talk about social difference and the (il)legitimacy of relations of epistemic authority. Though I caricature these positions here, the quotes reflect a field of contention that continues to shape education discourse at the national level in Bolivia today.

We sat around the worktable in the offices of TEKO: scribes, experts, NGO staff, and Guarani leaders. The topic: Where was Guarani education going? What was interculturalism? The Camiri heat was sweltering, as usual. A metal ceiling fan twirled slowly above us, fanning us with hot air. Mónica, the curriculum expert, led the discussion. She pointed out that a curriculum "takes shape around formalized practices, materials, and times," something all curricula, indigenous or otherwise, had to have. Citing the Russian psychologist Lev Vygotsky she said that learning was a process of scaffold-ing.[8] Through social interaction in a cultural context, she noted, children built on the known to gradually "construct" new knowledges. An inter-cultural curriculum would thus build on local learning practices and cultural knowledges. New skills (literacy and numeracy) and cultural knowledge (of science or Spanish) would build on this local base. The anthropologist would help figure out what children knew and how they learned it so as to help establish the cultural base on which new knowledge was constructed.

Though some read Vygotsky through a Marxian lens, others saw this constructivism as insufficiently political. A karai NGO staffer with experience in popular grass-roots education chimed in, invoking Paulo Freire's liberation theology rather than Vygotsky's constructivism. "Respect for sociocultural difference is important, but the curriculum should be about how the Guarani *learn to recognize their reality and act on it.*" This was classic Freire. Education should be used for consciousness raising and collective action. I sympathized with the position, and even had a Spanish copy of Freire's *Pedagogy of the Oppressed* on my shelf. Here the anthropologist would not just try to understand children's cultural base, but would compile experiences of subjugation and deconstruct hegemonic knowledge like racism to create a corpus for critical reflection. Schooling would ideally spur collective action by erasing the ideological barriers assumed to keep subjugated people like the Guarani politically docile.

Both perspectives allowed space for indigenous knowledge (itself assumed, but not specified), whether as a foundation (in constructivism) or as a critical lens (in popular education). Yet in both theories an implicit dualism persisted between indigenous knowledge and that pursued by formal schooling (i.e., a "better" knowledge or critical praxis). These dualisms took other forms too. The conversation turned to Father Pietro, a priest on TEKO's staff. He was an institutional descendant of Franciscan missionaries who hailed from the same region of Italy that produced nineteenth-century missionary fathers. A gravelly voiced chain smoker, Pietro had a long history of struggle alongside the Guarani and faced constant excoriation by the region's landed elite. Yet he was a teacher at heart, and from this view those with whom he worked needed schooling. He chimed in with Italianate Spanish, "the man of the rural area [*el hombre del campo*] doesn't abstract, they think and live in the concrete." The view invoked the "the great divide" between modern (literate) and premodern (oral) cultures and cognitions (Goody 1977). In the crudest version of this view, literate societies are composed of individuals possessing rationality, the ability to communicate outside of immediate context, and cognitive skills of abstraction that allow them to act on, rather than merely respond to, reality. Nonliterate societies, on the other hand, do not have these mental faculties. Writing is assumed to spur this great leap forward, though the strong version of the so-called great divide is now questioned in literacy studies (Collins and Blot 2003:9–33). Still powerful in the Andes, this view nonetheless construed EIB as the means to ease the transition from orality to literacy (i.e., from primitiveness to modernity). This notion resembled that of the Freirian passage from illiterate subjugation to critical praxis, yet it remained devoid of its transformative politics. Anthropological research, it seemed, would help access this "concrete" Guarani, bringing instances of context into the texts to facilitate the passage into literacy and higher thought. Though recognizing indigenous knowledge in a way, this dualist position assumed a natural psychological (almost biological) inferiority. Literacy was a transformative remedy for a lack: an evolved cognition. The paradigm situated literate subjects and their cultures in an unassailable position of authority, with little space for oral subjects to question the normative value and effects of schooling.

Another karai present was of the rare Guarani speakers among the rural teachers' union leadership. As a karai ally like the scribe José, he endured the enmity of some of his fellow teachers due to his support for bilingual education. Yet his was a less reflective support. A thin rail of a man, he fit the image of the schoolteacher to a tee. Formality embodied a desire and claim for authority: polyester slacks, fine socks, brightly polished shoes, a short-sleeved linen shirt (ironed and tucked in), and at his belt the de rigueur counterfeit Ray-Ban sunglasses (with case). Not unlike military officers, teachers commonly marked their status with these shades (until cellphones appeared in the 2000s). With the authority-seeking pedantry of the teacher, finger pointed skyward, he accentuated each point with a jab, saying, "It's good [jab] to talk about rescuing culture! [jab] But colleagues [jab], we must not [jab] lose sight [jab] of the technical [jab]!" Less progressive than Vygotskian constructivism or Freirian liberation, his call reasserted the civilizing mission of schooling and the authority of those who espoused science (known by teachers) over language, culture, or the kind of knowledge brought to the table by the grass-roots leaders. "Yes," he allowed, "the Guarani are different in the linguistic-cultural [jab]," but "education must be based in the technological-scientific [jab]!" Anthropologists, I thought to myself, would be useful if at all to identify and organize that indigenous difference to folklorize it, test it for scientific validity, or keep it out of the way. Experts would take care of the technical. Here bilingual education was not a creative or resistant project, but as in the "great divide" paradigm, a bridge or a moat between two hierarchically positioned knowledges. I coded him DIPSHIT in my field notes. In my naïve self-righteousness, I did not then know that behind the scenes he represented a crucial political alliance for the Guarani. As Bolivians would say, "había que soportarlo" (one had to put up with him).

The Guarani scribes remained silent as they listened to these outsiders talk about Guarani language and knowledge. Attuned to the fact that their projects relied on outsider funds, and having largely been denied any authority by everything said up to that point, they waited. Another staffer asked, "If we have Guarani who know their culture, why do we need an anthropologist at all?" Uh-oh, I thought. I asked myself the same question often and cringed at the possibility of anthropology's (and my) irrelevance. Fortunately, Elsa Aireyu then spoke up. She did not call for the defense of culture or the mobilization of resistance, but justified my presence by verifying the uncomfortable meanings of discipline that underlie academic positions. "We know our culture," she said, "we just need someone to help us systematize it."

TRANSFORMING SOCIAL CATEGORIES

The notion of systematization made for a problematic way to think about capturing cultural difference to transform education, even though it described, as I discuss in the following chapter, what one kind of anthropology might contribute to Guarani schooling. Yet Elsa's comment, offered gently to the karai arguing about the knowledge of the Guarani, suggests a useful way to think about how the Guarani perceived the utility of outsiders involved in their education: as providers of a potentially useful resource, not as possessors of one or another liberatory or civilizing knowledge to which they aspired to submit. Elsa's own background is also illuminating of how EIB unfolded within Guarani social lives and political worlds. I sat down with Elsa six years later to reflect back on EIB as she had lived it.

By 1999, when I shifted from working with the Guarani to "systematizing" EIB for academic reasons, Elsa had gone from writing schoolbooks to becoming the first Guarani to ever occupy a position as district director.[9] This was both a political feat and a measure of the slow transformative effects of Guarani education activism. She took the post in her home district of Gutiérrez, a karai-dominated municipality north of Camiri that encompassed her rural home community of Eiti. On a field visit that year, I had come down on the bus from Santa Cruz. Unable to find her in Camiri, I hitched a ride back north to the dusty little town. I found her negotiating education budgets with the karai mayor, a remarkable role for a Guarani woman. Over the next few days I accompanied her as she made the rounds of village schools to check on teachers. Over beers in the evening, we looked back at bilingual education, her work during the early years of mobilization, and our changing roles.

Elsa was born in Eiti (honey place) in 1950. Her Aireyu lineage links her to a long line of Guarani leaders of the zone called Kaipependi-Kaarovaicho, one of the areas where the captaincy as a leadership institution persisted within the karai world. Destroyed by hacienda incorporation or absorbed into mission tutelage elsewhere, leadership structures in Eiti and in a handful of other areas were reconfigured through tactical accommodations with karai. Though now seen as traditional, these captaincies were strengthened and transformed through engagement with, rather than isolation from, karai society.[10] In the case of Eiti, Guarani land and labor were ceded to karai to maintain a semblance of local authority. Elsa's father even served for a time as a congressman during the military government of René Barrientos (Albó 1990:120–31).[11]

Light-skinned in comparison to most Guarani, Elsa, like many Aireyus, as she acknowledged, spoke and acted with the kind of authority tied to those born into power. Yet this power was relativized by her ethnolinguistic and gender identity. For both Guarani and karai she was still a *kuña*, a Guarani woman, though an anomalous Guarani woman who grew up speaking Spanish because of her family's trips to the sugar mills of Santa Cruz and her father's ties to karai society. Using a term learned in her EIB work, she said, "I'm bilingual from the cradle [*bilingüe de cuna*]. My mother spoke to me in Guarani, my father in Spanish. My grandmothers, all my aunts, my uncles, spoke to me in pure Guarani." Elsa indeed spoke Guarani fluently and with gusto, consciously avoiding loanwords from Spanish and exhibiting a self-conscious fascination with the intricacies of her language.

Elsa represented a rarity in a place where female Guarani illiteracy surpassed 70 percent and women and girls were less likely to attain higher education. In the rural areas, if anyone at all had a chance to study, it was usually an oldest son, even in the case of karai families. Yet with access to resources from cattle and income earned from labor contracting, the Aireyu family was able to send its children to study in the private schools of Camiri. Elsa thus became one of the first Guarani to finish high school, graduating in 1967, the year Che Guevara was killed after his failed pursuit of revolutionary followers among the Guarani. Even more than today, in the 1960s, Guarani kuñas in the city were expected to work as domestic servants. As a kuña studying in a karai urban space, Elsa struggled against boundaries of race and gender. She neither belonged among the townspeople, nor did she resemble most rural Guarani.

> In those times, I'm talking about 1960 more or less, I was going to a private school in town, and the only ones who went were the children of the hacendados, the ranchers [*ganaderos*], the landlords [*terratenientes*]. But [my father] sent me because he knew times were changing. He said, "they are going to discriminate against you there, but you do not let them." He gave me strength, saying, "we are Guarani, but we have the same rights as any other people, Guarani or not." . . . So that gave me strength, because there was a lot of discrimination. . . . [Other students] would hear my last name, and say, "aaa, that's a *kuña*." I ended up fighting a lot, but it made me stronger. I always wanted to show them that I was capable, and I always got the best grades. But then I would go home on vacations and show my father my grades, and I think he was struggling within himself, you know, to accept it. He would say, "You are smart, aren't you, my daughter, you're very smart. It's too bad you're a woman." My grandmothers were also against my studying. They said it was only for men. . . . But you know, if I had not studied, I would be just one more *kuña* sitting by the mortar and pestle waiting for her husband to come home from the fields.

Elsa also credited her father with pushing her to know the "written world" (*mundo escrito*) of the karai so that she would be able to walk "among the karai." This phrase in Guarani, "karai ipɨte rupi" (G. karai their-midst through), was often heard in Guarani discussions of the purpose of schooling and mobilization. (Recall the words of Mateo Chumiray in the epigraph, which equated Guarani resurgence with the capacity to walk through the town square while speaking Guarani without shame.) In Elsa's use, the phrase illustrated a vision of interculturalism as a double-sided process: in one sense to defend one's own identity, and in another to transform interethnic spaces so as to claim a place for difference within, rather than for isolation from or radical opposition to wider society. Education was imagined as the instrument for this process and as a metaphor that described the desired space itself. "My father used to tell me," she recalled, "if we don't insert ourselves into the written world, we will not be able to defend our rights. They have taken our lands because we did not know the *mundo escrito*."

Entering this written world proved no easy task, even for the daughter of a captaincy family. Elsa was less constrained because of her family's resources, but her educational path was still an uncertain struggle. She started her elementary education in an evangelical school in Camiri and ended up at a high school run by Catholic nuns in Charagua. Looking back, she saw these changes as transitions through different "knowledges" (*saberes*). "Can you imagine," she asked, "from evangelicals to nuns?!"

EA: I had the problem of three religions, the evangelical [Protestant], the Catholic, and the [Guarani] cultural beliefs. I think those were difficult times when I did not know what to believe. But in the end, I think inside me, those that overcame were those knowledges that my grandmothers, my grandfathers, my uncles, and aunts taught me. That's why I am the way I am. I believe in the *ñanderu* [our fathers] as our ancestors did, and in the *kaa iya*, the masters of nature.[12] And besides, the Catholic [priests] did not accept the captaincy; they said we were autocrats, authoritarians. From their vision they have to think that way. We are still fighting over that with them today. . . . [13] The [priests] told me that my father exploited his people; that he earned on their backs. But I would hear the priests telling the poor that they would earn their paradise in heaven and the nuns talking about poverty and chastity, and there they are having sumptuous breakfasts with meats and jams. I stopped being Catholic in the end. I think I have antibodies [laughing] against the evangelicals, the Catholics, and the karai.

BG: But you married a karai.

EA: Well that's another story.

Elsa did end up married to a karai schoolteacher, and she worked as a schoolteacher herself. She had initially dreamed of studying law, though the idea conflicted with her father's desires. "Those professions are for men," he told her. "They involve *peleas* [fights]." Instead, he sent her to study the more "womanly" profession of nursing at San Simón University in Cochabamba. These studies floundered when the dictator Hugo Bánzer closed the universities in 1971. Elsa returned to eastern Bolivia and entered the Rural Normal School at Charagua, later transferring again to the Normal School at Portachuelo, near Santa Cruz. Awarded her rural school teachers' certificate in 1976, with Bolivia still under the dictatorship, she returned to the Guarani region to begin teaching in Eiti. By then her community had managed to build its own school, staffed, excepting her, by karai teachers. She married one of them, a loud-talking hulk of a man from Abapó. Despite her sometimes conflicted relationship with the karai—and a husband not enthralled with her activism—she defended her marriage saying, "A Guarani woman like me? There was no Guarani man who would have me!"

From the perspective of national society, schoolteachers, especially rural teachers, form part of the popular working class. Yet in regions like rural eastern Bolivia, the teacher came closer to the provincial elite than to the peasantry. Most rural teachers were male, and nearly all were karai. Most of their students were rural Guarani. For all of these reasons the very idea of a Guarani teacher, like the phrase "lettered Indian," seemed oxymoronic. Schooling and Guaraniness were opposed in every way. Though in some ways her family's status placed her closer to the rural elite in class terms, in every other way Elsa entered into a category that negated her identity and language by placing her on the side of the karai "civilizers" of rural Guarani, her own people.

Looking back on their early teaching practices and understandings of the Guarani language, Guarani teachers like Elsa are often self-critical. Another scribe recalled how he was "different back then, worse than the karai [*peor que los karai*]." He acknowledged having used the most sadistic punishments against children who spoke Guarani in the classroom, despite it being his language too. In contrast, EIB led Guarani scribes to construct new visions of themselves and their work. Most now narrate a past marked by points of "awakening" when they began to question the hispanicizing and violently anti-Guarani school. At these points of conversion, Guarani scribes say they began to see their languages as worth defending, or at least as useful to their task as educators.[14] These moments are retold today as instances in which the relationship between students and teachers was reframed in the terms of shared identity, rather than as distance between civilizers and indios. Both shifts—recognizing the value of language and the shared identity between teacher and student—subverted the existing idea that schooling necessarily entailed castellanización and evolutionary transformation.

For example, another scribe, Silvia, told of an "awakening" that shifted the relationship with her students:

> I was a teacher who came out of the Charagua Normal School with a pretty rigid, squared perspective [cuadrada]. But I watched as my brother spoke and fought in the early meetings about how the organization should be. I read some of the history he wrote, and I said, "Brother, I read what you wrote, and I wonder how you know so much history?" And he used to say, [she laughs] "Damn, sister, I read! And you being a teacher and you do not read?" And those things motivated me, and I think I understood. I said to myself, as a teacher I should work differently. It changed my attitude. I thought I should fight for my brothers and sisters, for the people where I work. [Until then] I was one of those teachers who stood in front of the [Guarani] children and would not let them call me "aunt." They had to call me "professor." But I started to take consciousness and then started to work in a different way.

Elsa says her awakening and her experience in bilingual education came from the "struggles of her work." I had heard one component of Elsa's conversion story several times and asked her to let me record it, since she was fond of retelling it. She often told the story to non-Guarani consultants as a way to demonstrate to them that she had understood the pedagogical value of bilingualism long before the foreign experts arrived. She told the story to younger Guarani as a way of highlighting the underlying distinctions of language and culture that subtly questioned the translation paradigm.

As she began to speak, her energy and demeanor took on a kind of amused satisfaction. She embellished the Guarani portions of the story like a good storyteller—raising the tone of her voice, imitating sounds and moments of surprise, and laughing at her discoveries. Since we had been speaking in

Spanish, she narrated in Spanish while switching to Guarani to recreate the dialogue between her and her students (in italics below). The story began with Elsa working as a young teacher charged with teaching first-graders the letters by way of animal sounds. The texts were in Spanish, and the animals were karai animals that, as it were, spoke Spanish. She recalled how the lesson suggested that the letter *o* be taught by asking what sounds were made by pigs (in Spanish, pigs say "o o o o o").

> That lesson never came out for me like the book said. When I asked what sounds the pigs made, my students said *"kui kui kui kui."* So I used my Guarani. I told the children, *"Well, that is what our pigs say, but do you want to know what karai pigs say?"* And so it went, all the animals [she details the chicken, the dog, the hungry calf, and other sounds: children crying, water splashing]. They all are different. It even came down to our Guarani flies that say *"mou mou mou."* I said to the children, *"Well, that is what our flies say, but do you want to know what karai flies say? The flies of the karai say 'mmmmm.'"* [She laughs]. So I used my language to help me. That was in 1983, there was no bilingual education yet.

Like Silvia's shift marked by kinship metaphors, Elsa's entailed repositioning herself as someone who shared the language of her students in a classroom context in which Spanish was sacred and "our" Guarani was still forbidden entry. With phrases like "our" animals, an inclusive Guarani "we" or *ñande* invaded schooling practice. The epiphanies were personal, pedagogical, and political. Elsa's colleagues, she recalled, were critical of her turn because it undermined the authority of Spanish (and its speakers).

Elsa said that with this realization she began to work harder for the Guarani students struggling with all-Spanish schooling. If they sought a life distinct from that of their parents, she argued to me and to them, schooling offered the best means of countering economic and racial hierarchy. Schooling allowed one to escape manual labor associated with being Guarani and to pursue the footing necessary to "walk among the karai." Elsa again intertwined Guarani with Spanish as she talked about the implications of her new relationship to students. Yet in these recollections she distanced herself from her students, using the language of "I" (*che*) and the plural "you" (*pe*). She spoke to them, she says, in "their" language, in "simple" terms:

I was the only teacher who spoke Guarani. Even though my husband said I was wasting my time, I made an extra effort to help students with their homework. I explained square roots, conjugations, division, numbers, everything I explained to my students in Guarani. . , . I used to ask them, [she switches to Guarani]: "*Do you want to grow up and cut sugar cane like your fathers? Do you want to waste your strength in others' lands? Do you women always want to be sitting on a goat skin or stuck to the angua [wooden mortar for grinding corn]?*" I told them, "*How do you think I got to where I am? I want to see you as teachers too.*" . . . [back to Spanish] I spoke to my students in their language, in simple terms."

Elsa's experience illustrates two dimensions of an emergent ethnic and educational project. On one side, it affirmed links of linguistic and cultural identity between teacher and student, links broken by the colonial ideology of schooling. On the other, it confirmed an understanding of schooling as creating social distinctions, always gendered, between rural workers and those schooled. The discourse of mobility outlined a field of multiple potential outcomes, simultaneously casting schooling as a process tied to class differentiation, ethnocultural affirmation and struggle, and individual mobility. When EIB was formalized years later, these tensions returned as EIB articulated in different ways with processes of indigenous resurgence and state transformation: Was EIB to be a platform for broad-based ethnopolitical mobilization and revival? Was it an instrument of managerial reformism and individual mobility? Or was it a vehicle of class struggle?

TRANSFORMING TEXTUAL PRACTICE

Elsa's atypical history placed her in a unique position to take advantage of the UNICEF-financed EIB project in the late 1980s. Until 1995, when textbook production was moved to La Paz, Elsa and the scribes wrote about twenty books in both Guarani and Spanish for language, math, history, and the life sciences. The scribes also worked politically to cultivate support for EIB and the buzzwords *interculturalism* and *bilingualism*. Elsa became a central figure locally and nationally and took on a new public role in movement processes. While her linguistic skills, credentials, familiarity with the karai world, and social status in Guarani communities did not all emerge from EIB, in its context this cultural capital allowed figures like Elsa to take new roles as intermediaries between development projects and Guarani political processes.

The convergence of indigenous organizing with new meanings of indigeneity and schooling made of Elsa something more than "just" a rural teacher or an educated Guarani. She and other scribes embodied and symbolized an emergent collective territorial, social, and political formation, that of an indigenous Guarani people and movement. This development challenged karai understandings of Guarani as racially subordinate rural laborers, and it also began to reshape Guarani socioterritorial imaginaries. EIB, unified around the language, presupposed the construction of a wider pan-Guarani unity through educational practice. Textbook writing served as the anchoring vehicle for this process.

If one visited sites of textbook production during these years, one went to Guarani and NGO offices in Camiri. From there one could follow Guarani scribes to rural villages as they tested their books in classrooms or to community meetings where they socialized the EIB agenda, creating support by uprooting colonial ideologies about Guarani and arguing in pedagogical and political terms for bilingual schools. At one such meeting in Itavera, Edmundo, the scribe and former rural organizer, eloquently used the metaphor of blood to claim equality and to call on Guarani to demand their rights: "If you cut us [Guarani and karai], we all have the same red blood." Elsa was herself fond of recalling how their singing of the national anthem in Guarani for rural communities conceptualized EIB as a path to equality, not to continued subordination. One might also find the Guarani scribes in workshops at the national level with other indigenous organizations or bilingual schooling experts from other Andean countries. Scribes also brought Guarani leaders and elders to town, generating a dialogic space across the boundaries of credentialed and noncredentialed knowledge. These events encouraged discussions about how to write the language, how to create new words, and about the best possible contents of the schoolbooks. Such events included the 1991 "Arakuaiyapo" ("Makers of Knowledge") conference that convened Guarani elders to create new words for mathematics. Another meeting to discuss writing conventions in 1993 and again in 1997 generated discussions about pan-Guarani linguistic unity and critiques of diglossia.

These events, all justified by the process of textbook production, created a new communicative space among Guarani intellectuals. They thus in one sense created an alternative or "counterpublic sphere," much like that described by Marcia Stephenson (2002) for the Aymara case. Following Nancy Fraser, Stephenson argued that counterpublic spheres were spaces in which indigenous intellectuals "could create and circulate counterdiscourses, which in turn permit them to formulate oppositional interpretations of their identities, interests, and needs" (Stephenson 2002:100–101). As Stephenson points out, these alternative spaces are not simply about the construction of interests to be channeled through existing institutional forms but about creative and generative projects that seek to transform existing territorial, social, and institutional orders. For the Guarani, EIB was coming to mean reconquering the right to speak and the right to know in their own ancestral territory, transforming dominant society as they sought to walk among the karai without shame.

Two texts illustrate how this process unfolded in the books themselves. A multisubject second-grade text of 1991 was called *Eireká* (*Honey Seeker*, a boy's name). A later (1995) fifth-grade social studies and history text was called *Kuarasɨ* (*Sun*, a source of knowledge). The cover of *Honey Seeker* showed a Bolivian flag and two light-skinned children (who did not really look Guarani) wearing uniforms and playing ball in front of a school, the traditionally acknowledged center of knowledge. The cover of *Sun* shows children who look more Guarani playing in a natural setting (now understood as the center of knowledge) with the sun above. Guarani artists painted both covers. Both books also bear the seals of UNICEF and the Bolivian Ministry of Education. The title pages credit the APG as one of the agents behind EIB implementation, positioned *beneath* the state, the church, UNICEF, the NGO, the district educational office, and the rural teachers' union. From within this tutelary space the Guarani organization used schoolbooks as a platform for protagonism.

The texts echoed Guarani heterogeneity and a pragmatic merger of translation, creativity, and mimetic transformation not easily reduced to any one curricular paradigm. For example, most of the exercises, cartoons, and dialogues in *Honey Seeker* focused on disciplinary imperatives familiar in Bolivian pedagogy (be clean! eat well! go to school! be on time! obey your teacher! boil your water! do your homework! sing the national anthem!). However, *Honey Seeker* also bore messages of Guarani resurgence. These came in the form of comic-strip dialogues on poverty, land inequality, and the APG movement aimed at Guarani parents through their second-grade children. Lessons also included calls for the respect of Guarani knowledge (*arakuaa*) alongside school knowledge (*yemboe*). Images like the smoking shaman stood as explicit markers of Guarani alterity alongside more familiar lessons on hygiene.[15] I see these instances as early exploratory incursions into standard schoolbook structures, paralleling the tentative incursion of Guarani into regional politics.

Following other texts in Guarani, math, and Spanish as a second language, the later text *Sun* appeared in 1995, at the apogee of autonomous Guarani educational activism just as the Bolivian education reform was getting underway nationally. Text writers felt emboldened by their victories against opposition to EIB. "By then, we had won the battle," recalled Enrique, suggesting that in five years they had changed public discourse on bilingual education. *Sun* also marked a shift from the imperatives of earlier texts like *Honey Seeker*, "you must do/be/speak," to a language of collective practice in the first-person inclusive plural ("we are doing/being/speaking"). The passage from "you do!" to "we are" or "we will be" is visible across the text. Enrique even marked the turn as a watershed, the "time when we starting using *ñande* [the inclusive 'we']." This shift further repositioned Guarani and their language and knowledge in relationship to meanings of schooling, as the scribes themselves had experienced with their students. With the inclusive *ñande* Guarani represented themselves as both the collective subject and the object of knowledge creation and teaching, rather than as silent, nonspeaking targets of discipline carried out by others.

There were other signs of the articulation between mobilization and pedagogy. *Sun* is punctuated by concepts that Guarani thinkers began to identify as central to an emergent ideological vision. These included -*mboroaɨu*, love, and -*angareko*, reciprocity, hospitality, and generosity. Both were associated with the cultivation of intra-Guarani solidarity and of exchange with others. The idea of -*yomboete*, respect, was highlighted as a kind of intergenerational glue. Against the cleavage that schooling historically sought to create between generations, -yomboete asserted a new relation between nonschooled elder Guarani and schooled youth. In discussions with Guarani leaders, the scribes also generated a tripartite notion of unity based on the metaphor of the *itakuru* (three stones used in Guarani fire pits). The three itakuru were *ñee* (language), *tëta* (home/family/community/people), and *yemboatɨ* (the assembly or movement). *Tëta* offered an especially rich semantic field. As evidenced in the epigraph to this chapter, the concept of tëta merged metaphors of Guarani kinship and community with powerful Spanish terms like *pueblo* (people, a word used in the popular sense associated with class struggle) and *nación* (nation, now in an indigenous sense of political territoriality and legitimacy). Accompanied by map drawings of the Bolivian state on which Guarani territory was imagined as transcending existing state jurisdictions, these new ideas recurred throughout the texts and emerged in Guarani political discourse at other venues.

Textbooks were thus simultaneously school lesson, social critique, and political manifesto. They were written, Enrique acknowledged, as much for parents as for students. In one lesson of *Sun*, the eighteenth-century Guarani war hero Aruma is celebrated for his resistance to the Spanish. Karai are excoriated for having tricked him into being captured. In another lesson, the narrative of the Kuruyuki battle returns as an allegory of resistance and as a counterpoint to new Guarani strategies. Then, the text details, Guarani used violent struggle. Today they use education, to recover "that which was taken from us." Lessons tied contemporary Guarani poverty to karai land grabbing. Drawings that accompanied one text on land loss showed a karai *patrón* (boss, rancher) whipping Guarani workers, a historical reality in living Guarani memory. Another image showed karai cowboys driving cattle onto Guarani corn plantations, also part of lived experience. A bold denunciatory and contestative stance emerged, easily visible as one reads from the earlier *Honey Seeker* to the later *Sun*. When I reflected on this later with Enrique, he agreed that they had increased what they called the political content, seeking a "reversion of history" through the texts. (In Spanish, to revert, *revertir*, means to take back, as when lands are taken back for redistribution to their original or rightful owners.)

The texts and images in *Sun* also signaled the historical taking back of domains of Guarani knowledge and language. A case in point is the reversion of the term *yemboe* (G. to make oneself be made to speak; school learning). As I discussed in chapter 1, yemboe was taken by the missionaries to refer to schooling and catechism as explicitly non-Guarani domains of knowledge superior to Guarani ways of knowing and speaking. The early *Honey Seeker* began the semantic reversion by elevating arakuaa (nonschool Guarani knowledge, wisdom) to the level of yemboe (Spanish school knowledge). *Arakuaa*, literally day-/time-knowing, refers to nonschool knowledge forms that range from social maturity to technical skills to supernatural knowledge of the world. Someone who possesses, or more accurately, is defined by *arakuaa* knowledge, embodies full and mature personhood through knowing in Guarani.[16] Arakuaa, for example, invaded the text in images like the shaman, placed on the level of formal school knowledge. Yet arakuaa in the earlier text still remained distinct from yemboe. Arakuaa was something Guarani; yemboe was something of the school, implicitly of the karai. In *Sun*, arakuaa began to merge with and absorb yemboe. Guarani, as Guarani, are portrayed as agents and producers of both types of knowledge. Guarani elders are shown teaching children in schoollike contexts. In one lesson grandmothers and grandfathers give advice on writing irregular verb prefixes and on conjugating nominal roots. In another, Guarani elders instruct Guarani children on the linguistic unity linking them to Guarani in Brazil, Paraguay, and Argentina. Distinct from lessons that portray elders transmitting knowledge through stories told around the fire (as occurs in real life), these new images intentionally reimagined Guarani as knowledge makers across a fused domain of arakuaa and yemboe.

TRANSFORMING STATE SPACE

The production and circulation of Guarani texts provided an anchor for the emergence of new actors and practices that unsettled the social and spatial order of the region. Similar to the slow incursion into and transformation of school knowledge, Guarani political mobilization unfolded as a gradual incursion into and transformation of public space. Bilingual texts were the vehicle through which Guarani sought to change and occupy the metaphorical plaza of citizenship in the lettered city.

The significance of the scribes can be gauged in part through reactions to them, clear in the battle of labels used to talk about who they were. APG leaders and NGO personnel saw the scribes as a nucleus of authority that formed an extension of the APG. In Spanish, movement supporters called them "those of the PEIB" (*los del* PEIB) or the "technical team" (*equipo técnico*). When commentators spoke Guarani in the communities, these labels morphed into a straightforward language of ethnopolitical solidarity. The scribes were referred to as *ñande vae* (we, our kind) or "our teachers" (*ñande oporomboe vae reta*) as opposed to karai teachers.

On the other hand, unsympathetic outsiders referred to the scribes as dependents of the NGOs with phrases like *los del* TEKO (those from TEKO). These phrasings sought to deny the possibility of autonomous Guarani agency, casting the scribes as subjects of church or NGO manipulation.[17] Rural teachers, quite reasonably, saw EIB as a threat because it licensed Guarani speakers to claim rural teaching jobs and undermined existing relations of authority.[18] Campaigns against the EIB, in large part waged to discredit the scribes themselves, occurred across the region. Karai teachers wielded significant authority in rural communities and could sway Guarani parents to oppose EIB through browbeating, the coercion of leaders, or the subtle talk against the supposed backwardness of Guarani schooling. They attacked EIB as substandard pedagogy and said scribes and Guarani teachers were poor substitutes for "real" Spanish-speaking teachers.[19] The scribes faced an uphill battle for community support for the legitimacy of EIB and their own authority. The most effective argument described the scribes as hypocrites. As Elsa often recounted, they were questioned because they lived in town, their kids studied in Spanish schools, and they got to where they were because of Spanish, not Guarani. Karai teachers thus contained EIB by referring to Guarani teachers simply as "bilinguals" (*los bilingües*) and avoiding phrases like "Guarani teacher" (*profesor guaraní*) that invoked a wider sociopolitical entity beyond teacher-union authority.

Another scribe who got his start as a bilingual teacher found himself on the frontlines of this struggle. Fernando Segundo, referred to as "Fernandito," graduated from the Charagua Normal School (having constituted part of the first wave of subsidized students there) and took a job teaching first-graders in Itanambikua, a Guarani village across the river from Camiri. The school was like an experimental plot for EIB. Visiting experts carried out evaluations there since it was close to Camiri. For the same reason it was a coveted post for older rural karai teachers awaiting retirement. Seniority in the union meant having privileged access to such schools, which allowed one to live in an urban center while commuting daily to a rural school. Itanambikua, even more so than other Guarani schools, thus became a space of epistemic warfare. Through a negotiated agreement with the teachers, the EIB team set up a control group (for Spanish education) and a bilingual group (for EIB) that served experimental needs. The ensuing battle over the validity of EIB played out in competing evaluations of the children's successes. (Most official documents concluded that EIB won.) Fernandito worked in the midst of this.

Fernandito's awakening came after he took courses in linguistics with UNICEF support. It was then that he realized that if he did not "defend his language," no one else would. In his work at Itanambikua, he recalled how Guarani were subject to constant attacks on the validity of EIB by the karai teachers who questioned the suitability of the language, the teachers, and the whole proposal. Schoolbooks gave young Guarani teachers a way to show karai that their language *did* have a grammar that acquired equality through its textualization, much as its speakers pursued equality through mobilization. Fernandito recalled how karai teachers also associated textbook writing with the erosion of karai claims on space: "The karai teachers told us EIB was a false project, deceiving the people. They said that there was no way Guarani could manage their own educational project. And they said, 'How are they going to send us [the karai] somewhere else [to work]?' The more bilingual education advanced with a new textbook through the third to the fourth grades, the more they were afraid of it."

The scribes' work and EIB also had ripple effects in the territorial and geopolitical order of the state. In his work *Seeing Like a State*, James Scott (1999) described how states seek to impose policies through top-down knowledge gathering. Though such large-scale projects generally fail, they rely on the mapping of local spaces and social worlds to make these "legible" and amenable to intervention. Conversely, Tania Murray Li (2007) has suggested that state rule in practice more resembles a Gramscian struggle of give-and-take through which "official" knowledge emerges out of negotiation between top-down visions and local ways of knowing. Education reform, writ large, resembled both Scott's legibility and Li's negotiation. Yet neither view allows for the Bolivian dynamic in which the far-off state was less present than an array of NGOs and increasingly assertive social movements. Here knowledge politics went beyond top-down visions and Gramscian struggle. The Guarani themselves used statelike knowledge-making tactics to legitimate and sustain EIB, redeploying "official" knowledge and ways of seeing as a social movement tool that made transformative demands on the state itself. Writing official textbooks constituted one such practice. Another example was a sociolinguistic study carried out in 1990 through which statistics on Guarani language use and attitudes were compiled to make legible a bilingual territorial space (López and Robles 1990). With this data, the APG began to redefine schools and communities as "Guarani-bilingual" and "Guarani-but-Spanish-speaking." Scribes spent time like generals at war, looking over maps that lined the walls of TEKO and discussing strategies for inserting a teacher in different communities, removing a karai teacher who opposed EIB, or negotiating with the union leaders to trade budget spots in one school for another. Between 1990 and 1995 the number of rural village schools with Guarani teachers increased from twenty schools with 23 teachers to sixty schools and over 140 teachers. By 1997, Guarani bilingual education had expanded to over one hundred schools across three departments (Tarija, Chuquisaca, and Santa Cruz), four provinces (Cordillera, O'Connor, Hernan Siles, Luis Calvo), and nine of fifteen municipalities with Guarani communities. At this writing there are more than 500 Guarani teachers. Arising in part through local tactics of knowledge production that mimicked state practice, Guarani schooling activism began inscribing a new reality and exercising a de facto authority in and on regional territorial orders.

Guarani sought to decolonize state territorial jurisdictions superimposed on their ancestral lands by claiming this de facto authority through their oversight of bilingual schools. A saying among leaders was, "Wherever there are Guarani, there is the [jurisdiction of] the APG." Such transgressions upset what James Ferguson and Akhil Gupta (2002) have called state spatializations. These anthropologists argued that daily routines of statecraft (often waged by state surrogates like NGOs) conjure the imaginary of vertical hierarchy and spatial encompassment that are crucial to the symbolic reproduction of the state. The centrally organized and pyramidally structured Bolivian education system, a template of the state itself, stands as a quintessential example. Teachers internalized this order and were intensely sensitive to their geographic and institutional place in hierarchies that reached upward (vertically, toward La Paz) and outward (from rural school to urban districts and on to departments). They embodied this formal order (e.g., in their dress and way of speaking) and in rituals of monitoring. Metaphorically, Ferguson and Gupta argue, the "dust" raised by one bureaucrat's jeep as it approached a local village to monitor a development project served as a symbol of this vertical and horizontal encompassment that always exists outside and beyond local fields of practice.

Drawing indigenous peoples into such spatial and bureaucratic orders while breaking up other social and territorial references was the primary goal of colonial and corporatist state schooling. Yet the scribes, the APG, and EIB unsettled these spatializations. Language as a political marker and the scribes as claimants on epistemic authority facilitated the conjuring of new concepts of geographic space, hierarchies, and centers. This development played out through transgressive routines tied to the physical movement of scribes (and Guarani books) across administrative spaces controlled by karai authorities. Here the "dust" raised by the UNICEF Land Cruiser as it carried scribes across the region generated uncertainty and the destabilization of authority rather than a routinization of the state. Scribes called community meetings, gathered teachers for training, or delivered supplies—all seemingly mundane yet actually deeply political events in usually quiet rural villages in which historically only ranchers and politicians held the power to do so. That Guarani scribes could arrive in a town, notify the karai school super-intendent of their impending work with a Guarani teacher, and then pro-ceed to the community to work in the classroom or hold a multivillage meeting constituted a profound transgression. Seeing like an NGO-backed movement, rather than (only) seeing like a spatializing state, is one way to rethink the emergent meanings of bilingual education as a transformative project. Whether and how these putative indigenous gains were congruent with the state-fragmenting goals of neoliberalism is a question to which I return below.

When I went to Gutiérrez to interview Elsa in 1999, a decade had passed since the EIB and the APG had come into existence. I hitched a ride in a truck driven by a young karai working at a natural gas service company. On the way we passed a group of Guarani farmers walking beside the road. Un-provoked, he waved his hand toward them and began to complain angrily: "With the uprising, they gave them an entry. Now they do not want to work! In the past they were eager to work, now they're tricky, uppity, they work slow[ly]." From the young man's perspective, the Guarani, incapable of determining their own actions, were led by others [donors? NGOs? the church? gringos?] to enter spaces where they did not belong. Now they were talking back, raising dust, and subverting order. Such comments were signs that change was real—unsettling yet also unsettled. Cultural-political resurgence, the advent of new vehicles for creative transformation, and the creation of new social categories, actors, and territorial orders together represented the ongoing transformation of state space at the heart of indigenous organizing in Bolivia. An intercultural space was under construction. Still resisted by those who perceived it as a threat, it remained unclear whether it would dismantle or intensify colonial ideas about difference. Nonetheless, Guarani were again becoming speaking subjects in their ancestral territorial space.

In the following chapter I return to this period from another location, the village where I went to do research to "systematize" Guarani knowledge. I arrived in Itavera (shining rock) at the same time as Ernesto José, the first Guarani teacher in the recently established school. He brought bilingual intercultural education and a vision of APG unity. I brought an earnest urge for anthropological solidarity.

In the 1990s the two-day trip from Camiri to Itavera involved first catching a rickety bus to Villamontes—a dusty, rocking eight-hour journey over one hundred miles of sandy roads and dry streambeds. There one waited for a bus or truck bound for Tarija. Out of Villamontes, the road, a winding track carved into a cliff, crawls along high above the narrows of the Pilcomayo River. An hour later the road turns south into hills crossed by old gas lines, and new gas exploration transects. It was usually dark by the time the bus got to the little town of Palos Blancos. There I always had a big plate of beef and eggs to load up for leaner times in Itavera. Three hours beyond Palos Blancos, I tick off landmarks in the darkness. The temperature drops crossing the cool heights of Lagunitas. Shortly thereafter come the seven turns where the bus must negotiate a nerve-wracking, hairpinned descent. I then watch for the highway workers' camp and a little shack where they drink at night by lamplight. From there it was up and down again to Cañadas, a creek crossing that rocked the bus and splashed water loudly under the tires. An oil lamp burned in the window of a small roadside restaurant there, the cue to gather my bag. Two hills beyond was the turnoff to Itavera, an unmarked dirt track leading north to the river.

I made my way to the front of the bus to stop the driver.[1] He and his helper, mouths bulging with coca, eyes red from the night driving, watched curiously as I got off in the night. To them, heading to the city of Tarija, it must have seemed like the middle of nowhere. Here the trip continued on foot to the river eighteen miles north. The sandy road reflected what light there was on a cloudless night, so I walked in darkness. The light yet sturdy tire-rubber sandals I wore made a crunching sound on the pebble-strewn road. Otherwise, all was absolutely silent. The Guarani were consummate and rapid walkers. Airase, Itavera's captain and my host, was always talking of lightness, -*vevɨi*, of foot, of bags, of body. After my first arrival he chided me that sandals were better than boots and that my pack was overstuffed. "*Ipoi ko!* Too heavy!" he used to say. I took his advice. I later carried a large cotton flour sack rigged as a shoulder bag with a change of clothes, shorts for river bathing, a water bottle, blanket, and a hunting knife. I kept a bag of coca, raw tobacco, and cornhusks for rolling papers in a smaller bag, all as Airase taught me.

Anthropologists seem clownish mimicking local practice. Yet the simplicity of bag and sandals, the buzz of a chew of coca, and deep pulls on a cornhusk cigarette were by then part of my way of engaging the field. I once told Airase that gringos said smoking was bad for you, and he scoffed, "Ñapëtɨ ñamae täta vaerä!" (We smoke so we have a firm gaze!). His statement reflected tobacco power in Guarani country. I had several yards of red and blue taffeta that would become beautiful *mandu* dresses for the older women. Extra tobacco plugs, coca, fishhooks, and line were appreciated by the men and boys. Dried pasta, rice, yerba maté tea, and sugar were also crammed in. Between Guarani generosity and my own fishing, these provisions would last for the few weeks of the visit. Burdened with getting things on paper, I also had a small spiral notebook.

About three kilometers in I saw a flashlight in the distance. I was edgy about the nighttime hike and my heart pounded. Itaverans were always talking about *ikuatɨro vae* (from S. *cuatreros*, highwaymen). Ikuatɨro vae were one expression of violence that marked stories about boundaries between Guarani and karai worlds. Yet, ikuatɨro vae, real or mythic, were said to get you out on the highway. I was well into the bush. Plus, highwaymen would probably hide their light, right? Rather than turn back to the lonelier highway, from frying pan into the fire, I kept walking. Soon I came on a lone, elderly karai. He had also heard my steps. A bit edgy himself, he had sat down to wait with his light, hoping for company from a fellow traveler.

This was Guarani country, but also that of the Spanish-speaking *chapaco* of the Tarija region. Most chapacos in these rural parts were small farmers or cowboys only slightly better off than the Guarani. Yet they maintained ethnosocial distance with the aggressive use of Spanish and racializing talk about cambas. Since he was not on horse or mule, this fellow appeared relatively poor, neither rancher nor patrón. He greeted me in the sing-song of chapaco Spanish, and we exchanged travelers' information: Good evening, *Guapo*?[2] Where are you coming from? Where are you going? I am coming from Camiri, heading to the river. He was coming from a karai town to the south, heading to a Guarani village three leagues in. (Leagues are three miles, a common measure here.) He says he is "visiting" an older Simba Guarani. I say I am "visiting" the school in Itavera. I imagine his visit has something to do with labor, debt, or trade, though I do not pry. He accepts that I am visiting the school and does not pry either. He offers his name, Don Gabriel Ferrufino, and shakes my hand with a sturdy dignity. Someone with "name and surname" (*nombre y apellido*) is worthy of respect. Guarani were not as ceremonious about names and rarely asked or offered them except in dealings with karai. Guarani greeted each other with terms like *tëtarä*, "relative" and shook hands lightly, with barely a clasp at all. "They call me Gustavo," I offered, using my local nickname. My Spanish could pass as local, but this introduction and whatever he discerned of my features marked me as different. He asked about my *pago* (where I call home).

"Estados Unidos" (the United States), I answered.

"That's another country, right?"

"Sí, es otro país" (Yes, another country).

He grunted. We shared coca and tobacco and walked on in the darkness. Like all good travelers, he passed the time telling *cuentos*, stories of the Chaco. "There are lots of *tapados* around here, buried treasures," he said. "But you have to know how to find them. You can get the riches, but you have to *entregar* something, hand over men, mules, blood, to the *Tío*." The Tío is the Uncle, an entity who controls underworld riches. Tíos were common in the Andes, but less so out here in the Chaco. Having studied the Tío in school and heard Guarani tell such stories, I affirmed his knowledge. I said, yes, I had heard that. He told me of working in the sugar mills in

Argentina. Probably alongside the Guarani, I thought. He recounted how managers found orphans or *opas* (idiots) among the workers and handed them over to "feed the Tío" in a special room. "There's a room full of bones there," he said. "Only those who can fight the Tío with knives can get out." The Guarani also told stories about knife fighting and violence on the plantations, about hidden treasures, and about offerings of mules and opas. I responded eagerly to his story, and the walking was made easier, lighter.

After a few hours we stopped to sleep. We laid out our blankets on the roadside, and I kicked off my sandals, stretched out, and folded my cover over me. The Chaco sky was full of stars, and I mused about the Tío. One expected Andean Aymara and Quechua to talk of things like the Tío. Yet here the karai Don Gabriel told stories that blurred boundaries between indigenous and nonindigenous knowledge. If interculturalism assumed that the indigenous were the ones who were non-Western believers in such things, where would Don Gabriel and much of karai Bolivia fit with their embrace of knowledge like that of the Tío? Anthropologists made much of the South American devil figure as explicitly indigenous, yet here the Tío crossed epistemic, linguistic, and ethnic boundaries.[3]

The older Don Gabriel stretched out beside me, grunting as he settled in. He also looked up at the sky musing to himself about his encounter with an Other, wondering about people and places in the world. Shortly he spoke in the darkness from beneath his blanket. "So the United States, huh? Do you have these Guarani [*estos Guarani*] there in your *pago* too?" Said without malice, he talked of "these" Guarani as if they were a distinct species of plant or animal.

> "No," I said; "no hay" (there are none).
> "Oh, then it [yours] must be a more advanced people [*gente adelantada*], a
>   more powerful country [*país más potente*], no?"
> "I don't know," I said; "it is a wealthy country."

He understood the Guarani as signs of backwardness, as inhabitants of any place and time that had not yet moved *adelante*, forward. It was a curious understanding. As I interpreted it, he delinked indigeneity (in his experience "these Guarani") from particular places and histories and made of it a universal marker of evolutionary backwardness. The United States, perhaps like a big city free of Guarani, was more powerful and *adelantado* than rural hinterlands like his. After some silence he ventured an even more perplexing question: "But these *simbas* here, they must be a little gringo too?" He was referring to the Guarani men of this region who wear their hair long, as in the past. Local karai lore cast them as distinct from and more powerful than the racially degraded, short-haired Guarani peon. I saw simbas as traditionalists, but all in all, still as just Guarani with long hair.

> "I don't know," I said; "No creo" (I don't think so).
> "They must be," he argued. "You know, the *simba* are whiter, taller, than these Guarani."

This curious twist juxtaposed a purer, whiter, simba Guarani of the past with a darker, degraded Guarani of the present. I knew some lighter-skinned Guarani who were simba, but this seemed more perception than fact. Race and time were inverted again, moving both backward and forward through whitening and darkening processes, unsettling clear hierarchies between the local karai and an indigenous Other.

I acknowledged him with my own grunt. This confused my simple notions of colonial racism and karai-Guarani hierarchy. It explained why karai and missionaries were eager to get rid of the long hair of the simba or the women's mandu dress. Both were signs of a more autonomous, more potent Guarani past, one thus cast as whiter and best entombed in statues or in folklore. Here the simba, a different, purer Guarani, imagined as whiter, was thought to survive in remnants representing resistance and power.

Ideas about racial improvement and degradation reflected the colonial ideology behind Don Gabriel's understanding of people. On the other hand, shared knowledge like that of the Tío flowed across these boundaries, suggesting intercultural, interepistemic exchange in practice. Such knowledge emergent from shared social experiences of residence and labor could in fact bridge interethnic schisms . . . such was the basis of popular nationalism . . . or . . . my thoughts faded into sleep.

A couple of hours later we got up in the predawn light and walked on. Don Gabriel turned at the trail leading to the old Simba's house, and we shook hands again, exchanging "que le vaya bien" (may it go well for you). After walking a few more hours, I heard the river's roar. I passed the local karai cowboy's house and his howling dogs and came to Salty Creek. The shallow river ran into the rolling Pilcomayo several hundred yards north. Sandals in hand, I rolled up my pants and picked my way across, smooth rocks and sandy mud under my bare feet. Passing village cornfields and fences, a mile or so on I made my way up the steep path to the plateau of Itavera.

Chapter Three

GUARANI KATUI

Schooling, Knowledge, and Movement in Itavera

The Pilcomayo River flows down from the Andes and winds south-easterly through Guarani country into the Chaco. At one point, the river traces the northern border of the curiously named O'Connor Province, the southwestern-most edge of Guarani country. Guarani in O'Connor work as subsistence farmers and laborers who live amid karai ranches and farms. Much reduced from their historical extension, Guarani populations today are limited to the northern edges of O'Connor, pushed back from the south and the west by karai *chapacos* and *kollas*, and from the southeast by Chaqueños, all labels for settlers of diverse regional origins. At this writing Repsol and Petrobras have also moved into the area to extract immense gas reserves under Guarani land.

O'Connor Province got its Irish name in the nineteenth century. In 1832, after the independence wars against Spain, the victorious liberator Simón Bolívar awarded the land to one of his Irish mercenary officers, General Frank "Francisco" Burdett O'Connor. The Guarani, seen as "errant barbaric inhabitants," were included (but not liberated) (Saignes 1990:175; Dunkerley 2000:145–67). The region still largely remained outside effective karai control, but eventually O'Connor's descendants and other karai established themselves as feudal overseers of the Guarani. According to some Guarani accounts, the patrons were not all bad. Some let the Guarani maintain subsistence lands in return for seasonal collective labor in salt and limestone outcroppings, much like the *mita* (form of compulsory Indian labor) in the Andes. Older Guarani recall stories of captains mobilizing ava workers to mine limestone for "old man O'Connor." After the 1952 revolution, an influx of karai and kolla settlers claiming land accelerated the displacement of

Guarani to the province's dry northern edge. Today new landowners graze cattle and grow corn on the best lands. Some Guarani still live in conditions of debt peonage, and all deal with poverty, drought, and land scarcity. The O'Connor family lives on in Bolivian and Tarijeño circles of power (O'Connor 1977; Dunkerley 2000).[1]

For Guarani, the river and region are known neither as Pilcomayo nor as O'Connor, but as Ɨtɨka Guasu (G. waters-raging big). Ɨtɨka forms part of the Simba region. *Simba* describes both the long hair that some men maintain here and the variant of Guarani they speak. Simba, called *oyepɨkua vae* (G. those who braid) in Guarani, tie their hair up around the head and cover it with a handkerchief like a small Sikh turban. Neatly trimmed side locks peek out from the kerchief, and these men strike handsome figures wearing white shirts and dark pants with the broad-rimmed chaqueño cowboy hat perched on top of the head. Like Don Gabriel, Guarani associate the simba with power. The long hair represents a Guarani past associated with vitality, autonomy, and proud resistance to pressures of schools, karai, and missionaries. For karai, such symbols serve as reminders of an unfinished project of domestication and unsettled racial hierarchies, as Don Gabriel suggested. The simba was thus often attacked by rural karai and treated as a folkloric object by urban karai, both attempting to silence what it represents.[2] Yet the pressure and power of schooling increasingly displaces the distinct power of the simba. The majority of young Guarani men of the region no longer follow the practice of keeping their hair long.

As a marker of power and autonomy, the simba is paralleled by the women's one-piece *mandu* dress. A wide, two-meter length of taffeta is doubled and sewn to leave arm and head holes, making a simple sack that slips over the head. Guarani women like red, blue, or green, unless a woman is in mourning and wearing black. Guarani desire for cloth like this has its origins in early colonial trade relations between karai and Guarani (Langer 1997). Yet with mission expansion the dress (like the simba) became associated with backwardness, and the priests urged the women to replace it with "the *pollera* [dress] like that worn by mestizo women" (Nino 1912:305). Like the simba, the dress is no longer used in Ava and Isoseño areas, having given way to cheaper secondhand clothing. Urban karai have also folklorized the mandu.

The simba and the mandu are understood in opposition to schooling. To my knowledge, no children from simba-using families study. I rarely saw schoolgirls wearing the mandu. Girls who wear the mandu are expected to "be made to dress" (*omovestiru*, from the Spanish *vestido*) like a karai *señorita* if they go to school (or if they marry a karai). Only on festive occasions do they dress in a mandu thereafter. The condition of being schooled supposes an irreversible transformation. These pressures come from karai discourse, but Guarani families have also internalized them. A maintenance of these symbols accompanies a total resistance to schooling. One community, Tëtayapɨ in the Simba region of Igüembe to the north, rejects schooling altogether, and the entire community from infants to elderly people is marked by mandu or simba (Acebey 2005). Most who hear about Tëtayapɨ say, "How can they refuse schooling? They have to have education!" Yet the community is better off than most. Access to land and a strong communal organization, not literacy, have emerged as the crucial determinants of well-being.[3]

The maintenance of these markers and the vitality of the Guarani language here have generated references to the region as a place of *Guaraní katui*, or roughly "true Guarani." The morpheme *-katu*, with the additional emphatic suffix *-i*, means something akin to *par excellence*, and it is most frequently associated with language vitality.[4] In contrast, communities where schooling or mestizaje have led to a linguistic shift to Spanish are referred to as *oyeayea* (G. mix-mixed). Spaces of language vitality were imagined by urban scribes like Elsa as socially and temporally distant from their own spaces of Guarani life. As Elsa told me, "When we go to communities like Itavera, we feel like we are in the time of our grandfathers."

Such essentializing and temporalizing of rural Guarani by the more urban and biliterate Guarani mirrors colonial and developmentalist ideologies. These phrases seem to glorify rural Guarani, but may frame them as backwards people that need guidance and control (Fabian 1983; Escobar 1995). Yet for the Guarani scribes, the idea that Simbas are modern representatives of the past made them powerful icons, not silent objects. The simba and mandu became ubiquitous symbols of Guarani authenticity, gracing posters, banners, and, of late, school textbooks. They are icons now deployed to arrest their folkloric appropriation by karai. There was still intra-Guarani inequality tied to schooling and a risk that scribes would collude in the folklorization of their own people. Yet bilingual education established communicative spaces between Guarani katui and the biliterate leadership that bridged different modes of knowledge and power. Scribes had school knowledge but were contaminated by the experience. Elders invited to key events in Camiri to contribute to EIB were illiterate, but they were defined by *arakuaa*. Though -katui spaces were usually economically marginal, they were symbolically (at times even supernaturally so) more powerful. These reservoirs of knowledge and language were deemed crucial to infuse EIB with authenticity.

Of course the Guarani here were neither pure artifacts nor silent icons. They were embedded in regional market relations and entangled in their own NGO-mediated organizational processes. They sought unity with, but some autonomy from, the APG in Camiri. Most men and some women spoke rudimentary Spanish. Even simba families on the river who rejected schooling and proudly combed their long hair each morning did so while chatting with me about the World Cup (heard on the radio), the gas companies on their lands, their visits to Tarija to collect their Bonosol (a pension for the elderly), and run-ins with evangelicals and Alcoholics Anonymous in Argentina (encountered on visits to family there). Being Guarani katui did not mean being stuck in some idyllic past or radically other episteme.

Movement Stirrings, NGO Networks

Organizing in Itika emerged locally as leaders with their own history of struggle and links to NGOs began to cultivate ties with the APG leadership in the 1980s. A team of Catholic aid workers in Entre Ríos assisted this process. At its core was a group of American Sisters of the Presentation led by the tall Iowan Maura McCarthy. Sister Maura had been working in Itika since the 1970s. By early 1993, when I first arrived, her Aid Team (Equipo de Apoyo) was loaning coca, tools, barbed wire, and food to Guarani to create communal work groups. The model, borrowed from the CIPCA approach in the west, promoted cooperative production to increase income and was a political tool that encouraged the formalization of organizations and claims on land. Amid myriad other activities, the sisters also set up health posts, helped build schools, and launched basket-weaving projects for Guarani women, generally working as a surrogate for a largely absent state.

Bilingual education expanded into the region through these movement-NGO connections. The 1992 Literacy Campaign brought awareness of the larger Guarani territory and organizing beyond the local region. When EIB expanded into primary schools, scribes and the APG targeted Itika to make a tactical expansive leap across state jurisdictions. Along with three other communities on the river, Itavera, a rugged place where few karai teachers wanted to go, was chosen as a beachhead for a new bilingual teacher.

Connections among ideas of authenticity, NGO networks, and Guarani organizational processes also shaped my arrival in Itavera. Guarani scribes argued that "real" knowledge and language thrived in Itïka. Following Elsa's call for systematization and the scribes' immediate goal of writing a Guarani natural sciences text, I would go to Itïka to compile Guarani knowledge of the natural world. I prepared by reviewing documents collected by a literacy warrior who worked in Itïka, an Isoseño named Valentín Ñanduresa. Assessing the situation of rural Guarani constituted part of the political knowledge-gathering strategy of the campaign, and Valentín had compiled notes on the communities along the river. Back in Camiri, I leafed through his files meticulously filled with figures on population, livestock, water supplies, housing conditions, the presence or absence of schools, kinds of political organization, and numbers of people in the literacy classes. In Itavera's file, under language, Valentín had penned a comment that drew my attention: Guarani katui.

With this information and letters from the APG leader Silvio Aramayo and Father Pietro at TEKO-Guarani, I traveled to O'Connor's provincial seat, Entre Ríos, where the sisters were based. There was no Guarani office (as there is today), and it was through outsiders that one contacted Guarani leaders. Sister Maura went out of her way to help. She escorted me to an assembly of Guarani leaders in the community of Ñaurenda and offered me frequent rides in her Land Cruiser pickup, which she wrestled over the twisting, rocky roads of the region. At the first gathering with Guarani leaders I described my plans and presented my letters. (Sister Maura clued me in, saying, "You better just read them out loud"). The leaders were familiar with the idea of EIB and had embraced the ongoing adult bilingual literacy campaign. My Guarani was then rudimentary, but I managed to suggest that I would learn about Guarani life to help bilingual schools. Based on my association with the literacy campaigners, the support from the APG, and most likely, the connection to Sister Maura, my presence was given a nodding approval.

Back in Entre Ríos, Sister Maura later introduced me to Airase, the captain of Itavera. He had missed that first meeting and come to town for another event. Airase was unaware of my existence, plans, or the wider context that had brought this gringo into his life. Again mixing Guarani and Spanish, I explained that I hoped to learn about Guarani knowledge to help write books for schooling in two languages. I also said that I had heard that Itavera was Guarani katui. I later found Airase to be proud that his community was "being talked about" (G. *jeräkua*) elsewhere, especially for being Guarani katui. I was arriving on the heels of the new bilingual Guarani teacher, and Airase, seeing productive linkages to outside institutions, acquiesced to my request to live in Itavera as a guest.[5]

The young schoolteacher who arrived was Ernesto "Tüi" (Parakeet) José. He explained his nickname saying, "I was small, but my parents knew I would fly high." Tüi was one of the first to graduate from the high school in his (and Elsa's) home village of Eitɨ, and like Fernandito (quoted in chapter 2), he was among the first group of Guarani teachers who graduated en masse from the Charagua Normal School in 1991. He was the first bilingual Guarani teacher in Itavera, which had only had a school at all for two years. In all of these ways Tüi occupied uncharted ground: he was a new kind of subject (a Guarani teacher), charged with a new kind of schooling (EIB), in the midst of a new process of political mobilization (the APG).

Tüi was not an ethnic militant. He embodied contradictory influences like most Guarani teachers. He bore the burden of all-Spanish training (we called it deformation) at the Charagua School. On the other hand, he brought ideas about bilingual interculturalism and Guarani rights espoused by the APG. In contrast to his hosts, seen as Guarani katui, he was an evangelical, having gained educational mobility in part through missionary tutelage. In all these ways, he differed from Itaverans who knew neither schooling nor missionaries and were new to EIB and the APG. Yet he shared their language and had grown up working as a poor Guarani under a karai patron, something that Itaverans certainly understood. He often reminded me of this when commenting on our differences. Though we were both twenty-three and educated, only one of us, he said, knew what it was like to be a campesino. Tüi spoke Guarani with zest and humor, quickly earning the acceptance of our hosts. Itaverans called him *tëtarä*, *mbɨa*, *ñande vae*, or in Spanish, *hermano*: family, a Guarani man, one of our kind, brother. For me Tüi was a roommate and tutor who deserves much of the credit for what I was able to do.

In Itavera, Tüi embodied what observers called the "Guaranization" of education in this part of Bolivia (López 1997). I represented the movement and collaborator networks intrinsic to the process. I experienced that time as youthful solidarity. It was research conceived not for academics, but for Guarani uses and audiences. Now with a different audience and temporal perspective, I return to Itavera here, a visit that means shuffling through dog-eared field notes that still bear the rich smells of the river: coca, fish, and wood smoke.

My interest in this chapter is not to expose and systematize closely pro-tected Guarani forms of knowing. I did compile a guide to the natural world in Guarani, one still used by Guarani writers (Gustafson n.d.). Yet here I take up the question of indigenous knowledge as a social phenomenon and consider again the (en)textual(izing) and social mobilizing dimensions of EIB as these articulated with wider patterns of indigenous resurgence (Briggs 1996; Gupta 1998; Escobar 2001). I do so by considering practical questions about EIB. First, what did it look like in practice and how did local Guarani view EIB? Second, how did EIB (and the new bilingual teacher) articulate with the nascent process of Guarani organizing? Finally, what can we learn about engaged anthropology from the (mis)(ad)venture of anthropological solidarity? My main viewpoint here emerges through the words of Airase, my unforgettable host.

Airase, Itavera, and Organizing Agendas

Airase was in his fifties then. He had a bronzed and weathered face lined by years of hard work under the Chaco sun. His black hair was cut short, covered most of the time by a worn cowboy hat. His mood shifted from concerned and serious to energetic and boisterous while in Itavera. Yet he was reserved when in town among the karai. When we traveled to town or to regional meetings together, he wore a slightly worn suit-type jacket, a long-sleeved cotton shirt, and his best pants. Back at home he wore clothes stitched and patched after years of wear from riverbed stone washing. His hat was also stitched from years of repair, with a string pulled tight under his chin like a cavalryman when he was out on the river fishing. Among the karai in town he substituted his handmade sandals, "like the elders used to wear," for a store-bought pair with tire soles. Like most men, he carried a shoulder bag where he kept a plastic bag of coca for chewing and a small plug of tobacco for cornhusk cigarettes. When at work or fishing, he kept a large knife in a leather sheath on his belt, as did most Guarani and chapacos of the region.

In Itavera Airase reiterated how he *ovɨa*, felt at ease, at home.[6] There he was *tëta iya,* the master of the house. When visiting other communities, Guarani depended on the hospitality of others and were attentive to social etiquette so that underlying rivalries did not turn to conflict. If meetings dragged on or led to arguments, Airase would say quietly, "yajaye tëtape" (let's go home). We would quietly pack our things and leave. By acquiescing to my presence, he took on a new burden and as village leader performed the role of generous host to me and Tüi as "visitors." He went out of his way to make sure that we would also ovɨa in Itavera.

Itavera was about the size of a football field, a clearing on a plateau that rose beside the Pilcomayo River to the north and overlooked miles of bush to the south. There were no orderly lines of houses, only a wide, hard-packed dirt patio and twelve thatched-roof structures dispersed haphazardly around its edges. Airase's house occupied a prominent place on one edge of the patio. It was the largest and the first that appeared to anyone coming up the main footpath. Most houses were rectangular, usually just a roof with no walls. Airase's had an oval shape with two rounded ends called "facing testicles." The front door opened eastward, greeting the sun as it rose across the river. Airase often boasted, "This is how the ancient ones lived, the *antiguo reta* [S. ancient G. plural]."

As the oldest of the village, Airase became captain after his father-in-law died. He had married the man's eldest daughter, and his mother-in-law, whom everyone called Yarɨ, Grandmother, still lived in the village. Her now deceased husband had been a simba, and in many ways he was still present, popping up in stories and buried in a huge clay pot right under their old house. "They folded up his arms and legs tightly," Yarɨ recalled for me, "and planted him where he would not get wet." Complaining about karai who criticized Guarani for this burial practice, she told me angrily—thinking of her own future—"we are not like the karai who throw their dead away like trash in the woods. Our pots never rot like their wooden boxes." Decaying house posts now marked the old simba's burial site, just behind where Airase's house now stood.

The other households were spread around the large patio known in all

Guarani communities as the *oka*. Here and elsewhere it doubled as a soccer field. Itavera's oka had a large tree at one end under which community assemblies were held. Around the oka, houses formed a roughly discernible periphery, some more, some less visible due to patches of brush and trees. Guarani were as concerned with privacy as with marking their shared orientation to this public space. The pattern was distinct from Guarani ex-mission towns where the grid of the plaza invoked the centralized hierarchy of church and state. The pattern also differed from karai settlements. Karai lived on isolated ranches or towns that were basically lines of houses built along entry roads. Closed to the road with patios (and livestock corrals) in the rear, karai households reflected an outward orientation toward market extraction (along roads or as outposts of absentee owners). In contrast to these karai points and lines, Guarani communities were clusters oriented around domestic centers surrounded by bush and farmland. These were spaces of experience, residence, and knowledge that represented a tenuous hold on territory in the face of karai expansion. The pattern was revealing of Guarani social structure, reliant in part on ties of community cultivated through shared space and exchange, but resisting formalized structures of sociopolitical order.

Guarani villages were not communitarian enclaves. Each Guarani tëta had multiple internal centers and each household had its own oka, a domestic micropublic space that could be remarkably detached from goings-on in neighbors' houses. Well-trodden paths connected and skirted houses and traced their way down the plateau walls, to the river, to trails leading to other villages, or to the dirt road out to the highway. To avoid drawing attention, Guarani walked around the village rather than across the central oka, which was like a stage when one traversed it at midday. My hosts were always speculating on others' comings and goings—who was going to fish? to work for the karai across the river? to another village? bringing corn? leaving for a few weeks of labor? being visited by a karai trader? Children, licensed to move more freely, ran and played between houses, taking note of goings-on and delivering messages back to their parents. At times a mother would whisper to her child, "Ekua emae!" (Go look!) to find out about something happening at another house. If a child from another family wandered into a house patio, an adult might say, "Mbaepa reeka?" (What are you looking for?) The same question was posed to others who visited the village— traders, ranchers, the anthropologist—"What did they come looking for?"

Daily discussions revolved around access to food, wages paid to Guarani workers by different landlords, prices of crafts paid by the nuns or karai women, the cost of goods, the going rate for fish sold to karai truck drivers, whether the capitán received extra benefits from the NGO, causes of illness, and the possibilities of drought and rain. The tenor of daily life, marked by scarcity, highlighted a sense of communal sharedness in contrast with the karai world beyond, yet it constituted a communality in tension with the Guarani penchant for sociopolitical autonomy and concerns for household survival within. Social relations were, to say the least, delicately crafted and recrafted on a day-to-day basis.

These tensions existed even though Itavera was basically an extended family structured around Yarɨ and her daughters. All the adult women were sisters, aunts, or nieces of each other, born and raised in Itavera. Following an uxorilocal pattern, these women brought husbands from elsewhere when they married, as did their daughters. Their brothers and sons, for the most part, would move away to marry women elsewhere. Though women here were closely related, men were not. The community ostensibly revolved around male leadership, but in practice the ties between figures like Airase and other village men remained weakly structured. His three sons-in-law were putative allies, but he was surrounded by the husbands of his sisters-in-law, ties marked by tension. Most did not call him captain or *mburuvicha* but just a respectful "uncle."

Through mastery of oratory, control over women's labor (having multiple wives to make corn beer), and generosity, figures like Airase in the past *might* have become influential leaders or *juvicha*. A juvicha, a big one, might cultivate temporary alliances between communities to become a "really big one" (*mburuvicha* or *juvicha guasu*). Yet these represented ephemeral kinds of leaderships that relied on the redistribution of surplus production and the convoking power of political or prophetic speech. While language use is still central, few Guarani leaders have the capacity to muster surplus. Polygamy, the underlying foundation, was attacked by missionaries for this reason. Economic scarcity today means that few if any Guarani have access to the land or labor to sustain strong leadership positions in the traditional pattern.

These patterns of flexibility and autonomy contributed to the acephalous society that Pierre Clastres (1987) famously characterized as the "society against the state" (see Saignes 1990). This decentralized society, never congealing in more than a dozen federated villages for any durable time, both facilitated and frustrated Guarani resistance to karai. Pan-Guarani movements were virtually nonexistent, but neither could karai easily co-opt Guarani leaders, whose significance could quickly dissolve when abandoned by their putative followers. The pattern persists in contemporary Guarani politics: at times flexible leadership clusters unite in moments of mobilization, but they rely on the constant recrafting of exchange and on support through symbolic or material redistribution.

NGO networks complicated this phenomenon. With the arrival of new ideas about Guarani organization, NGO resources refigured inter- and intra-community relations. Airase, who may have once relied on cultivating favor with a karai rancher to exert local influence, saw his captaincy formalized as both the APG and its allied NGOs relied on institutionalizing leaderships. The APG convoked regional assemblies that called for delegates and captains to be sent by local organizations. NGOs mobilized captains like Airase to help mediate the distribution of tools, coca, and food for communal projects or to deal with anthropologists.

Leaders like Airase had to convince other families that work groups, NGO resources, and the efforts of organizing benefited everyone. Some village men were more inclined to leave to help kin in other places than submit to the captain-mediated organization. Others were not convinced of NGOs and called them new *patrones*. Airase tried to set the example by being the first in work projects and the first in leading long walks to assemblies elsewhere. I often heard grumblings about demands placed on him by those trying to "help" (grumblings no doubt voiced about me when I was not around). I came to read in his lean, weathered face a constant sense of concern for the demeanor of others as he pondered how he would juggle myriad issues: tending to visitors, dealing with inter- and intravillage rivalries, hurrying his wife to stoke the fire or prepare food for NGO staff visiting the village, worrying over pigs straying into the cornfields, wondering how he would get to a meeting in town, dealing with demands of karai ranchers to clear brush from the roads, fretting over the weather and talk about witchcraft upriver, and commenting on the prospects of yet another year of drought, all while trying to keep his own family fed with fish and corn.

EIB arrived amid these complexities. I quickly learned that one effect of the NGO boom was that organizing was as often a means of seeking outside resources as it was a reflection of a sustained political agenda. On the other hand, NGO resources were crucial for pan-Guarani mobilizing, though competition between NGOs undermined the process. NGOs based in Tarija and Entre Ríos pulled the Itïka Guarani into their orbit and highlighted their particularities for European funders. NGOs like CIPCA and TEKO based in Camiri pulled Guarani in that direction, relying on them for similar reasons. NGO actors like Sister Maura supported EIB, which originated in the Camiri sphere, yet she and her Aid Team had many priorities. Without dedicated monies, local leaders could not engage EIB like the Camiri-based scribes. In short, amid tensions of internal autonomy, economic scarcity, karai pressures, and the geopolitics of NGO activity, indigenous organizing and the arrival of EIB did not erupt spontaneously, but represented feats of cultural and political (net)works riven by multiple lines of dependence. Mobilizing and EIB were as apt to fail as to succeed.

A few days after I moved to the village, I squatted with Airase behind his house, watching him deftly gut and scale a bagful of fish. A little boy, not his son, wandered by. Airase called him over, handed him two fish, and said, "Take them to your mother." Having read NGO tracts on indigenous reciprocity, I thought I was seeing Guarani communalism in action. I asked if he always gave fish to other families. "Oime yave," he said simply, if there are fish to be given. As I continued to observe expressions of sharing and tension tied to scarcity and the emergent organizing politics, I began to understand better the challenges to indigenous mobilization and, by extension, the challenges to EIB.

Observers of Latin America tend to write of indigenous peoples as ethnic blocks that represent "communitarian" identities, interests, and "cleavages" (Van Cott 2000). As the anthropologist María Elena García succinctly argued from work in Peru, there is an assumption (usually by those of the dominant society who wrongly see themselves as generic nonethnics) that indigenous peoples, like ethnic communities generally, naturally tend toward communalism and are "awaiting the right conditions to emerge through the cracks of uneven states" (García 2005:8). The assumption is that communitarian (i.e., indigenous) politics, if not contained by the state, is apt to erupt automatically under the right conditions (see Yashar 2005). Yet as García points out, indigenous movements emerge through long-term political and cultural labor that neither reflects preexisting collectivities nor reacts only to external pressure. Opportunity structures such as democracy or NGO aid are crucial, but the critical factors are the cultural and social interconnecting of heterogeneous identities, histories, places, and divergent interests, in short, articulations. This process faces internal (localized identities and leadership patterns) and external (state or karai pressures, NGO tactics) obstacles. New strategies of self-representation and institutional capture like EIB and the wider APG project served as potential articulators, but they did not automatically resonate with local lives. Locals embraced EIB, but they did so in relation to their own histories, ones different from the vision of unity and historical-territorial reversion imagined by the scribes, and quite different again from the textualizing urge of anthropological solidarity or simplistic theories of emancipation.

Exchanging Words and Knowledge

Tüi and I were relatively young, and Airase could have been our father. Had we been local Guarani, we would have shown him deference. Yet our connections to the school and to the institutions that sent us there from far beyond the community, and our relative wealth (mine more so than Tüi's), made Airase often show us deference, to my discomfort. Airase and his wife saw themselves as hosts (*tëta iya*, owners of the house) and us as their *mboupa* (G. visitors). As they had done for the young literacy campaigners, they demonstrated hospitality (*mbarareko*) and generosity (*mborerekua*), characteristics of a good Guarani, and for Airase, of an able leader.[7] Still a formidable fisherman, Airase was up before the sun on his way to the river or bringing firewood back from the bush around the time Tüi and I rolled out of bed. Unsolicited, his wife often prepared food for us, an extra task amid her daily chores. She usually made fish soup (water, rock salt, chopped fish, a little hot pepper, sometimes a smattering of rice) and offered us the coveted head. Toasted corn or corn flour, when available, was also offered. In return we shared pasta, rice, and potatoes. As I learned more of local etiquette and taste, I returned from trips to town with scarce goods like sugar, cooking oil, and cloth. We also learned to fish (Tüi better than I), and hand-casting from the shore we would catch and share fish with others in the village. I gave most of what I caught to Grandmother's household. They were always short on food, and "visiting" Grandmother was one of my recurring activities. On a daily basis, these relations of visiting and exchange set the stage for my pursuit of Guarani knowledge.

Being a good visitor and knowing how to speak constituted the preconditions for knowing anything at all. In light of the relative freedom from formalized social structures that one finds in Guarani contexts, ethnologists have argued that public speech played a primary role in organizing Guarani social life (Meliá 1988). This supposedly meant that "eloquence and verbosity," as noted by Silvia Hirsch and Angélica Alberico (1996:127), proved central to the establishment of authority, a fact noted by early Spanish chroniclers and discernible in Guarani political speech today. Ethnographers like Curt Nimuendajú (1978), Egon Schaden (1998), León Cadogan (1992), and Pierre Clastres (1987) have all highlighted the role of public oratory as central to the social order and the cultural ethos of Guarani peoples across South America. Though exchange and alliance building tied to cycles of war, revenge, and peacemaking have also been seen as central to Guarani society and ideology (Carneiro da Cunha and Viveiros de Castro 1985), the end of these cycles of war and revenge meant that ritual speech, traditionally yemboe, took the forefront. This is clear in Paraguay and Brazil, where *paɨ* (religious) leaders are known for their songs and prayers. In Bolivia, where formal religiosity has also waned in the face of missionizing pressures, Jürgen Riester (1984) has nonetheless argued for the persistent centrality of ritual speech tied to the arete carnival and to the words of petition exchanged with spirit masters while hunting and fishing. Bartomeu Meliá, one of the gurus of Guarani ethnography and linguistics, argued "for the Guarani, the word is everything" (1995:31).

However, the centrality of the word as the articulator of social relations and of a moral ethos was not only tied to formal oratory for the Bolivian Guarani. Rather, talk was tied to moral constructions of personhood and proper sociality in day-to-day life. One's way of speaking could make people laugh, be happy, and ovɨa; or it could bother, bore, worry, and embitter, eroding ties between selves and others. Kind and well-spoken Guarani were said to be *iñee kavi, ipɨa kavi* (one of good words, of good being or liver). One who was biting, rude, or ill spoken was *iñeeasɨ, iñee kachi,* or *iyuru kachi* (one of bitter, ugly words, an ugly mouth). The former was a desired interlocutor, the latter an undesirable actively ignored, avoided, and forgotten. "When we know how to speak, we are happy to encounter each other. Not knowing how to speak," a Guarani scribe said at a 1997 language congress in Camiri, "can only make people bitter."

The Guarani language thus occupied a central place in the production of intra-Guarani sociality and of a moral ethos at the same time that colonialism —and contemporary schooling—repositioned it as a marker of subjugation and racial inferiority. The school-based assault on language in fact constituted an assault on Guarani sociality and personhood. Both this valorization of language and the stigma generated by the violence of colonial racism shaped local understandings of language, as well as ambiguities toward EIB.

A conversation I recorded shortly after our arrival in Itavera illustrates the work of talk and exchange in constructing sociality, knowledge, and the histories of colonial violence that generate ambiguous acquiescence to schooling. One night Tüi and I sat with Airase, his wife, his daughters, and his son-in-law around the fire next to their house. Tüi was asking about the history of Itavera, and Airase consented to my request to record the conversation. He was narrating geographically, coming down the river village by village through Ñaguañaurenda (Ñaguañau-place, of mischievous little river beings with tightly curled hair that grab fishermen's hooks); Chorokett (*choroke-*cluster, place of many choroke trees); Ivope+tt (*ivope+* tree-cluster); and Tëtaguasu (village-big, an etymology Airase rejected, preferring to gloss it as deer [also *guasu*] village). Airase and Tüi talked their way downriver to Itavera, whose own name, meaning stone-brilliant, refers to minerals, some say gold, that glisten in the cliff walls above Salty Creek. I take up the talk as Tüi asked Airase about his own connections to these places.

> "You were you born right here [in Itavera]?"
>
> "No, I was born in Stone House," answered Airase, referring to a community upriver.
>
> "Aaa," interjected Tüi, repeating courteously, "in Stone House?"
>
> "Yes. My deceased father was a cowboy there, that's where I was born. But I grew up, I came up knowing just above Ivope+tt,[8] in a place called Rock Cluster."
>
> "Taaa!" Tüi exclaimed, politely showing surprise that Airase had grown up in a village that no longer exists. He engaged that place's name to keep Airase talking, "There must be lots of rocks there?"
>
> "Lots. . . ."

"The rocks are cluster-clustered there?" repeated Tüi.

"Itatɨ, Rock-Cluster." Airase paused. "Ita iyatɨ" (the rocks gather there). He broke down its etymology for the teacher.

Airase's story then took a serious turn. His simba father, working as a cowhand for a karai rancher, had come from Stone House down to Rock Cluster with his family. Later the family moved south across the river and up Salty Creek to a settlement named Little Salty. Though Airase did not elaborate, with this move his father had been trying to escape a labor bond to the karai, probably tied to the hook of debt or to violent intimidation. Airase explained his and his father's return to Stone House with little emotion, "The karai [came and] took him back."

Tüi politely declined to pursue this sensitive event and brought the conversation back to where we sat, "And you, well, this village was always already here for a long time then, no?"

"When I lived around here?"

"Jöo" (Yes).

"Yes, it was always already *ndeeeechi* [ollllllllddd]." Airase stretched out the word *ndechi*, emphasizing oldness beyond the present, but still within the memory of the living.

"Aah, it was already old, huh? And it was just Itavera? That was already its name?"

"It was always just Itavera. It never had another name."

The conversation continued through other villages. Airase said most were large in the past, although many had now been abandoned. With poor harvests and karai encroachment, the Guarani simply "died" or went to Argentina, memories echoed in early accounts. When the Swedish ethnologist Erland Nordenskiöld and his wife Olga traveled through the area in 1913, he wrote of Itavera that "it was the biggest Chiriguano village he had ever seen." He praised the beautiful pottery made there and collected items along with bows, arrows, and other artifacts (Nordenskiöld 2002b:46).[9] The French ethnologist Alfred Métraux also came through Itavera in the 1920s, collecting "material culture." These early traveler-ethnologists upheld quite different relationships with indigenous peoples and Bolivian power structures. They negotiated their expeditions with Bolivia's military governments, who had an interest in their knowledge gathering. Nordenskiöld even received armed escorts. Métraux negotiated his access to the Guarani through the missions and local karai. On the river, he stayed with a karai rancher "who intervened on his behalf with the Indians" (1930a:298) and whose son still lives there today. There were no formal indigenous organizations like the APG then, and missions most closely resembled today's NGOs. Like Nordenskiöld, Métraux was aware of the exploitation of the Guarani and of their shrinking territorial base, yet he described the Guarani communities along the river as large and numerous (296). Familiar with the Guarani of the cordillera (recall his description of Santos Aireyu), Métraux also imagined the Guarani of the Itika River region as purer, writing that they "had preserved better than the brothers of their race the traditions of their ancestors."[10]

Tüi tried to bring me into the conversation. I had been thinking and struggling to understand when I should have been talking. On the tape I hear Tüi say to me in Guarani in an off-stage yet clearly audible whisper, "You talk some too!" I mumble, "Jae ikavi" (That's OK) in response. I could not keep up. I managed to interject a few questions about some of the place names, but I did not have Tüi's linguistic and social competence. Despite my intentions, I was doing more taking than giving.

The older Airase politely pretended not to hear Tüi's prompting and continued, repeating what I later heard often.

> "All these people have gone to Argentina, they have died. This place [Itavera] used to be a big community too, but its people began leaving."
> "It was a big place then, huh?" asked Tüi.
> Airase answered emphatically. "Oh yes, it was a big place. But I cannot leave. My father-in-law said, 'When I die you better not go anywhere,' he said to me. 'Why will you throw away our home?' he said. 'If you leave, our home will be lost. We should not leave our home,' he said."

He reiterated his connection to the words of the old simba frequently, over the years, and in the fervor of drinking often tied these words to the school. He reminded me that he oversaw the building of the school and that he had not left the community. In fact, he would be remembered for having made his community bigger.

> "Your deceased father-in-law said the village would be lost [if you left]?" asked Tüi.

"Yes," continued Airase, "I was going to leave, but I have not left. That's why all my daughters were born here, like his daughters."

Tüi confirmed his moral stance and his authority, saying, "That's true. If you were to go somewhere, the village could disappear."

"That's what he told me, long ago," said Airase. "'If you go somewhere, this village will disappear,' he said. 'This land is ours,' he told me. 'This land should never become the lands of karai,' he told me."

"That's right," said Tüi.

Tüi had heard others in the village talk about the past and the loss of land, so he pursued the question: "Back at the beginning, it is said, there was no one here saying 'this is my land,' no?"

"No one! This [land] was all purely [*katui*] that of the old ones," said Airase.

"There were no karai here?" Tüi asked.

"Absolutely none. Not even in Tëtaguasu, not at all. It was pure Guarani, *Guaraní katui*! In Little Salty, in Clay Place, there were none at all. There were a few in Timboi, but here there were none. There was no one at all who was saying 'this is mine.' "

Like other older Guarani, Airase imagined a past when Guarani with a very different relation to territory did not have to confront karai claiming ownership. "Even in the days of O'Connor," an old simba leader told me angrily during one drinking event, "we farmed where we wanted, we left it, and someone else could farm it later. Only after Victor Paz (the MNR revolutionary president of 1952), did the karai go around saying 'my land, my land, my land.' " He echoed Kevin Healy's (1982) study of land dispossession to the north. By the 1970s and 1980s, the Guarani along the river had been pushed onto marginal lands, though they recalled good areas their forebears farmed. When we walked out toward the highway together, Airase always pointed out a place he called *kookue*, (G. field-past; what was once a planted field). Now occupied by karai cattle, it was a plot that his old simba father-in-law had once irrigated and farmed.[11]

As land bases shrank, Guarani who stayed in the region combined labor on their small plots with work for karai, harvesting, planting, building fences, herding cattle, or transporting goods. Airase himself worked in his youth as a mule skinner for karai, taking mule trains of lime or corn to Tarija, a month-long journey before truck transport. Even at his age, he still left the village periodically to work for karai elsewhere. Women earned a bit making baskets and selling them to the nuns or exchanging corn-flour sifters for clothing with karai women from Entre Ríos. Some women and girls also "helped"—as work was euphemistically called—a rancher's wife cooking for laborers, washing clothes, or grinding corn.

This sense of precariousness and subjection to karai contrasted with stories of abundance in the past. Grandmother, blinded by age, used to sweep her hand outward in an arc indicating the village oka, a space she knew intimately but could no longer see. "There were *jeeeeeta* [maaaany] people who used to live here!" She said often. "There were many jars full of *kägui* [corn beer] lined up at every house for the *arete*. But now they're all dead, they have all gone to Mbaaporenda [the work place, i.e., Argentina]."

Back in Airase's story, Tüi asked who the first tëta iya was, the founder or master of the village. "Grandmother's deceased grandfather," Airase said after a moment's thought. "He was a simba."

Tüi picked up on the reference. "Everyone was a simba in the old days?"

"Everyone was a simba!" Airase countered quickly. "Nobody cut their hair. We said when somebody cut their hair, they turned into a karai." Here he reversed old Don Gabriel's reading. While Guarani joked that short hair might make you like a white man, karai saw those with short hair as racially degraded Guarani, less white for that reason. Ever the jokester, the young, short-haired teacher turned to Airase's short-haired son-in-law, "I guess that makes us karai, huh?" We laughed. Thankfully I had caught the joke.

> "And you, when was it long ago that you came to no longer have a simba?" ventured Tüi to Airase.
>
> "When I was little, I was a simba-*tëi*." The suffix -*tëi* marked what was meant to be but did not come to fruition. "When we lived around here, when I was a boy, I was also a simba-*tëi*."
>
> "Ummm," murmured Tüi.
>
> "And so, from there, my now deceased father brought me here, as we were to live as cowboys. And by then I had a *patrón*."

Airase marked his life trajectory with terms that indexed decreasing autonomy through time: the intentioned but not achieved simba; his and his father's destined future as cowboys; and a final status that had permanence in time, as he came under the control of a karai patrón.

For Airase, much of this passage to subjugation occurred while he was still a boy.

> "I had a karai *patrón* then, and he took me around on horseback, to far places, [where I worked for him]. One day, 'cut your hair!' he told me, and I cut my hair."
>
> "Your patrón made you cut your hair?" Tüi reframed the question to ascribe culpability to the patrón.
>
> "Yes, my patrón made me cut my hair. And that's it. No more. I cannot braid [grow] it back again."

The life trajectory from simba (autonomy) to *empatronado* (patronage) was unsettling and contradicted claims to authority and authenticity in the present. Airase seemed resigned but defiantly reconnected himself to this marker of power. "My deceased father was a simba. My deceased grandfather was a simba. My little brother is a simba." Tüi reminded him that his eldest son was also a simba, the only one raised that way in the village.

Guarani men's speech often revolved around assertions of masculinity in a region marked by intensely gendered ethnic boundaries and the emasculating violence of dispossession and subjugation. Airase took up his authentic masculinity again by way of memories of his youth. He retraced his skill in shooting a bow, taking target practice on rolling cacti, and learning to fight with wooden knives. He recalled food taboos and forms of repose (*oyekuaku*) through which Guarani disciplined their bodies to be, in his words, "light of foot, agile, quick, and nimble."

"We were true men, then!" he exclaimed. This macho nostalgia was interrupted by laughter from Airase's wife and daughters, overheard scoffing at the absurdity of their husband and father playing with wooden knives. Airase ignored them. "That's the way we played. Our simba gave us power [*ñandembaepuere*]. We were light-footed. We had no fear. We ran when we walked. We did not sit on rocks or eat pork, these things made you slow and lazy. These days the children play other games. They just say 'I'm a man,' but they are not really."

Tüi collaborated in the reassertion of Airase's authority, asking,

"So you played those games, in case there were enemies?"

"In case there were enemies."

"That's what they call a *kereimba* [warrior], right?" said Tüi.

"I do not know," offered Airase, politely evasive. "We played those things. That's how we were schooled [*yemboe*], you might say, in those days."

Meanings of a Guarani School

Airase's memories of power and autonomy linked to knowledge of the past contrasted with understandings of schooling today. Schools were not seen as a way to revive the knowledge and power of the simba. In fact, they were understood to further movement away from that past. They offered a different kind of power—the possibility of gaining a semblance of voice in the karai world—yet this required sacrificing other forms of knowing, speaking, or embodying personhood and sociality. Against this understanding, EIB, we imagined, should offer empowerment without the violent shedding of other modes of being.

Yet this notion required changing the meaning and practice of schooling, and I soon came to understand that against the backdrop of precariousness, instability, and violence, schools were not primarily seen as changeable things but also as a means of claiming physical and juridical space precisely for what they were, extensions of the karai state. Against the longer history of dispossession narrated by Airase, one widely shared across Guarani country, schools in their current form constituted a means of acquiring space. With great local sacrifice, the little one-room school was built about thirty yards from Airase's house. On a slightly crooked and leaning wooden flagpole out front fluttered the red, yellow, and green Bolivian flag. It had power precisely because it was *not* Guarani.

The little school reoriented daily life in Itavera. Full-throated roosters and flatulent goats served as alarm clocks that started going off around four in the morning. Well before the sun most of the village was up. When corn was available, a rhythmic thump . . . thump . . . thump echoed across the oka in the predawn darkness. Women in pairs or threes ground corn into flour by pounding long, heavy pestles into mortars carved from the hard wood of the *urundei* tree. Women took advantage of cool morning air for the heavy, sweaty work. The thumping was a good sound. It meant there was corn in the cribs and children would be *oyerovia*, happy with food. Women re-kindled the embers of fire pits into small flames in the cooking area beside each house and put on a pot for tea. Men ate quickly and left to fish or to work, talking loudly to each other for good humor on the path, calling their own and shooing neighbors' dogs who barked ferociously as they passed.

A typical school day began much later when the sun was well above the horizon. Children had already let out the goats, looked for eggs or firewood, scattered corn for the chickens, or played in the predawn hours. As the young teacher started getting ready, mothers wet cowlicks on little heads, smoothed little dresses, or tucked little shirts into well-worn pants. Worn notebooks and little pencil nubs went into little handsewn shoulder bags like those their fathers carried to the fields. Little more than point and eraser, pencil nubs were treated as the preciously scarce objects that they were. Tüi and I heated water on our own fire for coffee with bread. Tüi turned on and up his transistor radio to hear the broadcast of Padre Pérez, the host of a national morning news show, the *Hour of the Country*. The priest's voice crackled into the air of Itavera from La Paz via Radio Tarija, tying us to the nation. Inculcated with the discipline of the rural teacher, Tüi shined his shoes while he listened to the radio. I kidded him about this, since most of his students came in sandals or bare feet. He put on his slacks, socks, and shirt, kept clean with the help of local women. Around eight he rang the bell, the ubiquitous symbol of school and state time across Bolivia. Itavera's bell was a chunk of iron kept in the crook of the main village tree. Its clapper was a large stone. At the sound, children came running from around the village.

On Mondays the girls and boys gathered branches to sweep the hard-packed dirt patio of the school. Tüi supervised his little charges, cradling his radio like a baby as he watched them or strumming his guitar and singing songs in Guarani and Spanish "to motivate" them. Most days began with children lining up in formation in front of the flagpole. Tüi called out "Pesïmbi! Pesïmbi! Pekirïi!" (Get straight! Get straight! Be quiet!) until they stood like little soldiers (see figure 3). Divided by gender and height, they kept their hands at their sides, rubbing feet against bare calves to shoo stinging black flies. Tüi inspected their hands and fingernails for cleanliness. Mondays also saw the raising of the flag (taken down on Friday) and the singing of the national anthem.

The national anthem is sacred to Bolivian school culture. Students and

FIGURE 3 "We will never again live as slaves." Students line up for the flag raising and national anthem in Itavera.

teachers are drilled in the anthem and its attendant ceremonies, and Tüi was no exception. The anthem was one of the first texts translated by the scribes, an unquestionable necessity to legitimate EIB. One of Tüi's first tasks after he arrived was teaching it to the kids in Spanish and Guarani. Though the lyrics are impenetrable, even to Spanish-speaking Bolivians, the last line in Guarani was always emphasized in performances and commentary: "Tembio-kuairä ngaraama yaikoye" (We will never again live as slaves; in Spanish, "morir antes de esclavos vivir").

To me, these rituals appeared colonialist to the core, and I saw their embrace by Guarani as internalized subjugation. Yet Tüi, like most Guarani, was less critical. He enacted schooling as he had experienced it, and for most the mere use of the Guarani language to sing the hymn, like other incursions into the karai world, seemed itself radical. By mimetically performing these national rituals as and in Guarani, Tüi and other Guarani teachers were not reproducing the same old thing but formulating a radical claim on the transformation of the nation. Here we see how translation generated shifts, not direct parses. Even the last line of the anthem, which for Bolivians invokes a metaphorical past of slavery that never existed, differs for Guarani.

Slave is translated as *tembiokuai*, "something ordered, controlled," the same word used to refer to Guarani peons, in other words, life in the present for many Guarani. The nominalizer (tembi-) usually refers to inanimate things that do not have agency. Singing this in the face of the karai school was deeply disruptive. As Michael Taussig wrote of mimesis, "a copy . . . is not [just] a copy," but rather entails the working of power in its execution, the absorption of some characteristics of that copied, and transformation in its effects (Taussig 1992:52).

Tüi's disciplinary concerns were also strategic. Against my vision, insulated by foreignness and detachable mobility (I could leave, he could not), Tüi knew that he was being monitored: by local karai, by karai teachers, and by the landlords. Speaking Guarani in the school already constituted a threat to the social order. He was careful to demonstrate his mastery of Spanish and of civic rituals like the anthem. To have any hope of sustaining a polemical bilingual education project and the APG agenda behind it, one had to perform subtle subversions of order. One need only imagine what might happen if Tüi decided one day to stop singing the national anthem, raising the flag, or celebrating civic rituals altogether.

After formation the thirty-five first- through fifth-graders poured into the schoolroom. In the mornings I would sit transcribing tapes or going over notes, turning one ear to Tüi as he taught on the other side of a low wall that divided the classroom from our sleeping area. To work in such conditions with the resources available proved challenging, to say the least. I did not envy him his labors. Yet Tüi took on his task as best he could. He used the new textbooks and creatively improvised. Since there were three Spanish-speaking children in the school (of the karai family who lived across Salty Creek), Tüi was forced to carry out a back-and-forth bilingualism, not exactly ideal. He repeated in both languages, "Good morning children! Good morning professor." He would start a group of older kids on their lessons and then try an oral lesson with younger children, again switching between Spanish and Guarani. One Spanish lesson helped children practice gendered nouns and articles, and I often heard kids repeating, "mira un gallo; mira una gallina; mira una vaca; mira un toro" (look, a rooster; look, a hen; look, a cow; look, a bull). Lessons might then turn to neologisms created for math lessons. "Mbaeno?" (What's this?), shouted Tüi, and the children shouted, "Pɨyovake!" (a square!) And so it went. Trying to teach several groups at once in two languages seemed chaotic, and singing allowed teacher and children to participate in an activity that seemed to evidence learning and order. Between recesses and interruptions, the school day ended quickly, usually with a song. By noon the children were lined up at attention again, dismissed until the next day.

Transformative Effects

While school quality in general is low in Bolivia, comparative evaluations led UNICEF experts to argue that EIB had positive effects in schools like that of Itavera. This was a crucial concern for donors (Muñoz 1997; D'Emilio n.d.; Albó and Anaya 2003). Yet beyond the technical effects, school culture (the rituals and routines of classroom practice and teaching) proved resistant to change.[12] If one could turn off the sound and just watch the goings-on, Guarani classroom practice looked like that in any Bolivian school, or (despite the rustic conditions) like that in many schools around the world. Yet the most visible change noted by Itaverans was that Tüi did not beat the children. The teacher who had worked in the village school before was spoken of with phrases like *pochi* (bad, evil), "sambiai okiye chugui" (the kids were afraid of her), "oipotaä oyemboe" (they did not want to go to school).[13] Like the presence of the Guarani language in the school, the end of school violence represented a first tentative step toward the decolonization of state-indigenous relations.

In comparison with a school that historically offered them literacy (of sorts) and citizenship (of a second-class variety), paid for with violent assimilation, the arrival of a Guarani-speaking teacher and the end of school violence *did* mark radical shifts. The traditional karai-dominated school had worked to exclude the Guarani or to keep them in a subordinate place. In the hands of a Guarani the school could *potentially* engage the social, linguistic, and moral terms of local Guarani life and of the emergent political organization. Guarani frequently talked of EIB and Guarani teachers as being *ñande koti*, on our side (lit., toward us [rather than toward the karai]). Demands for bilingual teachers of "our" kind, *ñande vae*, were often heard at assemblies. Education in *both* languages, another leader emphasized, was good. Yet of more interest to him was that the teachers be "our" kind. Guarani wanted to engage the school on their terms and in their language, even if they were not yet thinking of substantive shifts in school practice. The

EIB school resembled the conversation between Tüi and Airase detailed above: it initiated a dialogue constructed on mutual ascriptions of authority, rather than a one-sided enunciation of karai state power imposing silence and shame. Though neither epistemic utopia nor Freirian liberation, the bilingual school served as what indigenous activists call a *reposicionamiento*, a repositioning of the Guarani place in local relations of power and meaning.

These effects became visible in local organizing and in karai reactions. At village assemblies, new bilingual teachers assisted young, semiliterate Guarani who recorded and read minutes. (Assemblies were primarily in Guarani, though minutes and agendas were kept in Spanish.) Guarani teachers helped read, translate, and prepare letters sent to and from NGOs and state authorities. Teachers helped keep records of food or tools supplied by the Aid Team. Spanish was still preferred for literacy—since communication with karai was its immediate purpose—and these uses of writing privileged younger Guarani over elders. Yet EIB unsettled assumptions about the incompatibility of literacy and Guaraniness. Tüi raised eyebrows among Guarani and karai alike when he once kept and read minutes entirely in Guarani. Though far from practicing decolonization, the Guarani teachers moved literacy "to the side" of the Guarani.

Defensive reactions from karai illustrate what EIB activists confronted in practice. One karai teacher in the large Guarani village of Ñaurenda told me of his Guarani students: "You can't take away their culture [*quitarle la cultura*] that quickly, you have to do it little by little. That's why we need a bilingual teacher, just for first grade. After that we're fine."

Landlords like the powerful Dino Palacios, the putative owner of most of the region, also questioned EIB. Palacios reminded me of Ben Cartwright, of the old show *Bonanza*. Playing the part of benevolent patron, he would ride into Itavera on his mule, whip in hand, whenever he needed workers. As with any arrival, dogs started barking and mothers sent children running out to see. They would hurry back whispering, "Don Dino, Don Dino." Figures like Palacios were the law in these places, a law to which Guarani did not hold equal access. When another landlord sent a thug to intimidate a Guarani captain in Suarurito, I naively asked Airase why they did not complain to police in Entre Ríos. "Ñande Guaranivi," was his densely meaningful answer: because we are Guarani. On learning about the bilingual school and teacher, Palacios was wary. He told his Guarani workers, as they told me, "there was no economy in Guarani [language schooling]." In other words, there was nothing to be gained by it. Karai who had their children in the school also threatened Tüi. Afraid that learning Guarani might contribute to their degeneration, the local karai cowboy demanded that he not teach their children the language. One karai's ten-year-old son told me himself, "Yo no soy ava para estar hablando guarani" (I'm no Injun to be speaking Guarani).

Tüi negotiated these attacks through skillful diplomacy, demonstrating his teaching ability in ways familiar to locals (with singing, civic rituals, and nationalistic displays). He cultivated relations with non-Guarani teachers. He accepted the proselytizing of rural party bosses during campaign times, receiving T-shirts, pencils, and soccer balls for his students. Rather than enacting frontal resistance, Tüi, like the Guarani scribes, subtly maneuvered. Endowed with state capital yet facing durable resistance, EIB had mobilizing potential and unfolded gradually. Such is the slow flow of successful movements of political-cultural transformation.

Coda: Visiting and Knowing

I went to Itavera to compile knowledge on the natural world for the Guarani curriculum. The APG vetted the work, and I was paid $250 a month by UNICEF. The work yielded several written documents (e.g., Gustafson n.d., 1996) and a sustained conversation with the Guarani scribes. I learned to speak Guarani pretty well, a skill widely appreciated. I accompanied the Guarani in their political organizing, as a witness more than an intervener. This meant going on long walks to meetings in other villages, standing (silently), or speaking when prompted as Guarani confronted disputes over land and debt. I also did scribes' tasks like those of the teachers.

Yet Guarani sociality demanded relationships between hosts and visitors (*mboupa*) that transcended anthropological solidarity as I understood it. Much of my practice in Itavera, what I understood as knowledge gathering, was locally understood as "visiting." Airase understood my task, but I never —and perhaps this was a mistake—objectified the task through interviewing. As we fished, walked, or smoked in the evenings, he offered his knowledge on history, trees, plants, animals, soils, and so on. He was treating his visitor generously. When he did not know something or was bored with me, he sent me to others, an ipaye, a woman potter, a good fisherman. As I jotted things down in my room, I was doing what Elsa imagined, "systematizing."

As Guarani knowledge went, my hosts had it and lived it. Yet Airase, never schooled, knew that my writing things down did not mean that I kept this knowledge in my *pɨa*, my being. I often forgot things (scores of tree and plant names were impossible for me). I sometimes pleased yet often disappointed him with my embodiment of knowledge. Walking at the brisk mile-eating Guarani pace behind him, I was always wary of stumbling on rocky, cactus-filled trails. I was oblivious to bird songs, plants, or fruits that might have some use, animal or sandal tracks of others who had passed by, or wasps' nests hanging from low branches. Airase scolded me to walk like a Guarani: "We look up, we look around, we look there, we look here, listen! Don't just look down at the trail!" Nor, by virtue of my task, or by virtue of whatever shortcomings I had as a young anthropologist, did I always speak and socialize in relation to this knowledge in ways that would have made me a mature knower in Guarani. Just as writing did not make me know, sitting in my room compiling notes did not transform me into a knowledgeable social actor. Airase, ever the generous host, used to send his young son to sit with me. "My father sent me to accompany you," he would say, as he sat quietly watching me write. My solitary way of knowing as fieldworker, however engaged I fancied myself with the Guarani movement, did not constitute a good way to ovɨa. For the scribes and EIB, recovering knowledge required getting it on paper. In Itavera, living and speaking knowledge required maintaining relations of exchange, talk, and reciprocity, anathema to this entextualizing work.

In conclusion, EIB articulated politically and epistemically with Guarani organizing and life at two levels. Both were distinct from what I had imagined. Both were articulations with ambiguous meanings that did not respond to a clear-cut narrative of decolonizing interculturalism. At the political level, the articulation was complicated by geopolitics linking NGOs, local Guarani nuclei, existing state and school jurisdictions, and logistical and political challenges to EIB. There was an increasing synchronicity between EIB discourse and Guarani political discourse, but the practical forms of Guarani mobilizing—and attendant knowledges of state, political strategy, and relations with diverse allies and enemies—meant that no straightforward synergy existed between new Guarani EIB schooling ideas and practices and the complicated messiness of resurgence.[14]

Epistemically, the anecdotes about my collaborative task illustrate a second problematic of articulation tied to indigenous knowledge. The visiting and exchange on which socially embedded Guarani knowledge practices relied were undermined, or at least bypassed, by the form through which we sought to strengthen and defend this Guarani knowledge: schooling. Many EIB activists saw indigenous knowledge as an ideational corpus that could be decontextualized (taken out of context), entextualized (written down), and recontextualized (recirculated in schools).[15] Writing traditional stories for schoolbooks or diversifying the curriculum could be done by incorporating this indigenous content. This was understood as cultural, linguistic, and epistemic preservation.

Yet this reproduced schooling forms more than it did indigenous knowledge. In some cases it bordered on sacrilege, resituating religious narratives or ritual speech genres in children's fairy tales. It delinked speech from social relations, spaces, and practices. Sitting in a school "being made to speak" by a teacher differed from sitting in the forest speaking with spirit masters, contesting or acknowledging a leader's authority during an assembly, engaging in multivoiced story production around the house fire, conversing with an *ipaye* shaman about one's illness, or generating beautiful weaving designs after dreaming of snakes and ancestors. When I suggested to one old simba that the histories he was telling me might be good to pass onto the children in the school, he hinted at this by saying dismissively, "Those [stories] are things of the *antiguo reta* [the old ones]."

A parallel view of indigenous knowledge as a cognitive corpus rooted in distinct mentalities, philosophies, or cosmovisions opposed to Western thought is also frequently invoked in EIB debates. Such cosmovisions invoked through tropes like the Aymara pachakuti constitute powerful political and epistemic models and metaphors. Yet it is not clear that their entextualization in curricular forms necessarily reproduces alternative epistemes, subjects, and bodies. In addition, such concepts must negotiate heterogeneity in practice, or they risk hardening into artificial binaries of indigenous knowledge (holistic, local, substantivist) and Western knowledge (compartmentalized, universal, formalist), both abstract forms distant from the messiness of their practice (see Sillitoe 1993).[16]

Based on years of work in an indigenous teacher training school at Iquitos in the Peruvian Amazon, Lucy Trapnell (2003) has described how anthropologists and linguists dedicated to defending culture generated the unreal-

izable goal of recovering historical purity through teacher training. Indigenous teachers in training found themselves constructing idealized notions
of self and culture that did not fit their own complexly layered experience. Eventually indigenous students themselves sought to construct a more
multidimensional vision of knowledge that reintegrated the past into future
horizons, pursuing more control over pedagogical processes and standards of
validation and authority, rather than debating essential purity. This is not to
say that EIB was misguided, but that a deeper process of reflection, only then
slowly emerging, was needed to rearticulate Guarani knowledge practices,
schooling, and mobilization.

These comments should lead toward an understanding of how indigenous knowledge exists as socially mediated communicative practices that are
historically produced (rather than timeless mental constructs), internally
heterogeneous, articulated with nonindigenous social and symbolic forms,
and reproduced through gendered social, political, and economic processes
(Gupta 1998:216–18). EIB and anthropological engagement were best suited
to strengthen Guarani movement when they focused on forms of knowledge production with more "organizing potential," rather than simply on
textual inscription (Rappaport 2005:21). Clearly, the scribes, Tüi, and Airase
recognized this consciously and unconsciously in their own domains. Hence
their pragmatic and often tentative embrace and active redirection of EIB in
multiple directions.

In hindsight, I believe that effective engagement would have meant not
only executing my task (producing written products) but sustaining relations
of exchange and political dialogue *in this place*, more like the NGO actors yet
without their ties of external dependence. Though placing often unrealistic
temporal demands on academic actors fretting about publications, tenure,
and the like, a real engaged anthropology requires the time and reflection to
strategically articulate research agendas with local processes and actors.[17] My
tape-recording, writing things on paper, and carrying the work to Camiri
were all reasonable and went beyond the engagements of most anthropologists. Yet as collaborative practice these actions did not satisfactorily articulate with local understandings of knowledge, political process, and the
school. In retrospect, my efforts were not hindered because I did not ovïa or
embody knowledge perfectly, but, as I later understood through Guarani
eyes, because I did not stay forever.

The following two chapters explore EIB through other scales of time and place. Chapter 4 looks back in time and up at the state to retrace the emergence of EIB as a project situated between state, development, and indigenous movement actors. Chapter 5 moves forward in time and into the halls of state power to trace EIB as it moved away from grass-roots Guarani resurgence into the official world of neoliberal interculturalism in the 1990s and early 2000s. I depart from Itavera much as I was pulled into it, through a research project that came crackling in by shortwave radio one day.

Part Two   TRANSNATIONAL ARTICULATIONS

Interlude

To La Paz,
via Thailand

In 1990, education ministers, NGO activists, and representatives of the big banks and aid agencies gathered in Jomtien, Thailand, for the World Conference on Education for All. It was the first in a series of United Nations-backed global development rituals of the 1990s, followed by the UN Conference on Environment and Development, or "Earth Summit" in Rio de Janeiro (1992); the UN International Conference on Population and Development in Cairo (1994); and the Fourth World Conference on Women in Beijing (1995). These events brought first world aid donors and recipient countries together to shape the terms of development discourse. What emerged were ways of speaking about countries, populations, issues, and policy prescriptions that, if adopted by recipient governments, donors would support. The anthropologist Akhil Gupta described these events as "instruments being forged for global governance that have grave implications for the current world order of nation-states" (1998:292).

Jomtien, as the conference was later referenced, intensified the globalization of public schooling, traditionally the domain of sovereign nation-building agendas. Schools and children were reaffirmed as targets for aid, and education reform moved to the fore of development talk. Participants agreed that education for all to meet basic educational needs should be reached by 2000. This agreement sought to shift attention and resources to primary schooling (away from universities) and spoke of including traditionally excluded populations—especially girls, women, and the poor—whose education was deemed crucial to development (WCEFA 1992; Torres 1991). Though the goal went unmet (it was later pushed ahead to 2015 at the 2000 World Education Forum in Dakar, Senegal), the slogans of education for all and of basic needs took root in places like Bolivia.

These ideas were not entirely new. UNESCO had staged regional conferences on education in Latin America in the 1950s, arriving at similar conclusions about the need for education and its contribution to social and economic development (Blat Gimeno 1981). Yet a shift did occur. In the 1950s, the prominent paradigm was one of "inward-oriented development." Intellectuals saw their countries as peripheries situated in unequal positions of dependency in relation to capitalist centers (Sikkink 1997:231). To address this condition, so-called developing countries, many of them former colonies, promoted literacy expansion alongside nation-building agendas (e.g., Coe 2005). Though education quality and access declined during the debt crises of the 1980s, even countries like Bolivia attained near complete school coverage. In the 1990s, the paradigm shifted toward outward-oriented development. The rhetoric of liberalization, competition, and market-led growth displaced ideas about dependency and nation building. Education for all and basic needs now became ways to talk about paring down state schooling to the supposed basics. Universal schooling remained a universally unobjectionable goal. But the policy prescriptions that emerged from "universal" and "basic" schooling rhetoric were, in their approach to national public education, similar to neoliberalism's wider approach to the state. These policies did not simply privilege the market over the state, but expanded and transformed some state components while dismantling or downsizing others. New paradigms coexisted and collided with old, leading both state elites and indigenous educational activists to embrace and resist the idea of reform, albeit for very different reasons.

In the late 1980s Bolivian elites had begun to rethink the nation and education in these basic terms. Aided by the big banks and catalyzed by Jomtien, their efforts culminated in the creation of a national education reform proposal in 1993. A World Bank–funded team called ETARE, the Technical Team for Aid to Education Reform, spearheaded the plan, which called for the national adoption and expansion of bilingual intercultural education (ETARE 1993b).

In September of 1993, before this proposal became law, the shortwave radio that ran on a solar-charged truck battery crackled in Itavera's little health post. The health promoter's wife was listening and tracked me down. "*Ndiringo* [gringo], they're calling you from Camiri." I followed her back and raised my friend Tomás at the NGO TEKO-Guaranií.

> "Come back to Camiri," he said, "I need some help with a research project. Over."
> "What is it? Over."
> "To help promote bilingual education at the state level. Basic educational needs. Over."

Curious and ready for a shower, I packed my bag a few days later, trekked out to the road, and caught a Tarija Expreso bus heading toward Santa Cruz.

In the midst of neoliberal reform, academics like Tomás faced a shrinking state bureaucracy and a miniscule private sector. Social scientists became increasingly dependent on aid-funded NGO jobs. Research, as I later discovered with the "basic needs" project, was largely determined by development imperatives. As Julia Paley suggests based on work in Chile (2001:202–4), this echoed the paradigm shift described above, from an era in which social scientists generally allied with movements for social change and nation building (tied to support of and for large public universities) to one in which academics became agents of a depoliticizing, technocratic approach to development in support of the market.

Yet this held only partly true in Bolivia. There were certainly NGOs and think tanks funded by pro-market agencies and teeming with technocrats. Yet many NGOs were linked to grass-roots movements *and* development agendas. In addition, the education field was charged with discourses of anti-imperialist nationalism, liberation and decolonization, and a notion of the state's moral obligations to provide schooling. Social scientists like Tomás, who worked on education issues, were inseparably entangled in the politics of schooling. Researchers in the NGOs, often receiving support from progressive European sources, acted as mediators rather than as simple technocratic agents. Some NGO research was central to social movement formation and the politicization of public issues, while some was indeed deployed merely to legitimate policies already adopted (Paulson and Calla 2000). Academic knowledge constituted a battleground in the unsettled war over the future of market, state, and nation in Bolivia.

The World Bank–funded education reform plan emerged amid intensifying political debate over structural adjustment. Teachers, backed by the Catholic Church, opposed reform for its links to the World Bank and the "damned laws" of neoliberalism, deemed anti-union and ultimately seeking the privatization of schooling (Gill 2000). On the other side, the World Bank had viewed EIB and its implications for curricular reform with some skepticism. It wanted to "restructure" curricula, rather than complicate them with native tongues and issues. Yet European donors, especially Sweden and Germany, had already been funding EIB and supported the idea of indigenous education. They joined the Inter-American Development Bank (IADB) and the World Bank to support reform, but spoke of the need for more participation, especially by teachers (e.g., SIDA 2000). Reform discourse, apparatus, and practice were thus internally complex and faced multiple tensions: accusations of antidemocratic imperialism by teachers; demands for public participation by Europeans; and skepticism about bilingual schooling by the economist-dominated banks. ETARE confronted these challenges by deploying social science research.

A national "Basic Educational Needs" research project was designed and put up for public bidding (ETARE 1993a). TEKO-Guarani, because of its work in EIB, was chosen to do the work in Guarani country, and Tomás called me in to help out. As prescribed by Jomtien, the research proposed an empirical identification of the "basic educational needs" of the country. To deflect teachers' accusations of neoliberal imposition by calling on the legitimacy of social science, these needs would come as data from the ground up, echoing methodological phrasing in Spanish that speaks of *levantando datos del terreno*, lifting data from the ground (or field). These data would reveal Bolivia's multicultural and multilinguistic reality and justify EIB as a policy response. By virtue of its method, focus groups, it would perform participation by way of public consultation, "socializing" discourse about—not just capturing inputs for—reform.

Only when I retraced this history several years later did I understand the context described above. At the time, we did not talk about Jomtien or the

World Bank. Out in Guarani country we talked about the research as a means to critique the current state of education and to construct a Guarani demand for EIB. After meeting with Tomás and the rest of the team in Camiri, I returned to Itavera. Tomás planned focus groups with teachers and Guarani leaders, and I modified the research protocol for local use. Imbued with a sense of speaking truth to power I gathered interviews to denounce the dismal reality of schooling for the Guarani. One such conversation unfolded with Cristina, one of Grandmother's adult daughters in Itavera.

It was October and the heat intense. I sat on a bed of woven leather under the shade of the thatch in Cristina's open-walled house. Tiny *mbarivi* black flies were thick, looking for exposed arms and feet. Out back the corncrib was practically empty. February's harvest had nearly disappeared, and Cristina's husband was across the river working for the rancher in exchange for corn. Cristina was weaving cornmeal sieves to sell. She sat cross-legged on a goatskin hide on the dirt floor, the bottom edge of her green mandu tucked over her feet to ward off the flies. With her youngest child in her lap, she worked on the thin strips of palm while dealing patiently with my "visit."

Like most women of the village, Cristina understood but did not speak Spanish. She had never been to school. Now speaking Guarani in the words of far-off actors, I translated the first question on the protocol: "How do parents conceive of the purpose of schooling?" In my Guarani this came out: "Why do you send your children to school?" She answered:

> C: The children are all going to know [*oikuaa*]. We [parents] are stupid [*zonzo*]. We don't know how to look at paper. The other teacher used to say to us, "You all are stupid, you don't know how to read, send your children to the school." That's why they have to study.
>
> BG: What do the children study [*oyemboe*] in school?
>
> C: I don't see what the children study. I see the papers they bring home, but I don't know. I just look at it. They learn to read paper. You know, the teacher speaks to them, and teaches them, makes them speak [*omboe*]. They study in Spanish, and they learn Spanish in school. It's good what they learn in school, but I don't know what those things are that they study.

She used the Spanish word *zonzo* for stupid, referring to herself as many karai referred to unschooled Guarani. My asking the question seemed to affirm this prejudice, and I wanted to acknowledge her knowledge. Never much of a disciplinarian when it came to research, I strayed from the protocol, asking if she had not been taught (-mboe) by her mothers and grandmothers. "No," she answered flatly. She used her thumbnail to push the split palm into a tight parallel weave, pausing briefly to sit up and stretch her back. Checking the infant asleep in her lap she looked toward the kitchen area, thinking of what she could offer her visitor.

"But another kind of learning [yemboe]," I insisted. "Did you not *learn* how to make cornmeal sieves, how to make. . . ." She understood my misuse of *yemboe* and cut me off. "Yes, those kinds of things we learned [-*kuaa*]. . . . We learned how to make woven bags, pottery, sieves, dresses." She set off men's learning as distinct: "The men learn how to do what they do too. They go and make their fields, their fences. . . . My grandmother made us knowledgeable [*oremboarakuaa*]."

I asked, "And that knowledge [*arakuaa*], they don't make them knowledgeable like that in the school?" She answered quickly, as if it were obvious, "No. Because [in the school] they learn [*yemboe*] like the karai."

She dipped her fingers in a bowl that sat by her knee, flicking water onto the palm to make it pliable. Examining her work, she looked up again and told an older daughter in a quiet voice to get a pot boiling. I had been visiting long enough, and they would invite me to some tea like good hosts.

As we drank yerba maté I finished the protocol, though school talk was laborious. How long should kids study? "Three years is good they say." What did they need to learn in school? "Spanish reading and writing and numbers." What was good and bad about teachers? "Those who beat the children are bad, those who speak Guarani seem to be better." And so it went. I finally turned off the recorder. She was happier chatting about other topics—biting flies (a sign of good fishing), rising waters (more labor for women to deal with turbid water), karai merchants who brought alcohol to trade for fish (fish prices seemed low, men were drinking too much), and the clothes she would get for her sieves (calculating days of labor for a few pieces of clothing).

Back in Camiri we drew on these interviews and focus-group materials to produce a report with charts, actors, and discourses neatly arranged (Robles, Gustafson, and Rojas 2002). Our conclusions supported the Guarani demand for bilingual intercultural education and denounced poverty, land scarcity, and the racism of the education system. I felt satisfied that we had spoken. Tomás went to La Paz to present the work. In July of 1994, the day I flew back to the United States, the government passed the education reform into law. Bilingual intercultural education was approved. The national teacher unions were still enraged, but the Europeans and the banks had come together.

Through press accounts, later interviews, and reviews of reform documents I learned that the basic-needs research was less relevant for the knowledge it gathered than for its conversion into a polysemic token. It was cited to defend the legitimacy of reform as national and Bolivian (intercultural and multilingual, like the country), universally valid (following a global consensus on basic needs), and participatory (these needs were constructed from the ground up.)

Had we spoken truth to power or had development made us speak?

Chapter Four

NETWORK ARTICULATIONS

EIB from Project to Policy

> Bilingual education is not yet a solid policy of the state with an
> assured permanence in the future. We have more achievements
> than other countries in the educational, the legal, the administra-
> tive areas. . . . [But] there are distances that remain to be traveled,
> and we must not let down our guard. Those of us who are loyal
> militants of bilingual education have won battles, but bilingual
> education must be made irreversible. . . . We are strengthened by
> diversity. However, in 1952 [diversity] was interpreted as an ob-
> stacle to development, and in 1955 the educational reform sought
> linguistic homogenization. After forty years we are living the fail-
> ure of those policies. Now we want to recognize, value, and fulfill
> the potential of cultural and linguistic richness of the country, not
> just as a revindication, but as a pedagogical resource.
> —*Amalia Anaya, vice-minister of education, public statement, La Paz,
> 1998*

While living in La Paz in 1992 I studied Aymara with Vitaliano Huanca, a schoolteacher and language activist. Eager to get involved
with indigenous movements, I asked Vitaliano for leads on bilingual education. He sent me to the Lazarte Building in downtown La Paz, home to the
Ministry of Education where Aymara were working on the PEIB pilot project. "Maybe they can use your help with something," he said charitably. I
knew little about the wider processes underway that explained the existence
of bilingual education as a development experiment situated between rising
indigenous movements and plans for market-oriented school reform. As that
visit eventually led me to the Guarani, the Lazarte Building is a good place to
start exploring this history.

Back then, the building housed the Ministry of Education, Culture, and Sport (MEC-D). It is a large, gray mass that rises up over the Prado, the main avenue of downtown La Paz. A simple state seal over its looming front door read Ministerio de Educación, Cultura y Deporte. A monument to the centralized national education system created forty years earlier, Lazarte also symbolized the historical and institutional space of state power held by the national teachers' unions. Education reform was not yet law, but by 1992, EIB had already entered this historical space. Guarani scribes were working out in Camiri, and Quechua and Aymara scribes worked on their own text-books here in the General Directorate of Rural Education. Their physical presence in the Lazarte Building reflected the insertion of donor aid and indigenous organizations into a field previously monopolized by school-teachers, party elites, and the Catholic Church.

I recall trudging up the dimly lit concrete stairwell. Like many buildings in La Paz it was chilly inside, unheated and dank. People worked bundled in coats and hunched over against the cold. I wove my way through teachers hurrying up and down the steps, their polished shoes scraping and tapping the bare concrete. Most held long folders under their arms. Small groups stood on landings conferring with *colegas* (colleagues) in tones of hushed urgency. Others knocked on office doors to pursue some *trámite*, the mar-shaling of papers through bureaucracy. Andean peasant leaders waited out-side different offices. Wearing bright ponchos and *lluchu* stocking hats with silver-tipped staffs of authority slung over their backs, they were probably engaged in trámites too, sent to La Paz to change a teacher or seek resources for some community school need.

To my gringo sensibility the building felt run down. It represented the general situation of public education. Public schools were perennially under-funded and treated with disregard by the ruling class. The ministries of Fi-nance, of the Interior, and of Defense surely had polished and well-appointed offices, but public education (*educación fiscal*) had become the underside of the state that dealt with the masses and the teachers unions.[1] In the intensely class- and race-conscious view of public status, teachers occupied a social caste below university graduates and professionals. Urban teachers were only slightly above rural teachers, and in elite criollo eyes, all were scarcely a step removed from the rural peasants and urban workers whose children they worked to educate (Luykx 1999). Those who could afford it distanced themselves from these categories by going to private schools, called *particulares*. The Lazarte Building was thus also a monument to a wider structure and history of racialized class struggle built into the apparatus of the state.

Save the minister and high-level appointees, the six hundred function-aries who staffed the Lazarte Building were all schoolteachers. They had been credentialed by a rural or urban normal school and affiliated with either the rural (CONMERB) or the urban (CTEUB) union. Energized by Trotskyite leadership factions, the unions were disciplined, *contestatario* (contestative), and *combativo* (combative) in the courageous, Bolivian sense of the words. The teachers' occupation of the Lazarte Building thus signified symbolic power as well as quite real control over jobs, budgets, and money.

Despite its hard-line rhetoric, the teachers' union did not constitute a revolutionary vanguard. Its power relied on an institutionalized stability that tied it to the elite-dominated party system through cogovernment (*co-gobierno*). The Trotskyite call to intensify contradictions to bring down the state masked concerns with defending union power within the state itself. Elite parties competed to control factions within the union to support their candidates, offering jobs or concessions to union leaders that trickled down if their party won. The union in turn had oversight (*aval sindical*) over appointments, generating internal struggles over union leadership.[2] Cogov-ernment relations extended downward through departments, provinces, and districts, where party-union battles often led to opposing factions physically removing their opponents from contested posts.

Regionally and ideologically complex, the struggle over public schooling at the national level structurally manifests class struggle. It involves a give-and-take between elites who control state resources and public sector em-ployees whose interests are tied to the defense of public education for poor Bolivians. Against the state, the unions often mobilized as one. As salaries were announced each year, the teachers mobilized through strikes to defend their space. In times of relative power imbalances, as during military regimes, the state imposed itself more forcefully. In times of relative labor power, when ruling parties could not afford repression, teachers demanded more concessions. The Finance Ministry ultimately controlled education budgets, with the general disregard for public schooling reflected in the acknowledg-ment by one former ministry official that the school budget was the "adjust-able" variable. If needs arose in other ministries, he told me, amounts were taken from education. If there was any money left over, public education might get more.

This ritualized cycle of conflict and cogovernment defined the national politics of education. Reformists used the cyclical strikes, which led to many days of school lost, to argue that teachers had little interest in education and that the crisis of education was largely the fault of the teachers (Grindle 2004). For teachers, the struggle testified to elite disregard for public schooling. With neoliberalism—which sought not simply to privatize but to decentralize schooling, open teacher training to the market, and dismantle the cogovernment model of administration—education reform came down to a political war between reformists and teachers. As other state industries were privatized and labor unions hit by draconian laws that removed labor protections, the schoolteachers—and to a lesser extent, public health workers—were the last line of defense against the neoliberal turn. Teachers saw themselves as doing nothing less than battling against the privatization of society.

This history situated in the Lazarte Building was the product of the 1955 Education Code, the first reform of the postrevolutionary era that expanded public schooling and teacher training and created the unions (Contreras 2003). When bilingual education was initiated as an experimental project funded by UNICEF in 1989, it crafted a tactical place within this teacher-run state education apparatus and within the rural space assigned to indigenous schools. Though opposed by local teachers out in Guarani country, EIB as an aid-funded project had the tacit support of the national rural teachers union, backed by the Andean peasant-indigenous union (the CSUTCB). Both had been demanding bilingual education in their manifestos since the 1970s, a position nurtured in the Andes by Katarismo and other indigenous intellectual movements that were rethinking the relation between ethnocultural difference, linguistic identity, and class struggle. There were still deep schisms between some sectors of the teachers unions (especially urban) and the decolonizing projects of indigenous teachers and scholars like Vitaliano Huanca and the Guarani scribes. Yet EIB opened a space of dialogue, and on the eve of education reform this tentative articulation between a history of teacher union activism and indigenous schooling projects was already embodied in the little office I went to find in the Lazarte Building.

With the 1994 school reform, this emergent articulation of union protagonism and indigenous intellectual projects collided and converged with global initiatives like Jomtien, market-oriented policy networks, and the elite-led rethinking of state education. Bilingual interculturalism was at the center of this contentious convergence, and the 1994 reform converted it from experimental aid project into state policy. We celebrated the news, clearly an indigenous victory, as did others working on bilingual inter-cultural schooling in Latin America (Hornberger 2000). Yet reform did not just ratify indigenous movement views of intercultural education. It re-located EIB to new spaces and meanings distinct from its historical articula-tion in the Lazarte Building and its unfolding significance within resurgent movements like that of the Guarani. Like the miners who found themselves digging ditches or migrating to grow coca in the Chapare after neoliberal privatization, bilingual education had been *relocalizado*, relocated by the structural adjustment of reform.

When I began returning to Bolivia as a graduate student researcher after 1994, the Guarani scribes had also been relocated, from Camiri to La Paz. But they did not go to work in the old Lazarte Building. Further down the Prado were the new offices of the Education Ministry near the Radisson Hotel. Teachers with folders still milled around outside the building, yet a high iron gate and olive drab–wearing policemen controlled entry. A huge billboard outside showed indigenous children in native dress, reading: "Our Diversity is our Strength—Bolivian Education Reform." Beyond the Radis-son, just off the main thoroughfare, one continued to a shiny new glass-windowed building that eventually came to house the education reform's technical staff. These offices became ethnographic stopping points when-ever I passed through La Paz on my way to or from Guarani country. It was here, far from the teachers' old domain, that indigenous writers, EIB, and education reform were located.

The building was shared with one of Bolivia's many new private univer-sities, another outgrowth of the deregulation of private higher education that paralleled reductions in public university funding and increased atten-tion to the "basics." Riding up the mirrored elevator, I always felt I should be wearing a tie. It was a far cry from the bare concrete steps of the Lazarte Building and its histories of class struggle. It was distant further still from Guarani country. Writing about river spirits and weaving seemed artificial here, far from the political assemblies, jovial discussions, coca chewing, and sandy trails through which these things took meaning out in the Chaco.

With a gentle electronic tone, the elevator opened and emptied you into a warren of cubicles.[3] It was a busy atmosphere of phones ringing, secretaries carrying messages and trays of coffee, staffers walking to and fro, and posters proclaiming, "If Education is for All: Then it is Bilingual and Intercultural" and "Bolivia Reads! National Reading Day." Memos on timecards and new lunch-hour rules were pinned along the entryway. Most working here were middle-class, university-educated Bolivians who had studied pedagogy or related fields. Only a few, mostly indigenous scribes, were schoolteachers. On a typical visit, I would peek over a cubicle wall to say hello to two women working on teachers' guides for constructivist methodologies. Constructivism was to replace conductivism, the authoritarian, teacher-centered methods of dictation and memorization that had dominated classrooms of the past. Across from the women another friend, Ana, labored over manuals for school projects. Borrowed from Chile, whose transition to semiprivatized schooling had occurred under the iron fist of Augusto Pinochet, the school project idea aimed to inject local "autonomy" (*autonomía*) into school "management" (*gestión*), both reform buzzwords. Local communities would generate ideas (projects) for school improvement and seek funding. School projects were touted by reformists as a mode of democratization and local power. Critics saw them as devolving state responsibilities to local parents and a prelude to privatization. I jokingly asked Ana once if she thought she was an agent of neoliberalism. "If it makes education better, so be it," she retorted. Across the way a young economist fresh out of La Paz' Catholic University was redesigning the curriculum for teachers' schools. In one interview he distinguished his work from the chaos of the "bloated-six-hundred-strong-teacher-controlled-bureaucracy," gesturing toward the Lazarte Building with the words rolling out as one breathless epithet. Further on, two teachers were redesigning math and science curricula, seen as central to the creation of competitive, technically minded human capital. Thanks to European donors, the reform was also shaped by "transversals": democracy, gender equality, and the environment. Another cubicle represented the special budget line for gender equality that came from the Netherlands, with two Dutch staffers posted here to debate textbook representations of gender with Bolivian planners. If liberal elites imagined their Indians as little Swedish pacifists at the turn of the century, now they were refitted as gender-sensitive, democratic, and green Europeans.

On the floor below computer experts compiled information deemed crucial for administrative modernization. World Bank analysts concluded later that improvement in knowledge gathering (and the removal of the teachers' union from effective control) were the most notable achievements of Bolivia's education reform (Soares et al. 2005). The information department maintained a flashy Web site, managed databases, and tracked enrollments, infrastructure, dropout rates, gender ratios, test scores, and so on. According to staff interviews, new technologies of mapping, tracking, and monitoring brought an end to the opaque haze of the teacher-run system. "Education budgets had to be an adjustable," the ex–Finance Ministry official cited above argued to me; "you never knew how many students or teachers there really were." The enthrallment with numbers also found its way into the new curriculum. Argentine consultants hired to advise the team told the press in 2004 that a "statistical culture" would soon emerge in the Bolivian classroom.[4]

On the floor above staff restructured the school-district system to "rationalize" the distribution of teachers and schools according to population, territory, and the recently decentralized municipal government system. On the lighter side, a clutch of artists and graphic designers also worked up there. They were always busy drawing fantastical illustrations for the books, manuals, posters, and the new school modules produced on the floor below. These Bohemians represented the freest thinkers in the place, and my chats with them were laced with critiques of bureaucratic inanity, the ex-dictator they worked under (Hugo Bánzer, from 1996–99), and the dictates of their managers.

Back on the main floor at the far end sat the *jefa* (boss). She frequently complained of stress-related pain in her arms and hands. Smoke wafted up behind the glass that separated her office from the cubicles, and an ever-present pack of Marlboro reds sat on her desk. It helped ward off the stress of teacher conflicts, foreign consultants, a constantly ringing cellphone, monitoring by donors, critical newspaper articles, staff malcontent, and the ever-present possibility that political instability might leave her jobless from one day to the next. I wave through the glass as I stop in to see the Guarani scribes in the cubicle they share with their Aymara and Quechua counterparts. The Aymara and Quechua are also old acquaintances from the EIB networks, and they show off some Guarani they learned while I dust off my rusty Aymara greetings. I exchange news with the Guarani, and they share samples of their latest work, pointing out new writing dilemmas or showing me how stories like that of the Massacre of Kuruyuki are being refitted in the new modules. After a chat I take the elevator back down into the streets of La Paz.

EIB had emerged in a history in which movements forged in the language of class struggle were being reshaped in the context of indigenous resurgence, seeking to change a decrepit schooling system tainted by colonial ideologies and the rigidity of corporatist centralism. Yet now it seemed to enter another history, as a culturalist appendage to a managerial project, much like the diversity department of a corporate business office: contained, managed, and monitored in its own little cubicle. How had this happened and to what effects?

In this and the following chapter I pursue this question.[5] I explore the recent history of bilingual education to see how practices of translation and articulation worked to relocate EIB away from its grass-roots and academic origins and toward an ambiguous position as an appendage of state reform. The discussion considers a polemic of great significance in Bolivian education today: Was education reform a neoliberal imposition or did it represent —especially in its intercultural and bilingual turn—something authentically Bolivian and popular? This question is impossible to resolve analytically. Ethnographers so often invoke neoliberalism that it has become a totalizing bogeyman, specifying little while masking much complexity in state and cultural processes. Yet the public battle over reform legitimacy must be appreciated to understand the disputed location of bilingual interculturalism therein. Clearly, the relocation of EIB was neither total nor complete. As the epigraph to this chapter suggests, EIB maintained its "revindicative" meaning for movements, even as it was refitted, and never with great zeal, for an elite-led project that saw diversity only as a pedagogical resource or a cynical legitimizing tactic.

In what follows I trace EIB's emergence amid new network articulations among movements, donors, and state education actors. In the next chapter I connect this recent history with an ethnography of the present. My purpose is to understand more and less durable effects of the officialization of bilingual intercultural education, while showing how it maintained heterogeneous manifestations across interlocking domains of indigenous resurgence and state process.

EDUCATIONAL PROJECTS AND ARTICULATORY NETWORKS

In her work on Brazilian literacy, Lesley Bartlett (2003:87) proposes the concept of "educational project," "configurations of theory, pedagogy, philosophy, training and institutions, plus a variety of social actors and social practices," as useful for thinking about the relationships among schooling, nation-state formation, transnational flows, and social movement struggles. Educational projects viewed thus are not uniform instruments of the nation-state, but clusters or matrices of schooling practice with complex linkages to states and other entities engaged in the cultural politics of subject making and knowledge production. The concept of educational project allows us to consider how schooling may or may not articulate in a functional way with nation-state discourses or institutions in a given historical moment. Thinking of the distinctions between Elsa, Tüi, Airase, and Amalia Anaya, introduced below, is one way to recognize the heterogeneous, uneven effects of multiple educational projects unfolding across different historical locations of a single nation-state. Against the more familiar approach to school-state relations as dynamics of reproduction and resistance, the idea of educational project, especially in postcolonial settings like Bolivia, opens up space to consider the embeddedness of different schooling practices in multiple temporalities, spaces, and processes and the incompleteness of state hegemony and sovereignty as these relate to schooling.[6]

Ernest Gellner, reformulating the classical Weberian definition of sovereign stateness as rooted in the monopoly over legitimate violence, has suggested that nations and elites must necessarily seek a similar monopoly over legitimate knowledge production and subject-credentialing (1983:34; Weber 1978:56, 904). This aspiration is reflected in a long history of centralized nation- and school-building projects reproduced even amid neoliberalism's ostensibly decentralizing liberalism.[7] Yet even in highly industrialized societies, literacy-bearing education projects—religious, private, alternative, or public of various forms—reproduce multiplicity and contention, not singular hegemony. Attempts to inscribe state sovereignty over knowledge often constitute efforts to legitimate what one cannot oppose (see Collins and Blot 2003:87). The neoliberal turn has furthered this fragmentation, as states themselves, once pursuing national school systems, are creating differentiated education projects that target people and territories variously through distinct modes of schooling (Ong 2006). The question is no longer so much how schooling reproduces hegemony or national culture, but through what cultural translations and contingent articulations historically emergent educational projects engage territorial, institutional, and discursive power struggles occurring across state and transstate scales pulled between centralizing control and the centrifugal pull of decentralized complexity.

Understanding the contemporary location of EIB in Bolivia requires unpacking historical articulations among educational projects, state processes, and movement dynamics. Articulation echoes network theory by drawing our attention to the means and junctures through which differentially positioned actors, discourses, and resources come together in nodes of practice. Networks are products of heterogeneity, not of homogeneity. Nodes are sites of translation and interconnection where difference itself becomes productive and functional to the articulation (Latour 1993; Tsing 2005). The education infrastructure itself resembles an articulated network, with official messages transmitted downward from central ministries, passing through multiple sites of translation and ultimately mediated by schoolteachers before reaching students and classrooms (Wilson 2001). Yet state apparatuses also articulate with other networks of donor aid, elite circles, indigenous movements, and radical or technocratic intellectuals. Schools do not always reflect a clear linkage between states and subjects, often transcending this relationship entirely. Islamic *madrassas* or the occupation of wide swaths of Peruvian public schools by the Shining Path in Peru—both ostensibly under the purview of the state, yet possibly undermining its purposes—offer a case in point. Though distinct from madrassas or the Shining Path, EIB similarly emerged as a translocal network reflective of movement, state, and intellectual articulations. I turn now to consider the shifting spaces of these articulations in the wider education field.

The past thirty years have seen a dramatic rise of indigenous intellectuals and their allies in Bolivia and across Latin America. They are demanding protagonism in the education arena, demands that both preceded and paralleled the wider political effervescence of organized indigenous movements.

These movements have called for the inclusion of indigenous languages in state schooling (Maxwell 1996; Warren 1998; García 2005; Rappaport 2005). Arguments for bilingual education from both nonacademic indigenists and indigenous movements emerged in a context in which state and nonstate educational projects were disputed between those who called for a critical transformation of society (the popular education approach) and those who described their mission in the narrative of modernization (the developmentalist approach). Competing Christianities filtered through all three—the indigenous resurgence, the popular left, and the developmentalists.

In the Bolivian lowlands, Catholic missions (and later NGOS) and American Protestant missionaries have historically dominated programs of native language literacy (Castro Mantilla 1997; chapter 1 this volume). Competing religious projects were generally divided between conservative and anticommunist Protestant organizations like the American Summer Institute of Linguistics (SIL) and progressives (mostly grass-roots Catholics) espousing liberation theology. Both pursued evangelization through tactical work with native languages. State school expansion after the 1960s tended to pursue aggressive castellanización, rather than continuity with these early bilingual efforts. The 1970s and 1980s saw the appearance of more secular approaches to popular education, including what I call the left-agrarianist and neo-indigenist approaches.[8] I addressed some effects of Catholic and Protestant schooling projects in chapter 1. Here I consider the legacies of popular, new indigenist, and state education projects.

Popular education projects viewed literacy training as a means to generate critical reflection on social exploitation and to raise political consciousness to generate collective struggles for change. Across the Americas, popular education was largely conceived in class terms, yet because most of the poor in Bolivia were indigenous, class and indigenous issues became fused. Popular education merged the particular histories of indigenous peoples (*pueblos*) with the notion of the national "people" (*el pueblo*) as a subaltern class resisting an elite-dominated state. Indigenous languages were sometimes mobilized as instruments in this process, yet a tone of peasant organizing for land, communal solidarity, and production reflected the left-agrarianist approach underlying rural popular education. Though framed as a means of resisting the state, popular education projects were also executed as official state projects to produce legitimacy and support for a nationalist response to economic dependency and imperialism during left-leaning regimes (Urioste 1982).

Some popular education projects leaned more toward neo-indigenism, influenced by notions of indigenous cultural autonomy rather than by ideas about national (class-based) organizing. These approaches pushed for the reconquest of the colonial space of state schooling and for the defense of territory as an expression of indigenous rights to self-determination. This step beyond Paulo Freire was reflected in a piece that circulated in those days in Camiri, an article by the Mexican anthropologist Guillermo Bonfil Batalla on cultural control (1991). Ideas like "cultural control" focused on the defense of alterity and autonomy rather than on the mobilization of class interests. Overlapping with the counterhegemonic essence of popular education, cultural autonomists nonetheless emphasized indigenous languages and cultures not (only) as indices of class domination but as markers of historical alterity outside national structures of society, culture, and polity. In this view, indigenous languages were vehicles of alterity and spatial markers of collectivity, mobilized (as were nations themselves) to legitimate demands for epistemological and territorial autonomy. The defense of a distinctive space within the state, especially in the lowlands where native peoples constituted territorial, political, and demographic minorities, was as or more significant than the mobilization of indigenous masses as peasants with national-popular movements, the dominant trend in the Andes.

At the national level, indigenous languages faced a more difficult scenario. During the short populist Juan José Torres interlude (1970–71), a conference on indigenous languages took place in La Paz. Official policy declared support for "institutions dedicated to the study of the aboriginal languages, especially Aymara, Quechua, and those of Arawak and Tupi-Guarani roots" (MEC 1970:44). During the military dictatorships that followed, there were two short-lived bilingual education experiments, including a USAID program with a small group of bilingual schools in the Aymara region (1976–81) and a World Bank project (1978–80). These efforts were shaped by the rhetoric of modernization and not by the languages of popular education or neoindigenism (Urioste 1982). During the Luís García Meza dictatorship (1980–82), Bolivia became a violent narco-state, and activist teachers and indigenous leaders were largely, if temporarily, silenced.[9]

Beneath these shifts in official education projects, linguists and academics working on Andean languages were merging the language of popular struggle with the actual languages of indigenous peoples. Xavier Albó's seminal 1974 piece on the future of the "oppressed languages" (*lenguas oprimidas*) called attention to language diglossia as a means of critiquing social inequality and ethnic exclusion. The paradigm, though criticized by some indigenous leaders for its victimizing slant, shaped discourse on language for more than two decades. Attention to indigenous language and ethnocultural difference was also linked to the more clandestine rise of the Aymara-centered Katarista movement, which questioned assimilationism and pushed for the inclusion of the ethnic component alongside discourses of class struggle in the national peasant union (Rivera Cusicanqui 1984; Albó 1990). With ethnicity foregrounded alongside class, language was refigured as a terrain and marker of class struggle, and bilingual schools as part of the political demands of indigenous peasants. Furthermore, as the Aymara language activist and schoolteacher Felix Layme recalled (2002), indigenous languages could be talked about not as obstacles to liberation and equality, but as markers of historical difference worthy of cultivation.

With the democratic opening of 1982 this array of religious, popular, neoindigenist, Indianist, and state educational projects began to rearticulate in relation to resurgent movements in the Andes and the lowlands. In the lowlands, indigenous movements shifted away from the tutelage of the SIL. In the Guarani case this period saw the intensification of activities of the NGOs CIPCA (Commission for the Investigation and Promotion of the Peasantry) and APCOB (Aid to the Peasant Peoples of the Bolivian East) (Riester 1985). Both facilitated the formation of lowland organizations, made forays into Guarani language issues, and explicitly sought to dismantle the SIL's conservative legacy. The German-run APCOB espoused a more neoindigenist approach through its linguistic and historical work with the Isoso-Guarani (e.g., Riester 1984). This revolved around the celebration of the traditional captaincy leadership structure and the use of language as an icon of a people in the sense of *pueblo indígena*. CIPCA's more national-popular approach focused on the creation of peasant union–type organizations that also spoke of "people" yet did so in the framework of the *pueblo boliviano* shaped around the peasant-indigenous-worker alliance. For instance, the Guarani literacy primer of 1992 was modeled on Freire's idea of key "generative words" (like well-being, corn, knowledge, food, culture, reading, work, and organization) to stimulate reflection on living conditions and political organizing. Though APCOB was secular, CIPCA, tied to the Jesuits, also pursued work on Guarani liberation theology at the institute known as Arakuaarenda (knowledge-place) in Charagua. Competing in many ways with the kind of training state schoolteachers were receiving in the nearby normal school also in Charagua, the language work carried out by Father Gabriel Siquier at Arakuaarenda combined catechism, Guarani spirituality, and explicit liberation theology. As reflected in the narratives of leaders of thirty to forty years old today, scores of young Guarani leaders emerged out of this popular Catholic-Guarani consciousness raising project and the NGO-backed fusion of indigenist and national-popular education.

At the state level, the return to democracy brought the return of the popular left. The Popular Unity government of Hernán Siles (1982–85) launched a program called SENALEP, the National Service of Literacy and Popular Education. With UNESCO support, SENALEP mobilized Andean intellectuals to design bilingual literacy projects for adults. SENALEP also mobilized indigenous scribes of the earlier period, many of them former Bible translators, to write materials for popular literacy training. When asked about the origins of their work in bilingual education, a handful of older Guarani scribes invoke this SENALEP experience. Though centered in the Andes, SENALEP organizers sought connections with indigenous groups in the lowlands, leading to a collaboration between Andean organizations and CIDOB, the new lowland organization. Lowland indigenous leaders traveled to meet with Aymara participants in the SENALEP project in La Paz, and various workshops were held in Santa Cruz. At these workshops, the Guarani, Guarayu, Chiquitano, and other new indigenous organizations discussed their languages and generated manifestos that demanded bilingual education. The umbrella organization CIDOB incorporated a demand for bilingual education in its platform of 1982 (Riester and Zolezzi 1989). CONMERB and CSUTCB, the national rural teachers' and peasant unions, would do the same in 1983 and 1989, respectively (Choque 2005:22–23).

These early connections led to growing contacts between the lowland movements and the Andean CSUTCB (G. Chumiray, personal communication, 1994). These processes also reinforced bridges between discourses of social liberation and Indianist and neo-indigenist discourses focused on the particularity of indigenous peoples. For example, one Guarani leader spoke out at one of these early workshops in the 1980s in support of an education that "would also be a process of true social and economic liberation," as well as a "reconstruction of Guarani understandings of their history, as a means of understanding who they were" (qtd. in Riester and Zolezzi 1989).

This convergence of indigenous resurgence and EIB discourse unfolded amid emerging articulations between local and state education projects and foreign aid flows in education. For example, UNESCO funded the state SENALEP program that created space for indigenous assemblies and introduced new development and state actors to the indigenous education setting. Events brought together figures like the Guarani leaders cited above, Aymara linguists like Felix Layme, donor agents like the Italian anthropologist Lucia D'Emilio (a UNESCO, later UNICEF, functionary), and activist anthropologists like Xavier Albó. As during the Popular Unity government, the national political elite also sought to engage these processes. By 1985, when the MNR government came to power, then education minister Enrique Ipiña began to play a major role in talk of both EIB and education reform. Beyond the level of grass-roots practice, the emergent discourse spoke as often of social development and inclusion as of social and economic liberation and historical recovery. As the prospects of becoming official policy improved, these developmentalist articulations tended to absorb and mute the more assertive language of popular and indigenous struggle and of the meanings of bilingual education therein.

Popular Neo-indigenism to Social Development

In 1989, UNESCO's diminutive dynamo D'Emilio was transferred to UNICEF Bolivia. She helped oversee the establishment and financing of the pilot projects in bilingual education in Quechua, Aymara, and Guarani. It was then that EIB was inserted into the Education Ministry in the old Lazarte Building through negotiations between rural teachers, the peasant-indigenous organizations, and the Catholic Church's education arm, all on the scaffold of Swedish aid. Conferences on native languages and education multiplied in frequency, presaging the continental turn to interculturalism. Consultants arrived from Peru, Ecuador, Germany, and Sweden. Workshops and meetings convened indigenous intellectuals, peasant-indigenous organizations, and neo-indigenist experts to discuss bilingual schooling. Even as 1992 saw the failed attempt to unify indigenous movements, these education events provided a context in which Andean and lowland organizations could come together to cultivate a shared demand for bilingual schooling.

UNICEF efforts provided mobilizing resources and communicative platforms that proved useful during the formative period of indigenous resurgence. Yet UNICEF and other aid also brought constraints. This assistance was a resource deployed in the context of neoliberal structural adjustment, largely coming from states (like Sweden) and used at the service of states (like Bolivia) to defend their legitimacy during increasing social discontent. Unlike a handful of progressive European NGOs or labor unions that funded activist NGOs directly, entities like UNICEF did not directly support contestative agendas or radical critiques of inequality. UNICEF sought to transform state policy, not generate an indigenous pachakuti. Entities like UNICEF represented the soft side of structural adjustment or social development. They drew attention to health, education, gender equality, and indigenous poverty, but they did so through an accommodation of those in power, often even filling gaps in state functions in the midst of neoliberal downsizing.

Popular indigenism confronted social development in the field of education over several years during the 1980s and early 1990s. One example is the CSUTCB position on bilingual education, *Toward a Bilingual Intercultural Education*, published in a newsprint pamphlet with UNICEF assistance in 1991 (CSUTCB 1991). As the outcome of various meetings, the text highlighted demands for participation and the defense of public education, merging Indianist discourses of class and ethnic resistance with demands for "respect" and "language rights" of the "original peoples." The pamphlet also broadened the traditional Andean-centered frame for speaking of the indigenous in Bolivia. Usually dominated by "Quechuas and Aymaras," "the debate," the text argued, was "about education among the Quechua, Aymara, Guarani, Mojeño, and Chiquitano peasant workers [*trabajadores campesinos*], among others."

This fusion of concerns for class and ethnic inequality and an anticolonial stance of resistance articulated with the language of social development. Phrases like "peasant workers" sustained the history of popular struggle, while demands for "more education of a higher quality" resonated with development discourse. Social development buzzwords like *educational crisis* and the pursuit of *educational quality* merged with indigenous political visions that saw education as a way to "leave our legacy to our sons and daughters: an education born of our cultures, languages, and history. In that way our sons and daughters will not suffer as we have suffered" (CSUTCB 1991:1–2). The document also denounced historical indigenous exclusion from literacy (i.e., citizenship) and historical violence against indigenous people. This critique of the coloniality of power engaged the technical critiques of development agency reports. These included a detailing of low access rates to schooling, high dropout rates, an antiquated curriculum, high illiteracy rates, the exclusion of girls, and the exclusion of parents and communities from participation in school administration. This hybrid stance—which culminated in a demand for bilingual intercultural education—legitimated itself by invoking state law (decrees of the government in favor of bilingual education), international covenants on indigenous rights (ILO 169), and even Jomtien.

The pamphlet emerged out of seminars and assemblies in which indigenous leaders dialogued with academics and development organization representatives. One outsider was D'Emilio, the anthropologist and UNICEF education officer who took up the banner of bilingual education when she came to Bolivia. She had done doctoral fieldwork with the Kandoshi in the Peruvian Amazon and like many European aid actors, voiced public support for indigenous rights claims, a position distinct from the generally pro-business bent of most government-affiliated American aid workers. She used her position to channel resources and support for bilingual education. This involved funding events to connect figures like the anthropologist Xavier Albó with Guarani and Andean intellectuals and leaders. International experts like Luis Enrique López, a Peruvian linguist and the "guru" of EIB in Latin America, was also brought into this circle. Given her ability to make things happen, D'Emilio was informally christened the "Fairy Godmother" (hada madrina) by the Guarani scribes during our time in Camiri. Seen as a friend of the Guarani, she was also adept at cultivating support in Bolivian political elite circles. Some of these allies like Ipiña of the MNR had long held an interest in education. Others like the future education minister Anaya were newcomers. For distinct purposes and from distinct social locations, a heterogeneous network crystallized around bilingual education.

With regard to the formulation of indigenous demands, D'Emilio recalled later that it was a time when "they" (the translocal intellectual, indigenous, development, and state actors) took advantage of "currents to create alliances, new and old, and to create a movement of opinion around certain things [i.e., bilingual education]." As she wrote me in an e-mail from her new post in Cambodia in 1998: "Even the World Bank had directives on working with indigenous peoples . . . though as we began to work with the CSUTCB on a programmatic educational platform [in the late 1980s], the CSUTCB leaders were still [making references] to the origins of the family and private property. There was a super-idealized education, pre-Colombian tout court, [and] thousands of discussions about whether they were indigenous, ethnic groups, peoples, or nations" (November, 1998; my translation).

As reflected in this note and the summary of the CSUTCB document above, the articulation around EIB was not seamless, but rather dialogic, contentious, strategic, and hybrid. Various temporalizing imaginaries tied to education merged loosely: ideologues of modernization and social development actors, contestative anticolonial indigenous movements, and an assortment of indigenous and nonindigenous academics. The lingering presence of Friedrich Engels merged with millennial visions of Indianist revival were mixed up with languages of interculturalism and critiques of educational exclusion and quality. As D'Emilio recalled, the indigenous leaders, "at the end, agreed on more education, better education, and bilingual education." This constituted the narrow yet productive space that allowed articulation between movements and transnational aid and state actors. Radical critics saw such articulations as the neoliberal absorption of EIB. Yet from the perspective of pro-EIB indigenous leaders, such documents were icons of indigenous agency. Froilán Condori, at this writing a senator of the MAS party, was then a Quechua leader of the CSUTCB who participated in the elaboration of the document. In our frequent conversations, he invariably cited the pamphlet to me as a demonstration that "we [the CSUTCB] were the first" to "demand the participatory implementation of bilingual intercultural education."

It was in this articulatory space, with less talk of Marxian struggle and bold indigenous visions and more talk of social inclusion and education quality, that one was made to speak publicly about EIB during the neoliberal era. It was the space of official interculturalism in which the pro-EIB education minister Anaya could—or had to—say that indigenous languages were not just about revindication but were also pedagogical resources. These network encounters and their textual residues were also spaces of transformation. As Anna Tsing suggests (2005), articulations may imply subtle transformations (social development agents learn to talk about indigeneity and indigenous intellectuals begin to use terms like *quality* and *efficiency* in new ways). Yet this does not evidence a seamless hegemonic discourse at work, but rather, what Tsing calls a contingent articulation across difference, facilitated by the semantic, technical, and ideological flexibility of EIB. Beyond these public ways of speaking, multiple agendas continued to unfold.

Neoliberalism and Interculturalism

Neoliberalism came to Bolivia in 1985 with Decree 21060. The macroeconomic adjustments were followed by second-wave social and institutional reforms that accelerated in 1994, including education reform. Promarket, but by no means antistate, neoliberalism required a leaner, meaner state to impose unpopular reforms. It was not simply the case that the state was rolled back (nor did all elites embrace neoliberal ideology and policy). Rather, as Lesley Gill (2000) suggests, the state was targeted for restructuring with new forms, meanings, and categories, in short, with new languages of citizenship and state practice.[10] Though in part large-scale and institutional, neoliberalism also pursued microcultural change. The latter included shifts like the imposition of the continuous 9–5 workday. (My colleagues complained of having to eat at their desks, a radical shift from two hours home with their families.) Newly minted management and public policy wonks took roles in public offices, using the business-speak of entrepreneurial rhetoric in fields heretofore dominated by social activists. State functions were recast as services to be delivered and citizens reimagined as consumers or clients to be satisfied through market-oriented solutions. Though I caricature somewhat, the language was clearly shifting from corporatism (political centralism) to corporate (business) logics.

The rise of neoliberalism in Latin America is associated with the ascent of segments of the elite whose changing economic interests, ideological orientations, and professional ties delinked them from traditional mass-based party and patronage bases of legitimacy and tied them to U.S.-based political, financial, and academic entities backing the so-called Washington Consensus (Eckstein 1983; Conaghan, Malloy, and Abugattas 1990; Sikkink 1997; Babb 2004). In Bolivia, these new elites—often old statists recycled as new market-friendly technocrats—were bolstered by the decline of the left after the end of the Cold War and public exhaustion with hyperinflation between 1982 and 1985. The most ambitious programs of reform came during MNR regimes (1985–89; 1993–97). The same party that had ushered in state capitalism and corporatism after the 1952 revolution now sought to relegate those supposed truths to the dustbin and began speaking new truths of competition, market solutions, and liberalization.

Students of Latin America invariably associate the rise of neoliberalism with the ascent of the Pinochet dictatorship in Chile and the associated embrace of economist technocrats espousing the free-market economics of Milton Friedman, a network known as the "Chicago Boys" (Sikkink 1997). In neoliberal Bolivia the networks claiming technocratic legitimacy in a later period also sought epistemic legitimacy in a northern university, yet they were called "the Harvard Boys."[11] In the public eye, the key icon (or villain) was the then pro-market Harvard economist Jeffrey Sachs, the main advisor of Gonzalo "Goni" Sánchez de Lozada and, later, of the former dictator Bánzer. Aspiring Bolivian technocrats peppered their résumés with Harvard connections, while Sachs's prescriptions helped give intra-elite legitimacy to policies that had little popular support and about which elites themselves remained divided.[12]

The rise of neoliberalism thus did not come in the form of a magical hegemonic discourse, but rather in that of a cluster of actors, ways of speaking, resources, and connections—in effect, a set of articulated networks—that linked Bolivia and the United States. In these circles, political claims relied on epistemological claims of "universal" (i.e., economic) knowledge that claimed validity precisely because they came from elsewhere, from outside Bolivian territory. Policy networks linked actors and resources based in universities (Georgetown, Pittsburgh, Notre Dame, Harvard), U.S.-based government funded agencies (USAID, the National Endowment for Democracy), and Bolivian social and political circles (like the ADN and the MNR parties) (Grindle 2004). Think tanks tied to these parties (ADN's Fundemos and the MNR's Fundación Milenio) were funded in part by U.S. government sources and worked with U.S.-based academic advisors (Van Cott 2000:141–44). These networks had privileged access to foreign support and ties with the military, elite-led parties, and the president's inner circle that assured insulation from political pressure. Beyond their claims on truth, the networks relied heavily on state violence, a fact conveniently erased when reformers argue about the supposed success of these reforms.[13]

The popular indigenous-social development networks that coalesced around EIB were geospatially and ideologically distinct from this neoliberal network linking political-economic and intellectual elites in La Paz and the U.S. northeastern power corridor. The EIB network was geospatially oriented more along a European-Andean-indigenous axis. It was discursively hybrid and dialogic in its engagement with indigenous and social scientific claims to authority and epistemological validity. It was socially variegated in public instantiations. Imagine an often rowdy and ritual-laden conglomeration of indigenous leaders, and an assortment of indigenous, non-indigenous, and foreign anthropologists, linguists, and pedagogues that might gather around an EIB alphabet workshop, chewing coca, and burning incense for the blessing of the Pachamama. On the other hand, the neoliberal network operated in the coat-and-tie world of economists, financiers, and politicians. One might spot them at Club of Paris debt negotiations, a conference at Harvard's Kennedy School, or the plushly appointed finance ministry offices of La Paz. Both networks sought to strengthen themselves through capturing the symbols and institutions of the state. They would converge around a contingent and tenuous link: the neoliberal acquiescence to a limited role for state education and its rhetorical turn toward interculturalism.

Interculturalism, a public discourse widely examined in Latin America, is a bridge between these networks. It is commonly argued that interculturalism as imagined by Latin American cultural activists differs from U.S. and European ideas about multiculturalism. Rather than the multiculturalist model of cultural difference imagined as a mosaic of groups who tolerate and respect each other, interculturalism, its proponents argue, encourages relations of exchange and dialogue across cultural borders to create a "pluralistic dialogue among equals" (e.g., Rappaport 2005:4–5, 130–33). The former seems to suggest a hierarchy of cultures, something like a national space dotted with immigrant cultures (the "multis"). The latter hints at a more fluid notion of a society, nation, or citizenship comprised of equals, shaped through dialogue among and across the differences constitutive of Latin American nationalities and modernities.

Indigenous educators and advocates spoke of interculturalism as a response to the assimilationist models of the past with particularly Andean and Latin American roots. Even before the neoliberal turn, interculturalism was used in the 1980s to counter both the mestizaje paradigm of assimilation and racial improvement and the "bicultural-bilingual" model of assimilation through evangelization pursued by the SIL (Hornberger 2000). As mestizo or bicultural, indigenous peoples as indigenous peoples were denied real space. Interculturalism's proponents argued for the creation of spaces of dialogue and exchange, suggesting that difference was not a problem to be erased, but a foundation on which new knowledges and social formations could be constructed. Interculturalism, as will become clear in chapter 7, did not take the more assertive step toward the plurinationalism demanded by native movements. It did, however, constitute a way of speaking that indigenous movements could share.

The neoliberal reformers saw interculturalism as a managerial tactic, a rhetorical flourish more than a sign of deep philosophical complexity. Official interculturalism ostensibly recognized Bolivia's linguistic and cultural pluralism as a constitutive and legitimate part of the nation. It introduced a new idiom for restructuring and legitimating forms of political participation that appeared to allow for indigenous uses, customs, and forms of organization (Gustafson 2002). Yet as Diane Nelson describes for the case of Guatemala, state technocrats generally made selective instrumental use of popular understandings of culture as something inhering in local groups and individuals. Indigenous culture was traditional and local as opposed to the (superior) culture of liberal modernity and rationality (D. Nelson 1999:115; Povinelli 2002). The Harvard Boy Goni made this clear as he stood alongside Sachs describing interculturalism to an audience at Harvard's Kennedy School in 1998: "We've overlain a Western system of government onto an Oriental [sic; indigenous?] base." Like missionary biculturalism, neoliberal interculturalism hoped to cultivate some icons of difference while excising others.

The articulatory power of interculturalism for neoliberal reformers was less in the details of its content than in the discursive associations and silences that it facilitated. It allowed for an expression of recognition that appeared to echo indigenous demands without conceding radical structural, economic, or political changes. It evoked a sense of grounded authenticity—in "our cultures"—that proved a useful nationalizing anchor for reforms whose epistemological bases were rooted in the United States (figuratively and institutionally). Finally, "culture" had a sense of diffuse locality that could be contained either in circumscribed local communities or in individual citizen-subjects. It had neither the structural connotations of class (like indigenous peasants) nor the political weight of self-determination (indigenous nations). Like an earlier model of hierarchical citizenship built on the idea of race, elite uses of culture reproduced a sense of Western-indigenous hierarchy and the management of difference, thereby transcending an older model of homogenization yet avoiding a more utopian model of intercultural dialogue, equality, exchange, and the political-economic redistribution of wealth and power (Sanjinés 2004).

Neoliberal Interculturalism and Bilingual Education

As the unpopularity of neoliberal reforms became clear, reform projects in the 1990s took up the discourse of poverty reduction as a legitimizing mantra. Euphemisms like *human capital, social equity* (never *equality*), and *poverty reduction* were deployed to justify a limited state role and simultaneous strategies of marketization in fields like health and education. Here an economistic view of social policy became an instrument for facilitating the workings of the market, a view through which EIB would have to pass. During the 1980s development and state actors shared space at cocktail parties of the La Paz elite, and discussions emerged around the need for educational change in Bolivia. In 1988 the MNR under the guidance of the education minister Ipiña produced the so-called Pink Book (Libro Rosado), that outlined a plan for educational change (pink is the party color). Ipiña had already been involved with EIB events in association with UNESCO. Around the same time, the MIR party and intellectuals like Anaya were also introducing education into the social policy areas of their party platforms (Anaya, personal communication, 1998).

Though reform-minded elites had both ideological and material interests in reform, the field of education—that "thing" still housed in the old Lazarte Building—remained politically untouchable. Public health and education were bastions of labor power and of opposition to neoliberalism and could put people into the streets (or close hospitals and schools). Yet health and education also provided resources for the party-dominated patronage system. As other state industries were being privatized, party elites began intensifying their squabbles over access to the dwindling public resources there.

Even the banks, which expressed a desire for educational structural adjustment, saw a chaotic governance structure incapable of profound change (anonymous interview, World Bank, 2000; Anaya 1995).

While I use the 1990 Jomtien World Conference on Education for All as a symbolic anchor in this history, participants credit the event with having real effects in bringing together Bolivian and World Bank and Inter-American Development Bank (IADB) representatives. Jomtien convened proponents of educational change, NGOS, state ministries, and donors at a luxury beach resort. The Bolivian delegation, financed by UNICEF, included a group of high-level staffers from the country's Ministry of Education. By that time the MIR had taken over the presidency and the Education Ministry had come under the control of the right-wing ADN party, which opposed reform for pragmatic reasons. With no interest in change, the Education Ministry delegates to Jomtien were perhaps enjoying a meaningless junket.[14] Yet real power resided in the Bolivian delegates from the Ministries of Finance and Planning, colloquially called the "structural adjusters." Planning was then led by the MIR big man, the millionaire Samuel Doria Medina. UNICEF had funded the creation of an office of social policy within that Ministry, headed by Anaya, who also made the trip to Thailand. The delegation included segments of the EIB network, the pro-indigenous D'Emilio, and the EIB guru López. D'Emilio—evidencing the parastatal role of agencies like UNICEF—recalled that sending finance and planning technocrats to Jomtien proved crucial, since if "we [UNICEF] had only sent the education delegates, I don't think there would have ever been a reform proposal" (e-mail, October 1998). As these networks congealed into a series of high-level agreements, European bilateral agencies (Sweden, Germany, and the Netherlands) also approached the World Bank and the Bolivian government to participate in funding school reform. The World Bank prioritized managerial overhaul (decentralization, marketization, deunionization), referred to as "sectoral structural adjustment" (SIDA and World Bank interviews).[15] The most explicit targeted support for EIB came from the European side.

European agencies performed a more indigenist and rights-based stance, tying their aid to support for the poor and the excluded. Though the promotion of something that sounds like "ethnic" resurgence may not play so well in the United States and Europe today, especially in the wake of 9/11, European donors emphasized cultural difference, especially "indigenous" difference, that played well to audiences back home. In a pamphlet I picked up in the SIDA office in Stockholm, the Swedish government could claim with a touch of humane exoticism that through Swedish support for Bolivian education reform, "growing numbers of poor children in the mountain villages [i.e. Andean regions] are now being taught both in Spanish and the local Indian languages" and that "Bolivian Education Reform has meant that poor children are taught in their own language, and also have a say in the teaching." The document, titled "Education for All—a Human Right" invoked Jomtien and highlighted SIDA's global education aid. In light of Sweden's strong teachers' union, the brochure even hailed SIDA's "union solidarity," a preemptive defense, perhaps, against the government's association with Bolivia's union-busting school reform (SIDA 2000).[16]

At the World Bank, EIB reportedly faced entrenched opposition from those who saw it as expensive and impractical. One staffer told me of World Bank employees who said "chemistry books in Guarani were unrealistic" and "it was too expensive to have textbooks in every language." According to one advisor of Bolivian education reform, the justification of EIB at the World Bank depended on cost-benefit analyses, not debates about indigenous epistemic or linguistic rights. Others within the World Bank had published studies linking linguistic difference to poverty and argued that bilingual education could address opportunity differentials between indigenous and nonindigenous peoples to promote inclusion, and ultimately, poverty reduction (Harry Patrinos, personal communication, 2006; Hall and Patrinos 2005). Resituating EIB in the terms of bank-oriented knowledge was crucial to its support, as surely was less public talk about the political "costs and benefits" of addressing an issue of indigenous movement concern that could be deployed to legitimate wider World Bank roles. The Bank gradually turned toward backing EIB and, at least in its local manifestation, approached the issue pragmatically. As one staffer in La Paz framed it, "the reality is that the people speak indigenous languages, and our position is that the best kind of education is in the language people speak" (anonymous interview, November 1998). Whether astute development strategy, cynical appropriation, or a valid recognition of indigenous demands, the Bank- and donor-funded support of EIB did generate tentative support among indigenous leadership circles.[17]

Back in Bolivia, these network articulations were embodied in local histories and actors. The World Bank backed the creation of ETARE, which was appended to the Ministry of Planning to circumvent the Education Ministry, the main target of change. Amalia Anaya, whom I quoted in the epigraph, was the Bolivian most closely associated with education and eventually took over leadership of ETARE, later rising to the post of Education Minister. With an eye toward alliance building that reflected her new ties to the EIB circles, she worked closely with D'Emilio (the anthropologist) and López (the linguist) and hired the Aymara pedagogue Victor Hugo Cárdenas, a popular indigenous leader and intellectual of the Katarista movement. Evidencing an emerging elite consensus on reform and a new logic of power detached from traditional party-mediated patronage and now more dependent on foreign aid, Anaya also crossed party lines to hire the MNR intellectual Ipiña. ETARE set about elaborating a proposal for education reform and mobilizing public events and discourse on interculturalism, bilingualism, and participation, the pillars of school change. Like Decree 21060, which launched structural adjustment in 1985, the name ETARE—and later, EIB itself—was vilified by reform opponents as another manifestation of neoliberalism. It was then that Bolivian schoolteachers—and many NGO actors in education—started a long march of opposition to education reform.

It was in this context of rising tensions over reform that Jomtien and the basic needs research were deployed as symbolic instruments of discourse and public action to legitimate bilingual education. Likewise the understanding and practice of indigenous education as grassroots struggle was made more complex through its absorption into a deeply conflictive process of state transformation. EIB as an indigenous agenda had now shifted from its local conflicts in Guarani country, where it was arrayed against the conservative racism of landlords and the assimilationist mestizaje of traditional schooling, to a distinct national frame, where its officialization tied EIB to the "damned laws" of a "neoliberal" regime. Reform opponents attacked EIB as a World Bank imposition aimed at busting unions and balkanizing the country or as an inauthentic and cynical embrace of indigenous languages that masked western ideologies (Patzi 1999; Arnold and Yapita 2006).

Anthropologists have debated at length whether "multiculturalism" is a progressive or neoliberal agenda, often relying on distinctions between redistribution of material power (progressive) and symbolic recognition (neoliberal), sometimes associating EIB with the latter (Hale 2002; Postero 2006).

This is a valid critique for assessing the proposed dimensions of state policy or discourse, but it does not entirely capture the meanings, forms, and effects of EIB as these emerged through multiscalar networks crossing nodes of translation and articulation that linked distinct histories and actors. As such, the above discussion seeks to provide a corrective to simplistic anthropological readings of states, movements, and ideas in relation to neoliberal reform and bilingual intercultural education. Yet beyond theoretical concerns and my own discomfort as EIB became "neoliberal" policy, indigenous leaders and movements faced a more concrete, weighty, and complex political dilemma as they negotiated an unsettling process created by foreign donors, Bolivian elites, and their own historical mobilizing. These dynamics, as I describe in chapter 6, would have repercussions in local movement practices and forms. Yet as I discuss in the next chapter, these complex articulations also show the fissures and instabilities of state power, as criollo Bolivian elites were neither wholly convinced by, nor entirely enthusiastic about, bilingual interculturalism.

Interlude

Bolivia or Yugoslavia?

In early 1994, in the presidential Palacio Quemado on La Paz's Plaza Murillo, the cabinet of President Gonzalo "Goni" Sánchez de Lozada met to discuss ETARE's education reform proposal. Goni, elected in 1993, was a white criollo and one of Bolivia's richest mining tycoons. He headed the MNR party and stood at the fore of neoliberal reforms initiated in the 1980s. As president he pushed through the second wave of reforms that included his pet project of municipal decentralization (popular participation), the privatization of state industries (capitalization), and the rationalization of land markets (land reform) (Gustafson 2002). Education reform was not one of his "babies." It arose in part through the efforts of the MIR, a competing party. Yet due to foreign loans, outside aid, and the international recognition of education's importance for development, Goni supported school reform as his "adoptive child," embracing it in his Plan de Todos, the "Plan for All."

Echoing the rhetoric of "education for all," the Plan for All relied heavily on interculturalism. "All" implicitly meant that the indigenous and poor would be included too. Indeed, his coalition included left-leaning parties sympathetic to peasant struggles, and decentralization was a fairly popular reform. Capitalization, on the other hand, was largely unpopular, and despite Goni's embrace of land reform, its more progressive components emerged only after indigenous pressure. Interculturalism provided one means of countering the taint of the neoliberal and Harvard Boy labels.

Interculturalism was physically embodied in Goni's vice-president, who also sat at the table full of cabinet ministers that day. Victor Hugo Cárdenas, the Aymara intellectual and EIB supporter, left his work for the education reform team to become part of Goni's campaign. Born of indigenous struggle and an early proponent of resurgence, Cárdenas joined Goni in a risky alliance between his faction of the Katarista movement and Goni's MNR party. To his detractors he was a traitor. A popular joke portrayed him as the silent indio Tonto to Goni's Lone Ranger. To his supporters, he represented a bold move to occupy space in the fortress of elite power (Albó 1994).

The cabinet met to discuss and approve the education reform legislation for its presentation to Congress. Despite rituals of public participation (like the basic needs research), the reform had arisen within a narrow circle of experts. Though Congress would vote on it, it only required executive approval, since Goni's coalition had a disciplined majority. If jobs to be created by legislative change like the richly funded education reform were divvied out among the parties beforehand, a majority of Congress would vote however the executive ordered. Thus, "democracy" happened in cabinet meetings. It was here that Goni considered the opinions of his team to decide his position and thus, via executive authority, the law.

Goni defended education reform that day speaking in Spanish inflected by American English, a product of his upbringing in the United States. Cárdenas also supported reform, speaking in Spanish inflected by Aymara, a product of his upbringing in a rural community on the shores of Lake Titicaca. The pair embodied the strategic articulation of interculturalism in the neoliberal mode. Cárdenas could be seen as rooted in the national, indigenous, and local (for La Paz—centric politics, crystallized in the figure of the most proximate Indians, the Aymara), while Goni represented the denationalized, Western, and universal (usually imagined as a reference to the United States).

Those present listened while the ETARE team leader Amalia Anaya described the draft education law. They had little reason to support public school change. Save Cárdenas, they represented social sectors educated in elite private schools. Yet the party elite had incentives to bring the teachers' unions to their knees. If the Trotskyite-led teachers were brought to heel, the balance of power would shift toward the economic and political elite. It would weaken a nucleus of opposition to market liberalization. And reform was cheap. Funded by international loans and aid, education reform would displace teachers and open spaces of patronage for new professionals in the bureaucracy.[1] Some of these elites may have seen reform as a national project of inclusion and public good, perhaps even a human right. But judging from loan documents, ideological support was closely tied to the belief that a limited investment in human capital would contribute to market-led growth. Besides, Goni was enjoying a wave of popularity, and teachers—sure to raise hell—could be managed. Education reform should not have been a hard sell.

But one point of contention made the elite criollos nervous. It was tied to the article that legalized a shift in educational policy away from *castellanización* (the imposition of Spanish) to *bilingüismo de mantenimiento* (bilingualism aimed at the maintenance of indigenous languages). This insertion of indigenous languages into the reform project appeared to be "prodding nerves" (Willis 1977:176) that a more orthodox plan might hope to deaden. That a state with aspirations to global knowledge, competition, and modernity (imagined as desired whiteness, as represented in Goni) would embark on teaching Indians in dialects limited by orality and locality, writing books in languages without grammars, and supporting anthropological fantasies about the Indian (all tied to past darkness, much like Cárdenas) created real elite discomfort. Introducing indigenous languages into public schooling was akin to having a servant join the master at the table, much like the Aymara vice-president speaking cholo Spanish amid this lighter-skinned inner circle of power.[2]

That day an MNR party ideologue, Guillermo Bedregal, then the president of the House of Representatives, voiced these discomforts. In response to the article officializing the teaching of indigenous languages, he reportedly interjected: "This is an attempt to resuscitate dead languages of defeated cultures!" He went on to argue that indigenous languages had no writing, no grammar, and no alphabets. He intimated that neither these languages nor their speakers had any claim on political space in a modern nation. And the nation should not admit such absurdities. Bedregal was an old-timer, one of the generation called the "dinosaurs." Unwilling to accept linguistic and cultural equality, he also failed to grasp the possibility that recognizing difference might actually facilitate the neoliberal turn. Nor, one suspects, did he understand the technical or economistic arguments that better schooling (leading to the acquisition of Spanish) could be achieved using the language children actually spoke.

At this outburst, Goni is said to have turned to Cárdenas, waiting for a response to the blatantly racist insult. Those who told me this story said that the vice-president responded with a cautious defense of grammatical equality. The ETARE team then argued the technical merits of bilingual pedagogy. Goni himself finally ended the discussion. Representing the new liberal awareness of culture, though it overlay a lingering nervousness about Indians, Goni told his own story. He recalled his experience as a Spanish speaker challenged by English schooling in the United States, saying, "I don't want children to suffer in their own land what I suffered in a foreign one. Besides, you know, Guillermo [Bedregal], I have a sister in Bosnia, and I don't want Bolivia to become another Yugoslavia. I think we should have bilingual education. Next article."

Bilingual intercultural education became state law.[3]

Chapter Five

PRODDING NERVES

Intercultural Disruption and Managerial Control

The Bolivian government has proposed a twenty-year Education
Reform Program to establish an efficient and equitable system of
education which would provide 100 percent coverage at primary
and secondary levels and offer the range of scientific, technical,
vocational and higher education opportunities needed to meet
the nation's demand for skilled manpower.
—*Inter-American Development Bank, 1994, on approval of the first
$80 million loan to the Bolivian government*

I think most [nonindigenous] people say you have to civilize the
Indians, and if it takes teaching them in their languages to do it,
then so be it.
—*Bolivian anthropologist and functionary of the* IADB, *La Paz, 1999*

The education reform is sold to the public, to the donors, it's a
political show [*un show político*]. . . . We talk about quality education,
interculturalism, etc., etc., but in the long term it is about economics (*lo económico*). With the education reform you get resources [i.e.,
money] and you get the attention of the political parties.
—*Private statements of an Education Ministry official speaking over
drinks about education reform, La Paz, 2002*

W hether one interprets bilingual education as the expression of neoliberalism in indigenous languages or the voice of indigenous movements making the state speak on their terms, the cabinet meeting story
highlights tensions created by EIB as it infiltrated the criollo-dominated state.
EIB disturbed a paradigm of criollo rule that relied on the unquestioned
supremacy of Spanish as the language of the nation-state. It disrupted right-
and left-wing stories of mestizaje that privileged the criollo as the bearer of

superior knowledge and racial substance that would rule and guide the indio into modernity through education (Sanjinés 2004). Even in its neoliberal expression, interculturalism raised the possibility of cultural and linguistic equality, undermining evolutionary understandings that conflated race, culture, and language as organically linked traits of more and less superior beings. These narratives of language, nation, mestizaje, and race-culture evolution were crucial to the structures and idioms of state power and social order, and EIB brought them under subversive scrutiny.

EIB also generated practical problems. One was the challenge of producing materials and teachers to implement bilingual pedagogy. The state vetting of indigenous languages and knowledge in the sacred template of public schooling might also imply that language was a valid marker of social and territorial—and why not political?—collectivities within the state. Neoliberalism could benefit from the decentralizing urge of indigenous pluralism, but it sought to contain this possibility within manageable frames.[1] By mobilizing translocal linguistic territorialities, EIB could create—as it effectively did—decentralizing demands not contained in existing municipal jurisdictions (Gustafson 2002). "EIB is too risky!" elites seemed to say to each other. On the other hand, elites felt pressured by the rising tide of indigenous movements. "What might happen if we do not acquiesce to EIB?" Goni seemed to say in that cabinet meeting described in the preceding interlude. In the end, I interpret the rulers as saying, "We can manage this."

Discussions of neoliberal interculturalism often assume the existence of a strong hegemonic bloc that shares an ideological consensus (Hale 2002). In fact, Bolivian power holders and institutions were fragmented and entering a period of crisis during the 1990s. The education reform, cobbled together from diverse political agendas, exemplified supranational development flows that brought new pressures to bear on structures of rule and narratives of nation building. Dinosaurs like Guillermo Bedregal failed to see the deterritorializing logic applied through the discourse of education for development. In this logic, the creation of flexible and mobile workers to compete in global markets was more important than the sculpting of national mestizo citizenries who glorified Spanish. Goni, the enlightened tycoon, accepted this turn, perhaps facilitated by his own deterritorialized linguistic biography. Yet his was an embrace of difference at arm's length, a multiculturalism that reproduced hierarchies between "us" and "them." Elites were unable to see the country through the eyes of citizen majorities frustrated with the course of change in the country.[2] Their acquiescence to EIB was spurred by nervousness and fear, reflecting blind weakness rather than absolute power.

Well-positioned figures like Goni found themselves privileged by the neoliberal shift, but others were weakened. Neoliberalism did offer some support for elite rule. It was a story of triumphal capitalism wielded like a hammer to silence utopian political visions. It proposed marketizing problematic areas of government (public health, education, pensions), and it promised to maintain a role for traditional parties while crushing their popular counterparts (unions) through privatization and decentralization. On the other hand, most elites had made of party politics a lucrative business of "milking the cow" of the state. Political fortunes relied on clientelist networks dependent on the corporatist structure. Neoliberal downsizing thus left elites scrambling for new bases of power and patronage. Meanwhile, neoliberalism intensified social movement resurgence. Neoliberal interculturalism thus emerged not as a powerful shift but as a piecemeal process of reordering that many traditional politicians feared and that attempted to reshape the state in a context of uncertainty and intra-elite conflict.

As James Collins and Richard Blot (2003:76–86) have pointed out, school reformers in the United States from the 1800s to today have voiced enlightened ideas motivated both by (racialized) fears of the underclass and by desires for its control. Similarly, Bolivian EIB generated fear and desire. Criollo elites feared an indigenous Other emboldened by the linguistic subversion of the quintessential tool of colonialism: the monopoly of Spanish as the official language of literacy, knowledge, and citizenship. They feared the opening to explicitly indigenous control over a key instrument of state capital and legitimacy: the school system. Yet these fears were coupled with desire— as expressed in the epigraph—for an orderly, civilized Indian shaped by testable, standardized knowledge. As in the early twentieth century, reform aimed to improve the Indian to create useful subjects ("skilled manpower") while embracing a new secular theodicy based on knowledge and merit rather than race or class, a theodicy that could rationalize inequality in the new global order.[3] In addition, education reform and EIB brought resources sought by parties. EIB was thus absorbed into state process as disruptive containment, juxtaposing fears of indigeneity and desirable forms of managerial governance.

In this chapter I examine disruptive containment through three state-centered lenses: The first is the figure of Amalia Anaya, a person central to EIB and education reform. Anaya's trajectory reveals transformations within the criollo-led state project and in the nature of articulation between this project and the EIB networks. The second is that of new education professionals whose occupation of roles formerly held by schoolteachers reveals the racialized class struggle unfolding within reform. The third lens focuses on textual regimes, the new schoolbooks that scribes produced in the offices of the reform.

SCENE I: THE IRON LADY

Anaya began work in education as the subsecretary of social policy (1989–91), led the ETARE team during much of its existence (1992–95), and later held the positions of vice-minister (1997–2001) and minister of education (2001–2). Her story provides a useful lens onto the inner workings of the state and the social histories through which reform took shape during the 1990s and 2000s.[4] Anaya served as a node of articulation between education, indigenist, and development networks and the Bolivian party apparatus. For a time, Guarani leaders viewed her as one of their friends in La Paz. Andean indigenous organizations also saw her as a sometime ally. She represented a contingent state opening around and through which indigenous agendas were pursued. Within the villagelike public sphere of La Paz, where the state became personified through individuals like her, Anaya also stood for education reform and EIB. Those who opposed reform vilified her as a neoliberal villain; those who supported it, praised her as a heroine. After one interview, a journalist dubbed her the Thatcheresque "Iron Lady" of education reform, using her own words to portray toughness and dedication to change: "I come from a generation that entered the university during the military dictatorships. . . . We were a generation of social awareness. . . . We sought a utopia that would change the world" (qtd. in Calderón Magaña 2001:57).

Like Elsa, Tüi, and others attached to EIB, Anaya was a lightning rod for attacks because her support for EIB put her into an unsettling place that did not sit comfortably among the existing order. She was a former leftist activist, but she now worked within regimes on the right. She came from a traditional criollo family, yet she voiced support for indigenous rights rarely heard among criollos. She was a woman and a sociologist in a patriarchal world dominated by businessmen and caudillos. She was also in between a generational and historical shift. Having cut her political teeth in the world of criollo-led cogovernment between parties and unions, she now cultivated webs of support in relation to the media, foreign donors, and a cluster of intellectual and indigenous activists. Anomalous figures like her were crucial to the articulation of EIB into the state apparatus.

Anaya, a woman in her forties, had a surname that located her as part of a respected lineage of public figures from Cochabamba. In her words, hers was a "simple" middle-class family with schoolteacher parents, distinct from the landed oligarchs and the mining elites. As a teenager, Anaya entered the public university in Cochabamba. Like many youth of the 1970s, she planned to study sociology, a radical field during that era. At that time most students mobilized, as she did, in opposition to the military dictatorship of Hugo Bánzer, who ruled the country from 1971 to 1978. At the age of eighteen she became a student leader at Cochabamba's San Simón University. Her public visibility as a critic of the regime and her association with leftist or "red" ideology made her the target of death threats from paramilitary units. "They spray-painted things about me as a woman on the walls of my house that I cannot repeat to you," she told me. Her father tried to protect her by sending her to La Paz to study. Unlike wealthier criollos, "he didn't have money to send me any further [i.e., abroad]." She continued her political work as a student in La Paz, leading the Center of Sociology Students. During these times she characterized herself as part of a generation that saw Bolivia's future as one of radical change and itself as the vanguard in search of a new society. In her belief, the language of revolutionary struggle was clear: the students represented an intellectual vanguard that would lead the workers and (indigenous) peasants to liberation. Bánzer did eventually succumb to popular resistance after four miners' wives started a hunger strike in La Paz's Plaza Murillo in 1978 (Rivera Cusicanqui 1984).

Yet democracy proved short-lived, and the country soon returned to military rule. The day Luís García Meza took over in a violent coup in 1980, Anaya joined a new party called the Movement of the Revolutionary Left (MIR). Modeled on the homonymous party of Chile, the MIR was then leftist and somewhat revolutionary. (It is not anymore.) MIR leaders and activists suffered persecution under García Meza. In addition to assassinations of nonparty activists like the priest Luís Espinal, the most notorious event was the Harrington Street massacre in the neighborhood of Sopocachi in January of 1981: an entire cadre of MIR leaders was machine-gunned to death in a paramilitary attack. As a clandestine leader of the MIR, Anaya had gone into hiding and left the country before this tragedy. She traveled to Peru over the rugged Andean cordillera and returned later through Brazil during carnival season, pretending to be the wife of another MIR exile who accompanied her, Juan del Granado (who later split from the MIR and at this writing, in 2007, is the mayor of La Paz).

With the return to democracy in 1982 Anaya continued her MIR "militancy," as loyal party activity is called. By then the party was shifting rightward, much as the MNR had done years before. It began fissioning along factional lines and created rancor between former *compañeros*. Party splits "are like a divorce," she recalled, suggesting why some of her former compañeros on the left were so critical of education reform. She stayed with the MIR, which went from revolutionary struggle to accommodations with power when its leader Jaime Paz Zamora made a strategic pact with Bánzer's ADN party to take the presidency in 1989. Anaya thus found herself in a party allied with the dictator she had opposed as a young student.

Anaya worked on the MIR social policy platform for the 1989 elections, four years after the country began its plunge into structural adjustment. She also took a post as the subsecretary of social policy in the new government, a position funded by UNICEF given wide state cutbacks. By 1991, Anaya had become disenchanted with the MIR. Paz Zamora found himself accused of having received campaign monies from suspected drug traffickers. In addition, Anaya had promoted internal criticism aimed at combating party corruption that exploded after the party's electoral victory. Frustrated with corruption—and facing the closure of her subsecretarial post in 1991—she abandoned the party.

However, during her work in social policy and education, she came to know the EIB network—also associated with UNICEF—and traveled to Jomtien for the World Conference on Education for All in 1990. Moving in circles with donors and the big development banks, she also cultivated alliances outside traditional party structures. She further maintained the support of one of the MIR party's heavyweights, the cement mogul Samuel Doria Medina. Doria Medina, later named the minister of planning, backed her appointment to ETARE when it was created with World Bank support in

1992. From there she spearheaded reform until 1995. In the office of social policy she had also made friends with a young technocrat named Jorge "Tuto" Quiroga, a member of ADN. In 1997 the old dictator Bánzer returned to power as a democratically elected president with Quiroga as his running mate. Though not affiliated with any party by then, Anaya accepted the job of vice-minister of education, once again working under the old general she had once risked her life battling. When Bánzer resigned in 1999 and later died of cancer, Quiroga ascended to the presidency. Anaya was moved up to the post of education minister, which she occupied until the return of Goni in 2002. Overall it was a time of remarkable stability within the process of education-reform implementation.

As her experience reflects, ideological distinctions between the parties and the tradition of rewarding only party militants were becoming increasingly irrelevant as a younger generation of technocratically minded reformists came to the fore. Anaya gave meaning to her own work not as a party cadre, or a new technocrat, but as one whose support for education expressed a longer trajectory marked by the pursuit of social change and, when necessary, accomodations with power. "Those of us on the left used to refuse to engage the state," she recalled, "but things have changed." She reflected on the generational shift in political actors, from old-guard dinosaurs to the new businessmen that created conditions for these paradoxical articulations: "Even though the old dinosaurs still see me as a red, I have support among men like Samuel Doria Medina and Tuto Quiroga. They are businessmen. They are not leftist, never have been, and won't live long enough to become [leftist]. But they see education as a contribution to growth and they are good allies."

This ascent through layers of power reveals party fission, alliance making and breaking, and power contests tied to intraparty struggles over the shrinking war booty of the state. It also reveals a broader set of patterns—the intra-elite contest over the reduced state apparatus, the generational shift from party militancy to technocratic fealty within the dominant parties, and the shift away from old forms of party patronage to new networks of transnationalized, aid-dependent support. Neoliberalism chipped away not only at the livelihoods of the poor but also restructured the workings of state rule at the highest levels.

These dynamics were not unique to Anaya's story, but Anaya was unique in her defense of bilingual education in a context in which most of her peers scoffed at the proposal. Anaya argued that her stance was not new and that she had always held alternative ideas about indigenous language education. As a student leader in La Paz in the 1970s, she had proposed that the study of indigenous languages be incorporated into the sociology curriculum. "It was defeated by majority," she recalled bitterly. She pointed out that Hugo Carvajal, a fellow student leader and former party compañero in the MIR, had argued to her back then that "learning Aymara or Quechua served him no purpose at all."[5] She also incorporated a proposal for bilingual education into the MIR platform of 1989. Yet the party then supported neither education reform nor bilingualism. Both proposals threatened clientelist relations with the teachers' union, and bilingualism had little support, despite Paz Zamora's demagogic overtures to the lowland indigenous movements.[6]

Anaya traced her convictions about indigenous language education through a family history that reached back into the era of incipient criollo intellectual expressions of Bolivia's truncated *indigenismo*. "I grew up under the influence of my father," she told me in one conversation. Anaya's father, Rafael Anaya Arze, was born in 1915, the youngest of five brothers whose father was a noted jurist. Like many of that generation who lived in close interaction with Quechua working on the haciendas, Rafael Anaya grew up speaking Quechua in addition to Spanish. He studied to become a school-teacher in the country's first Normal Teachers' College at Sucre (the one founded with the support of the Belgian expert Georges Rouma in 1917). With French government support, Anaya the father later traveled to France and studied linguistics in Paris. A musician, pedagogue, and admirer of Quechua culture and language, her father, Anaya said, "inculcated admiration and affection for indigenous cultures" into his children.

As Javier Sanjinés (2004) describes in his study of Bolivian intellectuals during this period, rising middle-class and radical movements in the 1940s became increasingly critical of traditional liberal oligarchs in the wake of the Chaco War. They saw themselves as defenders of the working and indigenous classes, which formed part of their own strategy for accessing power. As one of this generation, Anaya's father lived in the shadow of his oldest brother, Ricardo, who in 1940 founded the PIR (Party of the Revolutionary Left), one of Bolivia's earliest communist parties (not to be confused with the later MIR). Competing radical parties—the MNR, the POR (Workers' Revolutionary Party), and the PIR—played prominent roles in the twists and turns of Bolivia's mid-twentieth-century upheavals that culminated in the 1952 revolution. These movements, with origins in the urban middle classes, took root in the radical ferment against the tin and agrarian oligarchs who dominated the country. Fueled by theories of revolutionary change circulating in the wake of the Mexican and Russian Revolutions, these intellectuals thought Bolivian revolution not only possible but inevitable. During the 1940s, the PIR, following a Stalinist line, played a significant role in the radicalization of urban workers prior to the 1952 revolution (Malloy 1970:95–96). Led by Ricardo Anaya, the PIR and the competing Trotskyite POR were eventually eclipsed by the more conservative middle-class reformism of the MNR.

Rafael Anaya is remembered by his daughter for making a key contribution to the PIR, in which he was also a militant. Far ahead of his time, she said, he sought the introduction of bilingual education into the party platform. This idea, she argued, resulted from his Quechua studies. Though not linked to a radical proposal for decolonization, it represented an enlightened position for the time. Though Bolivian indigenism never expanded as it did in Peru or Mexico, the nascent vision of Rafael Anaya echoed a phase of the criollo valorization of indigenous languages, especially Quechua, with its associations with the glory of the Inca past. This oppositional stance questioned the Eurocentric view of liberal positivists who saw these tongues as markers of the irredeemable racial inferiority of their speakers.

After the 1952 revolution, the PIR proposal for native language education entered the public debate on schooling. Yet the opening to indigenous languages would have undermined the class-centric discourse and the narrative of liberation through mestizaje that sustained the MNR revolutionary agenda. The Education Code of 1955 discarded the idea of bilingual schooling and adopted castellanización. The PIR eventually dissolved in the internecine battles that characterize party processes in Bolivia. Her father's work, Anaya later ruefully wrote to me, had been forgotten in the anonymity of history. The future of the country would have been different, she insisted, had more elites recognized what her father did: that the indio was stoic, intelligent, and hard-working, thus deserving the same opportunities as other Bolivians. Instead, she said, we are "living the consequences of fifty years of failed assimilation."

Like her office manager who complained of carpal tunnel syndrome and smoked incessantly to ward off stress, Anaya exuded an intensity marked by sharp-witted, ribald joking and a strong-willed leadership style. Her demeanor, crucial for political survival, led to her reputation as *dura* (tough, strong, and obstinate). This was reflected in the Thatcheresque label—the "Iron Lady"—given to her by a reporter. "I have always been contestative, one who talks back," she told me proudly. She butted heads often with Bánzer's education minister, the doltish Tito Hoz de Vila, who feared she would outshine him in the public eye. This demeanor—*dura* and *contestataria*—came out when she spoke. She blended the rousing style and metaphors of one who had worked in party-union activism with the new terminologies of the transnational education and development networks that called for firm, efficient, and technically sound decision making. She dismissed teachers' complaints about not participating in education reform design. "You can't make effective decisions in a popular assembly," she told me; there are "some things, like budgets, that just don't lend themselves to that." As she reminded me later, "if we had sought the approval of the teachers' unions, there would never have been bilingual education."

I often heard her use the word "passion" (*pasión*) to describe her work, so I asked her about this in one conversation. Her answer outlined the contested historical shift underway in the meaning of the education field. It also mapped a contemporary social topography of intra-elite battles for prestige and the war booty of the state. "In my day [*en mi época*, referring to her era of student activism] what we called *mística* [mystique], today I call passion.[7] Reading attacks against your work every day in the press is tough. That's why I say you need passion in this job." Barely taking a breath, she launched into a laundry list of opposition to reform, and thus to her own person. These battles played out both in backstage maneuvers and in very public airings. The "newspapers publish notes on this stuff every day," she said, "they write barbarities about you!"

> We have enemies on all sides. This is not just a left-right issue. Take the Iturraldes for instance. This is a provincial country and surnames are surrounded by an aura like that of Iturralde. Deservedly or not, in a tiny little country like this, they become like oracles.[8] They may have some merit, like Iturralde [the father]. But their children inherit their prestige

[undeservedly]. After a [World] Bank and foreign donor evaluation questioned the work of one of the Iturraldes on our staff, she resigned in protest, and that earned us the wrath of her father [a prominent lawyer]. And then you have Gutiérrez [an ex-minister of education], intellectually dishonest, a plagiarist, yet lining up against the reform. . . . I cannot explain why, with all the evidence that supports education reform, you have other intellectuals who criticize the reform, or try to *desprestigiarla* [discredit it], sometimes ignoring it, which is another way of attacking it. Take LH, who wrote a book about social policy and only gave two lines to education reform, undoubtedly the most significant social policy in recent years. He writes an entire book about the [World Bank] Social Investment Fund that was nothing more than a political instrument to make the New Political Order [neoliberalism] viable, to support structural adjustment. They buried waterlines that led to nowhere just to create jobs! And he devotes two lines to education reform! And take AM or LR, university professors who say that bilingual education is retrograde, that you've got to incorporate the Indians into Spanish. . . . I am attacked from civil society, even from the progressives from whom we expected support. The feminists, the leftist leaders write editorials against bilingual education any chance they get. If you don't put passion into this, you either go home or you end up on the Americas Bridge. That's what I am talking about when I say "passion."

She raised her hand to point over my shoulder in the direction of the suspension bridge that crossed a deep ravine between La Paz and the Miraflores neighborhood. It was a popular spot to commit suicide. Returning her active hands to the table, she again took up the paper on which she had been doodling as she spoke. An assistant came in to ask her a question about a budget figure, whispering into her ear. She waved to me to turn off the recorder, and I obeyed. While I waited, I rested my gaze on a poster hanging behind her desk. It was one of UNICEF's, of a little Quechua girl, sporting the words, "If education is for all, it is bilingual and intercultural."

Anaya's historicization of her place in education adds to our understanding of this transformative moment in Bolivian history. From her position, education was an apparatus for distributing knowledge and for ordering power relations that emanated out and down from La Paz at the same time that new prescriptions for governance called for increased decentralization of school administration—in part stimulated by fomenting the creation of new indigenous actors by responding to the demand for EIB. In Anaya's view, this represented a turn away from deeper traditions of verticalism, centralism, and authoritarianism. And like Anaya herself, education was under reconstruction. She and the education field were increasingly detached from the old form of party-union apparatus and increasingly reliant on new ways of speaking and new external props like foreign aid and EIB network allies, including the new players on the scene, the indigenous movements.[9]

A testament to the tenuous position of EIB (and Anaya) within the liberalizing project was the way in which it was subjected to two equally colonial perceptions stemming from Bolivia's elite crisis of power. On the one hand, it was viewed as the only domain in which state authorities and indigenous subjects were making progress. On the other, reactionaries, old-guard leftists, and racists saw it as stoking the fires of indigenous mobilization. Both perspectives are colonial in that they maintain a racialized distinction between rulers (criollo) and ruled (indigenous). Both are blind, since they were unable to rethink the state, but rather viewed short-term policy shifts like EIB and interculturalism as managerial solutions rather than processes for opening democratic and dialogic space. Indigenous movements, on the other hand, saw these policy shifts as a moment in a much longer history of struggle. EIB and the articulation represented by Anaya marked the beginning, not the end, of decolonization. One event reported in late 2001 illustrates this tension beautifully.

Between 1999 and 2002, Bolivia entered a period in which the dominant mainstream parties—ADN, MNR, and MIR—were rapidly losing credibility. In hindsight, we know that this marked the beginning of their end. Yet even then the country was trembling. The past two years had seen violent conflicts over coca eradication in the Chapare region. The so-called Water War in Cochabamba in April of 2000 had sent privatization into retreat and energized urban movements. The "bloody September" of 2000 saw an Aymara-led siege of La Paz tied to the rise of new leaders like Felipe Quispe. Lowland indigenous marches surged out of the east in 2000 and 2001, its participants demanding the rewriting of the constitution and an effective implementation of land reform. These were just the more remarkable events. Cyclical protests, including those by schoolteachers, continued to enact a democracy of the streets against a state seen as retreating from its obligations to the people.

The urban media evaluated the work of ministers like Anaya according to their ability to deal with these protests. This view of legitimate rule reflected the corporatist logic of governance in which authorities managed sectors, a view that had never disappeared under neoliberalism. The state center in La Paz intensely felt the pressure, particularly in relation to the Aymara of El Alto and the surrounding altiplano. State authorities tried to maintain prestige (and their jobs) by defusing conflicts. Ministers were called *ministros bomberos*, fire(wo)man ministers, who spent their time *apagando fuegos* (putting out fires). This meant resolving hunger strikes, blockades, marches, and protests through dialogue, concessions, co-optation, cash payments, or the use of force. In the midst of these tensions, EIB and education reform became a way for then president Quiroga to say that something was going right with indigenous peoples.

The event in question coincidentally fell on Columbus Day, October 12, 2001, nine years after I snapped the picture of the two Aymara demanding epistemic justice. The next day a headline in *La Razón* read "Indigenous Peoples Show Advances of Education Reform" ("Los pueblos indígenas" (2001). As reported, adults and children from Aymara communities had visited the presidential palace in La Paz. Dressed in Aymara fashion, they showed their support of indigenous school projects, a component of reform touted as a model for local participation. Anaya was quoted lauding bilingual education. Yet reporters gave more attention to a poem recited in Aymara and Spanish by the young Alvaro Quispe Chiri, an eight-year-old Aymara boy. President Quiroga, they noted, was "moved" and "playfully smiled" as he listened to the boy recite. He must have been smiling uncomfortably:

> I am a child who comes from the countryside; I live with the sheep and the cattle
> And with them I have grown, with the sun blazing, with the cold whipping
> I have come today to learn to read and write, to confront the thieving q'ara [criollo, white].
> Where are those thieving q'ara? With fire I will burn them

As they did to Julián Apaza, exactly the same I will do to them.

As the great *mallku* [condor, leader; i.e., Apaza] said dying, I am dying but on

my body millions will rise.

The poem epitomizes the image of the *indio letrado, indio alzado*, the Indian who learns to read and write to contest the corrupt, thieving, and exploitative *q'ara*, mestizos, whites, or criollos. The invocation of literacy here was not tied to the formation of docile human capital but to the reproduction of a longer relationship of exchange and resistance between indigenous peoples and the state. Schooling constituted a vehicle for contestative memory, in this case memories tied to Julián Apaza, also know as Tupak Katari, the Aymara revolutionary leader drawn, quartered, and burned by the Spanish after laying siege to La Paz in 1781. Katari, referred to in the poem as "the mallku" (A. condor, leader), left a prophecy before his execution that energizes Andean resurgence today: "I am dying, but on my body millions will rise."

Even when attempting to show the "advances of education reform" and the new techniques of school management (the school project), these unsettling words surely prodded nerves among criollos. It was precisely this kind of anticolonial imagery that elites feared would accompany projects like EIB. Even so, as ritual the performance demonstrated the durability of the colonial model of rule. Aymara traveled to the colonial center (La Paz), enacting a relation between criollos (the rulers) and indios (the ruled). Aymara, at least those who had not rejected education reform, performed a resistant loyalty. As a campaign effort for Quiroga, the show proved limited. Other Aymara and indigenous movements were busy knocking on (and down) the doors of power.

Anaya's position thus reflected a contingent opening in an unstable field. She told me on several occasions that some accused her of coddling the indigenous. Yet she was clearly no romantic. "The indigenous movements," she said, "are [education reform] allies, but not reliable ones. I recognize the five hundred years of oppression, and all that," she added, shaking her head in frustration, but "I know from experience that indigenous leaders are still working in the logic of the unions." Indeed, indigenous movements were ultimately unwilling to sacrifice alliances with the peasant and teachers' unions to express loyalty to a state project (and a criolla subject) that represented the colonial relationship they sought to overturn. Indigenous leaders, especially in the Andes, tactically engaged EIB, but they were building their own new networks increasingly articulated with the rise of the MAS. From the indigenous lens, EIB was a wedge into the state, a place-holder of sorts. Their apparent support for that aspect of reform did not make them earnest allies of the criollo hegemonic project. The more distant Guarani, somewhat detached from the Andes-centered conflicts by virtue of their location, would remain more reliable allies, at least for a while.

SCENE 2: REFORMISTS VERSUS TEACHERS

As I pointed out above, the opening to EIB was marked by instability in elite power arrangements and nervous fear about what this might yield in the way of indigenous responses. In this view, instabilities offer a useful way of thinking about state process. Yet in another view we can see structural and cultural change taking place within education that has more potential durability. It is amid layers of bureaucratic power, not in the public rhetoric of interculturalism, the shifting battles of elites, or the struggles of indigenous movements, that the workings of reformism played out most effectively. Yet neoliberalism fails to capture completely the meaning of these changes, which relied on and even intensified traditional languages and structures of racial hierarchy and social order. The new, as such, intensified expressions of the old.

I hinted at these changes at the beginning of chapter 4. By 1998 the Lazarte Building had been shut down and much of its six hundred–person-strong staff of teachers relocated. Their offices were replaced with the buzzing cubicles of the new professionals in the building farther down the street. Though many of the new staff revolved in and out with party shifts, eventually this new administrative field underwent "institutionalization." Institutionalization, financed by foreign donors, aimed at creating a professional technical class based on merit rather than union and party politics. Open competition for jobs, merit-based exams, and the routine evaluation of staff formed part of the process. Cast as apolitical, since it would do away with political appointees, institutionalization was nonetheless deeply political. Institutionalization sought the consolidation of certain "rules of reason," the new *doxa* of educational knowledge that would be insulated from shifting political tides (Popkewitz 2000). In a context of intensifying competition for scarce jobs where access to university credentials were beyond the material capacities of most Bolivians, institutionalization was not based on neutral merit, but in fact promised to harden existing inequalities of class. This proved doubly political in public education, a field historically open to upward mobility from the lower and lower middle classes. A space traditionally abandoned by the elite now became part of the narrowing field in which middle- and upper-class professionals sought to appropriate a portion of shrinking state capital. Schoolteachers, in short, were losing ground to technocrats.

What we see, then, is not merely a technical improvement brought by the ascendance of experts but a combination of political insulation, social displacement, and discursive infiltration that sought to redefine the state through an overhaul of the bureaucratic field. It is here, within the more densely institutionalized and monitored center of state power, more than at the village and school level, that certain neoliberal imperatives could take root through what development ethnographers refer to as "governmentality" from beyond the borders of sovereignty (e.g., Gupta 1998). These changes contributed to and relied on the redefinition of education professionals as no longer colegas and compañeros engaged in a struggle against the state, but as docile, competing, and self-regulating individual experts or *técnicos*. As Cris Shore and Susan Wright suggest (1999:559–61), and Michel Foucault intimates (1990:125–28), new political technologies are not always deployed on or through subalterns, but work most effectively at mediating levels of power. For Foucault, this was the bourgeoisie. In the Bolivian case, the change targeted the upwardly mobile professional classes. Controlling, disciplining, and redefining the identities and loyalties of educational técnicos—more than the difficult control of indigenous children in schools—was the immediate objective of educational structural adjustment in Bolivia.[10] My stressed-out interlocutors on the reform staff and the Guarani scribes who went to work in the cubicles were the people the changes addressed.

The vignettes that follow show how this new managerial class narrated itself in relation to idioms of state and schooling. What we see is a Bolivian manifestation of racialized class struggle shrouded in the new terms of schooling as a complement to market-led modernization. The new professional class sought to embody a claim to modernity, a world iconicized for some in the image of the cocktail party of "heavyweights" (*pesos pesados*), a ruling class frequently celebrated in the society pages:

> Last Tuesday, the resident representative of the World Bank in Bolivia and his wife offered in their elegant and distant residence a cocktail in honor of the new director of the World Bank for Bolivia, Ecuador, and Peru. Original and appetizing tidbits were enjoyed by various ministers and vips, particularly from the economic area; there we saw the members of the cabinet, the president of the Bolivian Central Bank; the ambassador of Argentina; the ambassadors of Germany and the Netherlands; the business attaché of the United States Embassy; the representative of the Inter-American Development Bank and his wife; the director of usaid; and many others. It appears that many do in fact work, as their suits were wrinkled after many hours at their desks; some fatigue was also noted in their faces, but the good drinks and comforting canapés helped to dissipate it. A very good reception of heavyweights. (Ficho, qepd, *La Razón,* October 13, 2002)[11]

These professionals were closely monitored and evaluated (recall Anaya's invocation of World Bank "observation"). They were not to fall into the trap of popular or indigenous utopias that flowed through the educational field, and to that extent knew they were being watched. Interviewees invariably cited foreign donors and consultants as those who "observed us" or "told us" or "evaluated" or "monitored." On the other side, the referential point of repulsion in the self-representation of this new class was a social figure cast as unsuited for the modern future: the excluded object of reform, the Bolivian schoolteacher.[12]

Most reform discourse cast schoolteachers as relics of the past. They were frequently spoken of as technically and politically unsuited for participation (Anaya 1995; Contreras 1997; Gill 2000; Grindle 2004). Technically, teachers were seen as nonexperts, the bearers of antiquated methods, irrational ideologies, and distorted logics. "Irrationality" was a label frequently used, since teachers continued questioning the model of free markets and free elections (Contreras 1997). In fact, teacher opposition to reform was immanently rational, as reform sought to do away with union power. In political terms, their exclusion was justified since they only knew how to operate in large popular assemblies where discourse, but not decisions, thrived.

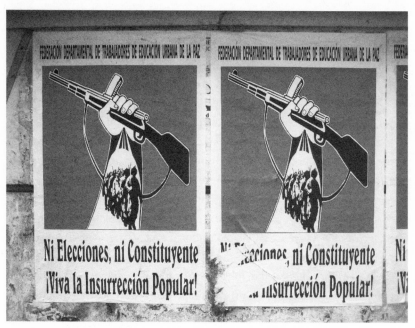

FIGURE 4 Revolutionary or sindicatero? Poster of La Paz's Trotskyite-led urban teachers' union, 2005. "No elections, no constitutional assembly, long live popular insurrection!"

The *asamblea* (assembly) frequently invoked in interviews represented a past kind of democracy and inefficient cogovernment that structural adjustment sought to dismantle (see figure 4).

Development aid contributed to the exclusion. For some donors, ironically, arguments about sovereignty, the very condition brought into question by the workings of structural adjustment, justified this exclusion. One World Bank staffer denied any culpability for teacher exclusion, telling me, "We let the Bolivians [i.e., reformists] carry this out the way they wanted." Analysts sympathetic to reform also replicated stereotypes about teachers as preternaturally violent actors, ignoring many decades of state violence deployed against them and other representatives of the working classes (Grindle 2004:151–53). Finally, this violent, irrational, political relic was imagined in racial terms particular to Andean meanings of social class, which see economic hierarchy as racial hierarchy. Whether indigenous or not, teachers were often spoken of as indigenous or *like* the indigenous in quotidian discourses on reform. Despite the rhetoric of interculturalism and utopian visions of liberal market democracy, class struggle within reform intensified and mobilized exclusionary corporatist and colonial discourses on race.

Reformers who constructed themselves in opposition to the school-teacher depended on this language of exclusion since they sought to occupy the teachers' space within the state. Reformists saw themselves as moving away from that perceived as anachronistic (a teachers' union that thrived in chaos, outmoded politics, inefficiency, corruption, violence, and proximity to indigeneity) toward that perceived as modern, global, and professional (upper-class, university educated Bolivians wielding a discourse of social progress that echoed the latest in universal knowledge and speaking English at will). The establishment of distance from teachers worked primarily through a class-inflected language of prestige constructed in relation to the criollo public of La Paz. By extension, education and the temporalizing narratives of the nation-state associated with it were also undergoing redefinition. At the risk of simplifying a heterogeneous mix of professionals, I highlight this in the sections below.

A generally shared concern among reformists was that education was stigmatized and that their work received little public respect. In the recent past, those who had aspired to ascend social ladders did well to disassociate themselves from public education. One high-level administrator said, "My friends made fun of me when I took this job with education."

> [For me, an economist,] we were taking our first bath in education, we were afraid! You know there is a norm, a categorization of the [Education] Ministry, that to work in education was to work in the lowest of the low. Because of the level of quality of education [*formación*] of the people, because of the importance that professionals and people in general give to the ministries, the Education Ministry was on the lowest floor, right along with the Ministry of Peasant and Agrarian Affairs. Health was a little higher, because doctors have more prestige. At the *top* [said in English] are finance, planning, the Foreign Ministry. (Anonymous interview, 1999)

Dropping English words like *top* also marked distance from those subjects and languages identified as traditional actors and objects of schooling. The manager went on to tell me how he had been attracted to the job by the professionalism of the reform-team leadership, as well as the prestige of the donor agencies behind it. Working with the "banks," the World Bank or the IADB, he said, helped him make the change, since it was, in his words, a marker of "prestige" (*prestigio*).

Some reformists were sympathetic to teachers' positions, and a handful themselves worked as teachers. Yet others marked distance from school-teachers in daily speech. Teachers were referred to as *maestritos* or *maestrillos*, diminutives that cast them as lesser subjects.[13] One staffer referred to blunders of her colleagues by labeling them *maestros rurales* (S. rural teachers), that is, cretins. I also heard teachers referred to as *sindicateros* and *politiqueros*, actors who made of schooling a political business (*negocio político*) rather than a pedagogical process. Schoolteachers' yearly strikes, never accompanied by alternative proposals for reform, fed into these accounts. "I sat at all of the negotiating tables with the teachers," said the economist quoted above, "and not once did I hear them propose a technical solution for schooling." After one massive teachers' strike against the ministry, another reform manager suggested to me that the only solution lay in firing at least fifty thousand teachers.

A Bolivian working as the education officer for one of the funding agencies also described the education field as undergoing a shift from ignorance to knowledge, in short, one away from the traditional schoolteacher:

BG: In the social spheres of La Paz, in Bolivia, to work in education was always something . . .

Anon: [interrupts] Very low [*muy bajo*].

BG: Very low, you mean speaking in terms of prestige?

Anon: I think so. All changes take their time. And I am going to speak to you as a Bolivian [i.e., not as an employee of a foreign donor]. I always had that perception, that the people who worked in the educational sector, were . . . [pause] . . . unionists [*del sindicato*], conflictive people [*gente conflictiva*], with low levels of education [*con menor formación*]. . . . Though now there are very well-educated people, very capable. Even though many [in the public] still associate education with the teacher-politico [*docente politiquero*], now there are respected figures, people who are at the vanguard of improvements. But that preconception still exists. There just are not many specialized people in education in Bolivia.

The framing placed Bolivia and its education system in a position of temporal lag, marked by the absence of university-trained experts in pedagogy. This backwardness was further marked by the fact that teachers and unions were until recently still in control of education. The term *vanguard*, more familiar to the language of unionism itself, was appropriated here to refer to this new professional cadre.[14]

Another young economist working on the transformation of Bolivia's teachers' colleges (*escuelas normales*) placed all of us in a similar evolutionary narrative:

> You know, there has been an evolution of the ideal teacher profile: In the sixties, it was in fashion that the teacher would be a sociologist, a revolutionary, who had in mind the model of society that they wanted to build, to come from their trenches, those kinds of terms. In the eighties, it came into vogue that they should be anthropologists, right? Cultural diversity, linguistic diversity, responding to the context, you know? That was the style [*onda*]. In the nineties, the teacher should be a manager [*gerente*], an administrator, someone who makes decisions, decentralized, autonomous, right? There's no reason to make stereotypes of it, and maybe we need a little of each, *but* [emphatic] considering the necessity that the teacher be a decision maker, a manager . . . in the end, the ultimate responsibility for the educational process in the classroom lies with the teacher. We want them to be trained to make decisions in the classroom . . . that is the modern manager-teacher [*docente-gerente moderno*] of the nineties. All that intercultural stuff is fine when they are inside their community, but when they come out of the community, they have to be more neoliberal than Bill Gates!

I raised an eyebrow. This was great for field notes, but it was also a jab at my own discipline: I—we—anthropologists—were stuck in the 1980s! Many of us do dress that way. Yet while I cringed at an anthropology deemed irrelevant, I found evocative his conviction that schooling would no longer turn indios (and teachers) into national, mestizo citizens, but would transform, whiten, and globalize them into a million little Bill Gates. In the past, the Indian was told to abandon difference and access citizenship (never attained); defend class struggle for liberation (not forthcoming); or buy into the liberal myth of equality (unachieved). Today the myth of schooling said the Indians

could have their difference at home but would access the universal by transcending the state entirely, in the form of a geeky, thick-framed–glasses–
wearing billionaire, the iconic body of (trans)national modernity. Devoid of
its critical social content and marked by an entrepreneurial, rather than a
revolutionary, hero, schooling had a new utopia. Yet competing millenarian
visions still swirled between the Andean Bill Gates and the Tupak Katari
imagined by the little Aymara poet.

The struggle between neoliberalism and public-sector unions has unfolded across Latin America and the globe. Yet these are not merely battles
with winners and losers where the key to reform is balancing short- and
long-term "costs, benefits, and incentives" (Kaufman and Nelson 2004).
Rather, these are racialized class and cultural struggles in which the education field as a set of relations, hierarchies, and modes of determining legitimate knowledge is being transformed, along with those bodies that occupy
it (Bourdieu and Wacquant 1992:17–20). The struggle against teachers was
thus a struggle over the state itself, including the aesthetic and corporal forms
of the ideal bodies who would inhabit spaces of power. It was here—for a
time—that the more durable effects of reform seemed to take root.

SCENE 3: CURRICULAR REGIMES

In 1994 several of the original Guarani scribes—including Enrique Camargo
—as well as some of a younger generation moved to La Paz to write textbooks in the offices of education reform. Elsa, my jocular friend whose story
I recounted in chapter 3, also went for short stints. These temporary migrants charted new paths for the Guarani and took up residence in a less
expensive neighborhood of La Paz. Their organization, the APG, continued
to gain national prominence. Other Guarani leaders were gaining access to
state posts in the new Ministry of Ethnic Affairs. Unlike in 1992, by 2000
one could find a fair number of Guarani in La Paz. When I visited them, they
were always joking about the cold, about new foods, about office routines,
and about *kolla* (Andean) customs. One young text writer joked how he was
a "country" Indian who had trouble figuring out how to punch his timecard
and balked at the thirty-minute stay-at-your-desk lunch rule. They were
also being targeted for disciplinary adjustments.

What I saw as detachment from local struggles, these Guarani saw as a
conquest. They began calling one shared house the Embajada Guarani, the

Guarani embassy, joking that they were Guarani envoys dispatched to the Bolivian state of kollas and criollos. Now they were walking among the karai, not only in the provincial sphere of Camiri but in the center of state power itself. Those residing in the "Guarani embassy" who went to work in the cubicles of state reform were still influential political and intellectual figures of the Guarani movement, yet they were now also state functionaries and técnicos. Working alongside Aymara and Quechua scribes created an intercultural and interlinguistic space, to be sure. Yet all three language groups worked with a national curricular template in a cramped cubicle that produced official EIB. Their task was defined as the translation and the contextualization of the national curriculum. In this final portrait of state change, I examine this curricular practice through two textual regimes that served as templates of knowledge, indigenous subjects, and the intercultural state. The first are the new schoolbooks (called modules, *módulos*); the second is education-reform legislation on curricular organization.

Guarani Modules

The reform launched a new series of textbooks called modules. Modules for language, math, and the social sciences were written for three cycles of primary education in four languages, Quechua, Aymara, Guarani, and Spanish. By 2005, fifteen modules in each subject had been written and covered the first and second cycles (six years). Modules were based on the child-centered paradigm called "constructivism" (*constructivismo*), locally referred to as the *enfoque* (the focus, approach). As one reform document states, "[the module design] builds on the autonomous and cooperative work of the children, in accordance with their own level and rhythm of learning" (Las lenguas 1997). Reform staff referred to the enfoque as curricular modernization, juxtaposing it to *conductivismo*, the rote memorization and the teacher-centered approach of the past. Constructivism was visible in the books themselves, which had very little text. Modules were not conceived as depositories of knowledge to be transmitted. Rather, the newly empowered child would learn to construct knowledge with the help of the teacher, relying on vivid images and instructions to make, construct, or produce his or her own texts. This approach moved away from the letter-based or phonemic model of reading instruction and promoted comprehensive-whole reading methods with authentic texts (*textos auténticos*) from an early age.

Authentic texts were to be derived from local experience and knowledge (animal names, local songs, accessible texts like food wrappers or signs) rather than from artificial or contrived borrowings. Other prescriptions included classrooms designed for small-group work instead of children formed in rows of desks; class libraries that encouraged children's independent exploration; work in cycles instead of grades to encourage collaborative learning; and an end to physical punishment. Circulated in training workshops, policy statements, media accounts, and teachers' guides, the progressive bent of the enfoque was crucial to the justification of reform and acknowledged as positive even by vociferous critics of neoliberalism.

Constructivism gave EIB activists a way of justifying interculturalism and indigenous knowledge since indigenous children were no longer seen as bearers of something that had to be erased. Rather, they were little knowledge bearers and producers who had a legitimate base (the known) on which to construct new knowledge (the unknown). Guarani scribes even sometimes argued that constructivism was like their own method of dialogic knowledge exchange and autonomous knowledge production.[15] Yet constructivism was not a particularly indigenous pedagogy. It was an academically based theory that could be cited to defend indigenous language and knowledge, but when embedded in a particular processual and institutional matrix, it did not in itself allow for radically alternative epistemologies. Ideologically flexible, constructivism could as easily defend the creation of the autonomous, self-regulating individual, a very Western understanding of literacy. The Aymara sociologist (later the first education minister from MAS) Felix Patzi (1999) argued that children could easily construct themselves through a transition from the known (indigenous languages) to the unknown (Spanish universalism) as a path to assimilation. For example, as envisioned by the staffer who was a fan of Bill Gates, a child might begin with context (in their own *local* space) and later pass to the construction of new knowledges (via schooling) and the transference of these knowledges to new concrete situations elsewhere (the deterritorialized labor market). In short, the constructivist paradigm was as suited to the creation of flexible labor as it was to the decolonization of knowledge.

In the modules, the enfoque took shape as a dialogue between the universal (national and scientific context) and the local (the indigenous linguistic and cultural context). This legitimated yet contained indigenous knowledge and language as variants of a spatially encompassing state standard. The state was metaphorically represented as a common curricular trunk (*tronco común*). Variations of place, culture, and language were referred to as diversified branches (*ramas diversificadas*) (Albó and Anaya 2003). This paradigm set up criteria for the ascription of legitimacy and authority in the educational field. More than translators yet something less than autonomous producers, the Guarani and other indigenous scribes found themselves in a politically and spatially subordinate role as *contextualizers*. The sovereign authority of the state was reasserted over Guarani knowledge and truncated the incipient autonomies (the reversion of territory, history, and knowledge) emerging during the earlier phase of EIB. Camargo, who worked on the new modules under state supervision, remembered the shift as one away from Guarani culture (*ñande reko*) and toward the pedagogical or technical (G. *mborom-boeete*; S. *lo técnico*).[16] He was not overly critical of the shift, acknowledging that the scribes' early work may have been weak in the pedagogical. Yet the new relationship of authority was clear. An extended excerpt from his reflections in 2005 shows how constructivism and autonomy for children differed quite markedly from indigenous constructions of knowledge and autonomy on a territorial, cultural-political, and epistemological scale:

[In Guarani:] I believe that pedagogy was a bit weak for us [back then], but our strength was *teko* [culture]. Nowadays, when the reform came, with reform the strength was that constructivism, pedagogy, but Guarani ways were weakened there. . . . What the reform said was this: this will be for all of Bolivia, all the same. Guarani culture will be dealt with there [locally]. But they did not give us help to do those things [promote Guarani curricular diversification]. So when they began to write the modules, this teaching toward the outside was what was strong, other cultures were emphasized. True, that would have been fine, but not without a balance between our culture and other cultures, that's no good. So with this, the culture toward the outside was strengthened, and Guarani culture was slowly weakening. True, we still used the language, the new words, the language was still going forward, still strong, our language was no longer going away. . . . But a lot of things were done since the reform said "like this, like this, like this" and we said, but it should be done this way. [Switches to Spanish] "We make the decision," the reform people said, "we make the decision." [Back to Guarani]. But we are the culture masters [*teko iya*], we are the language masters [*ñee iya*].

Camargo separated language as a vehicle from culture as form and content, but the use of the language itself was now subject to a new censorial procedure. Scribes were not free to create their texts in Guarani (or Quechua or Aymara or any of the Amazonian languages). All lessons had to be translated to or from Spanish so that reform staff could approve them. "They said, 'that's OK,' or 'that's not' and sent it back to us. We were now all one [curricular] structure, Quechua, Aymara, Guarani," he said. "The reformists argued for universal knowledge, and we argued that our knowledge is also universal knowledge. That is to say," he summed up for me, switching back again to Spanish, "the reform gave a matrix, and one could only negotiate so far. Back [in Guarani country] we had an indigenous pedagogical matrix under construction."

A cursory comparison of the modules and the books I discussed in chapter 2 illustrates this repositioning. The texts from the earlier era had names like *Eireká* (*Honey Seeker*), *Ararundai* (*Cloudy Sky*, a girl's name), *Kuarasí* (*Sun*); and *Yaeka ñande raïkuere* (*Let Us Find Our Tracks*). The new titles were *Ñeeregua 1, 2, 3 . . .* (*On Language*) or *Papakaregua 1, 2, 3 . . .* (*On Mathematics*), with the same title translated into Spanish, Quechua, and Aymara. The state logo for educational reform (an outline of a school bell) is the only seal on book covers. The phrases "Educational Reform–Bolivia" and "Support Module" are translated into Guarani. There are no references to transnational donors, teachers' unions, or indigenous organizations. The state is positioned as the sovereign arbiter of language and knowledge. Individual Guarani and various nonindigenous experts are credited as contributors, but the APG as a political entity has been erased.

Within the module, curricular form also reflected new visions of knowledge and its subjects. A first-grade module shows children dancing in and around a corncrib. The children are guided by a Guarani woman in a mandu dress and a Guarani man. The page reads, "We have an *arete* festival for the little corncrib," in reference to the harvest celebration. The text and image represent a core cultural practice in Guarani life, the *arete*. Yet little girls play the flute and drum, reversing the gendered and aged norms that make of these activities the domains of adult or young men. The progressive discourse of gender equality here redirected indigenous knowledge and practice. The images to generate discussion guided by the teacher read, "Let us look in the books about food to find writings (recipes) about how to make food" and "Let us read and make food." Here children engage familiar practices like cooking through new modes of textual interpretation and production. Distinct, for instance, from the politically charged use of *food* as a generative word to promote the discussion of land scarcity in the literacy primer, food talk here reveals the enfoque at work as writing recipes, something not immediately familiar to Guarani or rural Bolivian children, the new skill to which children should aspire. To do so children can explore the resources at their disposal (ideally a classroom library) and generate new oral and written texts based on their observations.

As usual, the Guarani seemed less critical of all this than me. They took the work, well paid, as bringing them a step closer to assuring the permanence of EIB as state policy. The modules were not wholly depoliticized, and Guarani language and historical visions certainly made their way in. They included texts about the violence of Kuruyuki, stories about the Guarani arete carnival and about reciprocity and solidarity, and discussions of Guarani spirit owners and ancestors. The new modules put interculturalism into practice since they furthered an (unequal) epistemological dialogue and, compared to conductivist modes, constituted a leap forward from the past. Yet native languages were forced into the straitjacket of a standardized curriculum. In an extended critique of the reform, Denise Arnold and Juan de Dios Yapita (2006) argue that EIB effectively privileged a Western, text-centric notion of literacy that erased or displaced locally rooted practices of knowledge production and exegesis. This is partially true at the textual level. Yet the politically weighty issue here concerns less text centricity than the wider process that detached EIB from indigenous movement praxis. For the Guarani, the officialization of EIB and the scribes' relocation to La Paz had a weakening effect on EIB back in Guarani country. This did not result from one or another focus in the textbooks, but from scribes' geographical and institutional detachment from local processes. Arnold and Yapita seem to suggest that EIB could be remedied if texts were only written with more attention to cultural and linguistic authenticity. I, on the other hand, argue that the spatial and political orders embedded in textual production as a political and intellectual process are more central. As Camargo conceded to me reflecting on the old days, "we used to talk with the true knowledge masters about these things [and] we were just the ones who put it on paper; the real knowledge masters [*arakuaa iya*] were in the communities." In La Paz, the process was far removed from territorially situated social and episte- mological worlds.

Curriculum and Context

For Ernest Gellner, a shared cognitive orientation and communicative skills constituted the means and ends of successful nation building: "But," he wrote, "some organism must ensure that this literate and unified culture is indeed being effectively produced, that the educational product is not shoddy and sub-standard. Only the state can do this, and, even in countries in which important parts of the educational machine are in private hands or those of religious organizations, the state does take over quality control in this most important of industries, the manufacture of viable and usable human beings" (1983:38). Control of schools and teachers proved central to this, making the state's "monopoly of legitimate education . . . more central than is the monopoly of legitimate violence" (34). Though Gellner's some- what dated formulation still imagined nation-building to be at the core of quality control, neoliberal globalization replicated the centralizing and stan- dardizing logic. As Nelly Stromquist observed,

> the special role of education under globalization will be subject to contra- dictory expectations. On the one hand, it must serve to provide both basic and advanced skills. On the other hand, it must do so at minimum cost to the state. Arguments about the decentralization of state power will generate a profusion of forms of educational institutions, yet the prefer- ence for the development of identities friendly to market economies will press educational systems and programs toward greater uniformity. In consequence, substantial tensions may be expected between local and global expressions in the educational field. (2002:16–17)

The idea of interculturalism seemed to break down the old-fashioned Gellnerian model of the nation-state built on a "unified culture." Yet in a state like Bolivia, fraught with instability and pursuing an illusory sover- eignty, neoliberal intercultural education shaped by global flows generated new tensions and paradoxes. EIB made for a modest proposal in this sense. Far from weakening the state as nervous elites feared, EIB repositioned the state as the arbiter of knowledge with control over indigenous and nonindigenous knowledges in its space. Reformists and their supporters acquiesced to EIB precisely for this promised containment of something that was still opaque, indigenous tongues. Yet there was still a risk of too much context, that pesky epistemological and contestative locality that elites hoped would stay in its place. This idea reflected wider colonial fears about unraveling racial privilege: that EIB would become a vehicle for radicalization and reverse racism, spinning out of state control into indigenous *revanchismo* (revenge seeking), a fear that plagues Bolivia as much as it does Guatemala, the other indigenous-majority country in the hemisphere (D. Nelson 1999:1; Hale 2006).

In the era of the transnationalized state, this fear of, and desire for protection from, context reflected shared concerns of state elites and bank monitors. The message was: Watch out for too much "I" and "B" of EIB. Just three years into the reform, the World Bank voiced this colonial concern, again couched in the ironic language of centralized Gellnerian sovereignty over quality control:

> With respect to the concern that too much emphasis was being given to cultural diversity, and less to contents of a universal nature, a common curricular trunk has been developed which is now present in the program. It is under discussion in which form the design of contents that reflect cultural diversity will now be taken up: if this is to be left for local communities or to the Districts, or if it will be the role of the technicians of the reform team. The Mission [the banks and donors] recommends that *even when there is an open space left for the teachers and the community to introduce their interests, that attention be paid to the establishment of clear criteria for the definition of local contents, so that these are related in organic form with the contents of the common trunk.* (World Bank 1998b; emphasis added)

As Nelly Stromquist (2002) predicted, and despite neoliberal paeans to local autonomy and participation, the common curricular trunk and the programs for its application, evaluation, and permanent updating became recentralized. The autonomy of local parents and communities was contained. These were the limits of interculturalism, stuck between the decentralizing mantra of neoliberalism, the individualizing discourse of self-regulation, and the centralizing needs of a totalizing form of market-friendly governance.[17] The standardizing urge of the market attacked the idea of a strong state by celebrating the individual consumer, but it required a strong centralized state, especially in the validation and control of credentialed knowledge, to sustain the discursive regimes within which the self-regulating consumer-laborer comes to see the system as legitimate. In Bolivia this involved reproducing the colonial hierarchies of place, knowledge, race, and language. Against the fears that EIB might break apart the state, I am simply pointing out that as implemented between 1994 and 2005, it proved disruptive more in the imaginaries of criollo elites than in the actual shape it took in practice.

Indigenous intellectuals argued instead that the state should be reimagined, so that diverse languages and knowledges could find a space within a state articulated across differences rather than homogeneity. This was in part the meaning of plurinationalism, a concept increasingly offered by indigenous people when talking of a new Bolivia beyond interculturalism. Nonetheless, it should be clear that some national control—that is, sovereignty—was useful, even if it proved constraining to the Guarani and other indigenous peoples. On the one hand, it guaranteed their right to a distinct education against powerful regional (and national) elites. It also, ideally, promised the public resources needed to carry out this education. Note Camargo does not criticize any absorption into national curricular templates, but rather the imbalance between those forms and the search for and funding of a Guarani pedagogical matrix. In exchange for this access to state capital and public education, Guarani ceded aspirations to radical epistemological autonomy. Yet it was an unequal exchange with the Bolivian state, which made much of its intercultural opening and plastered the Guarani and other indigenes on Web sites, posters, and billboards.

When Goni and his cabinet acquiesced to EIB, it was for the sake of stability, not of indigenous transformative agendas. Goni's support suggested what Paul Willis (1977), in his classic study of schooling and working-class culture, called a "wager of uncertainty." As Willis argued, mass education was a field where the reproduction of power was disputed rather than seamlessly attained. Elites made wagers of uncertainty by creating systems of mass education that—like EIB and constructivism—granted "potentially real freedoms." Yet elites could only hope they would "receive back a minimum consent for rule" (175–76). In fact, the openings to interculturalism ultimately represented insufficient overtures to difference.

These reflections set the stage for understanding the ongoing politics of knowledge that I examine in chapters 6 and 7. Chapter 6 shows how interculturalism was never just an issue of classrooms, context, and curriculum but was also constructed through creative and contestative political practice. Given the remarkable political upheaval that brought an indigenous-friendly government to power in 2005, chapter 7 explores how this development has not immediately translated into a radical embrace of EIB, but rather a radical polarization of ethnic and regional tensions and new challenges to the decolonizing project.

Part Three　　**RETURN TO STRUGGLE**

La Indiada, como para Dar Miedo

On a visit to La Paz in January 1998, I made my rounds through the education reform offices, catching up on news. The right-wing ADN was in power, with the former dictator Hugo Bánzer serving as president. Education reform continued apace, but critiques of EIB were on the rise. The vice-minister of education, Amalia Anaya, told me that her boss, the minister of education, Tito Hoz de Vila, knew nothing of EIB and cared little for Indians. Staffers said that Andean indigenous communities were questioning EIB. The production of Spanish-language modules was running behind schedule, and indigenous communities were said to wonder whether this was a tactic to keep them from learning Spanish.[1] Uncertainty about EIB was palpable. I stopped in at the scribes' cubicle to chat with the Guarani writers. They asked me what was new in Camiri, rather than the other way around. We speculated whether Guarani might take control of a new bilingual teachers' institute in Camiri. Nonetheless, higher-ups were secretive about restructuring plans for teacher training. It was a political hornets' nest of national proportions. I walked up to the next floor where a Paceña friend worked in the art department. She showed me her latest drawings for the modules, which were quite beautiful. She also spoke of uncertainty. The word among the staff, she told me, was that EIB was *k'encha*. K'encha, an Aymara word used in Bolivian Spanish, was a bird that marked a bad omen, or someone or something jinxed, bewitched, doomed to fail.

Maybe I was k'encha too, or so seemed my trip back to Camiri. The annual Guarani commemoration of Kuruyuki was to start on January 26. I was anxious to get out of the bustle of La Paz and back to the quieter Chaco. A flight got me to the wind-swept plains of Santa Cruz in an hour. There movement slowed. With no money for a chartered plane, I took a shuttle from the airport to Santa Cruz's central bus terminal, then a chaotic urban nightmare. Buses to Camiri left from one side of the station. Honking taxis and small microbuses pushed their way through narrow, litter-strewn streets. Small beer halls spilled tired drinkers out onto the sidewalk, while music blared to reel them back in. Competing bus lines hawked tickets, and young men hurried back and forth tossing cargo up onto roof racks. Passengers waited in the scrum with luggage, bags of grain, and baskets and crates wrapped in cloth and sewn shut. Now and then a chicken's head poked through a bag, clucking angrily at the chaos. In the mostly karai crowd, quiet Guarani faces could be spotted, perhaps heading south after work in the city. Heavy-set Aymara women in the abundant *pollera* skirt of the Andean chola were also present, standing guard over huge bags of goods being taken south for sale. They contrasted with lean Chaqueño farmers in cowboy hats and sandals carrying flour-sack shoulder bags. Wealthier Camiri folk waited too, set apart by nice clothes and the suvs that dropped them off. With sunglasses and polished shoes they stood talking loudly in the evening heat. I worked my way through the hubbub to find a ticket, settling on a bus scheduled for a 7:30 p.m. departure.

The bus did not inspire confidence. Nonetheless, bags were loaded, the hour arrived, and the driver punctually honked his horn. Passengers crowded around the door and into the narrow stairwell to board. I lifted my ticket and laptop bag above my head to make my way to my seat, squeezed in the aisle amid what seemed an especially aggressive crowd. A man smiled at me, joking about the "traffic." Oddly, he was trying to get out of the bus. I nodded and smiled back, finally settling into my seat. After we rolled out of the station I discovered that someone had relieved me of a wad of cash that I was carrying in a front pocket. The friendly jokester had orchestrated it flawlessly with a gang of pickpockets who had boarded with the passengers, probably complicit with the driver. Another passenger lost a wallet, but that was only slight consolation. As the bus rolled out of the city, I imagined the pick-pockets drinking away my money at the station and cursed my stupidity. If EIB was k'encha maybe it had rubbed off on me.

By eleven the bus had made some progress and was pulling out of Abapó, a town just north of the Rio Grande. A historical bastion of Guarani resistance to colonial expansion out of Santa Cruz, Abapó was now a dusty karai settlement built around the junction of the highway and railroad where trains and vehicles shared a long one-lane trestle bridge across the river. Traffic from either side took turns crossing, bouncing over loose wooden planks and straddling the railroad tracks down the middle. Our bus was lurching over the iron rails to make its way onto the bridge just as a loud pop sounded below. The driver stopped abruptly, the bus tilting awkwardly half on, half off the tracks. Passengers poured out, and the driver shined his flashlight on a rear wheel, cockeyed on the axle like a broken Matchbox car. This was definitely k'encha.

With the bus stuck on the track, travelers traded speculation about what time the night train from Santa Cruz to Argentina would pass through. Still swearing at the pickpockets, I peered nervously into the darkness to the north. Images played through my mind: the light of an oncoming train, horn blasting, passengers fleeing madly, train, bus, and bridge smashed into a heap and plunged into the river. I stepped back further from the tracks with my small bag. At least my laptop and field notes were safe.

After a couple of hours our k'encha luck turned. The driver announced the wheel fixed, and we reboarded. I held my breath as we bounced over the planks toward the other side. There we regained the rutted dirt road and rocked along for several miles. When the bus was well into a long stretch of empty countryside, far from what counted for civilization out here, the pop sounded again and a collective groan arose. Some passengers resigned themselves to sleep. Others, myself included, made their way outside. Dark Chaco nights are usually marked by a profusion of stars in the absence of city lights. As luck would have it, a light misty rain that Guarani call *jaivi* had set in. It was still cooler outside, so I sat down in a dry spot under the back of the bus. Heroically ignoring the mist and the rapidly muddying road, the chubby, coca-chewing driver and his helper labored over the wheel with an assortment of improvised, increasingly slippery tools. He cursed and groaned with his butt exposed like that of a plumber under a sink, alternating between pushing, tugging, and beating on the wheel. Sometime before dawn he announced it fixed again, so we clambered aboard, and he cranked the engine with ceremony. The bus lurched forward. After fifty yards or so the pop sounded a third time. The driver gave a look of surrender, and I went to sleep.

At daybreak the bus heated up under the rising sun and passengers bailed out again. We all peered north up a dreadfully silent dirt road and speculated about alternative transport. Back in the shade behind the bus, I shared cigarettes and complaints with some karai farmers. Eventually the conversation found its way to my work in Camiri. Usually any mention of Guarani organizing in such small talk unplugged fears about Guarani protagonism in the region. I dissimulated and answered with a standard line: "I work in education, with the Guarani." True enough.

"These *jochis*!" spat one fellow. *Jochis* are agoutis (G. *akuti*), a crop-eating rodent slightly larger than a guinea pig. My mention of Guarani had brought to mind the indigenous Weenhayek of the Villamontes area, his home. His frankness perhaps meant he saw me as an unfortunate employee of some agency forced to work with Indians.

> These *jochis*! They [the government] are giving them land, and they don't even want to progress. Look at the Matacos [Weenhayek] in Palmar [a town near Villamontes]. They work two or three days and then disappear. Jaime Paz [Zamora, the former president] gave them one hundred thousand hectares, and they just hunt parrots; they don't even plant. The missionaries have done a lot to civilize them, but they are *dañinos, perjuiciosos* [damaging, destructive]; they will cut down a whole tree just to get a piece of fruit.[2]

Dañino and *perjuicioso*: damaging and destructive like the jochi. Out here indigenous peoples were seen as subhuman obstacles to progress, coddled by a government conceding them huge land grants (or so it was imagined). Shaking his head, another passenger chimed in. "These *pata-anchas* [wide-feet]! I saw a Guarani who worked at TEKO. I'm sure his shoes split open when he tried to put those *pata anchas* in them." His joke suggested that Guarani in Camiri were out of place, wearing shoes and working in office jobs when their bodies were better suited for rural labor.

The first man finished off a laugh with the word "*mierrrda . . .* shiiiitttt," trailing off into the air. I tried to steer the conversation back to our shared misfortune, yet they lingered on the Guarani. The first man started in again. "Were you here in '92?" he asked me. Without prompting he invoked the first Kuruyukɨ commemoration, when the Guarani launched the 1992 bilingual literacy campaign. The huge public Guarani mobilization was the "rising from the ashes" that we all celebrated.

"No," I answered honestly. I was hurrying back for the 1998 commemoration, but I kept that to myself. My fellow traveler was less enthralled about Kuruyukɨ, Guarani resurgence, and 1992. "Puta mierda," he answered, flicking his cigarette into the ditch beside the road, "¡se juntó la indiada como para dar miedo!" (Whore [and] shit! The Indian hordes gathered in a way that could strike fear in you).

I let the conversation drop and made a mental note: jochis, pata-anchas, dañinos, perjuiciosos, indiada, mierda, miedo—rodents, wide-feet, damaging, harmful, hordes, shit, fear. None of this seemed very intercultural. EIB, k'encha, neoliberal, or otherwise, seemed a decolonizing miracle given such nervous anti-Indian sentiment. I looked up the dirt road to the north wishing for a truck to appear. My k'encha misfortune finally broke when a Toyota Land Cruiser rumbled by, slowing as it passed. An NGO acquaintance was at the wheel, and I waved him down. Offering luck, suerte, to the karai travelers, I asked the bus driver about my bag on the roof. Sweating over his tire, he shrugged, so I climbed up to get it, tossed it onto the Land Cruiser, and squeezed in to finish the trip NGO-style.

Chapter Six

INSURGENT CITIZENSHIP

Interculturalism beyond the School

M y fellow bus travelers, karai Bolivians of the region, feared indigenous resurgence (in the form of land claims, special attention from
government, or the occupation of urban jobs). Interculturalism nationally
and resurgence locally were unsettling to both power holders and nonindigenous citizens. This unsettledness created a sense of disorder, and disorder threatened to expose real and imagined violence—that which formed
part of everyday (unequal) social relations, and that imagined to reside just
beneath the skin of every indigenous body. I did not see my Guarani friends
as wide-footed *jochis*, nor did I imagine my interests opposed to or margin-
alized by theirs, and thus I did not share the visceral response of my fellow
travelers. Furthermore, I saw official interculturalism as distinctly unthreat-
ening and its effects exaggerated. By the late 1990s, I felt hard pressed to
find a school where EIB was thriving. Land reform did not restructure power
relations. Indigenous individuals had made inroads into municipal politics,
yet elite parties were still firmly in charge. Why then this sense of rising
fear and tension?

In the previous two chapters I argued that one reading of reformism
revealed new disciplinary effects of managerial technologies, while another
showed how interculturalism produced fear, uncertainty, and nervousness
among elites. Here I follow a similar approach to consider the ongoing
meanings and forms of indigenous resurgence in Guarani country. On the
one hand, bureaucratization and the relocation of the scribes as knowledge
producers weakened local EIB activism, suggesting that the epistemic insurgence was losing steam. This was a time about which the scribe Silvia
Chumiray reflected, "When the reform came, it was like a setback in the

whole process of EIB, just when it was on the verge of blossoming. Instead of helping us as we expected, the state actually sent us backward" (interview, August 1998). On the other hand, Guarani protagonism outside—but in reference to—schooling and EIB was intensifying. Foreign gas companies had begun to arrive, mobilizing new pressures and interests for leaders. Land struggles, given elite opposition to land reform implementation, were also intensifying. Indian inroads into municipal politics—a visible and radical shift to local karai eyes—began to unsettle the traditionally exclusionary patterns of mainstream parties. These were processes that together generated potential for transformative interculturalism and/or, as they rubbed against recalcitrant interests, backlash.

Borrowing the notion of "insurgent citizenship" (Holston 1999), this chapter illustrates how the Guarani deployed talk of education and its counterpart, violence, to claim and transform public space through the performance of alternative models of citizenship in practice. Education, I argue, beyond classrooms and texts, constituted a crucial mediating nexus through which the Guarani mobilized and sought to manage unsettled fears and tensions among regional karai. The significance of education, both in its intercultural and colonial meanings, remained central to movement representations internally and externally, even as Guarani knowledge production had, for the moment, been institutionally contained by education reform. The implication is that epistemic resurgence continued apace, but did so within terms channeled through locally resonant national(ist), regionalist, and popular histories, rather than primarily as alternative epistemological agendas.

I juxtapose three scenes to make the argument. The first is a Guarani school, the others large-scale movement events in 1998: the public commemoration of the Massacre of Kuruyuki and a Guarani hunger strike, the first of several such strikes that since then have become a core tool in Guarani repertoires of contention.[1] Both were staged on the eve of the economic and political crisis that began to unravel the neoliberal project. They reveal the beginnings of a broader surge of indigenous and social movement power amid signs of a rising backlash against interculturalism from those opposed to the decolonizing turn (Gustafson 2002).

In mid-1997 I went to visit the school in La Brecha, a Guarani town in Ɨsoso. I hoped to sit in on classes to observe teachers working with new modules. I was also helping organize the Ñeerokɨ language congress that year and used the visit to deliver invitations to the school's non-Guarani principal.

The principal and her staff were three Spanish nuns. As part of a long-standing *convenio*, or charter-type arrangement, the Catholic Church ran many Bolivian public schools with state monies and staffed them with national and foreign church personnel.[2] It was my impression that most church actors supported indigenous rights, so I waltzed into the office with a cheerful "Buen día." As I explained the nature of my visit, I was greeted with distinctly unfriendly Castilian accents as the sisters revealed their scorn for EIB. At the elementary level, one said, "it was senseless. What good would Guarani do these kids if they went to the university?" Besides, another added, "There aren't any texts in Guarani." Bolivian karai teachers had rational if racist reasons to oppose EIB. But I was surprised to hear the nuns speaking in similar terms. Bilingual education clearly undercut the authority of those who made no effort to learn Guarani or to appreciate its beauty. They continued in rapid-fire defensiveness, "In addition"—as if to say, worse yet—"those who have been in bilingual education in elementary levels come to junior high ill-equipped for Spanish." And—worst of all—"if you don't have literature, you don't have any reason to learn to read in Guarani!" They rallied in defense of what anti-EIB editorialists invoke as the "language of Cervantes." That an American and three Spaniards could sit arguing about how the Guarani should be educated suggested how far decolonization had yet to go.

Nonetheless, some Isoseño Guarani leaders had also distanced themselves from EIB and the Camiri-based APG. There was a historical dialect rivalry, to be sure. But more important, Ɨsoso leadership was involved in the management of a U.S.-funded national park and entangled in new alliances with the city of Santa Cruz and its satellite, Charagua. As with the Guarani of Ɨtɨka, geopolitics, other priorities, and the centrifugal effects of different development projects contributed to the multipolar character of pan-Guarani mobilizing. One Isoseño intellectual I had known for many years—and who was an early EIB activist—had of late begun to argue that EIB constituted a form of marginality. They did not want "special education," he told me. They wanted "education as good or better than the karai." This explained in part how the attitudes of the nuns could persist in a region known for its proud use of Guarani.

Having secured the begrudged permission of the nuns to observe class, I extracted myself from the disagreeable conversation and stepped out into the bright morning sunlight. Unlike Itavera's little one-room school, the large L-shaped structure here had a number of classrooms with real doors, a tin roof, glass windows, and a wide concrete playground with a steel flagpole. A young Guarani teacher in white uniform was overseeing the start of the day. She rang a real bell, and rambunctious children ran to line up in front of her, all with frocks that passed as uniforms. Under the watchful eyes of the nuns she faced the children. She held a long, thin stick, the infamous *palo* associated with the old kind of schooling. As my old friend Tüi had in Itavera, she scolded the children to line up: "Pesɨmbi! Pesɨmbi!" After a brief lecture in Guarani about good behavior and the importance of studying, she dismissed them to begin the school day. Guarani might not be suited for literature, thought the nuns, but like karai ranchers they had no qualms about the language's suitability for keeping order.

I had come to visit Petrona, an Isoseña, and Mateo, an Ava, both bilingual Guarani teachers in training. They met at the teachers' institute in Camiri and married across the much-exaggerated Ava-Ɨsoso dialect boundary. During the 1992 literacy campaign, Petrona had been a *kereɨmba* literacy warrior. Now thirty-five, she was working on her teacher's degree. Like all Guarani, she had experienced education as a struggle: a few early years in a village school, followed by a few years of work; a chance return to school when her parents migrated to Santa Cruz; then a first marriage; weaving hammocks to support children; separation and return to Ɨsoso; a chance to study with a Catholic NGO; then the literacy campaign; finally finishing a high-school degree through night and radio classes; then entering the teachers' institute with UNICEF aid. And now, at thirty-five, a second marriage.

In a previous interview, Petrona had spoken eloquently about EIB. Her memories of schooling were typical: an abusive teacher, quiet, scared children, and rules against speaking in "our language" (*ñande ñee*). She juxtaposed this against "what we do now." "Even the older Guarani leaders can know what is going on in the school when we [teachers] speak our language," she argued. Petrona believed bilingual education (*yemboe*) would give children knowledge (*arakuaa*). Underlying this was what all Guarani sought, to be able to "speak without shame," in a kind of intercultural existential space of well-being where linguistic alterity and other differences coexisted in the absence of humiliation. Shame, -*mara*, often cropped up in talk of Guarani mobilizing.[3] In her rich, rapid-fire Isoseño Guarani, Petrona expressed her ideas as new truths validated by her firsthand "seeing" and "watching": "I am seeing it happen, these little ones will become defined by *arakuaa* in/through their language [emphatic], so they will no longer be ashamed to speak! They no longer have shame [G. -*mara*]. I am watching it happen. That is why this *yemboe* is a good thing."

Back on the school courtyard, her husband Mateo called me to his first-grade classroom.[4] I followed the children as they crowded into the room laughing and shouting. Mateo spoke Guarani with a skill admired by less fluent speakers of the language. He greeted the children with a jovial, "Good morning, my little daughters, my little sons!" He laughed as I made my way through the throng of little ones. "Imachi no?" (They are monkeylike aren't they?)[5] They slowly settled into their chairs organized around hexagonal tables. This was a sign of reform: no more rows of desks facing an all-powerful teacher. Nor did Mateo wield a stick.

I moved to the back and took a seat. The walls were covered with papers and pictures labeled with Guarani text. Mateo had dutifully created the "lettered classroom" called for by education reform. A response to the scarcity of public text in rural areas, these stimuli were deemed crucial by reformists to make children readers of their surroundings. Mateo was working from the module *Ñeeregua 1* (*On Language 1*), the first written by the Guarani scribes in La Paz. As prescribed by the constructivist *enfoque*, students were building on what they already knew and using authentic texts derived from their own context. Mateo's students had learned to identify their written names and the words for domestic animals with which they were familiar (goats, chickens, pigs, dogs). That morning they practiced new word recognition building on the knowledge of their bodies. They traced their hands, sang hokeypokey-type songs, and talked about body parts and functions, all in Guarani.

As in my own child's preschool in the United States, the activities were designed around student-created projects. Today's was the creation of a song, in Guarani, about the body. The overall sequence—from what is known (the body) to an engagement with new knowledge (unknown written forms) to the collaborative generation of a product (a song)—outlined the underlying pattern of every module lesson. This was how the reform said students learned how to learn and acquired content as well as process to become active and autonomous producers of text.

Mateo applied the lesson energetically, trying to keep the equally energetic children's attention. He pointed out parts of the body saying "Mbaepa kuae?" (What is this?) The children shouted gleefully in Guarani, "Ñaneäka! . . . Ñandeyayu! . . ." (Our head! Our neck!) "And what is our hair for?" A quick-witted child piped up, "To give our lice somewhere to live!" "And what are our eyes for?" "So we can see our path!" "And what is our nose for?" "So we can smell things." And so it went. The module showed a silhouette with parts labeled as isolated words (head, neck, hand). The kids were asked to write the words for each body part, scribbling pretend letters with Mateo's help.

If one focused on linguistic and cultural authenticity, one could easily find weakness in the modules, the product of the constraints and criteria imposed by the técnicos of reform. Beyond the project-based template, which imagined Guarani as individual, order-taking laborers who find pleasure and self-satisfaction in production, there was also a linguistic error in this lesson, the result of the forced translation of Guarani into Spanish molds. Guarani body parts do not exist in isolation (e.g., *äka, head). They must always have a possessor. If spoken of in the abstract (heads in general) the inclusive plural "we" is used, as the children did above (i.e., ñaneäka, our head). Yet the textbook, as in Spanish, called for unpossessed parts. Children disembodied their language, quite literally, as they learned to write and speak of head, arm, and eye (rather than our head, our arm, our eye). Having come to see grammatical forms as a key locus of linguistic alterity to be defended by EIB, I often harped on such errors with Guarani colleagues. My view coupled a defense of linguistic authenticity with disciplinary pedantry inculcated by my own years of grammar-centric schooling. Yet scribes and teachers like Mateo did not overtly worry about such things.[6] What I saw resulting from underdeveloped linguistic militancy, some rationalized as a new mode of speaking for schooling. Others said, "If you can say it in Spanish, you should be able to translate it to Guarani." So Mateo dutifully helped the children write on little papers what in English might be akin to eck, houlder, lbow and eg. The kids stuck the little papers to the silhouette. After about an hour, they began to lose attention and my eyes were drooping, my notes trailing off into illegible scrawl. I was glad when Mateo turned us loose for recess.

Judging from numerous school visits like this, documents produced by reform evaluators, and discussions at the teachers' institute, similar scenes unfolded throughout the region during the late 1990s and early 2000s. Reform had brought change to classrooms. Those concerned with technical and cost-benefit analyses argued that EIB worked. Children got better scores, stayed in school, and learned Spanish (Hyltenstam and Quick 1996; Contreras and Talavera Simoni 2003). For those concerned for social rights, EIB made children into "happy" and "expressive" thinkers (Albó and Anaya 2003).

Even with the flawed modules the shifts were significant. The children's exuberance *was* a far cry from the silence of the past. This was what Petrona meant when she said children could speak out loud without shame. Yet beyond the desire to speak without shame, where was the mobilizing agenda of EIB? Did the work of teachers and the day-to-day labors of EIB now mean little in relation to the Guarani movement? Were these new indigenous militants or indigenous classroom managers? Had Western-style hokey-pokey replaced the Guarani search for a native pedagogy?

SCENE 2: JANUARY 28, REMEMBERING KURUYUKɨ

The answer to these questions does not lie entirely within the schoolroom but rather beyond the school, where the meanings of education intersect other expressions of mobilization. The effects on subject formation in classrooms like Mateo's—and on subjects like Mateo and Petrona themselves— were mingled with and molded by multiple other processes and practices that emerged not from reformist plans but from the varied struggles of life experiences and from movement tactics. As the articulation between the APG and EIB as a *core* field of epistemic struggle was temporarily weakened by reform, the movement was already rearticulating with other dimensions of resurgence through new fields of practice. One of these fields can be seen through the Guarani's annual commemoration of the Kuruyukɨ massacre.

In 1998, in the days leading up to January 28, Guarani delegations from throughout the region began converging on Camiri. As they had every year since 1992, they relied on assistance from NGOs to provide transport and help with room and board in the city. On the morning of January 27, the Guarani staged the first event in Camiri's central plaza. Several hundred Guarani women, men, and young people marched into the square and lined up in neat rows in front of the church. The scene resembled that of a school courtyard, where the children lined up to face the teacher. Guarani were in formation, almost military-style, grouped in blocks by their place of origin. Those in the front row of each section held handmade signs with place names like Itïka (Airase and a contingent from Itavera had also come), Ingre, Villamontes, San Antonio, and so forth. An NGO staffer handed out small paper Bolivian flags, and the red, yellow, and green fluttered in the hands of most Guarani. January in Camiri is hot, as it likely was back in 1892. The Guarani stood quietly under a blazing sun, while karai passers-by gathered to watch from the sidewalks under the shade of trees lining the plaza.

On the steps of the church, one found an array of local authority. Four or five uniformed military officers with close-cropped hair and spit-polished shoes lined up on one end. The balding, spectacled priest was at their side wearing a long brown Franciscan habit and rope belt, straight out of the 1800s. The director of TEKO, the NGO that had long accompanied Guarani mobilizing, stood off to one side. The pot-bellied provincial subprefect, an appointee of the ADN government, stood next to him in spotless white pants. A descendant of Croatian immigrants, the subprefect Drago Pavlovic was a local karaoke bar owner. He had an oversized disco look that fit the role, with meaty arms and hands and a gleaming gold necklace nestled in the hairy expanse of an exposed neckline. Among the state and nonstate authorities also stood Enrique Camargo, the former scribe and now president of the APG. In shirt and slacks, his Guarani features marked him as distinct, yet he quietly established a place amid local power. Huge speakers framed the entire scene, screeching and squawking as the emcee warmed up and tested his microphone.

The event got underway when a choir of Guarani schoolteachers took the stage. In button-down shirts, slacks, and leather shoes, they looked like good Bolivian teachers. The one conducting wore a Ray-Ban sunglasses case on his belt, and he raised his arms as the speakers crackled with the martial-sounding drums, tubas, and trumpets of the national anthem. The Guarani in formation and their karai watchers straightened up a bit when the music started, and the teachers started singing in Guarani. The military officers stood at attention, joining in on the second round when the teachers switched to Spanish. It was the only use of Guarani in the entire ceremony.

Like other Bolivian civic spectacles, which put the state, power, and order on visual display, the main content of this one involved different authorities taking turns making speeches, or *discursos*. The discursos were interspersed with musical interludes of Guarani pipe and drum and the booming voice of a practiced emcee who announced each point on the program. When Camargo took his turn, he spoke in Spanish without a word in Guarani. He described the purpose of the event and ended by situating Guarani mobilization within a frame that went beyond indigenous particularity: "This movement is not just for the Guarani," he said, "but for the entire Chaco region, for the entire country." The invocation of the "land without evil" had become de rigueur in such speeches, and he used it with flourish. "This means that the land without evil is not just for the Guarani, but for the whole society. We have a very clearly marked territory, that of the grand Chaco region, which we will make flower. . . . Now we will walk again toward the land without evil, where justice, solidarity, and love prevail." The Guarani, still standing in formation, applauded quietly.

Education, broadly conceived, was also a trope through which the Guarani could speak safely to karai. Daisy Melgar, then the vice-president of the APG, followed Camargo to the podium. She broke the stereotype of the mandu-clad woman, wearing Western dress like most. As a native of the Spanish-speaking Guarani communities of Yacuiba to the south, she often spoke Guarani with hesitancy. Yet here she spoke only in Spanish, with forceful, carefully selected words. After highlighting the importance of the event, she called on those gathered, especially the young people, to demonstrate their unity. She built up to her concluding remarks, saying: "We want to defend our people as our ancestors did." Here she paused for several seconds. The ancestors, as karai and Guarani all knew, had defended themselves with violence. "Our ancestors," she went on, correcting and containing the image, "they never knew how to read and write. But as young people now are learning more, and we are moving forward with education, it is important [to recognize] that we can no longer fight that way, that is to say," here again she paused as she found her words, "with," and she paused again, "with weapons [*armas*]. Rather, with the right kind of learning, we will be able to carry our education and our struggle forward. Thank you." The crowd applauded again, and a group of Guarani musicians took the stage behind her.

In the interim, the emcee read from a script: "The Guarani people are advancing in every way. Almost all of them now know how to read and write." For karai, I surmise, this could be interpreted ambiguously—as a positive sign of domestication or a troubling sign of rising claims for equality. I panned my video camera across the stage and picked up one of the military officers, head bent over, busy taking notes on a small notebook. The priest gazed toward the sky, hands clasped at his waist. Camargo also had his head tilted over, whispering to Pavlovic. He later told me he was prepping the karai for his remarks. Out among the Guarani in the sun, Airase stood at the head of the Itika contingent. He had on his going-to-town hat and had stuck the little paper Bolivian flag into the hatband. From simba to peon to claimant on citizenship, he stared back toward my camera with an expressionless gaze.

Pavlovic got his last bit of coaching from Camargo and stepped up to the microphone. With light-colored skin, the ruddy face of a heavy drinker, and a huge belly, he could not have been more different from the Guarani. Guarani saw such girth as a sign of wealth and easy living, and compared this kind of body to the *samõu* tree, which had a bulbous trunk that protrudes like a pregnant belly. Pavlovic spoke with hesitant uncertainty. He was clearly unfamiliar with words like *interculturalism* and *bilingual education*. He rarely had occasion to address Guarani as putative equals. He was known for his landholdings (and Guarani laborers) and for having refused Guarani entry into his bar. With the familiar order unsettled, it was clear why he had asked Camargo for coaching on what to say. He was made to speak now, as it were, by a Guarani.

He launched by welcoming the Guarani and pointing out that some were out of place, since they had come from beyond the province (his jurisdiction). Nonetheless, since all were ostensibly embracing education—and thus indirectly acknowledging the government of which he was a part—he latched on to education as the linchpin between rulers and ruled. "We see the new educational policies of the government, the educational reform that permits the education not just of young people but also of adults. It permits the bilingual interculturalization [*sic*], the. . . ." Here he paused, tongue-tied by *interculturalism*, a word he had probably never uttered in his life. He corrected himself and started again, "The exchange of cultural. . . ." Again he had talked himself into a corner. He restarted. "Because we are a pluri-cultural people." I exhaled sympathetically. Like Daisy with her "weapons," he had finally got something out. "Because we are a pluricultural people, we have assumed the responsibility to represent all Bolivians. This government is going to do it. That's why we feel satisfied to see your organization and its purposes."

Such were the tentative transformations of the new languages of the state, an exercise in hesitant, tension-ridden exchange. Pavlovic, however, re-covered his momentum when he turned away from interculturalism toward familiar ground. "But all of this must occur within Christian codes, ethics, the exchange of dialogue. Nothing justifies aggression! Nothing justifies any kind of action that brings the loss of human lives!" Beneath the façade of neoliberal interculturalism lay an anxiety-ridden social order. Behind the expressionless gaze of Airase, the flowery rhetoric of Camargo, the hesitant invocations of Daisy, and the clumsy acknowledgment of difference by Pav-lovic, a new Bolivia was confronting the older one.

This Was Our Land!

After the speeches ended, the Guarani left Camiri and were trucked south-ward toward Ivo, near the Kuruyuki battlefield. The next day, on January 28, the events would unfold there in a different setting. Several thousand Gua-rani, many more than had come to Camiri, gathered in the *oka*, the large open space of Guarani communities. A stage occupied one end, flanked by a huge banner showing a Guarani woman in mandu and a Guarani man with his head wrapped simba style. On top of a nearby hill stood the old mission, built in 1893 to contain the survivors of the massacre. Scripting what might have been said by Pavlovic a century later, in 1898 the Italian priest Doroteo Giannecchini (1996:230) wrote of the Guarani at the Ivo mission: "There are many difficulties that one must confront at the beginning of a mission that lacks everything except barbarous and savage people, people who first must be made rational, so that they can later be made into Christians, artisans, and citizens."

Against this historical backdrop, the captain of Ivo, Valerio Mena, played host to those assembled. A handsome, copper-skinned man, Valerio was a skilled Guarani orator. He held the microphone close to his mouth, eyes flashing as he leaned slightly forward to speak, one hand open at his side, a silver ring shining on his finger as protection against sorcery. This was Guarani country, and he spoke in Guarani with no translation.

> This day of remembering has come to us, and it comes with great pain
> [-jasɨ].[7]
> On a day like this one, at a time like this, our ancestors spilled their blood!
> That is what we are remembering! They spilled their blood right out
> here!
> But they did not spill their blood in vain.
> Now we have come together again.
> The karai could not disperse [-moai] us forever.[8]
> Kuruyukɨ will never happen again!

A young Guarani radio reporter held a tape recorder behind Valerio, capturing his words for later rebroadcast. Other leaders surrounded him on stage. There were no karai authorities. A sea of Guarani sat and stood around the field, no longer under surveillance, no longer in formation, listening to the words.

> And you young people will also become part of this movement.
> Truly this memory is painful to us. But it has given us strength.
> This memory is part of knowledge [arakuaa] left to us.
> Our ancestors knew this when they defended the land.
> They knew not to let us forget.
> We are many gathered again here today, we are from many different
> places,
> yet we are all standing here as one, we are living as one large family.
> On a day like this, in broad daylight, our ancestors suffered and fought,
> so that we might live, and so that we would use this land!
> But it will never be like that again.
> We now have education [yemboe], and through it you young people will
> come to know.
> We have our own teachers, they will give knowledge [arakuaa] to our
> children who are coming after us.

We should put these words into our being [*ñandepɨa*].[9]

We will repeat them again to the children, and they will do so again in the future.

. . .

Thank you, I am happy, we are happy.

That is that [*Jae jokuae*].

He ended in classic Guarani style, closing with a sense of unity, goodwill, and cheer, not of rancor and bitterness, with the simple "jae jokuae." That's that.

Following the 1992 March to Kuruyukɨ, the APG staged commemorations like this one every year. They continued to gain in significance and often served as meeting grounds between the Guarani and national authorities, including Jaime Paz Zamora (1992), Goni (1994), representatives of the MAS (2005), and Evo Morales himself (2008). The symbolic power of the events as loci for performing Guarani regional authority and territoriality is such that the narrative of Kuruyukɨ (and the date January 28) have been targeted for co-optation by the karai oligarchs of Santa Cruz, fearful of alternative centers of power within their orbit (Lowrey 2006).

The events also have a functional role in relation to the organization. They are staged as inaugural ceremonies at which newly elected officers are sworn in each year. They represent one of the few moments at which the collective reality of the APG as a movement is made visible for karai and Guarani audiences on a large scale. These are moments of public interethnic dialogue and encounter, as well as of collective self-representation and, as Guarani call it, of "remembering" (see figures 5 and 6).

In the urban space, where many karai fear that Guarani mobilization is a precursor to violence, the Guarani perform order, nationalism, and loyalty, much as they do at school. The ceremony acknowledged power (military, religious, civil, and NGO), while slowly transforming the position of the Guarani therein. A colonial version of indigenous evolution was highlighted to make this comprehensible to karai, yet beyond there are insurgent claims on space and public discourse. Interculturalism itself was a language through which the Guarani sought to *omboe*, to teach local karai like Pavlovic, to make them speak in new terms. The Guarani also modified their own claims to alterity, voicing interests shared with karai, especially the regionalist sentiment of the Chaco.

FIGURE 5 To walk among the karai. Guarani march into Camiri for the 1994 commemorations. Note the statue of the Guarani warrior, bow drawn, in the background.

FIGURE 6 El Plan de Todos. Gonzalo "Goni" Sánchez de Lozada (at left, speaking) visited the Guarani commemoration of Kuruyuki in 1994 to announce his three reforms: decentralization, land reform, and bilingual intercultural education. Compared to 1998, it was a time of rapprochement with the government.

In the more Guarani setting near the battlefield, eloquent speech evoked strong emotions and sketched a uniquely Guarani narrative of resurgence. Rather than the imaginary of the violent Guarani threat and paeans to literacy as evolution, the memories here are of karai violence and Guarani recovery of history, land, and memory, in short of epistemic and territorial authority. Education out here is understood not as a means of performing order, but as a vehicle for Guarani contestative memory, a way to rearticulate a history fragmented by the violence of Kuruyuki and to struggle for a new social order. The Guarani resignify one expression of colonialism (schooling) as a means of resolving another (violence).

In both cases we see beyond the façade of orderly resurgence the anxieties produced by the unsettling of the colonial order, what the Bolivian social historian Silvia Rivera Cusicanqui refers to as the "hidden violences" of colonialism (1993:123–24, 126): "The potential violence is an invisible . . . violence, which is present in the ways that collective identities are constructed in Bolivia. [It is] a constitutive process tied to processes of cultural disciplining [that] affects all cultural processes; in particular the formation of collective identities." EIB nonetheless plays a mediating and moderating role. *Bilingual* and *intercultural* posit a palatable notion of citizenship through difference, while *education* offers a counterpoint against specters of potential violence and the language of orderly citizenship.

Unlike in other contexts, such as Brazil, where displays of radically, often explicitly warlike indigenousness or linguistic alterity are deployed for the recognition or defense of "existential space" (Graham 2005; Turner 1991), in this particular setting the Guarani have elected for performances that mimic Bolivian visual and aural displays of legitimacy, space, citizenship, and power, calling on national frames, as in some Mexican cases (Stephen 1997). Yet by juxtaposing performances for karai and Guarani audiences, I show how code switching and speaking across multiple registers that characterize modes of survival and accommodation for colonial subjects perform both loyalty to order and an assertive, insurgent sense of legitimate authority alongside and against existing structures of power. Even on stage in Camiri, as in schools and in schoolbooks, these rites are more than just translations: they are constitutive transformations, enactments of an emergent intercultural citizenship in practice. With the Guarani on the stage, the stage itself is transformed.

In May, just four months after the Kuruyuki event, eleven Guarani and two karai working at the teachers' institute quietly walked into the Catholic church on Camiri's plaza. There they unrolled blankets on the floor and declared themselves on hunger strike. The Guarani included two women and eight men in their early twenties, all studying to be bilingual teachers. The two karai were rural schoolteachers affiliated with the union, but now teaching alongside the Guarani. An older Guarani leader named Felipe Román joined them. Familiar for his work with the APG as a kind of leader at large, Román (quoted in chapter 4) was a pioneer of Guarani mobilization in the 1970s and 1980s. That experience landed him in a military jail during the García Meza dictatorship. He was beaten and lost most of his front teeth to rifle butts, leaving him with a toothless grin and a smoldering temper. Román of late had been collaborating with another leader at large, Guido Chumiray. Both had experience in the language and practice of popular struggle and functioned as the intellectual catalysts of the action.

The hunger strike is a ubiquitous sign of the contestative nature and practice of citizenship in Bolivia. It emerged through many decades of corporatist and movement struggle defined largely by a logic of blockade and petition. But this was the first time that any Guarani—as Guarani—had staged a hunger strike. It was also the first time that anything tied to bilingual education had been performed as political protest, situated as it was within the aid and state process of reform that the Guarani had supported for nearly a decade. Now, however, local leaders sought to (re)inscribe a different kind of meaning onto EIB, one infused with a deeper tradition of popular movement struggle and contestative citizenship, rather than with that of the docile Guarani shown happily reading on the Web site of reform.[10]

Camiri had seen prior strikes of karai teachers and the region's once powerful oil workers, who often struck in their union offices. Yet for the Guarani, the church had high visibility in the center of Camiri, and churches were sometimes occupied for hunger strikes as they offered an aura of sacredness and some security against attack. This complemented the meaning of hunger strikes themselves, which perform a moral claim based on suffering against an unjust state refusing its obligations to its citizenry. Having little to do with explicit indigeneity, hunger strikes are part of national repertoires of contention that index belonging in a broader historical trajectory of contestative citizenship. Hunger strikes make for one way that citizen rights of diverse class-based sectors can be exercised collectively against elites. In provincial towns like Camiri, strikes previously also played out in an idiom of locality as the region could be framed as a collective body struggling against a distant government through its primary sectors (teachers, oil workers, Indians). The fact that indigenousness was explicitly *not* associated with hunger strikes was precisely the point. As Chumiray told me when I asked him why he chose this tactic, "this is not a traditional kind of protest."

After the fiasco of trying to train Guarani in the plantation-like Charagua Normal School, UNICEF had accepted Guarani requests to finance a Guarani teacher training institute. Launched in 1995, the institute was staffed by Guarani and karai teachers, with oversight by the APG. With the scribes in La Paz, the institute became the new epicenter of EIB activism in Camiri. Yet the arrangement did not prove ideal. Guarani were not sure if the state would credential their students, and a teachers' certificate was indispensable to acquire jobs. Moreover, UNICEF was scaling back support as the state prepared its national restructuring of normal schools. Teachers were concerned about job security, a topic of daily conversation. Meanwhile, EIB languished in practice. There were few resources to give crucial political and technical support for teachers like Mateo and Petrona, left on their own in rural schools. The state was supposed to supervise EIB directly, yet local ADN education administrators opposed EIB. I redirected my collaborative work to the teachers' institute in later years. Though we did write a bit, and organized a large language congress, most of our time was spent writing institutional plans to defend the institute when the state overhaul came. The state had produced a grand turn to EIB in La Paz, but at the grass roots EIB withered.

It was in this context that the strike emerged. The strikers demanded that the Ministry of Education immediately convert the Guarani teacher training program into a "Pluriethnic Superior Normal Institute" with state funding, official status, and Guarani control. They demanded more budget lines (items) to pay teachers for Guarani communities and the return of the Guarani scribes from La Paz. In short, the Guarani demanded the recuperation of the incipient autonomy they had experienced in an earlier period, while reasserting a collective claim to state capital, political authority, and public educational resources. This paradoxical stance—pursuing authority based on indigeneity while demanding state resources based on citizenship—outlined the broader strategy of most indigenous movements in Latin America. Beyond simple resistance or recognition, this marked the demand for plurinationalism that transformed the state. Much like the epistemic dialogue sought by Camargo in writing modules, Guarani and other indigenous peoples accommodated national structures of authority while seeking a reciprocal and balanced exchange given the legitimacy of indigenous claims on difference.

Marking Rupture, Claiming Space

A political hornet's nest nationally, given the combative unions and the coveted public resources that tied normal schools to multiple local fields of power, the struggle over teacher training for Guarani concerned regional and indigenous politics. There was a three-way standoff between the APG, the state reformists, and the Charagua school. Between Charagua and Camiri, only one teacher training institution would survive. Both were lobbying at the state level. We made constant calls to find out what was going on "up there" from allies in the ministry and from foreign aid offices. We heard only, "be patient, things are moving slowly." Charagua called on its allies: the Santa Cruz Cattle Ranchers' Association, Santa Cruz elites, ADN party cadres in government, and the education minister himself.

As geopolitics undermined indigenous unity, the Isoseño Guarani had also cast their lot with Charagua, whose anti-Indian faculty now touted their embrace of EIB. The Isoso-Ava split did not worry local Guarani too much since it was nothing new. More important, the karai were divided. Camargo later told me that making karai fight among themselves made for a tactic long used by the Guarani. By dividing the powerful (i.e., teachers, parties, authorities, donors, reformists), he suggested, minorities like the Guarani amplified their own space. It was a lesson that drew on centuries of alliance making and breaking that marked both Guarani resistance and internal tensions.

Guarani had been waiting patiently for the state to act, but this preemptive strike had obviously been brewing for some time. When I walked into the Guarani teachers' institute one morning, it was underway. Chumiray was leading a swearing-in ceremony of newly arrived teachers in training. With years of experience in the APG and the CSUTCB, much of it during periods of dictatorship and persecution, he was transferring experiential knowledge to youth who had come of age with the organization already established and a sense of struggle numbed by NGO aid and scholarships. He guided the students through the election of officers, president, vice-president, secretary, and so on. He then guided them through the election of a strike committee (*comité de huelga*). Distinct from communal Guarani organization, the hunger strike mobilized an organizational language that I had never seen used by Guarani.

Chumiray stood before the student leaders and showed them how to make the sign of the cross for their swearing in. The right hand is held vertically in front of one's chest, palm to the left, right forefinger bent at a ninety-degree angle across the middle finger, the forefinger's tip braced against the thumb. Like swearing on the Bible, the gesture was ubiquitous across Bolivia. My Aymara folklorist friends used to swear in like this when elected to leadership in their dance troupes, as did the president and the cabinet when they took the oath of office. The oath that followed situates sovereignty and authority between the moral rewards of God (if they fulfill their duties) and the accountability of the people (if they do not). Chumiray modified the oath slightly to have the students swear "in front of God, your *compañeros*, and the Guarani people" to carry out their offices: "If you execute your duties well, may God reward you, if not, may the Guarani people hold you accountable." He lectured them to lead a struggle that would defend the conquest of education. The reassertion of the language of a democratic and sovereign pueblo demanding accountability was that much more remarkable given that the entire apparatus of neoliberal reform was trying to erase these very idioms of contestation.

On the Strike Picket

In the small chapel beside the main church the pews were pushed to one side and the students put down their blankets and mattresses on the floor. Signs on the walls above their heads indicated their names, places of origin, and ages. After a few days, the chapel took on a heavy air with strikers passing time reading, chatting, chewing coca, or listening to the radio. On the second day, a local TV reporter arrived to interview Chumiray, who compared the students to Apiaguaiki Tüpa, the prophet whose followers were killed at Kuruyuki. He also linked their struggle to the region, asserting both protagonism and domestication in terms the karai TV audience could understand:

> GC: These young people are just like Apiaguaiki Tüpa, who fought for his people over one hundred years ago. He was a warrior, a young person like these students, a visionary who stood up for his people. Now we are standing up for the entire Chaco region!
>
> Reporter [turning to the camera]: We have reports that there are Guarani leaders from throughout the region now converging on Camiri to join this strike!

In Bolivia the hunger strike is referred to as an "extreme measure" (*medida extrema*). Other extreme measures include self-crucifixion (being tied to a public cross), the sewing together of ones' lips (often by prisoners, to denounce silence and injustice), and self-burial (to perform one's symbolic death at the hands of the state). These actions against the self are distinguished from *medidas de hecho* (actions of fact) such as the blocking of roads, the occupation of land or buildings, or the temporary seizure of officials. Extreme measures like the hunger strike usually come after other channels have been exhausted, including public denunciation to the press, temporary work stoppages, prolonged labor strikes, marches, or road blockades.

The moral plea made in this way constitutes a fundamental aspect of democratic and participatory politics in Bolivia, where institutionalized channels of representation and redress are weak and the understanding of the state as having moral obligations to its citizens bolsters claims against its inefficacy (Goldstein 2003). As citizenship exercises, the protests generally represent collective bodies and interests—since the exercise of individual, liberal citizenship through voting is, well, a myth. Yet for those who see collectivist, corporate, or communitarian models of citizenship as a mostly indigenous trait (or flaw), hunger strikes appear deeply Western. Hunger strikes, tied to unions and public workers, also generally represent urban strategies. Hunger strikes require access to a public stage, media attention, and the possibility of garnering sympathy among the wider political community. Lowland indigenous movements in Bolivia have relied primarily on the march. A hunger strike relies on the symbolic power of a few bodies made publicly visible at a key contested center of authority, while large-scale actions (like blockades or marches) restrict flows to or move toward centers of power, requiring significantly more bodies. Indigenous peoples, usually struggling from a position of rurality with little sympathy from urban audiences, are more apt to block roads or march than to set up hunger strike pickets.

As political wager and choreographed performance, Bolivian hunger strikes do not stop traffic and may or may not get results. A hunger strike started by four women miners in the main plaza of La Paz in 1978 helped catalyze the fall of then dictator Hugo Bánzer. In 2003 upper-middle-class Paceños (including the mayor and prefect of La Paz) went on hunger strike against Goni (who also fell). At this writing, conservative oligarchs of Santa Cruz are staging hunger strikes against the MAS government, reviving a corporatist, popular icon in the name of liberal, capitalist development. Yet hunger strikes are so common as to risk being labeled farcical and comical. Public commentary assesses strike legitimacy by whether the strike was "dry" (without water), "with coca" (which assuages hunger pangs, but is not actually consumed), or with "food" (smuggled to strikers in the form of liquefied soups). Hunger strikes can even be recharged. Those who begin to falter might drop out while others join in, diminishing a sense of urgency about the strike's resolution. Just as actions of fact have (until recently) never been marked by great civilian violence against the state, never have I heard of a Bolivian dying from a hunger strike. The significance of one's identity in sociopolitical space and time—on which moral pressure on elites relies—as well as multiple other modes of leverage, play into the success or failure of a hunger strike. For all of these reasons, calling a hunger strike for the Guarani constituted a densely meaningful wager that claimed contestative citizenship within and against urban-centered sites of power and national histories of struggle.

As the strikers settled in, I talked to a young Guarani reporter who had come to capture commentary for his radio show. We spoke in Guarani, and he took on a formal tone for my own camera.

Julio: Thank you for this conversation. I, as a Guarani, my parents are Guarani, you know. They did not know paper [how to read and write], my father did not know paper. And now, those of us coming behind them, we are going to know [how to read] paper. We have now begun to speak out with strong words [*ore ñeengeta!*]. All of us young people are looking for a way to get an education, an education in two languages to strengthen our language, our culture, our *arete* festival in our communities. That is why we want to strengthen ourselves. According to the laws that recognize us, there are laws through which we can become stronger.

BG: How do you see these young people? Are they OK with the strike?

Julio: We are Guarani, this is nothing [difficult] for us. All these relatives [*tëtara*] are *timakas!*[11] We are accustomed to working and feeling hunger, without becoming tired. Our women might get tired a bit, but with a bit of rest, they no longer feel it. In contrast, city people, when they are hungry, they just hit the bed. But these *tëtara* are not like that. We are tough, we walk long distances, we speak out loud, and we know we have in our hands the recognition [the law]. So these *tëtara* are happy, they are feeling good, in this place together they are really at home [*ovïa katu*], there is no sadness. There is no sadness visible here.

While Chumiray dramatized the event for karai, young Julio, an up-and-coming APG activist, framed it through the eyes of Guarani youth. He highlighted the generational distinction between past illiteracy and a present marked by claims for schooling, and cast these within the "law" and "recognition." Yet he also highlighted particularly Guarani idioms of struggle, kindred *tëtara*, *timaka*, rural origins, fortitude, talking strongly, and—in good Guarani fashion—the "happiness" and *ovïa* (feeling at home in a place) in this difficult moment. As Airase frequently prodded me back in the village, when walking toward an enemy, one always talked out loud, with laughing and strong words on the trail. Like words of joy in the midst of bitter memories, these phrasings invoked strength and the absence of sadness.

My own reading of the strike differed. As an allied observer of Guarani politics, I stayed on the periphery. I never played roles in decision making, much less in something as dramatic as a hunger strike. My gut instinct was that the strike was a miscalculation. I thought a hunger strike useful to support land rights or to fight debt peonage, but not for this bureaucratic mess of the teachers' school. What was the point? Yet just as I did not viscerally sense the racialized fears held by karai, my gut instinct indicated an embodied gringo reading. It was skewed by naïve faith in our allies in La Paz.

I thought the state, given that Guarani had pioneered EIB, would ultimately favor Camiri over the Charagua school. My reading of the political logic of the strike was *isolated* within a particular set of reform relations and temporalities. Guarani leaders saw these issues as *articulated* with scales, relations, and temporalities that situated the teachers' institute and EIB in a wider field and a history of struggle. On later reflection I realized how my corporeal discomfort with the strike shed light on my orientation to EIB (as something that was not perfect, but at least a sign of positive change). Conversely, Guarani leaders saw EIB as a process and platform, funded in their names, tied to a deeper movement history, and crucial to their place in a complex field of power struggles, an instrument now slipping from their hands.

I kept my mouth shut. Bitter words, critical questions about the strike (even as a researcher), or worries about hungry students were not called for. This was a time for unity, happiness, and fortitude. Even Guarani leaders who I knew shared my uncertainty stepped forward as vociferous supporters. I began to understand this more clearly after Camargo asked me to call my contacts in La Paz to get information and I sensed the limits of networks with the powerful. Even intimate friends refused to provide me with information. The power triad (state, donors, NGOs) closed ranks around the institutional process of reform. My contacts' comments included, "the [Guarani leaders] are screwed [*cagado*, lit. "shitted"]; "they are closing doors with this"; "they won't get any more information"; "they are going to bring down bilingual education"; "you should distance yourself from the strike"; and "they will achieve nothing." As Camargo later reminded me, "in the face of our enemies, we are one."

Several days in, with the striking students still in the church, I mingled with Guarani leaders in the APG office. We waited for faxed responses from the Education Ministry in La Paz, while, as expected, the ministry stalled. I snapped a picture (see figure 7). Posters lined the office—showing indigenous faces, multilingual maps of Bolivia, and calendars produced by NGOs, aid agencies, and state offices. Camargo sat at his desk, flanked by a red, green, and yellow banner embroidered with the name of the Asamblea del Pueblo Guarani. The banners were all over Bolivia, emblems of corporate rights to exist vis-à-vis the state. Silvia Chumiray, the former scribe and head of the Guarani educational council, stood looking over Camargo's shoulder. Guido Chumiray, the strike strategist, was at the center outlining responses

FIGURE 7 Not a traditional kind of protest. APG leaders meet to discuss strategy during the hunger strike.

to the state. Sabino, a Guarani language teacher at the institute, stood quietly in the background. Guarani captains had also arrived from the countryside, distinguished from the urban leaders by their worn clothes, sandals, and woven bags. A simba leader from Ingre sat quietly in the corner, somewhat excluded from the bilingual conversation. The group was discussing strategies for amplifying the strike, while they waited for a response from the state.

A few minutes later I spoke to Guido Chumiray again, filming as I asked questions about the strike. A careful reader will note how he detected a hint of (unintended) critique. Despite my faux pas, Chumiray, always joking, repositioned the conversation to one of humor framing serious business. I reproduce the interview at length because it illustrates the articulatory framing I describe above:

BG: Why was the decision made to begin, all of a sudden, this hunger strike?

GC: [laughing] Because we wanted to have an ugly pageant [*un concurso de feos*]![12] [We both laugh]. No, seriously, it has not been all of a sudden.

This is the vision of people who have experiences of struggle [*lucha*] in questions that aren't traditionally Guarani [issues]. This is because the government is not listening to the Guarani people. They are stalling us. We have been insisting on this for six months. Even though we have people in the government who have good intentions, the policies of this government are very different from these intentions. If seventy children in a community don't have a teacher, what kind of people are we going to get for the development of the province? If the teachers don't have adequate training, how is development possible? If there are no books in the schools, if there are no reform materials, no textbooks in accordance with our projections of the man of the future [*hombre del futuro*], then how is it possible to talk about development and the eradication of poverty? That's why we've entered into this hunger strike, to the final consequences [*hasta las últimas consecuencias*]. We've also done this, in a way, so that even the Guarani community will realize that this [bilingual education and teacher training] is something that's worth sacrifice, that it's a struggle, and that they will react.

BG: Where does this strike fit into a longer history of Guarani struggles?

GC: It was time. For nine or ten years we've been helping the education reform. We were the first to support reform during the previous government [Goni, 1992–97]. Then after reform became law, we continued supporting it. This made us look, in public opinion, like officialists [*gobiernistas*]. Throughout this period, everyone has been raising [us up like a] flag [saying], "the APG supports education reform and decentralization!" But in this government [Bánzer, 1997–2002] things are changing radically. They speak of reform and then take measures that are contradictory. . . . One thing is their discourse, and the other is our position to push forward with the defense of education that we began in 1992, in 1993.

BG: Some might say that the issue of education is a distraction from more serious issues, like land?

GC: I don't think so. All problems have a sequence. We came to understand the problem of land by way of education. We must be conscious of that. The [1992] literacy campaign awoke the consciousness [*despertó la conciencia*] of many people by associating the problem of land with the problem of education. [Before the campaign] the *compañeros* who had always lived in peonage did not know their condition because they did not know their history. That's the way we look at this process. Now we are fighting for education. The year before last we were fighting for land.[13] In the future we will have other struggles. I don't see it as a distraction. Rather, this is what we fundamentally seek: that within the problem of education we also speak of the problem of land.

My first question had betrayed skepticism about the strike, yet I often asked myself the other questions: What were the consequences of our labors in education? Where did this fit into the bigger picture? In light of Chumiray's responses, I began to understand the strike in ways not tied to its instrumental rationality. As the anthropologist Sally Moore suggested (1987), "diagnostic events" like the hunger strike are not necessarily significant because of their expressed intentions. On wider analysis they reveal patterns of change linking multiple local and translocal processes, interests, and relationships. We see clearly how a classroom view of EIB here confronts wider reality. For Chumiray the strike concerned a deeper struggle over the historical meaning of education, public attitudes toward the Guarani, visions of education in relation to territorial struggles, and the risks posed to Guarani consciousness by dancing too closely with the regime. What was happening was not just about the teachers' school but indicated a constitutive learning process aimed at relations with the karai, movement stances, and the political training of Guarani teachers to be. As a knowledge-producing event, the hunger strike rearticulated an indigenous agenda with the language and form of popular grass-roots politics (see Calla 1999; Regalsky and Laurie 2007). As interculturalism gave way to bureaucratization, the strike sought to recast the Guarani—both internally and in relation to their karai audiences—as more than obsequious executors of interculturalism and, rather, as bearers of a contestative popular stance.

This rearticulation emerges clearly in Churimay's comments. For him, "experiences of struggle" were mediated through a language of class and social liberation, experiences foreign to the young students. Phrases like *struggle*, *until the final consequences*, *compañeros*, and *the new man* mark this deeper trajectory of popular movement history. Chumiray's perspective complemented Julio's invocation of kindred solidarity, fortitude, and the jovial stoicism unique to Guarani languages of struggle. The strike rearticulated a

Guarani-centered politics of knowledge in dialogue with, but not determined by, official interculturalism or older exclusionary forms of corporatist
unionism.

Two blocks from the APG office in the chapel, the Guarani strikers silently
passed their days and nights. By day five, the two karai teachers had dropped
out. Román remained. Two other Guarani captains joined in. Chumiray,
negotiating with the state during the day, came in the evenings to speak with
the students. He brought videotapes of Indian mobilization in Brazil and
movies like *Platoon* and *JFK*. The students watched themselves on the local
news interspersed with nightly soap opera fare. Beyond contributing coca,
my efforts to help were exhausted. So I sat with the students, Chumiray, and
other leaders in the evenings, smoking and chewing coca and listening to
stories of the young organizers during the dictatorships. There was always
joking going on despite the long faces of the striking students.

The strike made a local splash. The Guarani garnered a rousing letter
of "proletarian support" from the sexagenarian leaders of the Departmental Workers' Confederation. Another statement of support came from the
Civic Committee of Camiri. The mayor and the ex-mayor dropped by to
express solidarity. (Both were interested in expressing opposition to the ADN
more than sympathy with the Guarani.) A local TV reporter covered the
strike with updates each night. The Guarani also had collaboration from
some members of the rural teachers' union. One bearded, beret-wearing
karai teacher worked at a rural high school where many of these young
Guarani had studied. He spoke eloquently of how the chapel held a history
of resistance. This was a "history of struggle in a sacred space," he offered
dramatically, a history that Guarani youth now had the "honor" of joining.

This rapprochement with the symbols and tactics of the rural teachers'
union appeared ironic given the longer history of conflict between the
Guarani and the teachers. The national structural and symbolic tensions at
play with reform—posed between the containment of ethnic militancy, on
the one side, and the assault on the unionized teacher, on the other—here
came to the surface as an intra-Guarani struggle. One of the former scribes
came into the chapel on the first day of the strike and gazed thoughtfully at
the students lying on the pews. He leaned over to whisper in my ear: "Estos
sí van a ser kereimba!" (These [young people] really are going to turn out to
be warriors!). He highlighted their prospects as Guarani militants. However,

he changed his mind as events intensified and Guarani factionalism reared its head. Several days later he visited again and questioned the strike, in a backstage whisper, of course. Again he spoke into my ear, using the pejorative term for teachers' union activists, "It looks like we are turning into *sindicateros*."

Crafting a New Schoolteacher

Based on an analysis of the Irish Republican Army (IRA) hunger strike led by Bobby Sands in a British prison in 1981, the anthropologist Begoña Aretxaga suggested that strikes be viewed not merely as political instruments but as a complexly layered "ritual event through which historical myth is transformed and created anew" (1997:80). Aretxaga described the elements of this mythic history, nationalist symbols with striking parallels to the Guarani framing of the hunger strike. Irish strikers privileged heroic masculine political agency over silent feminine support (invoking ancient Gaelic warriors as the Guarani did Apiaguaiki Tüpa). Strikers sought to establish a moral congruence between prisoners' bodies and the Irish nation (like the Bolivian pueblo). They performed a Catholic narrative of redemption through Christ-like sacrifice and ideals of social liberation (part of the Bolivian hunger strike's deeper meanings). Aretxaga argued that these codes of cultural continuity were central to understanding the performative effectiveness of the strike (1997:81–90).

The parallels illustrate how Bolivian and Irish hunger strikes emerge in a history of Western state formation shaped by colonialism, Catholicism, and Marxian-inspired idioms of struggle, all infused with patriarchal models of political agency. Yet while Chumiray situated the strike as a novel event in a deeper history of struggle, the strike sought performative effectiveness not through cultural continuity but through symbolic rupture. It sought both to reposition the Guarani in regional fields of power and to reorient the meaning and direction of movement practice. In doing so, it refit Guarani claims to particularity into locally familiar models of citizenship.

In the case of both the Kuruyuki commemorations and the hunger strike, bilingual education was the medium through which Guarani could speak simultaneously as different kinds of subjects (with particular rights and interests) and as corporate citizens who shared in a legitimate struggle in the Bolivian nation. There were two key axes of this reformulation: the indigenous as a new *regional* authority seeking to manage racial fears and memories of violence by demonstrating orderly engagement with karai spaces and actors; and the indigenous as a particular type of *national* actor operating from the position of an epistemically and historically distinct people and within the contestative language of popular struggle.

Neoliberalism sought to reestablish control over the state, in part by redesigning the key human agent of schooling: the teacher. I opened this chapter by discussing teacher practice in schools to juxtapose this site of subject formation with Kuruyukɨ events and the hunger strike. Reformists favored the image of the teacher as a gently progressive intercultural class-room manager. Indigenous teachers like Mateo and Petrona would quietly pursue quality in terms amenable to their culture, eschewing engagement in more unsettling politics. Yet Kuruyukɨ situated Guarani teachers within a project of historical recovery and movement unity, while the hunger strike sought to position them in a national history of popular struggle, revolution-ary vanguardism, and the *mística* of sacrifice.[14] The Guarani were building their own views of interculturalism and knowledge from the ground up.

For these reasons I see the events described here as examples of what James Holston (1999:167) called "insurgent citizenship":

> [These are] forms found in organized grassroots mobilizations and in everyday practices that, in different ways empower, parody, derail, or subvert state agendas. They are found, in other words, in struggles over what it means to be a member of the modern state. . . . Citizenship changes as new members emerge to advance their claims, expanding its realm, and as new forms of segregation and violence counter these ad-vances, eroding it. The sites of insurgent citizenship are found at the intersection of these processes of expansion and erosion.

Precisely because the Guarani found themselves in the midst of both expan-sion (with a growing regional and national significance and general success in EIB politics) and erosion (new state controls, the loss of local protagonism, and rising karai anxieties about potential violence) I find this characteriza-tion useful for thinking about movement performances like Kuruyukɨ and the hunger strike. Beyond simple models of resistance (to processes coming from elsewhere) or inclusion (into existing categories of citizenship), Hol-ston's notion draws attention to the self-conscious performances for transforming intercultural and interlinguistic spaces—such as the urban plaza of Camiri—where Guarani and karai come together. These are creative, partly mimetic tactics always staged in multiple registers and codes. They sought the negotiated transformation of meanings of knowledge, of schooling, and of the state and attempted to reposition the Guarani as distinctive kinds of citizens within these new ways of speaking. It was here, I suggest, rather than in the contained walls and texts of the rural school, that EIB was now finding new organizing potential in articulation with a new moment in movement history.

Coda: Partial Victory, New Challenge

The strike ended after fourteen days. Negotiators, including the chain-smoking lieutenant of vice-minister Anaya and two other staffers, came twice to Camiri to speak with the Guarani. The state yielded little. The Guarani attempted to force departmental prefects to assign more teachers (they never did). The Guarani hoped to return control over textbook writing to the APG (this did not happen). They demanded Anaya's presence in Camiri (she never came). The negotiated resolution included guarantees that the APG would be part of decision making on the new teachers' institute (they were not).

Anaya shrugged when I interviewed her several months later about the strike. "Personally, it was a low blow, like you say in boxing, from those [the Guarani] I considered my allies. . . . [In any case] the strike had no effect, and fortunately the [anti-indigenous] minister was out of the country and did not even find out about it." Acknowledging the workings of power in Bolivia, she added, "In this country you have to at least block a major highway or no one will hear about it. The press did not pick it up, it had little repercussion." Yet this distance between centralized state processes and Guarani regional politics facilitated precisely the local redirections that I described above, even as it illustrated the limits to effective institutional forms of participation and representation in the intercultural state.

Decisions about teacher training were made within reformist circles and time frames. A year later, the reform converted the Guarani teachers' institute into the Pluriethnic Superior Normal Institute of the East and Chaco (INSPOC). Thirteen of the country's twenty-four normal schools became Institutos Normales Superiores (INS). Others, like Charagua, were closed or transformed into vocational institutes. My colleagues mostly kept their jobs at the new institute. Yet new challenges arose. The Education Ministry arranged for public and private universities to bid on contracts to administer these new institutes. In the words of one reformist, "we want to diversify the supply of higher education and get the private sector involved in teacher training." The change was said to improve the quality of teacher training by subjecting it to the rigor of university standards and the market (and insulate it from the machinations of parties and unions). Teachers saw the outsourcing as a move to open teaching jobs to nonteachers, erode the teachers' union, and privatize higher education.[15]

For the Guarani, outsourcing led to an unexpected twist. The contract to manage the INSPOC was won by the private Baha'i-run Nur University in Santa Cruz. The Nur was known for training urbanites in business administration and technical fields.[16] The Guarani leadership acquiesced and received a consultative position on the executive board. The Catholic NGOs in Camiri were furious. It proved an ambiguous victory. The Guarani maintained some protagonism yet were placed into a new arrangement of surveillance, monitoring, and control.

In the Andes the restructuring and outsourcing of normal schools provoked a series of violent marches and strikes in 1999 and 2000, protests symptomatic of the deepening crisis in the neoliberal project. An Aymara student marching from the Santiago de Huata Normal School in La Paz to protest its transformation into a vocational school was quoted saying, "Behind these decisions there is racial hatred . . . they want to keep us Aymaras in a state of ignorance so they are closing the Normal School, on the other hand, for cities they are creating pedagogical universities" ("El gobierno anunció" 1999). Police turned out to repress the marchers. During one march a stick of dynamite was tossed at Anaya's office in La Paz. Though the tenor of struggle in the Andes differed from that in the lowlands, the Guarani hunger strike came ahead of a wider curve of escalating opposition. Guarani leaders who reminisced about the event in later years always argued to me that it had offered a valuable learning experience about both state and movement tactics. As evidenced in conflicts that began to unfold after 2000, in Guarani country and across the wider landscape of Bolivian politics, they were right. When I went back to Guarani country in later years, they *had* started blocking the highways.

Interculturalism to Decolonization

> September 21, 2003. La Paz: "A shootout at Warisata [Bilingual Intercultural Teacher Training Institute] ends with five dead, and various wounded. . . . Forces of order entered the zone to rescue 1,000 hostages that the peasants were holding in Sorata. In Warisata, the peasants ambushed the military and police who arrived and a serious battle ensued.
>
> — *"Una balacera en Warisata terminó con cinco muertos y varios heridos,"*
> La Razón, *September 21, 2003*

Warisata is an Aymara town about sixty miles northwest of La Paz. It is home to the Bilingual Intercultural Teachers' Institute of the same name. The town and school are located in the heart of Omasuyos Province, one of the most politically combative Aymara regions in the country. Statues of Tupak Katari and Bartolina Sisa grace the plaza in the provincial capital of Achacachi, home to the fiery Felipe "the Condor" Quispe, a radical leader who played a major role in the unraveling of elite power in Bolivia.

Embedded within this geography and history of resistance, Warisata as a place and name is sacred in the discourse of Andean indigenous education. Warisata was the country's first indigenous teachers' school (founded 1931). Warisata arose out of Aymara demands for education and state-backed pedagogical experiments of the early twentieth century. Called the *ayllu*-school, it was modeled around the territorially ordered kinship and political units (*ayllus*) that serve as the foundation of Andean society. At the time of its founding the town's *amaut'as* (knowers, wise elders, teachers) were key actors of local school control. Yet far from a radical Indianist pedagogy, Warisata represented an early intercultural experiment. Spanish literacy was of tactical interest to the Aymara, who sought to confront criollos and mestizos on the terrain of law. The curriculum was in Spanish and by today's standards would be seen as assimilationist. Though politically and territorially rooted in Aymara epistemic and political domains, it represented a space of intercultural engagement—rather than frontal confrontation—between indigenous peoples and the state. It even arose out of mestizo-Aymara collaboration. The founders were an Aymara leader named Avelino Siñani and a mestizo named Elizardo Pérez. Both names are part of the contemporary pantheon of heroes in indigenous education.

Nonetheless, just as karai see moderate Guarani letrados as a threat today, criollo landowners in the Andes saw Warisata as a threat in the 1930s. A provincial governor denounced the school in 1936 for "creating conflict between [criollo] *patrones* and [Aymara] *indios*" and for promoting the "extermination" of the mestizos and whites by the Aymara. Press reports in La Paz lamented that schooling increased the "idle laziness" of the Aymara. By 1941 the school had closed. Yet for indigenous intellectuals today, Warisata, like EIB in Guarani country, began to break the "siege" against indigenous education maintained by the hacienda class (Choque Canqui 1992:32–33, 58).

Operating intermittently in the years that followed, Warisata reopened as a normal school after the 1952 revolution. Like the Charagua school out in Guarani country, Warisata became what the anthropologist Aurolyn Luykx has called a "citizen factory" (1999). Teachers were often of rural indigenous origin, yet pedagogical practice attacked the backwardness of the Indian, pursuing racial improvement through castellanización and Bolivianization. As teachers, these new citizens, Luykx argued, were converted through education into the agents of their people's continued marginalization. After the restructuring of teacher training in the late 1990s, Warisata became a new bilingual intercultural institute, like the Guarani INSPOC in Camiri. Yet in a shocking turn that reflected a more intense atmosphere of conflict in the Andes, in September 2003 Warisata became the scene of bloody violence between the Bolivian military and Aymara that led to the deaths of two soldiers, a teacher, a student, and three other civilians, including an eight-year-old girl hit by a soldier's bullet.[1] Warisata marked the tipping point of events that cascaded into the ouster of Goni that October. Conflict at a bilingual teachers' school, it appeared, had instigated the fall of the neoliberal era in Bolivia. Compared to the Guarani hunger strike, the Warisata violence reflects its own kinds of political articulations and insurgent citizenships, illustrative both of the variegated shape of indigenous knowledge politics and the shared patterns of resistance and rule that link indigenous resurgences across Bolivia.

In early September 2003 Aymara farmers blocked the highway to La Paz, cutting off access to Sorata, a tourist town thirty miles beyond Warisata. The Aymara regional leader, Quispe, demanded the release of jailed leaders and the fulfillment of agreements extracted from the state during prior blockades. The event was polysemic and converged with other protests in El Alto and La Paz over taxes, public sector wages, and ultimately against the export of natural gas through Chile. Yet since 1999, these protests had become cyclical, underlain in part by the breakdown of regime legitimacy and by competition within movements now rearticulating across translocal fields. Quispe's region, for example, was jousting for leadership with the coca growers of Evo Morales and the MAS. Warisata was in the midst of these dynamics, and it eventually joined the blockade that September.

Gas and nationalism dominated later interpretations of the October 2003 events, now enshrined in history as the Gas War. Yet multiple transects of grievance and poles of contestation fed social discontent that went beyond gas. In the case of Warisata, students and faculty had been waging struggles against the outsourcing process for several months, and intensifying combativeness was fermenting in the school. Beneath the surface other structural bottlenecks undermined reform, and submerged ideological networks thrived below reformist discourses on constructivism and interculturalism.[2] Warisata's proximity to El Alto and La Paz proved a key factor. With the public university in El Alto facing budget cuts and new testing requirements, many urban Aymara students pushed to enroll in rural teachers' schools like Warisata, somewhat reversing a historic pattern of rural-to-urban migration. By returning to the rural school, periurban youth facing frustrated aspirations of mobility rearticulated with long-standing forms of rural indigenous militancy.

Since 1999 students and faculty at Warisata had also waged strikes and marches against the government. Like the Guarani, they had grievances linked to restructuring. Warisata was outsourced to the private Catholic University Saint Francis of Assisi, in La Paz. Students, teachers, and elders, the amaut'as, opposed the move, even though the state sweetened the deal with increased salaries for faculty that entered through selective, test-based competition. Reformists, not local communities, would now determine who worked and who did not. New entrance exams were locally interpreted as attempts to restrict access to schooling and to remove ideologically radical students and faculty opposed to reform. The neoliberal jargon of local participation and autonomy did not extend to these local conceptions of the indigenous historic right of control over Warisata.

Cells of nightly political discussion thrived at Warisata. Some were Marxian-inspired and linked to the Trotskyist teacher union leadership. Others were tied to the convergence of anticolonial thought and class struggle rooted in the public University of La Paz's sociology department (where some of Warisata's faculty had studied). Another group solidified around a culturalist yet equally anticolonial vision of indigenous resurgence, with a more radical version pushed by leaders like Quispe and a more moderate strand proposed by EIB activists. As if this were not enough, a delegation of Zapatista supporters from Mexico had recently visited Warisata. My interlocutor laughed recalling, "everyone wanted to be like the Sub," referring to Subcomandante Marcos, the Zapatista guerrilla leader. Black ski masks à la Marcos became a new fad among students. Far from a citizen factory, Warisata had become a node of hybrid contestative politics.

Judging by the government response to the Aymara blockade, there was blind arrogance in the face of impending regime collapse. Goni ordered the "rescue" of tourists at Sorata. Press reports suggested that U.S. embassy personnel were vacationing there, highlighting the sense that the once-popular Goni now just served as Washington's errand boy. His minister of defense, a Machiavellian operator named Carlos "the Fox" Sánchez Berzaín, directed the supposed rescue from a helicopter. Before dawn on September 20, an army caravan broke through the Warisata blockade on the way out, filling the town square with tear gas. At Sorata, angry crowds threatened the Fox and his officers with *chicotes*, horsewhips used for public punishment in the Andes. Backed by guns, the troops loaded several buses with tourists and the convoy headed back to La Paz. This now entailed running a gauntlet through Omasuyos Province, with the region's organized communities angry at the aggressive military intrusion. Stones—the government claims bullets—rained down on the convoy from Aymara farmers on the hillsides along the way. Quispe later said the provocation was answered in turn, "If they want war, we'll give them war." Aymara students, teachers, and farmers were also entrenched at Warisata, waiting.

As the military convoy approached the school, shooting began. At some point the confrontation shifted to the Warisata Institute's campus on the main plaza. Students and teachers threw rocks. The army claimed that Aymara snipers were inside the school. As proof, *La Razón* ran a photo of empty bullet casings, curiously standing in a neat row, on a desk in a Warisata classroom ("El gobierno denuncia" 2003). Five Aymara were killed, including the eight-year-old girl. Seventeen were wounded. At least two soldiers were killed—either by old rifles or by friendly fire—as the convoy pushed its way through. Several students and teachers were detained for "armed revolt" (*sublevación armada*). The next day, young Aymara armed with old Mausers and wearing ski masks posed for the press in the town square of Warisata. Cognizant of the fear of the Indian held by urbanites, they seemed to embrace the accusations of armed revolt in defiance of Goni's regime.[3]

Those killed at Warisata in September 2003 joined a long list of indigenous martyrs. Yet judging from the press, elites interpreted them not as martyrs but as illegitimate subjects, noncitizens, *indios alzados* (uppity Indians). This was the "legitimate" violence turned against subversive knowledge and tongues outside the state's sovereign control. Goni, who had defended bilingual intercultural education in 1994, was in retreat from his liberal interculturalism. He justified the killings by saying, "It seems like they were studying something else there besides how to be teachers." Yet contradictorily, as if to both legitimate the violence and to assure urbanites that Goni was not provoking peasant hordes, the culprits were unruly letrados: "The President of the Republic assures that the confrontation last Saturday was with students and teachers of the Warisata Normal School, and not so much with peasants of the zones" ("Goni acusa" 2003). Implying that bilingual schooling in particular was to blame, the president's interior minister added that "dangerous radical intellectuals" had been incrusted in the school for some time. The vice-minister of the Interior labeled them an "irregular, subversive, radical group, composed of highly ideologized persons with strong racism toward the *q'aras* [nonindigenous Bolivians]" ("El gobierno clausuró" 2003). Nonetheless, public outcry at the killings galvanized wider protests that congealed in the Gas War (Ari 2003). After several weeks of bloody street violence, with sixty-seven civilians killed by the army, Goni and the "Fox" fled La Paz for Miami and then Washington. The articulation between neoliberalism and interculturalism had ruptured.

Two years later, the Aymara coca farmers' leader Evo Morales and his MAS party swept to victory in an unprecedented expression of popular democracy. Morales chose as his new education minister Felix Patzi, an Aymara sociologist and a critic of education reform. Patzi promptly renamed the Ministry of Education, Culture, and Sport the Ministry of Education and *Cultures* (pluralizing knowledge with a decolonizing *s*). The government began work on a new education law to supplant the 1994 education reform. The new law would be based not only on interculturalism but on intraculturalism, the strengthening of indigenous cultures from within. It also called for the decolonization of education. The proposal was subtitled, after the founders of Warisata, "the Avelino Siñani and Elizardo Pérez Law."

Chapter Seven

SHIFTING STATES

¡Que hable cuando aprenda el castellano!
[Let her speak when she learns Spanish!]
—*Beatriz Capobianco, a delegate from Santa Cruz shouting down
her Quechua-speaking counterpart, National Constitutional Assembly,
June 2006*

What are the conditions of possibility for the exercise of democracy in a society where human beings are not equal, in a social
formation split by colonialism, the colonial legacy, and coloniality?
Is it not necessary, before speaking of democracy, before achieving
democracy, to resolve the pending problems brought into the
present by the colonial legacy? The rupture with the colonial
legacy appears to be one of the conditions necessary for speaking
seriously about democracy, of the exercise of democracy, of the
realization of the force of the *pueblo*.
—*Raul Prada, "The Articulation of Complexity"*

The election of Evo Morales in December of 2005 made for a watershed moment in Bolivian and Latin American history. Evo emerged
as a leader of the coca growers' unions of the Chapare region in central
Bolivia. He is an Aymara, originally from Oruro Department. Yet as a leader
he cut his teeth in the language of union politics rather than among indigenous rights movements. The coca growers are certainly indigenous,
most of them Quechua and Aymara settlers who moved into the Chapare
region over the past decades after the neoliberal privatization of the mines in
the high Andes. They brought with them indigenous roots and the combative spirit of the miners. Galvanized against the violence of the antidrug
war, by the 1990s the coca growers were developing ties to other peasant-

indigenous organizations to found the MAS, and Morales catapulted from being a thorn in the side of the United States to a charismatic national political leader.

Morales was elected with a clear majority in the first round (53.7 percent). This constituted an unprecedented mandate in Bolivia, where back-door intra-elite pacts have generally decided who would wear the presidential sash. As democracy goes, few presidents in Latin America can boast of such popular support. The MAS rolled into power calling for a "democratic cultural and political revolution." At the top of the agenda was the nationalization of gas, the acceleration of the 1996 land reform, and an education revolution. Fifteen years had passed since I first arrived in Bolivia and speculated about the possibility of pachakuti. Now many observers were using the term *pachakuti* to describe the unfolding events.

The symbolic shifts were immediate and dramatic. The most visible in body-conscious Bolivia was that of Morales himself. His features, skin color, and way of speaking challenged five centuries of light-skinned criollo-mestizo rule. He refused to wear a necktie, the symbol of the *doctor* (i.e., lawyer), an icon of colonial knowledge and the exploitation of indigenous peoples. At his swearing-in ceremony, he dressed in a neatly tailored jacket embroidered with Andean motifs and raised a clenched left fist instead of making the thumb and forefinger sign of the cross. He was also inaugurated through an Aymara ritual staged at the ruins of Tiwanaku near La Paz. Those gathered gave thanks to the Pachamama, the Andean spirit of the earth, and a llama was sacrificed. Conservative editorialists were aghast at this negation of the traditional symbols of authority.

While indigeneity is central to the MAS project, it is important not to exaggerate the ethnic nature of the party or its politics. The MAS emerged through myriad social movements, from urban poor to middle-class nationalists to old-guard criollo leftists to lowland and Andean indigenous communities. Morales and the MAS are products of the "articulation of complexity," as Raul Prada, a key MAS intellectual (and criollo) puts it. Unlike the top-down, clientelistic parties of the corporatist past, the MAS draws its strength from the groundswell of a multiplicity of local sites of grass-roots struggle—from coca growers to Chiquitano Indians to urban market vendors to the Guarani. Rather than an ethnic party, the MAS bridges indigenous histories and territorialities—which exert a decentralizing pressure and a discourse of plurinationalism charged with a deeply felt sentiment of popular nationalism, tied both to visions of a strong, developmentalist state and to active control over economic production, especially over Bolivia's strategic natural resources. Without hegemonic economic and military control, the MAS relies on balancing these sources of legitimacy, relying heavily on the mobilization of diverse movements to sustain the regime. It leads a social-movement state.

With the support of indigenous movements, urban popular organizations, and middle-class progressives and nationalists, the MAS pushed forward with its plan to hold a national constitutional assembly to refound the country. On the other side, the conservative elite quickly regrouped. Confronted with a democratic challenge, and no longer wielding the reins of the state apparatus, elites retreated to the discourse and locus of regionalism. Based in regional cities, first among them the agroindustrial and mineral-rich stronghold of Santa Cruz in the east, this new opposition generated a call for regional autonomy. The elections to choose delegates to the constitutional assembly coincided with a national referendum on autonomy for the country's departments (states). While the MAS saw the constitutional assembly as a vehicle for dismantling neoliberalism, the elites saw in regional autonomy a move for radical decentralization, in effect transferring most functions of state into the hands of elite-dominated departmental governments. Through the complexities of negotiated electoral design, the MAS managed to capture a solid majority of delegates to the assembly, while the autonomists won the "Yes" vote in most of eastern Bolivia's departments. The country was split (Gustafson 2006).

In this chapter I explore how the politics of knowledge are shifting in this current scenario. For the MAS, the language of redistributive nationalism—encompassing the fight against poverty, the reduction of regional inequalities, the recovery of sovereignty, and the address of the population's needs—functions as the principal tool. For the regionalist elites, a discourse of modern aspirations for first world consumption against the supposed third world threat of the masses marks an appeal for the loyalty and sentiments of the urban middle and upper classes and for those who aspire to join their ranks. The MAS builds on articulations of rural and periurban populations historically excluded from power. The autonomists make of cities and their masters the privileged locus of true citizenship, order, and rights.

I have two interwoven objectives here.[1] The first is to revisit EIB, both at the national level and in Guarani country, to assess where it stands at the eve of this new historical moment and how it might fare in the future. The second is to map the new geopolitics of knowledge in the country. Underlying this discussion are the questions I raised at the outset of this book: To what extent has—or can—educational transformation contributed—or contribute—to addressing economic inequality and dismantling the coloniality of power? By extension, how has the primary fault line of interculturalism—between indigenous resurgence and neoliberal reform—now been refigured as a battle between redistributive nationalism nurtured by indigenous utopias and a model of the state based on the radical federalism of urban-centered, regionally variegated citizenship rights?

ASSESSING EIB: AN OVERVIEW

What conclusions can be drawn about the radical experiment with bilingual intercultural education in Bolivia? I have argued that despite its emergence during a period of marketizing reforms, EIB initiated a decolonizing shift in regional and national languages of the state. It generated conditions for a new dialogue on citizenship, tentatively addressed indigenous educational marginality, and opened doors to those epistemes and languages historically relegated to the margins (Mignolo 2005:120), the voices that are now speaking from the centers of power.

In terms of cultural and epistemic difference, I argued that EIB constituted a vehicle for creative engagement across languages, epistemes, and visions of history. Though constrained by the institutional forms of Western pedagogy, it provided a platform for emergent intellectual projects that sought to reverse history. In the Guarani case, this was not pursued through cultural conservatism or radical ethnic militancy, but through a dialogue of knowledges based on a logic of reciprocal exchange and mutual recognition (rather than mutual exclusion).[2] In my early days, I engaged EIB with a notion of cultural defense and the "rescue" of language. This is a part of what EIB pursued. Yet as I learned early on—from the scribes' concerns with tactical mimesis and translation to Airase's interest in defending his land by creating connections with a symbol of karai power—EIB concerned strategic modes of transformative inclusion, not cultural preservationism. In the Guarani case, these changes were observable in the shift toward an interculturalism both thought and practiced where Guarani could "walk among the karai" and "speak without shame." As I concluded in chapter 2, I see EIB not as *the* privileged site for indigenous epistemic agendas, but rather as a way of clearing space for such projects to unfold elsewhere, by virtue of EIB's slow dismantling of colonial ideologies institutionalized in the traditional school system.

In linguistic terms, EIB also had potential yet remained burdened by constraints. Languages like Guarani and those of other indigenous peoples of eastern Bolivia, as well as Aymara and Quechua, are still at risk of disappearance. Ideally EIB would serve to further language survival. Yet school-based programs of language maintenance generally fail if wider ideological, economic, and social conditions remain absent. As with epistemic and cultural practices, languages must thrive beyond the school. By countering the stigma attached to native languages, certain advances were made. Yet EIB promised, ultimately failing, to thrive even in its modest form of a balanced bilingual pedagogy. This is not because of flaws in EIB as an idea, but because of the myriad political and practical challenges that I explored throughout this book.

Politically, EIB offered an articulatory scaffold. Against the logic of reform, which was to institutionalize and manage education as a narrowly conceived project for creating human capital, the logic of movements like that of the Guarani was to treat EIB as an instrument for an expansive social movement practice. The scribe and leader Enrique Camargo summarized this for me himself, saying, "ñanderembiporu ko," EIB was our tool, our instrument. EIB's potential lies in its possibilities for facilitating and mobilizing other kinds of change. Rather than represent a directed, classroom-based consciousness-raising agenda, EIB served as a networking and communicative vehicle, facilitating the movement of leaders, resources, symbols, and new practices like assemblies, marches, commemorations, and confrontations that emerged from multiple loci of talk, experience, and memory. As its political utility decreased, leaders shifted to other tactics and priorities.

On the other hand, many indigenous communities and leaders did not embrace EIB. I suggested that this derived in part from the weight of colonial history and in part from pragmatic understandings of schooling as a vehicle for accessing the Spanish-speaking power structure. Yet I argued that the nature of contingent articulations and variegated histories of the state—linking unions, movements, intellectual and leadership circles, and indigenous lives—nurtured or stifled support for EIB based on how it was conceived in terms of potential empowerment.

At the level of the state, EIB emerged as an appendage of a broader set of processes that sought to implement new forms of knowledge control and management broadly oriented toward the market-centric ideology of neoliberalism. Elite political objectives contradicted indigenous expectations about interculturalism. As reform proceeded, EIB was reframed from its origins as a culturally creative and socially liberating agenda into a special education that provoked distrust from its putative beneficiaries and generated nervous anxieties among the powerful.

Among the traditional ruling classes, EIB found tentative support among those willing to engage its possibilities but fearful of imagined extremisms. Rather than dismiss EIB as a Trojan horse of neoliberalism, I optimistically saw in the project the possibility for instigating a reflective learning process among political elites. While Prada (2007) suggests that a "rupture" with colonialism is needed before the democratic force of the people can be unleashed, at best EIB gave the possibility of mutual recognition between "epistemic contemporaries" (Benhabib 2002). This tentative learning process may now be truncated by rising polarization. As education reform and EIB enter the national agendas of countries like Peru and Guatemala, these lessons may prove useful, at least for the social movements and intellectual activists who must dance with stubborn and recalcitrant power holders reluctant to pursue even such modest transformative agendas.

A NEW GEOPOLITICS OF KNOWLEDGE

I am often asked whether or not Morales supports EIB, a question easy to answer (yes, at least by virtue of the MAS education proposal, he does). The new MAS proposal calls for decolonization, interculturalism, intraculturalism, and plurilingualism—for all Bolivians. Trilingual education has been proposed for all Bolivians (indigenous languages, Spanish, and English). I will return to these terms below. Yet a deeper set of processes underlies knowledge politics and the origins of the MAS. Understanding the current moment requires backtracking a bit to trace the social movement articulations that currently sustain the MAS regime and the resuscitation of older languages of assimilation and mestizaje that seek to counter it.

The Return of the Dinosaurs

By 1999, when EIB had begun to confront the limits of official interculturalism, indigenous movements, progressive NGOs, and various critical intellectuals were already engaged in deepening the project through their own rethinkings of interculturalism and their critiques of education reform (e.g., Garcés and Guzmán 2003; Regalsky and Laurie 2007). Alongside the intensification of indigenous and popular movement protagonism and neoliberalism's unraveling, there also emerged signs of reactionary entrenchment on the part of elites (Gustafson 2002; López 2005:473−77).

Between Goni's ouster in 2003 and before Evo's victory in 2005, I returned to Bolivia. The country was experiencing a period of intense political mobilization and uncertainty. Attacks on EIB both before 2003 and in the wake of Goni's flight were on the rise. For conservatives, bilingualism served as a metaphor of indigenous radicalism. Attacking EIB offered a way of denying the legitimacy of indigenous movements, since speaking in native languages was said to be a sign of the refusal of modernity, a marker of impenetrable differences that posed atavistic threats to universal knowledge, progress, and modernity. Such voices began to rise most strongly from circles of intellectuals in eastern Bolivia, where opposition to the national-popular-indigenous project arose around the city of Santa Cruz. Writers from Santa Cruz gained increasing coverage in the national media and set the tone for a broader urban and middle-class reaction suggesting that a MAS victory would bring indigenous revenge (*revanchismo*) and a racial war. For example, one Cruceño, a former diplomat and frequent editorialist, complained in late 2003 that promoting indigenous languages constituted an absurd retreat into ignorance (Saavedra Weise 2003): "In Bolivia we could begin by unifying teaching and schooling in *castellano* [Spanish], one of the great universal languages and in its own right an important point of access to the world. Later has to come English, for practical and convenient reasons, setting aside whether one likes it or not, if it is imperialist or not. It is useful. Period."

A Cruceño historian wrote in a similar vein, synthesizing the modern colonial vision so clearly that it merits reproduction at length (Prudencio Lizón 2004; emphasis original):

> When the Latin American Republics were born into independent life, all of them had indigenous populations that spoke their own languages. But the majority of these [republics] made efforts to culturally unify their countries around the massive teaching of Spanish, or Portuguese in the case of Brazil. The result has been their conformation into *true nations*, joined by language, religion, and historical tradition. But in the last years of the twentieth century, decisions radically changed this integrationist policy for another directed toward "indigenizing" the peasant. Such an extreme was reached that even in the Political Constitution of the State it is indicated that Bolivia is a pluricultural and multiethnic country. Consequent to that position, the educational authorities have made efforts to implant a system of literacy training based on the teaching of reading and writing in the autochthonous languages before it is done in Spanish. It was not taken into account that those languages are not written languages, and that the peasant child, when they learn to read in Spanish, will never again do so in their vernacular language. And in relation to the *indios*, it is enough that they learn Spanish or move closer to a city so that they become culturally Mestizos. Therefore, the origin and essence of being Bolivian is not pluricultural, it is Christian, Spanish, and our Viceregal and Republican Culture, eminently Mestizo.

Another frequent editorialist decried the "adulation of the masses," suggesting that democracy and interculturalism had gone too far and that it was time to reestablish an order where the "peasants" knew their correct place (Kempff 2005).

There was no place for indigeneity in these urban-centric visions of the future of Bolivia. These attitudes denied the right of indigenous subjects like Morales to occupy positions of legitimate power, since, by their logic, if one were so premodern, the election must have represented an aberration. If these were modern citizens they would be Spanish-speaking mestizos and have no right to clamor for difference at all. Intercultural reformists—even those of the donor agencies and elite-led parties—looked quite progressive when compared to these extremists.

Dismantling EIB

In the meantime, EIB as an institutional practice was undergoing its own slow decay. Between 1999 and 2002, social conflict virtually brought EIB implementation to a halt. By 2002 the façade of intercultural enlightenment among the elite parties had dissolved. In practical terms EIB survived hanging by a thread of aid from Denmark and Germany (López 2005:468–99). Amalia Anaya left her post after Goni's election in 2002. While many of the midlevel reform staff managed to keep their jobs, the Education Ministry entered a period of turbulent churning. A series of anti-EIB ministers followed, all of whom, according to EIB activists on the inside, either explicitly or implicitly began shutting down support for EIB.

Guarani scribes no longer worked in the reform offices. Textbook production, like the teachers' institutes, had been outsourced. Lucrative textbook-writing contracts—in the millions of dollars—were granted to private firms. Guarani (like their Aymara and Quechua counterparts) were now working as individual contractors for two Spanish publishing companies, Santillana Editions and Santa María Editions. Santillana is a subsidiary of the Prisa Group, a Spanish conglomerate owned by Spain's version of Rupert Murdoch (Jesús de Polanco, recently succeeded by his son Ignacio). The Prisa Group also owns Madrid's conservative newspaper *El País* and La Paz's own *La Razón*. Santa María Editions is a Spanish multinational firm affiliated with the Catholic Church. Outsourced schoolbook production occurred in the name of quality improvement, yet it represented the transfer of power to private capital and the erection of another firewall between indigenous movements and epistemic authority. Even more ironic—almost humorous, if not outrageous—is this paradox of colonial history: indigenous text writers were again serving as translators and contextualizers for Spanish institutions linked to the imperial spread of language, capital, power, and religion. It was as if the clock had shifted back to the days of Antonio Nebrija.

These companies were careful to defend interculturalism even as they worked to monitor and control indigenous writers and textbook content. Santa María's Web site (www.grupo-sm.com/inicio.asp) touts its focus on the "dialogue between cultures" along with "Christian values" and "liberty." Yet their business is business. In an interview with the editorial chief of one of the offices in La Paz, the primary concern voiced to me about working with indigenous languages did not concern linguistic or epistemic difference but the meeting of deadlines and controlled budgets. Elsa Aireyu, who worked briefly in one of the editorial offices, complained that the companies forbade Guarani from speaking with each other about their work, for fear that business secrets would be exposed. Of course, since they all lived together in the "Guarani Embassy" in La Paz, they spoke on a day-to-day basis (interview, 2005; also qtd. in Albó and Anaya 2003:164–65). Camargo, who also worked briefly as a writer, argued that there was indeed a valid concern with "quality" but that curricular content had moved further away from Guarani "masters of knowledge."

At the other end of the chain linking state policy to local lives, I traveled from La Paz back to Itavera in 2004. With continued aid from the local NGOs, the community seemed to be doing well on the surface. NGO monies had helped build new stucco houses, and there was a gleaming new brick schoolhouse, part of the infrastructural improvements brought by education reform. Yet a much older Airase was still frequently leaving the community to seek work, since local corn remained insufficient. In addition, the death of Yari had cast a somber mood over the community. Worse yet, a youngster who had been one of my fishing guides years ago had recently committed suicide. These were signs of hard times that generated speculations about witchcraft, a marker of rising social tensions. In the new school, the teacher was a young Spanish-speaking Guarani woman from one of the mixed communities upriver. She was an interim teacher with neither a formal teacher's certificate nor training in EIB. EIB was no longer practiced. Although the regional APG had grown significantly, its battles against gas companies—Brazil's Petrobras and Repsol's YPF—now largely shaped its day-to-day priorities and those of its NGO supporters.

Back in Camiri, the teachers' school survived in the midst of uncertainty. Each year saw the entrance of karai and Guarani students, and there was a real sense of intercultural dialogue underway. Yet the outsourcing to the Baha'i-run Nur University was of ambiguous benefit. As a colleague, Valentin Arispe, concluded in a master's thesis written about the INSPOC, the university was unable to displace the APG as a vetting organization, and the APG retained significant control over staffing and other decisions (Arispe 2006). Yet the constraints of outsourcing, new techniques of management, and budget limitations had restricted the politically crucial work of defending EIB in practice.

On my visit to the INSPOC in 2004, I sat in on a meeting between the faculty and the Nur University accountant who had come down from Santa Cruz to go over the yearly budget. He started the meeting with an assessment of the institute's progress on test scores. "We were in the lowest rankings in the national tests," he said, using the English word *ranking*, "but we are starting to make progress." Despite these low marks, he soon turned to cuts in the budget. "Unfortunately, budget-wise, we are going to be pretty short this year."

"How are we going to support bilingualism and social participation?" asked one of the staff. "We cannot produce materials in Guarani or encourage the participation of the Guarani communities without resources." For the Guarani, social participation was understood as the means for pursuing a diversified curricula (through engaging the *arakuaa iya*, or knowledge masters) and maintaining the link between the APG and the educational process. Both *participation* and *diversification* were legal terms of the education reform, but no mechanisms or resources existed to pursue either.

"The only solution is to look for help from outside," said the accountant. "Maybe NGOs? The Europeans? UNICEF?" The officialization of EIB did not bring robust state support. Guarani, who had struggled to end dependence on aid entities, were now told to turn back again to donors and NGOs.

The accountant later shifted the conversation to accreditation. "We will go through a process of self-evaluation," he said. The staff were to prepare for the arrival of outside evaluators. "This will involve establishing criteria, indicators, and indexes, those things that we can use to measure the quality of educational processes." These measures would permit the "management of statistics, crucial to making decisions." Perhaps for the benefit of the two foreign researchers present, he emphasized the importance of evaluation: "We have to be like any developed country in aspiring to achieve quality of educational services." This would require, he said, creating a "culture of self-regulation [*auto-regulación*] . . . [and it] is not always easy to incorporate this culture into an organization."[3] Guarani had been working to create a native pedagogy tied both to the exigencies of quality and to a cultural and political project articulated with regional transformation. With this managerial turn it was no wonder that the expansion of EIB had led to the loss of its organizing potential.

The main issue of concern to the staff was their paychecks. "The state [via the university] is already behind on our salaries two months," said a Guarani teacher. Nor, she went on, had promised infrastructure been built. Students studied and lived in sweltering open-walled garages and tin-roofed Quonset huts.

"Well," offered the accountant, "we're in a difficult situation. I don't think it will happen again." Fulfilling the role of political firewall, the accountant discouraged any thought of protest: "We're not going to get anything else out of the ministry with any kind of pressure. We just have to focus on our responsibility, which is teaching classes." The staff responded by sitting quietly in classic Guarani style. A few weeks later they mobilized again, marching, suspending classes, and threatening a hunger strike. Their move achieved a visit from the education minister, the release of paychecks, and the beginning of construction on the new buildings. Between new forms of control, older modes of contestation thrived.

Indigenous Rearticulations

The Guarani had in fact been intensifying their strategies alongside national processes. They marched in 2000 and 2002 to defend land reform and to demand the constitutional assembly. During the conflicts of 2003, the APG joined the national protest against Goni. The APG had also joined the Indigenous and Originary Pact, an alliance of highland and lowland indigenous and peasant organizations that began to congeal loosely around the MAS project. The expansion of Bolivia's natural gas industry with wells and pipelines on Guarani lands had also generated new sites of conflict. Between 2001 and 2005, there were yearly Guarani road and rail blockades, gas-plant occupations, and marches seeking to pressure gas companies to respect agreements or to pressure the government to concede a greater share of royalties. During visits in 2005 and 2006, I encountered the Guarani not in their offices but out on the highway, manning road blockades and squaring off against riot police sent down from Santa Cruz. The Guarani teachers' institute, faculty and students together, comprised the main bloc of protestors on both occasions.

Indigenous organizations were also involved in mobilizing nationally around education and EIB. Working through the structure of the Indigenous Education Councils, bodies created by education reform, workshops and meetings were held between 2000 and 2005 to cultivate a position in defense of EIB. These meetings were quietly facilitated by EIB-friendly international donors. One UNICEF event I attended in December of 2002 began with indigenous Aymara *yatiris* (knowers, priests) burning incense and coca in a ritual called a *q'uwa*. All participants—indigenous and not—were invited to share in the offering, and UNICEF's Italian director and the then minister of education, Isaac Maidana, both chewed coca and watched respectfully.

At the event, Xavier Albó, one of the longtime gurus and supporters of bilingual education, commented optimistically that despite the obstacles still in the path of bilingual education, the staging of the k'oa showed that at "least the country had now gotten to a point where things that were once only done in the home are now done in plain sight." Yet participants recognized that EIB had stalled and that mobilizing demanded a broader perspective. The Quechua leader Froilán Condori—whom I knew as an early EIB activist (see chapter 4) and who as of 2005 was a MAS representative in Congress—stated in his presentation: "If we are just going to talk about EIB, we fail. [We are talking] about economics, the quality of life, the constitution of a more equitable society [*una sociedad más equitativa*] . . . we are not doing this [EIB] so we can end up singing the national anthem of the United States."

Like the Indigenous and Originary Pact that backed demands for the constitutional assembly and eventually rallied behind the MAS, an Indigenous and Originary Peoples' Education Block also emerged. The block—including many rural teachers, the APG, CIDOB, and various Andean organizations —consolidated a position in defense of EIB and deepened it, introducing a new discourse on schooling as "a decolonizing bilingual intercultural education with territorial control and self-determination" (CONAMAQ et al. 2004). As the criollo ruling class retreated from its soft multiculturalism into an increasingly anti-indigenous stance, the indigenous and popular movements revived a deeper historical trajectory of education in convergence with a nationally rooted popular struggle.

The Indigenous Education Councils also began reformulating their vision of curricular knowledge. They criticized the reform's vision of indigenous knowledge as the "diversified branches" of a national "common trunk." New proposals argued for inverting the picture to place indigeneity at the center of knowledge production (the roots of the tree) and thus at the center of educational, territorial, and political authority. Knowledge from the "outside" was imagined as the complementary branches, while the trunk and its roots represented indigenous life and knowledge (Garcés and Guzmán 2003:29). These shifts were tied to expectations about the coming MAS victory, changes that future researchers and collaborators will ideally engage.

AFTER EVO: BETWEEN NATIONALISM
AND PLURINATIONALISM

When I returned again to Bolivia and Guarani country in 2005, just before the election of Morales, a sense of expectation had been added to the ongoing uncertainty. Mobilization continued as the rule of the day as state institutions were brought into question and social movements mobilized to put pressure on the elites of Santa Cruz, now the mainstay of opposition to the MAS. The following summer, after Morales's election, I returned again to Camiri to find the pro-MAS Guarani euphoric. Others, to be sure, were not so excited. Some Guarani were skeptical of the MAS and feared an onslaught of kollas into the region. The Isoseño-Guarani leadership, building on its long-standing orientation toward Santa Cruz, went in the opposite direction, cultivating an alliance with the oligarchic elite (Lowrey 2006).

Camiri was much the same as before, yet with Morales's victory came a small but very visible shift. I passed by the young conscripts outside the military garrison on the main plaza every day, and they were now carrying AK-47s, not the Belgian FALs from before. The global icon of third world anti-imperialist struggle—or authoritarian terror and violence, depending on one's view—had come to Camiri courtesy of Morales and his new ally Hugo Chávez.

Camiri also set the stage for one of Morales's first gestures as president, a national literacy campaign. The plan was to educate 1.2 million functionally illiterate Bolivians. For popular governments literacy campaigns aimed at adults sought to affirm the role of the educator state and ratify ideologies of nationalism, anti-imperialism, and popular democracy. When Morales came to Camiri to launch the campaign, a new generation of Guarani leaders stood at his side. The vice-president of the APG, Petrona Bruno, made a stirring speech. Back in 1992 a matrix of U.S. (World Bank), European (UNICEF, UNESCO), and Bolivian funds had launched the Guarani's own literacy campaign. Yet in 2005 the literacy plan was a Cuban-designed and Venezuela-funded campaign called Yo Sí Puedo (Yes, I Can), after the

FIGURE 8 For a new Bolivia. The modest "house of the popular campaign" of the MAS in Camiri. The names of its candidates for the constitutional assembly, including the Guarani leader Avilio Vaca (later elected), are painted on the outer wall.

highly-celebrated Cuban model. Bruno stood beside Morales, who had invited both the Cuban and Venezuelan ambassadors. Yo Sí Puedo sounded rather like any liberal individualizing Western vision of education, yet the associations with counterhegemonic revolutionary regimes and class struggle were foregrounded. The new president argued that schooling was about the "deneoliberalization" of the pueblo: "They [the nonindigenous elite] never took a chance on education in our country, because education is about the liberation of our peoples [*nuestros pueblos*]" ("Alfabetización" 2006; "Aspiran alfabetizar" 2006). As I talked with leaders later to catch up on these details, I was pleasantly surprised to learn—more for reasons of historical irony than any ideological conviction about the direction of the process—that one of the old APG leaders had gone to Cuba to translate the Yo Sí Puedo model to Guarani. The MAS had opened a modest office in Camiri, and a Guarani leader was also later elected to represent the party in the constitutional assembly (see figure 8).

In part because of the Guarani and in part because of the massive gas reserves under this territory, the region constituted a crucial point of articulation that echoed both the indigenous and the nationalist turn of the MAS. Yet the contradictions between a nationalist, state-centric vision of anti-imperialist education—following Cuban or Venezuelan models—and a plurinationalist indigenous model of multiple centers of epistemic and territorial authority has now emerged as one line of difference within the MAS project.

Criollo Anxieties, Redux

While broad swaths of social movements rallied behind Morales, the crucial loyalties and sentiments of the urban middle classes were up for grabs. Most criollos I knew were enthusiastic about the new president, yet they comprised a biased sample since most of my acquaintances were tied to the progressive work of NGOs. A few were guarded. They acknowledged the significance of an indigenous president, an expression of the interculturalism that so many had rhetorically supported. Yet they voiced concerns about the future of education reform and beyond. Beneath these concerns there lay a deep criollo anxiety about the end of race and class privileges. Some expressed doubts about whether indigenous peoples and the MAS had the knowledge to run the state education system (and the wider state itself).[4]

One left-leaning criollo philosopher working with bilingual education told me with a wry smile that in their coffee shop circles his friends joked about their support for Morales. "Yes, we all said we would vote for him; but then we asked each other, 'What if he actually wins?' " Another colleague who had gone from grass-roots EIB activist to high-level functionary in the Education Ministry was more conservative. He argued that radical Indians, especially the Aymara, were a greater threat to Bolivia than neoliberalism. The regionalists of Santa Cruz, he argued, were liberals in comparison to leaders like Quispe. Though he exaggerated the extremes (and Quispe is not a close ally of Morales), he did face the prospect of unemployment given that he was not a MAS militant. He questioned my cautious sympathy for Morales. "It's easy for you anthropologists to pontificate on the indigenous revolution from afar. But you don't know what it's like to live in the midst of this!"

At one dinner-table conversation before the elections, his teenage daughters echoed what they had heard in their private middle-class high school in

La Paz. In answer to their questions about my preferences, I told them that if I were Bolivian I might vote for Morales. They rolled their eyes in mockery and offered a litany of complaints: "Evo is ugly! Evo is a *cholito*. If we vote for him, the USA is going to close down everything. We're not going to have CDs, DVDs, or refrigerators! We're going to be the second Cuba! There are going to be pure *cholitos* [in government], and they don't have experience, they will take us to ruin. We'll be poor. And my dad won't have work anymore because he doesn't have very dark skin!" I turned to their family maid (and the girls' longtime nanny), an indigenous woman of around thirty-five who was washing dishes and eavesdropping on the conversation. "Who will you vote for?" I asked. On hearing her quiet "Evo," accompanied by a barely perceptible smile, the two daughters shouted, laughing, "Aaaaa! ¡*Traidora*! [Traitor]"

The breakdown of colonial hierarchies unsettled social spheres that extended from government to the markets and streets and the intimacy of the household. These vignettes reveal a deeper obstacle to interculturalism: the inability of elites and criollo mestizos to transcend their dependence on certain languages of the state, on ways of speaking of and viewing the nation as an order defined by criollo rulers and indio or "cholito" ruled. By appealing to aesthetic and consumer desires, central to middle-class attempts to stave off their own descent into poverty (and proximity to indigeneity), the conservative elite found a ready audience for a message of racial fear. Going with the MAS would lead to ugliness and economic ruin. Defending the status quo would provide the possibility of accessing the consumerist modernity symbolized in Western power.

DECOLONIZATION VERSUS AUTONOMY

The new government's proposal for the decolonization of education became front-page news as the country prepared for the National Education Congress of July 2006 and for the constitutional assembly. It was in this venue that the new law to replace the 1994 education reform law would be debated. Felix Patzi, a onetime critic of EIB, was the new minister of education and now its main defender. The proposed law, named after Warisata's founders, Avelino Siñani and Elizardo Pérez, would be "decolonizing, liberating, anti-imperialist, revolutionary, and transformative," a breathless leap from the managerial rhetoric of interculturalism and human capital formation (MECs

2006). The plan spoke of a deep overhaul of education reform while acknowledging that some of its tenets had been positive. Most important, decolonization was for everyone, not just for indigenous peoples.

Patzi explained decolonization through an epistemic critique—often impenetrable for journalists—frequently simplified into a vision of racial equality and opportunity. For example, in one interview, he argued that "the whites always monopolized education, work, and political opportunities, and the indigenous were condemned to occupations of lower hierarchy, or that had no prestige or status. That has to change" ("Nuestros estudiantes" 2006).[5] Furthermore, the new law proposed ending the official teaching of Catholicism in public curricula and the cancellation of the *convenio* through which the Catholic Church ran some fifteen hundred public schools with state funds.[6] The law and Patzi frequently invoked new values associated with Andean peoples (reciprocity, complementarity, communitarianism) that would enter into the practice and discourse of schooling. Interculturalism would be maintained as the dialogue between cultures, yet intraculturalism would be strengthened as the reconstruction of cultures, languages, and identities from within indigenous peoples' lives (MECs 2006:18).

These ideas marked distance from the 1994 education reform while reproducing some of its core tenets. These included the support for EIB, as well as calls for technological and scientific education "complementary to indigenous knowledges," education for production, and "educational quality" and "administrative efficiency," all more or less congruent with the existing law. Teachers mainly expected the reversal of marketization and decentralization. Morales himself made it clear that the fragmentation of schooling had come to an end. Invoking the body of Tupak Katari—drawn and quartered by the Spaniards—he transposed the indigenous rebel into a symbol of the new nation itself ("El gobierno decide" 2007): "I am an enemy of the [possibility] that four sectors be drawn and quartered by way of the constitutional assembly. I am talking about the armed forces, the national police, education, and health."

As expressed in the new law, decolonization envisions an education system rooted in part between and among different indigenous territorialities, but one still broadly Andean-centric. Decolonization was a relatively new way of speaking that emerged among university intellectuals in the Andes. It was clearly a project in phases of development and expansion that had yet to ferment beyond its Andeanist core. When I sat down at a discussion of decolonization with faculty of the Guarani teachers' school in late 2006, there was a palpable fear, especially among karai faculty, that it referred to a coming radicalism like that reflected in the Aymara mobilizations of Quispe. On the other hand, new Guarani leaders involved in the Education Congress had embraced the rhetoric, saying in one meeting, perhaps for my benefit, that "those with blue eyes would no longer have the first say in everything."

In part, the decolonization agenda extends the tentative experiment with bilingual intercultural education that emerged during the 1990s. However, decolonization goes beyond the liberal vision of interculturalism in several ways. First, it rejects the colonial divide maintained in official interculturalism. Decolonization is not primarily something indigenous peoples need— the way neoliberals imagined interculturalism—but rather something the q'aras, the criollos and whites, also need. How this might proceed is uncertain, given widespread skepticism among the nonindigenous middle and upper classes about the value and worthiness of indigenous languages and cosmovisions. The initial, very modest proposal to introduce indigenous languages into the curricula of all public and private schools met resounding opposition.

Decolonization also goes beyond interculturalism with *intra*culturalism. Interculturalism in the liberal mode was construed as a call for dialogue between and across cultural differences, largely interpreted as an attempt to get the indigenous to open up to the outside and the supposedly universal. The stance was based on a flawed sense that indigenous peoples and cultures were in fact largely closed (*cerrado*) to non-Indians. In fact it is probably more the other way around. Furthermore, intraculturalism, the strengthening of indigenous identities, histories, and languages from within, argued that there was a need to remedy the violences produced by colonialism, what the Guarani referred to as "dispersal." Creating and sustaining spaces— geographic, geopolitical, and institutional—for constructing alternative knowledges constitutes a key prerequisite for this process.

Another ministry official of the MAS (Huanca Soto 2005) imagined two challenges to this indigenous proposal. Decolonization assumed first, decentering the monopoly on theory currently held by European and Western pedagogical experts; and second, the establishment of democratic forms to manage knowledge with alternative subjects and intellectual practices (*gestionar el conocimiento*), precisely what the Guarani had attempted to do in their engagements with EIB. Against what R. Huanca Soto refers to as "epistemic normalization"—which continues the colonial dependency on the notion of universal knowledge—he argued for the notion of "epistemic insurgence." While derived from a critical anticolonial stance, the maintenance of concepts such as *gestión* (management) reveals the entanglement between traditional school administration and the intellectual circles of decolonization. As Huanca Soto argued, this was not a radical anti-Western stance, but rather an intercultural and intracultural stance aimed at generating an "epistemic *tinku*," a ritual encounter, conflictive, but ultimately based in mutual exchange. Much like EIB, decolonization was not about pursuing radically alternative schooling forms, but about seeking complementarity between standard curricular models and emergent indigenous epistemologies.

The Autonomist Challenge

The decolonizing thrust of the MAS project had a nails-on-the-chalkboard effect for the elite-led autonomist agenda. The recolonizing counterattack came quickly. Neoliberal discourse often glorified the community as an actor in the management of its own education. Yet terms like *communitarian* in the proposed law became flashpoints for conservative media assaults that associated decolonization both with indigenous primitivity and Cuban- (or Venezuelan-) inspired communism. On one talk-show broadcast just after the July 2006 Education Congress, the hostess and her guests (a representative of the Catholic University and two rectors of private evangelical universities) attacked the proposal for "taking the country back five hundred years" and attempting to "force us to change our forms of teaching."

The law, and the Education Congress which was supposed to generate mass support for it, met with deep opposition. The Catholic and evangelical churches, urban teachers, and private and public universities formed a conservative block against the so-called indigenous block. Unable to vote it down, this new cluster of conservative opposition abandoned the event. As would happen with the constitutional assembly, the autonomists took the tactic of disrupting or abandoning sites of dialogue given that they could not muster the votes to defeat the proposals democratically. The new law, at this writing, has yet to be passed in Congress.

The new foci of elite regionalist power in Santa Cruz also initiated a number of de facto assaults on MAS power in the name of regional autonomy. Now allied with urban schoolteachers whose loyalty to the region outstripped their loyalty to the union or to national education, the governor of Santa Cruz named his own state education superintendent. A parallel superintendent (of the MAS) also exists, and both battle—physically and legally—to manage regional school administration. Similar tactics of de facto (and illegal) seizures of state power unfolded in the allied urban city regions of Tarija, Trinidad, and, later, Sucre. In Santa Cruz tactics have also included the publication and insertion of their own textbooks and discourses in public schools, an intensified turn toward regionalist folklore in schools (demanding the display of regional flags, the insertion of regional foods in school breakfast programs), and calls for regional loyalty by urban schoolteachers. It is, in short, a grab for de facto sovereignty by way of control over legitimate knowledge. In Santa Cruz, representatives of the Catholic Education Commission—whose national office had pioneered EIB in the early 1990s—also allied themselves with the autonomist agenda. A new stance, more neoconservative than neoliberal, invoked universal paradigms of knowledge as science while rallying behind the symbols of Christianity. Marches of parents' organizations against the education law were staged in all major cities. The primary rallying points were the defense of children from communism and satanism. The emerging struggle over knowledge no longer pits a homogenizing neoliberal state against indigenous epistemic diversity, but generates regionalized fields of struggle in the colonial language of Christianity against savagery.

Finally, in late 2006, Morales was forced to capitulate in the face of other rising conflicts. The young sociologist Patzi was removed from office and replaced with Victor Cáceres, a schoolteacher and former union leader who came out of the urban teachers' union. The unions were temporarily mollified, as this was the first time that a schoolteacher had been named minister since before the advent of the neoliberal era. In a sign of instability and weakness in the education field, the MAS also dismissed Cáceres a few months later for showing more loyalty to the union than to the party. At this writing a progressive intellectual of the criollo left—tied to one of Bolivia's powerful intellectual clans—Magdalena Cajías, is occupying the post of education minister. The proposals for decolonization and intraculturalism are on hold. The MAS thus retreated quickly after two conflictive missteps in schooling change, from the radical decolonizing stance of Patzi to the failed rapprochement with union leaders. The embrace of the light-skinned intelligentsia is perhaps seen as a safer way of legitimating school control as the country has become more embroiled in violent conflicts over the new constitution.

Reconciling Decolonization and Nationalism: Plurinationalist Visions

The tension between indigenous and nationalist visions of schooling emerges in the debates over their potential mode of articulation, the discourse of plurinationalism. Its critics on the right see the concept of plurinationalism as merely a model for ethnic federalism, a kind of balkanization of the country around indigenous territories. On the left—even within the MAS fold—proponents of old-style nationalism see plurinationalism as an invention of NGOs, destined to break up the country and open it further to multinational capital and U.S. interests (Solíz Rada 2007). Plurinationalism is seen as a threat to existing state jurisdictions and has galvanized urban middle-class support for their own kind of territoriality centered around the departments and their primary cities. While indigenous "tribalism" and "fundamentalism" are seen as threatening the fabric of the nation, the autonomist agenda has also morphed into a racially tinged enclosure around regional identities—the *camba*, the *chapaco*, and so on. As these identities have their roots in the outright exclusion of native peoples, or in narratives of mestizaje that do not allow for the legitimate expression of indigenous difference, regional identities are converted into racially marked tribes themselves.

Yet reading MAS intellectuals like Prada (2007a, 2007b), it is more accurate to understand plurinationalism as the vision of a transformative *process* through which the traditional metaphors of the body associated with the nation are replaced with metaphors of maps. The state should be approached as a set of "manipulable cartographies," Prada writes, through which new geographies of power—diverse much like the fragmented topography of state territory—will be rearranged and emerge in new articulations. The shift away from the metaphor of the body is crucial, as within it lie the metaphors of blood, race, and homogeneity that were at the heart of the coloniality of power. In Prada's terms, admittedly a bit imprecise, plurinationalism emerges as the articulation of pluralities, a multisocietal view of the nation that may or may not imply simply rearranging territorial lines and boundaries.

Che Guevara

The challenges to the decolonizing project were also clear back in Camiri. In the summer of 2006, I made a point of tracking down leaders of the rural teachers' union, part of my own attempt to rearticulate this story with actors whom I had largely avoided in my early years in Camiri. I looked up a person from the days of EIB, the Ray-Ban–sporting professor I called "Dip-shit" in chapter 2. Now retired, but always eager to chat, he came to get me one Saturday morning in my hostel and took me to a teachers' union hang-out, a beer and chicken place named Chuy's.

I had a list of questions, yet as beer and cigarettes mounted, I found my attempts at systematization foiled by his grandiloquent tales of the old days. Professor Oswaldo, I will call him, told of having parlayed his alliance with the Guarani into a strategic embrace of education reform. He boasted that Amalia Anaya had been one of his close allies—and he hers—as they con-fronted local resistance to reform. While I hoped to capture a sense of how Guarani teachers were now engaging the union, he talked more of his successes in politics. He had eventually won a seat on the Camiri city coun-cil. Soon his cellphone, strapped to his belt where his Ray-Bans once rode, went off. He shouted into his phone, laughing, "Are you the ones who are going to teach Patzi how to speak Spanish?!!" Guffawing for my bene-fit at this jab against the Aymara education minister, he barked into the phone. "Where are you? Get over here to Chuy's Chicken! And bring Che Guevara!"

A few minutes later the rural teachers' union leadership arrived. Greeting us with a round of handshakes and a cheerful acknowledgment of the beer bottles arrayed on the table, they pulled up their chairs. Don Chuy came over with two more tall cold ones. The four were a composite of karai rural teachers. One, who I will call Durán, came from Charagua. He kept silent most of the afternoon. He distrusted me and cared little for the Guarani. The second was Rómulo, a math professor who had worked briefly in the Gua-rani teachers' institute and had even done a few days with them on the 1998 hunger strike. He was now the union president. The third was Santiago, the ex-husband of one of the Guarani scribes, a former national union leader who led resistance against bilingual education (and the work of his ex-wife) in the early 1990s. We knew each other by reputation, but knowing we disagreed on EIB, we had never sat down to chat. He remained critical, but we were open to talk.

Finally, there was the character the others called Che Guevara. Mario was a rural teacher from a small town south of Camiri. He intentionally sought to embody the image of the iconic revolutionary: bushy black beard, an unruly shock of hair with graying streaks, and a black beret with a shiny star pinned to it. Che images were ubiquitous in the region, as were memories of his passage through nearby towns. Guevara (the real one) continued to provide a reference point for masculine expressions of vanguardist heroism for many Guarani, MAS activists, and the rural teachers. Now here in front of me appeared his doppelgänger. I placed Mario—no deep ethnographic insight necessary—on the left side of the spectrum. A rough-hewn double of the "Comandante de las Americas," Mario was missing some front teeth and had rugged hands that dwarfed my own keyboard-sensitive fingers. These were signs of an upbringing in the hardscrabble life of the rural poor. He smoked filterless Astoria cigarettes that he said set him apart from the more effeminate Santiago next to him. The real Che, of course, had also requested one last Astoria to smoke before his execution.

Che was suspicious of me, though for different reasons than Durán. Later we warmed to each other as my criticism of education reform opened space for conversation. His conclusion was that reform was nothing less than the failed attempt by the United States and the World Bank to break the revolutionary consciousness of Bolivia: "They wanted to break our socialist consciousness" (querían rompernos la conciencia socialista), he said angrily, "but we broke them!" (pero nosotros los rompimos!). His fist slammed on the table. He later revealed (and my Guarani friends confirmed) that he was an important regional MAS operator. His political leanings had arisen because of the inspiration of his father, who led the karai-dominated CSUTCB peasant union in Cordillera Province for "thirty years." As a MAS activist he had at least transcended his doppelgänger's limitations, reaching out across the ethnolinguistic divide to engage Guarani MASistas and the Andean kolla taxi drivers, market women, and other migrants who were a key segment of Camiri's MAS.

Osvaldo, Durán, Rómulo, and Santiago were by comparison quite conservative. In 2006, Bolivians voted simultaneously to elect representatives to the constitutional assembly and on whether autonomy should be approved for their respective departments. While MAS dominated the assembly voting nationally, eastern Bolivian departments largely voted "Yes" to autonomy, seen as a vote against the MAS agenda. As Che was quick to bring up, all four of his colleagues had voted "Yes," placing them on the side of the regional elite. "You are all siding with the oligarchy," he complained. The four countered in different ways. Rómulo, the union president, defended his rejection of the MAS by stating his class interests clearly, "I have a piece of land south of Boyuibe! And they,"—referring to peasants, the MAS, the Guarani, or any others pushing land reform—"will get it only over my dead body!" Durán, also opposed to the MAS and annoyed by my questions about racism in eastern Bolivia, pointed out that Americans had slaughtered indigenous peoples and that Vikings—here he picked up on my surname—had raped and pillaged. Where, then, did I get the moral authority to question them? Osvaldo, now very drunk, raised his head from where it had been resting on his arms, to ask me whether I could not verify, as an anthropologist, that the Aymara had a genetic problem with the correct pronunciation of Spanish. Against my denial, he insisted that the structure of the throat of the Aymara was biologically different, a factor that contributed to the guttural nature of Aymara and the education minister's difficulty with Spanish.

The MAS articulation and the elite autonomist reaction hinged on these tensions of race, region, and class. Given colonial perceptions of indios as a race marked by biological inferiority and the equally emotive language of nationalist class struggle, this was an axis that could generate openings to dialogue in figures like Che and closures like that simmering behind Durán's silence. Even Che's support for the MAS was qualified. He ultimately agreed with Osvaldo: there was something genetic that kept the Aymara from speaking good Spanish. He also added a note of caution, "I support the MAS, but the MAS education proposal is going to take us backward," he argued. "The curriculum has to be universally socialized [i.e., validated], and who is going to validate an Indianist curriculum?" The narrow opening to indigenous difference could be quickly closed. Against what he saw as too much "Andeanism" in the MAS project—and here I must concur that he had a point—he said, "We all have the right to think. We fought against the impositions of the neoliberal reform, and we are not going to accept the verticalist imposition of the MAS either!" That "right to think" was, in this new juncture, interpreted in terms of regional authority, not in terms of indigenous epistemic rights.

This regionalist stance, whether of the Santa Cruz elites or of activists like Che, could be inflected with a nationalist sentiment, class consciousness, racist intolerance, or a little of all three. Guarani and other indigenous peoples made great strides toward decolonizing these regional milieus. Yet with the victory of the MAS and the reaction of the elite, the slow work of building dialogue and assuaging karai fears threatened to break down. Interculturalism and decolonization may thrive in this new space of pachakuti, or, in fact, they may wither away as the minimal conditions for interlinguistic and interethnic engagement collapse.

EDUCATION, INEQUALITY, DEMOCRACY

The general understanding of neoliberalism's embrace of interculturalism among many anthropologists is that it represented a very narrow, managerial view of culture that masked market-friendly policies with deeply exclusionary effects. Ethnographies of intercultural reformism, generally situated from the position of the less powerful, have highlighted the violent effects of reform and of resistance to neoliberalism. Outside anthropology, observers of processes like Bolivia's intercultural reforms, generally situated among the powerful and among policy makers, are more optimistic. They assume that social policies like EIB and education reform constituted attempts to exercise good governance directed toward social inclusion. If they failed it was a sign of weak incentives, faulty implementation, the absence of necessary conditions, or the strength of irrational, antireformist actors.

In this book I have attempted to engage both kinds of positions at different points in the story. Though my sympathies should be clear, I tried to go beyond a normative stance that exaggerates either the power and reason of good governance or the noble suffering and resistance of "good" social movements. The antistate tenor of much anthropological research, often made in the name of critiquing neoliberalism or of defending subalterns, fails to recognize the practice of social movements as engaged in a battle for the transformation of the state itself. Virtually all movements demand more schooling, embrace legal regimes, and willfully subject themselves to disciplinary forms of control while seeking to modify or redirect these in ways that respond to their lives and aspirations. These processes do not unfold only in dialectics between resistant subjects and a powerful state but rather also through multiple scales, and increasingly across multiple territorial poles of authority, in which power is neither all diffuse nor rooted in a singular hegemonic bloc.

Yet a perspective on what Prada calls the articulations of complexity must ultimately grapple with wider political-economic structures, among them the state, the market, and the role of knowledge. I have not offered prescriptive solutions—nor to the certain dismay of many education experts, have I grappled with the numbers. I considered the place of education in relation to poverty and inequality through a somewhat different path. EIB in the short term played out largely in changing discourses on citizenship and the reconfiguration of institutional geopolitics, what I saw as a democratizing effect. The effects of reform on economic inequality are unclear, and I do not think one could measure such effects in the short term. I suggested, however, that education and EIB only have real transformative potential in articulation with other processes of change (whether struggles over land and power from below or the turn to a more activist form of pro-poor state intervention from above).

On the other hand, conservatives appeal to a Malthusian vision. After the neoliberal regime crumbled, *La Razón* ran a story on Bolivian education and labor markets ("Bolivia tiene" 2004). The story cited an International Labor Organization report suggesting that Bolivia's population, in terms of skills, resembled a skewed hourglass. There were too many professionals at the top, too many nonskilled poor at the bottom, and not enough medium-skilled and vocational workers in the middle. This crude vision sees Bolivia's future in the global market as one of providing cheap resources and basic labor controlled by a small managerial class. The message to urban middle classes was like that deployed to generate fear of the MAS: "You are already struggling to compete for scarce professional jobs, and those dark masses coming from below need to be contained." There was no room for utopias of popular democracy, interculturalism, or industrialization, nor, for that matter, for the pursuit of "postdevelopment" alternatives (Escobar 2005).

So might education contribute to poverty reduction? A recent study carried out by the United Nations Development Program suggested that at current rates of growth, poverty in Bolivia would be eradicated in 178 years

(UNDP 2005). Economists concluded that to break the cycle of individual poverty, a poor Bolivian needs at least thirteen years of schooling, a figure that stands at seven or eight in Brazil (Andersen and Wiebert 2003). Development babble about quality education—with its testing, decentralization, quality control, marketization, and evisceration of the unions—as being crucial in the fight against poverty must thus be taken with caution. Rhetoric about education as the way out of poverty in isolation from other state interventions forms part of a market theodicy that only serves to legitimate the existing social order.

With or without education, real employment possibilities are limited by the capital-intensive pattern of export-oriented growth. As the Bolivian sociologist Ivonne Farah wrote (2005:228):

> It is clear that what is being overwhelmingly offered [in education] are skills and abilities that create conditions of "employability," but without necessarily guaranteeing productive employment. . . . It is thus not surprising that given the levels of social inequality and economic polarization that the Bolivian society is reaching its highest levels of division and conflict. Division manifests itself not only in difference of income and needs, but in an inequality that is compounded in its seriousness by ethnic, geographic, and gender differences. The rural and indigenous groups are those at the most disadvantage. This suggests that politics of recognition that are not accompanied by redistributive policies to counter inequality end up deepening these differences.

One need not share Farah's critical stance to reach these conclusions. Even the Inter-American Development Bank (IADB), which funded structural adjustment and education reform during the 1990s and 2000s, broadly agreed. A decade-long assessment of IADB policy in Bolivia reported that the bank did not "help the country address key development questions such as . . . the problem of ethnic inequalities." While health and education reform were "successful at producing better indicators, [the] youngest cohorts of Bolivians are faced with an unfavorable labor demand scenario in which to apply their human capital [i.e., work]" (IADB 2004:i–ii). Behind the neoliberal speak, in other words, there are deep structural inequalities and no jobs.

Progressive supporters of public education have always argued that schooling is not a stand-alone remedy but a component of wider-ranging changes. This may stem from a view of decolonizing rupture as a prerequisite for democracy as in Prada's comments above, or from a moderate Keynesian call for state intervention. What both entail is a rejection of market orthodoxy and an acknowledgment—rather than a silencing—of the historical depth and just demands of grass-roots struggles. As many indigenous peoples thus recognize, education alone is not a miraculous road to salvation, and nor was EIB necessarily a convincing way to make it so. Beyond EIB, access to higher education and productive employment requires rethinking education—and development—in ways that address both the anticolonial struggle for deep democracy and the realities of globalization.

Looking back on nearly twenty years of indigenous mobilizing and activism tied to education, it is obvious that the turn to what Joanne Rappaport (2005) called "intercultural utopias" is in its gestation stage, while neoliberal interculturalism appears to have run its course. Battles tied to racial, regional, and class inequality and the defense of democracy and public education are breaking out from Santiago, Chile, to Oaxaca, Mexico, and in the cities of the United States, including, as I write, in my own city of St. Louis. Attempts to redefine schooling in accord with the myth of meritocracy, corporate business practice, and market efficiency further the dismantling of democracy and heighten inequality. Education—if one follows the articulatory strategies of Bolivian activists—is a key field through which democratizing movements must challenge the theodicy of the market as the legitimization of exclusion.

The MAS regime now seeks to reposition the state to intervene in economic production and distribution and to pursue a more diversified economy. Given the unfolding violence in the country, whether the boom in natural gas might help eradicate poverty in less than 178 years is an open question. Bolivia could take the path of other resource-rich poor countries, in which politics devolves into rent seeking, corruption, and authoritarianism. If the traditional elite returns to power, the country will follow the path of other enclave economies, with widening gaps of regional inequality.

The distance yet to be traveled, as Amalia Anaya might have said, is evident in the outburst quoted in the epigraph to this chapter. During the early days of the constitutional assembly, a criolla assemblywoman of Santa

Cruz denounced an indigenous woman from Cochabamba for greeting the gathered assembly in Quechua, her native language. The Quechua speaker merely opened her speech (given in Spanish), by saying in Quechua, "We have come here to work." The outburst marked the disruptive, and desperate, tactics of the right in the one fragile space of legislative dialogue in the country. A few decades of grass-roots and official interculturalism do not so easily turn back five centuries of colonialism. Such denials of equal citizenship, humanity, voice, and a shared place in modernity are not propitious signs for a country embarking on the search for a new pluralist democracy.

Postscript

As this book went to press, Bolivia entered a period of intensifying civil conflict marked by regionalist opposition and clamor for autonomy on the right, and the rising tide of expectations for change from the indigenous, popular, and nationalist movements backing the MAS party. The new constitution was passed in late 2007, and after a series of violent illegal actions from the right, was slated for a national referendum vote in early 2009 (Gustafson 2008). The elites of Santa Cruz had successfully mobilized a near-hysteric level of opposition to MAS proposals, bolstered by the notion that urban-centered city regions constituted bastions of modernity arrayed against a rural, indigenous threat. The Guarani maintained in large part a strategic alliance with the MAS based on their own support of the proposal for indigenous autonomy. Bilingual education was returning to the grass roots as APG intellectuals took control over local NGOs. Yet the political stance of the Guarani teachers and the bilingual teachers' institution was clear. In mid-2008, ranchers opposed to Guarani demands for land attacked a group of Guarani accompanying a state land-reform official. A group of Guarani bilingual teachers in training had joined the group and also suffered the organized violence of the landowners. Scores were injured, and some were taken hostage by ranchers and beaten and tortured. As one EIB activist-turned–movement leader wrote me in the wake of the violence, "And now we continue in the struggle . . . working hard and doing things with even more dedication . . . and it is the time to make the world understand that there exists injustice . . . and it is time to end this situation."

A new conjuncture of mobilization and articulation is now emerging out of the congealed knowledge and experience of nearly two decades of resurgence. It is clear that the Guarani embrace of EIB generated durable transformations, while the unfinished history of the decolonization of Bolivia continues. As a Guarani orator might say as his people head out walking toward the future, "We should talk loudly and with happiness in the face of such struggles."

Jae jokuae.

Notes

INTRODUCTION: ETHNOGRAPHIC ARTICULATIONS

1. "Structural adjustment" refers to privatization, downsizing, decentralization, and market liberalization pushed by the IMF and the World Bank during the 1990s.

2. From a reformist perspective, see J. Nelson 1999; Corrales 1999; Contreras and Talavera Simoni 2003; and Grindle 2004. On reform as a Westernizing imposition, see Patzi 1999 and Arnold and Yapita 2006.

3. This ethnographic interest in the meanings of inequality and state legitimacy differs from quantitative studies of inequality (also called social exclusion or inequity) focused on statistical links between school quality, poverty, and individual mobility. See, for example, Reimers 2000; Anderson and Wiebelt 2003; Hall and Patrinos 2005.

4. I take the phrase "coloniality of power" from Quijano 2000. See also Mignolo 2005; Stepputat 2005; Rivera Cusicanqui 1993; Walsh 2005; and below.

5. I use *epistemic* to refer to knowledge, its social and discursive modes of validation, and to power relations that adhere to knowledge production. By "epistemic inequality" I do not mean unequal access to supposedly universal science or literacy, but the racialized epistemic inequality that emerged out of the colonial assault on indigenous languages, religions, and ways of being and knowing in the world. Epistemic equality demands epistemic rights to produce other knowledges as a form of political and territorial authority, distinct from multicultural views of *cultural* rights to individual difference (Mignolo 2005:118–20).

6. In 1989, 65.5 percent of public-sector spending depended on foreign loans (53 percent) and donations (12.5 percent). Between 1998 and 1999, 30 percent of public-sector revenues still came from foreign loans and donations. Neoliberalism maintained foreign debt payments that, along with costs incurred from privatization, made up 44 percent of state finance ministry expenditure by 1999. Bureaucracies were downsized, but ministries like finance—my friends called them the "structural adjusters"—maintained a sizeable staff. Dependent on aid, Bolivian functionaries thus became employees of foreign development agencies. Through this period education maintained a stable percentage of public expenditure around 12 percent (Fernández Terán 2004:82, 126, 134–39).

7. In rural areas, 86 percent of indigenous and 74 percent of nonindigenous Bolivians are poor (Hall and Patrinos 2005).

8. Q./A.: *pacha*, time, space, earth; *kuti*, turnover; as between seasons, epochs, or regimes.

9. Johannes Fabian (1983:32) critiqued early twentieth-century anthropology for placing its subjects of study into a distant place (the past) and denying them the right to speak and know as equals in the present. Yet this denial of coevalness is still central to liberal political theory. Seyla Benhabib (2002) asserts that democratic dialogue and pluralism is possible between those who recognize each other as "epistemic contemporaries" sharing similar temporal horizons of historical experience. This leaves temporality unresolved. Benhabib appears to suggest, like the Great Lie, that "indigenous peoples and native tribes" (135–36) are not "our" epistemic contemporaries.

10. On the early PEIB, see D'Emilio n.d., Muñoz 1997, and López 1997.

11. On Ɨsoso, see Hirsch 1991 and Combés 2005. On urban Guarani in Santa Cruz, see Postero 2006.

12. In the technical view, defended in a World Bank report (Soares et al. 2005), EIB is a selectively targeted program for monolingual regions that would be phased out as communities transition to Spanish, quite different from indigenous viewpoints.

13. To *hacer buena letra* (have good handwriting) is to obey subserviently. To be *mal educado* is to disrespect authority, like an unruly Indian or child.

14. On textualities and territorialities, see, among others, Lienhard 1992; Arnold and Yapita 2006; and Rockwell 2005.

15. On the *estado docente*, see Rama 1996; Sanjinés 2004:111; and Nuñez 2005. On the welfare state and mass public schooling elsewhere, see Collins and Blot 2003.

16. On governmentality and education, see Hunter 1996 and Popkewitz 2000.

17. On development and indigenous knowledge, see Sillitoe 1993 and Gupta 1998.

18. Stuart Hall (1986) theorized articulation to think about identities as assemblages of symbols that attach to (articulate with) subjects in a given social and historical position, without reducing these to class or other essentialisms. I am interested in networked articulations across scales of social practice, public space, and collective action. This builds on articulation in Hall's sense (what identity is) but focuses on articulation in the broader sense of how diverse identity projects work through interconnected, heterogeneous, social fields. See also García 2005 and Li 2007.

19. I also draw on a database of over eight hundred Bolivian newspaper articles collected since 1992 and scores of documents from government and donor agencies.

SOLDIERS, PRIESTS, AND SCHOOLS

1. I draw on Sanabria Fernández 1972 and Pifarré 1989.

2. "Colonial state" refers to the republic of Bolivia, whose patterns of governance largely reproduced Spanish colonial relations, laws, institutions, and ideologies (Rivera Cusicanqui 1993).

3. Pronounced Ah-pee-ah-why-kee Toom-pa.

4. The letter, like much of the Kuruyukɨ narrative, may have been the work of priests. Like many Franciscan accounts, the letter lauds the work of the church and denounces karai abuses, yet it ultimately vindicates the priests from accusations that they were behind the uprising.

5. Ipayes in Guarani country are often charged with "seeing" the weather. Not praying, strictly speaking, they see what or who is working to impede the rain so as to counter these efforts.

6. The name is also written Apiaike, Apiawaiki, and Hapiaoekɨ. The Jesuit writers prefer Hapiaoekɨ Tüpa, translated as "God removed his testicles" or "eunuch of God" (Pifarré 1989). This parse links a Christian template of heroic celibate masculinity (and the Jesus-like cultivation of a following, sacrificial struggle, and martyrdom) to expressions of Guarani prophetism. It echoes attempts to reconcile indigenous and Catholic symbologies through tropes like the "land without evil" (Shapiro 1987). Yet the translation "eunuch of God" is grammatically impossible. In names ending with Tüpa, like that of the deity Yagua Tüpa, *tüpa* refers to the named subject, not to a distinct agent. Naming a man "castrated" is also culturally improbable. It may have been given to Apiaguaiki after his execution, emphasizing a karai claim to superior masculinity (see also Saignes 1990). Airase, my (male) host at the village of Itavera, contested the label "castrated one," saying it must have been Japiavae ko, "one of true testicles." Another name was Chapia Guasu (colloquially, "young tough," but derived from the contraction of "my big testicles," *che rapia guasu*). On the other side, the karai leader of the Bolivian troops referred to himself as "Chapcha," a Quechua term for macho (Sanabria Fernández 1972). Verging on hyperbolic absurdity, these testicle-centered concerns reflect the gendered contests over power that fuel racial ideologies and Guarani-karai relations.

7. Even so, some criollo elites promised literacy in exchange for Aymara votes to be exercised in support of white politicians (see testimonies in Choque Canqui 1994).

8. Supposed witchcraft threatened church hegemony over the supernatural, polygamy was the root of captains' powers to convoke followers, and sloth—which we should read as a Guarani desire for leisurely pleasure—undermined disciplinary labor routines.

9. As with the "land without evil," writers as distinct as Eduardo Galeano and UNICEF filmmakers have made much of this false etymology of paper as the "skin of God."

10. On liturgy and schooling, see Arnold and Yapita 2006.

11. Being baptized, *oñemongarai*, "to-make-oneself-karai," also transformed a word once used to mark the emergence of a spiritual leader, *karai*, into a process approximating the identity of nonindigenous whites and their beliefs.

12. The name I-Have-Made-Myself-White, like "eunuch of God," may have emerged from the pens of missionary fathers, yet it still reflects dominant ideologies of literacy.

13. Alfred Métraux visited the region in 1929. Against the threat of secularization he called for protests by anthropologists, since the missions had "defended the [Guarani] against the violence of the whites [and] have made [whites] respect their rights and lives. . . . The destiny of the Chiriguano race is disappearance, and the closing of the missions will only hasten that end. . . . All ethnographers and Americanists will feel as I do, the sadness that this measure foretells for the Indian race" (1930b:315–16).

14. C. Bernand (1973) describes Guarani on the sugar plantations in Peronist Argentina. On Guarani migrations to Santa Cruz, see Simón et al. 1980 and Postero 2006. On

the Chaco War in Guarani country, see Hirsch 1991; Langer 1994b; Schuchard 1995; and Pifarré 1989. On Guarani who fled to the Paraguayan Chaco, see Grünberg and Grünberg 1975.

15. On the Bolivian revolution, see Malloy 1970 and Grindle and Domingo 2003.

16. Xavier Albó reports (1990:272–73) that the agrarian reform initiated nationally in 1953 got under way in central Guarani country in 1977. This was during the Bánzer dictatorship. Ninety-three percent of the titles went to cattlemen, not Guarani.

17. "La letra con sangre entra" is a phrase heard across Ibero-America, possibly attributable to St. Augustine (K. Woolard, personal communication, 2004). Among older teachers the phrase invokes conventional wisdom that unruly subjects can only learn through violence. In relation to indigenous subjects like the Guarani, the phrase links schooling to the work of evangelization, the extirpation of heresy, and racial purification through infusing the new blood of the letter. Impurities of sin, knowledge, race, or language are literally beaten out (see Mignolo 1995:73–74).

18. Historically karai towns displaced Guarani towns to peripheries as labor pools. Original Guarani place names were taken for the karai pueblo, and the Guarani community was renamed as "little X" or "X outside or up in the woods." These toponymic hierarchies persist today as with this place, "Little Ipita in the Woods," which is subject to dominance by the karai town of Ipita. Schooling intensified this extractive hierarchy as town-based karai began to work as teachers to discipline peripheral villages.

19. *Simba* (Q. braid) refers to warriors' long hair and to those men who wear their hair long today. Marking the cruelty of the slaughter, Yari emphasized *tairusu* (G. youngsters), referring to boys killed in their early teens, before marriage.

INTERLUDE: TO CAMIRI

1. *Chaguanco* is a derogatory label for Guarani laborers on the cane plantations.

2. Because men learn Spanish working for karai, male Guarani bilingualism is generally higher than female, furthering associations between indigenous language use and femininity (and marginality), a common Latin American pattern (see below, and Cadena 1991).

3. In colonial terms, speaking Guarani explains and justifies gendered violence against Guarani by karai. This is reflected in "jokes" linking language and gendered violence against the Guarani: "A camba comes back to his hut on the hacienda to find his wife being raped by the karai *patrón*. The Guarani picks up a stick, intending to beat his boss. In his stupidity, he does not want to hit the patrón in the head, fearing the karai will kiss his wife; nor in the ass, fearing he will penetrate harder. Confounded, he drops the stick and decides to scare the patrón, yelling 'culéela culéela!' (S. screw her, screw her)." At this point, those who understand markers of linguistic difference are expected to laugh. The Guarani intended to scare the boss by shouting "snake!" in Spanish (S. *culebra*). Linguistic interference assimilated the "br" sound to an "l," so that he cheered on the rape of his wife. A similar joke has a Guarani woman attempt to

stop her karai rapist by shouting, "Animo karai! Animo!" (in Guarani, No more, white man! No more!). In Spanish, *ánimo* means "with spirit."

GUARANI SCRIBES

1. Unlike progressive papers like *Aquí*, which expressed solidarity with Guarani, regional papers like Santa Cruz's *El Deber* sided with the status quo (e.g., "Los guaraníes" 1994).

2. PEIB began with similar numbers and thus less proportional weight in the immense Andean Quechua and Aymara regions.

3. The APG institutionalized the election of a female vice-president in the late 1990s and elected its first female president in 2004. Formal positions of captains at local and subregional levels were invariably held by men.

4. The scribes often laughed hysterically about a time during Enrique's youth when gringo missionaries snapped his picture in front of a world map. In the photo he points to a spot in Africa where he would go and spread God's word. Now more indigenous activist than Christian believer, Enrique, like many Guarani converts, entertained the notion that both God and Guarani deities were real. He also had fond memories of missionaries who stayed many years in the region. His father had worked with the Summer Institute of Linguistics' (SIL) Harry Rosbottom, who worked on Bible translation in Guarani country from 1957 to 1970.

5. Language planning seeks to make native languages functional for schooling in the name of their defense. It treads a fine line between emancipatory practice and the imposition of new techniques of control. These processes are shaped by dialect and institutional rivalries and battles over purism and authenticity (England 1995; Maxwell 1996; Silverstein 1998). The Guarani continue to grapple with these tensions (e.g., Gustafson, Manuel, and Gutiérrez 1998; Gustafson 1996).

6. Joanne Rappaport (2005:235–40) describes the Nasa's creative use of translation to reconceptualize law in Colombia.

7. Three examples prove illustrative. Tomás had worked for more than a decade with Peruvian Aymara peasant movements. By the 1990s he questioned his Marxian vanguardist approach, saying, "we needed to know something more about culture." Tomás now advised Guarani on a realpolitik of empowerment, which shared much with Guarani pragmatism. Mónica had a similarly activist youth protesting dictatorship while a university student in Uruguay. Yet she was not convinced of relativist or culturalist positions. She insisted that Guarani would improve their condition through better education, not (primarily) through cultural knowledge, a stance shared by some Guarani. I then saw education through a Freirian lens and imagined land recovery as the ultimate objective. How exactly EIB would facilitate this, I had no clear idea. Guarani constantly drew parallels between land and education, so I was reassured. Yet as I explore below, the complexities of EIB and movement politics transcend simplistic materialist formulas of practice and objectives.

8. Mónica kept at hand a Spanish copy of Vygotsky's *Thought and Language* (1934). Along with Brazil's Freire (1921–97), Vygotsky (1896–1934) was often cited by left-leaning pedagogues—and this although Vygotsky, unlike Freire, made little explicit contribution to the idea of class struggle and consciousness raising (see Lave and Wenger 1991:47–50; J. Wertsch personal communication, 2006). Thomas Popkewitz (2000) refers to such intellectual heroes as "indigenous foreigners." Decontextualized and dehistoricized icons invoked to bolster competing positions in national schooling projects, indigenous foreigners index hybridization and change in national education fields. The Bolivian education reform brought new indigenous foreigners like the Frenchman Josette Jolibert and the Spaniard Cesar Coll, constructivists who spoke of children as text producers (Jolibert) or of new literacies and the information society (Coll), rather than of social contestation (chapter 5).

9. After I gave in to the research imperative, palpable shifts occurred in the feeling of what had been a more collegial relationship. Elsa finished one interview by placing herself in the category of an indigenous woman vis-à-vis the anthropologist, telling me, "You should write a book about me like the one they wrote about Rigoberta Menchú."

10. Alfred Métraux (1930a:314) visited Elsa's grandfather Santos Aireyu in the late 1920s. Métraux's monograph included a photo of Aireyu in coat, tie, and boots, describing him as the "last grand captain of the independent Chiriguano Indians. Aireyu is completely assimilated and lives the life of a rich Bolivian planter." Earning the disfavor of Elsa's family, CIPCA researchers (Albó 1990:120–31) built on this assessment to portray the Aireyu captains (like Elsa's father, Aurelio) as exploiters of their own people. This was tied to CIPCA's attempt to influence the APG to pattern itself after communal peasant unions (*sindicatos*, as in the Andes) rather than after captaincies. Against Métraux's predictions and NGO desires, the captaincies maintained significant influence. During most of my work with the Guarani, Aurelio's brother Rogelio was a regional captain with significant popular support. Rogelio, whom Elsa called Uncle Choco (Blondie) because of his light complexion, passed away in 2002. Only then was his replacement named through communal elections. Elsa called this turn from inherited leadership to karai elections the true end of the captaincy.

11. Barrientos initiated the Military-Peasant Pact during the late 1960s to co-opt Andean peasant unions (Rivera Cusicanqui 1984). The overture to a rural leader like Aireyu fits into this pattern. Overtures may also relate to concerns about potential Guarani involvement in guerrilla movements during the period of Che Guevara (who operated in Guarani country while Barrientos was president). This sensitive history is not written, but see Albó 1990:127–35.

12. *Ñande ru* (G. our father) is sometimes "God," but also generic male ancestors seen as Guarani progenitors. *Kaa iya* (G. woods their-master) are ancestral spirits and other beings who watch over game and with whom Guarani must reciprocate when hunting and fishing.

13. Elsa referred to tensions between APG autonomy and NGO dependence.

14. Warren 1998, Nelson 1999, García 2005, and Rappaport 2005 describe upwardly mobile indigenous activists in Guatemala, Peru, and Colombia that share this sense of self-critique. At some point the expected trajectory of assimilation is brought under question and activists reposition themselves—in cultural, epistemic, or linguistic terms—on the indigenous side.

15. This concern for hygiene has roots in the genealogy of Western schooling and biopolitical rationalities for the management of healthy bodies. Within the colonialist paradigm the hygienic imperative intensified as a racialized mechanism of control over indigenous bodies seen as biologically and socially dirty (Foucault 1990; Stephenson 1999; Larson 2003; Zulawski 2007).

16. More than "having" knowledge, what western readers may see as a possession or commodity, in Guarani the phrase *iyarakuaa*, "her or his knowledge" is more accurately translated as "there exists socially valued knowledge in relation to her or his being" or "her or his being is defined by socially valued knowledge." Thus knowledge/knowing was as much a descriptor of one's essence as a person, as a thing possessed. Though arakuaa parsed as Guarani "knowledge" led to discussions about what Guarani "content" might be included in textbook curricula (such as shamanic knowledge), this deeper sense of arakuaa evaded schoolbook containment and for many might not be attainable through formal schooling.

17. Most locals did not know that the NGO was a conduit for resources that came from the Swedish government via UNICEF.

18. This reflected a split pursued by reformists who embraced bilingual education to drive a wedge between indigenous movements and teachers' unions (see Calla 1999).

19. Outsiders who support EIB explain indigenous opposition to EIB as the internalization of colonialist discourse or as the effect of teacher manipulation. Outsiders who oppose EIB suggest that indigenous communities are manipulated by NGOs. Finding a pure, unmediated indigenous demand for (or rejection of) EIB is impossible, though I illustrate the construction of demands on the national stage in chapter 4.

INTERLUDE: TO ITAVERA

1. This portion recounts a return visit in 1996, three years after my first arrival.

2. In chapaco Spanish, *guapo*, posed as a question, inquires about one's fortitude and good health, not looks.

3. June Nash (1979) and Michael Taussig (1980) debated the status of the Andean devil figure or Tío, a being whom workers supplicate with coca, alcohol, and ritual to extract ore and avoid accidents. The Tío found its way to the Chaco through Andean migration, where it became part of shared lore in the agroindustrial setting of cane plantations.

GUARANI KATUI

1. The old soldier's heirs salvaged the surname of the sonless O'Connor and fused it to that of his son-in-law D'Arlach to craft an aristocratic identity as descendants of

Catholic nobles. The O'Connor D'Arlach clan is prominent in Bolivia's business and political elite. The blue-eyed O'Connor sisters Elizabeth and Cecilia were elected Miss Bolivia in 1986 and 1993, respectively, representing the country in Miss Universe pageants in those years.

2. Missionaries cut boys' hair in mission schools (Nino 1912). Itaverans told stories of karai ranchers getting Guarani men drunk and then cutting their hair as they slept. The contemporary (white) racist and separatist "camba" movement of Santa Cruz, and karai in towns like Camiri, frequently deploy images of simbas in folkloric and carnival representations (Gustafson 2006).

3. I admired the resistance of Tëtayapeños, yet their position was not shared by other Guarani communities who accepted by force, if not by choice, the necessity of schooling.

4. Others translate -katui as "pure," though I avoid the racialized undertone of this usage. Guarani also say guaraniete (emphatically Guarani), añetetegue vae reta (the emphatically true ones), or borrow the Spanish puro (pure) or neto (pure, unadorned) to highlight individuals, communities, or practices deemed "very" Guarani.

5. I lived in Itavera for a total of nine months between March 1993 and June 1994, leaving for short periods to return to Camiri. I visited Itavera for periods of three to four weeks during the summers of 1995 and 1996, during extended fieldwork in 1997 to 1998, and again in early 2004 and in the summer of 2006. What follows focuses on the early period (1993–94) yet relies on hindsight accumulated over the decade.

6. I interpret the verb -vɨa as originating in the lexeme -pɨa (G. liver, seat of well-being). Both share semantic associations with mbɨa (Guarani man, person), which may derive from -pɨ (foot, base, foundation) and -a (locative, place of). In traditional usage, mbɨa also marked the rooting of people and place, such as Yukɨmbɨa (salt-community). One might ask a person, "Where is your mbɨa?" to mean, where do you call home, your place? So to -vɨa is to feel well-being and rootedness in a place, through exchange of intimate knowledge, words, and experience with others. Making guests ovɨa in your domain by talking to them and showing generosity to them is a hallmark of Guarani hospitality.

7. José Domingo Véliz (1999:162) defines mbarareko (alt.–parareko) as referring to "one who gives from their being (pɨa) to look well after another." The related term, mborerekua (alt.–pirerekua) is "when one looks well after or helps their kindred without expecting payment or exchange" (125).

8. "To grow" is to–kuaakuaa (know-know). The usage associates the gradual acquisition of knowledge, personhood, and maturity and is closely associated with place.

9. I later found these items in Stockholm's Etnografiska Museet.

10. Erland Nordenskiöld and Alfred Métraux pursued a comparative ethnology built on the collection of material artifacts and myth, items taken away for cataloguing to study cultural change and diffusion. Salvaging these items, what Métraux called the "traditions of their ancestors," was seen as urgent for the sake of science, since both traveler-ethnologists assumed that the Guarani were on the verge of disappearance. By the late

twentieth century, a similar sense of salvage motivated the Guarani scribes, now eager for a Guarani ethnopolitical and territorial project, not for science.

11. In 1963, a University of Wisconsin Land Tenure Center research team passed through Tarija to study the effects of the 1952 land reform. Interviews with Tarijeño elites yielded the observation that "these tiny bands [i.e., the Guarani on the river] are apparently quite autonomous, settling in semi-permanent villages wherever they feel inclined. Landowners [*sic*, occupiers] let them remain because they are glad to have them available as a potential source of wage labor when they need extra hands during seasons of peak labor load" (Erasmus 1969:76–77). Elites referred to Indians as "semi-permanent" to question their claims to the land, against which leaders like Airase sought some fixity and permanence.

12. See Whitman 2004 for a similar assessment of EIB schools in Ecuador.

13. The previous (Spanish-speaking) teacher left an assessment of her labors penned in the school's *libro de actas* (book of acts). It was a testament to her lack of preparation to work with linguistic difference and a typical karai dismissal of Guarani capabilities. Reporting on one year of labor, she wrote: "An advance was made up to the word *uña*, [i.e., we got through the alphabet to "fingernail," for the letter *U*], but since it is a new school, and in addition, they are all Guarani, all of them will have to go back and repeat the first grade."

14. While ethical considerations keep me from delving further into this issue, the tension between local NGOs and the Camiri-based EIB project also contributed to limitations on EIB's further expansion in the Itika region. In addition, when a conservative government party, the MIR, captured some influence within the APG in the late 1990s, Guarani leaders affiliated with that party sought to use EIB teachers for prosyletizing purposes, deeply undermining support for EIB in these other regions (where NGO activists opposed that party). What this reveals, as I discuss below, is that indigenous support or opposition to EIB is not ever entirely a question of militant linguistic loyalty or assimilationist desire, but often reflects shifting articulations with multiple other lines of cultural politics.

15. I have taken the concepts of decontextualization, entextualization, and recontextualization from Briggs 1996.

16. Ray Barnhardt and Angayuq Oscar Kawagley (2005) illustrate the dichotomous view of Western versus indigenous knowledge in curricular design. Bruno Latour (1993) questions the purity of Western science. Teresa McCarty (2002) offers an insightful comparative discussion of similar complexities in Navajo schools.

17. Charles Hale (2006) shares insights on why this desire for engagement often fails despite anthropologists' best intentions.

NETWORK ARTICULATIONS

1. This differs from the early twentieth century when prestigious public schools were associated with the emergence of an antiaristocratic middle class.

2. For parallels elsewhere, see Foweraker 1993; Torres 2000; Cook 1996.

3. I combine observations from between 1998 and 2004.

4. The consultants inverted the Freirian notion of schooling aimed at critical analysis and the transformation of reality, suggesting that schooling aimed at improving individual decision making through the recognition—but not the transformation—of reality. In their words: "When children leave school they should manage charts and pie graphs to perfection" ("El gobierno critica" 2004).

5. Based on interviews carried out between 1999 and 2002, media reports, and reform documents.

6. For a synthesis of reproduction approaches, see Giroux 1983.

7. Witness, for instance, the centralized, albeit neoliberal intentions of the testing mania tied to No Child Left Behind.

8. With "left-agrarianist" I refer to peasant activists and nonpeasant intellectuals who primarily focused on land reform. By "neo-indigenists" I mean nonindigenous intellectuals of the 1970s and beyond who supported indigenous struggles as partners, questioning the paternalistic assimilationist indigenism of the past.

9. The dismal state of education was epitomized by then minister of education, Colonel Ariel Coca, an army officer later indicted for cocaine trafficking (De Mesa et al. 1997).

10. On neoliberalism in Chile and Ecuador, see Paley 2001 and Sawyer 2004.

11. The phrases "Harvard Boys" or, for instance, the "élite tecnócrata de Harvard" (Harvard technocratic elite) were frequently heard in association with the circle of Gonzalo "Goni" Sánchez de Lozada (though few actors actually attended Harvard). The Harvard Boys' web extended into multiple realms as the second-wave social reforms hit Bolivia in 1994. Connections developed between Bolivian agencies and the Sachs-led Harvard Institute for International Development (HIID) (Grindle 2003:341; Van Cott 2000:141n7). Seminars on Bolivian decentralization were held at Harvard in 1995 and 1996. Goni appeared with Sachs at a Kennedy School event in 1997. With USAID monies, the Bolivian Catholic University in 1994 opened a masters program in development that was granted the rare privilege of using the Harvard name, a magnet for aspiring public policy students and economists. Bolivian think tanks such as UDAPSO (Unit of Analysis of Social Policy) and UDAPE (Unit of Analysis of Economic Policy) were connected to the Kennedy School and HIID, with Harvard graduate students researching Bolivian governance experiments. As with Harvard's dealings in postcommunist Russia, the links involved dubious allies and had debatable benefits for Bolivia.

12. When I lived in La Paz in 1992, the name Jeffrey Sachs was excoriated in public discourse. Sachs has reconfigured himself as a softer, gentler development genius these days, appearing with U2's Bono and radically modifying his market orthodoxy.

13. State violence was deployed against miners, teachers, and coca growers, among others. Among the most tragic events was the 1996 killing of eighteen Andean miners at Capasirca and Amayapampa. The final violences of neoliberalism were those of October 2003 (see chapter 7; Nash 1992; Gill 2000). On Bolivia's success, see "Harvard Helps" 1997.

14. The right-wing ADN minister (later implicated in illegal land dealings in eastern Bolivia) cogoverned with the left-wing teachers' unions. Both party and unions opposed education reform (the former to protect patronage and stability, the latter to maintain union power).

15. World Bank documents referred to education reform as a "sectoral structural adjustment," what one interviewee said was an "unfortunate" phrase that failed to capture the institution's (eventual) support for curricular change and EIB. SIDA (Sweden) had supported UNICEF's bilingual education program since 1989. Germany's GTZ had supported bilingual education in the Andes (Peru and Ecuador) since the mid-1980s. Both SIDA and GTZ worked with networks of linguistic and pedagogical experts who published on EIB in Latin America.

16. By tact or by conviction, European supporters did not often speak of native-language schooling as a political right, but rather as a nod to local languages of poor people engaged with the national Spanish. This meant that only insofar as these distinct languages marked the poor and unschooled—even better if this linguistic marginality attached to gender inequalities as well (as it does in Bolivia)—could bilingual education be justified as a state-development project.

17. The World Bank strategist Joan Nelson (1999:29) gives advice on making reforms successful: "Major reforms must be marketed beyond the circle of those with power to introduce them," and, "Often, reforms can be designed so as to create new stakeholders whose support may counterbalance ongoing resistance from old vested interests." It is obvious that indigenous movements like that of the Guarani represented such useful new "stakeholders" who might be expected to counterbalance resistance from unions—as they did, for a time.

INTERLUDE: BOLIVIA OR YUGOSLAVIA?

1. Aid monies came as low-interest loans and grants and were mainstays of the middle and upper classes. With teachers out of the way, funds could be captured by private ventures for book publishing, school building, consultancies, research, evaluations, training workshops, the provision of computer services, and the like. Complex state change cannot be explained by the crude calculation of incentives, but there are moments at which resources ease anxieties and grease the gears of contingent articulations. On incentive and choice, see Kaufman and Nelson 2004. On intraparty pacts, executive authority, and Goni's view of reform, see Grindle 2004 and Van Cott 2000.

2. I am invoking a tone accessible through any superficial reading of the criollo-controlled media.

3. Recounted to me on several occasions by Amalia Anaya and Luis Enrique López, both at the meeting. A version without the remarks on Yugoslavia was published in Albó and Anaya 2003:67.

PRODDING NERVES

1. As Mahmoud Mamdani (1996:90) suggests in the African context, colonial forms of indirect rule shifted strategically from "race to tribe" in attempts to confront popular

mobilization, since racial idioms (as in Bolivian corporatism) threatened to undermine rule by unifying the poor as a racially subjugated mass, while tribal idioms (as in Bolivian interculturalism) offered a new idiom for organizing and dividing alterities, though this also presented a new set of challenges to colonial (or neocolonial) control.

2. On Goni's pluralism and criollo ways of seeing, see Sanjinés 2004:159–64, 187.

3. On technologies of knowledge and rule, see Shore and Wright 1999; Popkewitz 2000; and Paley 2001. I take "secular theodicy" from Michael Herzfeld (1993:127–59) who applies it to nationalism. For a parallel view of schooling as racialized secular theodicy in the Andes, see Cadena 2000.

4. From interviews and e-mail exchanges with Anaya between 1999 and 2006.

5. At the time of that interview, some twenty-five years later in mid-2003, Carvajal, still in the MIR, served as Goni's education minister. In his short time in office before Goni's ouster in October 2003, Carvajal drafted a twenty-year education plan that eliminated EIB.

6. The MIR cultivated ties to lowland indigenous organizations in the 1990s, leading to later splits between pro-MAS and pro-MIR sectors of the movement (see Gustafson 2002, 2006; Van Cott 2005:94–95).

7. *Mi época* suggests the glory days of one's youth. *Mística* emerged during the revolutionary 1960s. Echoing Che Guevara's dedication to self-sacrifice and revolution, the term was widespread among movement activists and peppers teachers' discourses today (see Torres 1995). Anaya self-consciously temporalizes her relation to the term, highlighting her shift from the "mystique" of collective struggle to the individual "passion" necessary for political survival.

8. I have changed names and initials.

9. Props are support points (resources, ideas, actors) that sustain articulatory linkages (nodes) in networks spanning difference or territorial and institutional space (Latour 1993; Strathern 1996).

10. This is not to say that reform had no effect on children, but that they were not the most directly accessible target of change in the short term.

11. The words *drinks* and *VIPs* were in English in the original.

12. Lesley Gill (2000) narrates this moment through schoolteachers' perspectives.

13. *Maestrito* has a soft paternalism, while *maestrillo* connotes corruption, connivance, and incompetence.

14. This resembles Pierre Bourdieu's "avant-garde": "To impose a new producer, a new product and a new system of taste on the market at a given moment means to relegate to the past a whole set of producers, products and systems of taste, all hierarchized in relation to their degree of legitimacy" (1996:160).

15. Joanne Rappaport describes a similar interpretation of native pedagogy in Colombia (2005:130–32).

16. *Ñande reko*: our way, character, that is, culture. *Mboromboeete*: from *-mboe* (to make speak); *-poromboe* (to make persons speak in general, to teach); *mboromboe* is the nominalized form, hence mboromboeete suggests emphatic, true teaching, pedagogy.

17. After Michel Foucault (1991), individualization refers to the formation of self-regulating bodies and subjectivities who understand control as individual freedom. Totalization refers to how these bodies are subjectified in totalizing discursive regimes.

INTERLUDE: LA INDIADA, COMO PARA DAR MIEDO

1. Criollos skeptical of EIB created an image of the entire altiplano being at risk of "closing itself off" (*encerrarse*) with schools where only indigenous languages were spoken. Given the shift to Spanish and native language loss underway throughout the country, even without EIB this seemed absurd. Nonetheless, indigenous leaders and teachers demanded Spanish-language texts that were in a production bottleneck.
2. This quote has been paraphrased from notes.

INSURGENT CITIZENSHIP

1. Repertoires of contention are culturally encoded forms of protest (Edelman 2001).
2. The Catholic Church also influenced the curriculum, which requires a religion (i.e., Catholicism) class. Liberal reformers, including Anaya and members of the anti-neoliberal MAS, sought, but failed, to end this practice.
3. Recall the epigraph to chapter 2. -*Mara* also invokes the "land without evil" (G. *ivi imarambae*, lit, land without shame, unscarred, virgin). This was the earthly paradise historically pursued through migration (Clastres 1995). Talk of a "land without evil/shame" is not part of contemporary Guarani experience. The phrase has nonetheless been refitted for Guarani political discourse directed at karai audiences. Shame (-*mara*) associated with neocolonial racism *is* part of contemporary experience. We can thus read Petrona's "to speak without shame" as a contemporary pursuit of an intercultural land without evil.
4. Most beginning teachers were assigned distant rural schools teaching first grade, moving up and thus closer to urban centers as they gained seniority. Yet karai administrators placed the new cadres of Guarani teachers in early grades and hoped to keep them there. This kept the supposed threat of bilingualism from expanding, yet it also sought to maintain a karai-indigenous epistemic, linguistic, and political hierarchy within the union and teaching field. The practical effect was the atmosphere of containment within which Guarani teachers like Mateo and Petrona worked.
5. Little children and funny people are compared to chattering, rambunctious monkeys.
6. I have argued throughout that, in terms of indigenous knowledge, geopolitical and epistemic authority and their translocal articulations constitute more crucial questions than curricular authenticity, which in any case should be debated locally, not by anthropologists (see also Gustafson 2004 and Briggs 1996, from whom I draw). Authenticity dominates the classroom-centric debates on indigenous education in the English-language world. It is also crucial for essentialist critiques of Bolivian EIB (e.g., Patzi 1999; Arnold and Yapita 2006).
7. G. *jasï*: physical pain, rage, bitterness, and the feeling one gets, eyes closed tight and head jerking, from a gulp of pure alcohol.

8. G. -*moai*, disperse, scatter, like throwing out corn for chickens. Like that of shame, the metaphor of dispersal is common in Guarani discourse. It invokes collective social, linguistic, territorial, and corporal fragmentation as the result of karai violence.

9. G. -*pïa*: liver, self, consciousness, a conceptual center for notions of Guarani emotional and physical well-being, personality, memory, and character. The word has conceptual links to person and community (*mbïa*), the center (-*pïte*), the foundation (-*pï*). Putting words and memories into one's -pïa (and bringing them forth from there) is more legitimate than what Americans might call "getting it down in writing."

10. As of 2006, the ministry Web site (www.minedu.gov.bo) showed three indigenous children reading modules in the upper right corner. The Guarani girl is wearing a mandu. The Aymara and Quechua are also dressed in native clothing. The same photo of the girl appears on a pro-reform poster reading (in Spanish and Guarani) "In the search for the Land without Evil." A marker of the network that is Bolivian EIB, the poster hung in the Guarani movement office in Camiri, in state offices in La Paz, and in SIDA's office in Stockholm.

11. G. *tïmaka*, leg, calf; slang for "Guarani person." Like the n-word in North America, this term is used jokingly by Guarani and in a derogatory way by karai. Given the often muscular legs of Guarani men, I see its derogatory use and etymology possibly arising from karai designations of useful Guarani bodies (like heads of cattle, arms of braceros, or legs of Indians). For Guarani, *tïmaka* denotes toughness and resilience in forays in the karai world. Tïmakas, when visiting the city on NGO workshops, forgo a decent hotel and crowd with others in a cheap room to save per diem monies. Alternatively, a tïmaka might drink up all their per diem to enjoy the moment. In this interview, a tïmaka would have no trouble with hunger, as would a city karai.

12. Beauty pageants (*concursos de belleza*) are ubiquitous in eastern Bolivia. Feminine beauty (assessed in degrees of distance from indigeneity) is put on display, and beauty queens are construed as objects of desire and as silent, aesthetic tokens of ethnoracial citizenship, that is, those with rights to public space and visibility, conferred patriarchally by those with sexual access to such bodies (white men). Guarani are often referred to as "ugly" by karai who, even when eroticizing Guarani women, refuse them legitimate social belonging (Gustafson 2006). By joking about an "ugly pageant," Chumiray marked the tensions surrounding the reversal of this spectator-object-citizen relation in a karai space. We laughed, but beyond was a denunciation of the aestheticization of rights that shapes movement struggles across Latin America. See, on Bolivia, Sanjinés 2004; on Guatemala, D. Nelson 1999; on Mexico, Rubin 2004.

13. He referred to the 1996 march for land reform.

14. Recall Anaya's use of mystique. Carlos Alberto Torres (2000:83) links the term to a wider historical moment in which "many [teachers] think of themselves as the main public employees responsible for the transmission of a nation's collective values. . . . This self-perceived *mission*, coupled with similar roles attributed by the State in Latin

America, created a *mystique* of spiritual satisfaction, self-esteem, and professional status" (emphasis added).

15. Pablo Gentili (2000:15) writes, "The privatization of social policy by neoliberal regimes must be understood as a process of delegation. Through a variety of mechanisms, public responsibilities are transferred to private entities."

16. The Baha'i are influential in Andean education projects with associations to donors like USAID. Juan R. Cole (1998:191–97) suggests that the Baha'i represent liberal modernity dedicated to individual freedom and tolerance, yet they increasingly pursue a fundamentalist adherence to moral engineering.

INTERLUDE: INTERCULTURALISM TO DECOLONIZATION

1. I draw on Ari 2003; "Una balacera" 2003; "El gobierno denuncia" 2003; "Goni acusa" 2003; "El gobierno clausuró" 2003; Bolpress 2003; Radio Fides broadcasts of *La hora del país* (September 20 and 21, 2003); and a 2005 interview with an Aymara professor who taught at Warisata between 2001 and 2003.

2. Submerged networks (Melucci 1989) are social relationships constructed around symbolic production and the circulation of alternative frameworks of meaning behind the public face of political process.

3. According to my interlocutor, the community manning the trenches that day was the region's most combative. A few were armed with 1930s bolt-action Mausers from the Chaco War.

SHIFTING STATES

1. The chapter is based on annual field visits between 2002 and 2006, including six months in 2005 and 2006, correspondence with key actors, document analysis, and media reports.

2. Denise Y. Arnold and Juan de Dios Yapita (2006) argue that this logic of exchange and reciprocity lies at the heart of *all* indigenous peoples' cultures in Latin America. I do not share this essentializing stance, but rather suggest that EIB as an idea and a practice facilitated this as an intercultural possibility, precisely because of its rootedness both in Western models of nation building and in multiple indigenous visions and histories.

3. These comments highlight the inflexibility of orthodox models aimed at the technocratic management of knowledge. Though spoken of in terms of quality and efficiency, they are tools of political control (Mignolo 2005:119–24; Shore and Wright 1999; Paley 2001).

4. Commentators frequently noted that Morales and many MAS representatives had only an elementary-level education. That many MAS representatives spoke Spanish inflected with Aymara or Quechua accents further provoked criollo prejudices. (Goni's English accent and grammatical errors had the reverse effect, as it associated him with gringo power and knowledge.) The selection of the left-wing university professor

Alvaro García Linera as the MAS vice-presidential candidate was interpreted in part as a means to counter this discourse by adding an intellectual assistant to the Indian president, inverting the formula of the Lone Ranger and Tonto that ushered in neoliberal interculturalism in 1993.

5. The journalist reinforced the criollo public's racially inflected skepticism about indigenous actors in power by commenting on the disjuncture between Patzi's physical body (small) and the size of his new office (large). He also inserted bracketed corrections and "*sics*" to highlight Patzi's Aymara-inflected Spanish grammatical errors.

6. The 1994 education reform also tried and failed to secularize the curriculum.

Glossary

Word origins are indicated by Q (Quechua), A (Aymara), S (Spanish), or G (Guarani).

arakuaa	G. Guarani knowledge of time, space, the world (*ara*: time, sky, day; *-kuaa*, to know); sometimes opposed to school knowledge (*yemboe*) *Arakuaa iya*: master of knowledge; *-kuaakuaa*: to grow, mature
Ava	G. Guarani man; also refers to a Guarani region and dialect area, derogatory in some cases when used by karai
camba	S. Used in a derogatory way as a label for Guarani, also a regionalist label for people of the Santa Cruz city and region
Chaco	S. Region of southeastern Bolivia, western Paraguay, and northern Argentina
Chapaco	S. Person from the Tarija region
Chaqueño	S. Person from the Chaco region
cholo/a	S. Refers to urban indigenous Aymara and Quechua, often derogatory
constructivism	Educational theory that focuses on child-centered learning to construct knowledge, as opposed to teacher-centered dictation or rote learning
corporatism	Centralized state system in which public interests and identities are institutionalized through collective bodies of representation (or "sectors" usually organized by class or profession) that negotiate collectively through elected parties, pressure tactics, or the military to distribute public goods. Bolivia was largely corporatist between 1952 and 1985.
criollo/a	S. Person identified with the country's European heritage
Isoso	G. broken water. Guarani region and dialect area; compare to Ava and Simba
karai	G. Used by the Guarani for all non-Guarani mestizos, criollos, gringos, foreigners. Karai is gendered male. *Señora* is often used as a label for nonindigenous women.
Katarismo	A. S. from the Aymara rebel Tupak Katari (1781), an ideological

	movement that began in the 1970s and sought to fuse ethnic and class discourses of anticolonial struggle
kolla	A. Q. S. Also colla, Andean Bolivians, indigenous or not. Contrast with *camba*, which refers to Bolivians from Santa Cruz and the lowlands
kuña	G. Guarani woman. Used in a derogatory way by Spanish speakers, somewhat like *squaw*. *Kuñita* (S. little *kuña*); *kuñatai* (G. young woman).
mandu	G. Guarani woman's one-piece dress, also *tipoi*
mburuvicha	G. Guarani leader, also captain or *juvicha*
mestizo	S. persons of indigenous and European descent. Used infrequently in Bolivia, where regional labels usually predominate
module	Primary level textbooks produced by the education reform
ñee	G. language, word. *Ñandeñee*, our language, Guarani.
neoliberalism	Ideology centered around the free market as the solution to the distribution of wealth and social goods and the individual as the primordial category through which political representation, identity, and interests are determined
oka	G. patio surrounding a house, or the large open area of a community
pachakuti	A. Q. Time/space-turning over, a transition between epochs. In the Andes pachakuti invokes indigenous movements for political transformation
-pïa	G. Liver, center of being or character; *-vïa*: verbal form, to feel comfortable, at home, tranquil in a social or geographic space
popular	S. Refers to grass-roots, subaltern masses or the people as opposed to the elite
pueblo	S. A small rural town; also refers to the "people" in contrast to elites
simba	Q. braid. Label for Guarani men's long hair, or as a descriptor of men who wear their hair thus; as Simba, also refers to a Guarani dialect area
tëta	G. community, home, people, nation
tüpa	G. deity, God
yemboe	G. To learn or study in schools. From the root *-e* to speak; *-mboe*, to make another speak or to teach; *-yemboe*: reflexive, to make oneself be made to speak

References

Acebey, David. 2005. "La escuela de Tetayape." *Los Tiempos* (Cochabamba), March 6.

Albó, Xavier. 1974. *El futuro de los idiomas oprimidos de los Andes*. La Paz: CIPCA.

———. 1990. *La comunidad hoy*. La Paz: CIPCA.

———. 1991. "El retorno del indio." *Revista Andina* 9 (2): 299–366.

———. 1994. "And from Kataristas to MNRistas: The Surprising and Bold Alliance between Aymaras and Neoliberals in Bolivia." In *Indigenous Peoples and Democracy in Latin America*, ed. Donna Lee Van Cott, 55–82. New York: St. Martin's.

———. 1995. *Bolivia plurilingüe: Guía para planificadores y educadores*. La Paz: CIPCA / UNICEF.

Albó, Xavier, and Amalia Anaya. 2003. *Niños alegres, libres, expresivos: La audacia de la educación intercultural bilingüe en Bolivia*. La Paz: CIPCA / UNICEF. "Alfabetización se estrena con dudas." 2006. *La Prensa* (La Paz), March 22.

Anaya, Amalia. 1995. "La reforma educativa: Una visión desde adentro." Unpublished manuscript.

Andersen, Lykke, and Manfred Wiebelt. 2003. "La mala calidad de la educación en Bolivia y sus consecuencias para el desarrollo." IISEC Working Paper no. 02/03, www.iisec.ucb.edu.bo/papers/2001-2005/iisec-dt-2003-02.pdf (accessed January 15, 2007).

Aretxaga, Begoña. 1997. *Shattering Silence: Women, Nationalism, and Political Subjectivity in Northern Ireland*. Princeton: Princeton University Press.

Ari, Mariana. 2003. "Warisata en la masacre aymara." Bolpress, October 22, www.bolpress.com/art.php?Cod=2002073778.

Arispe, Valentin. 2006. *Mbaravikiyekua INSPOC regua: Como irradia el trabajo del INSPOC*. La Paz: PINSEIB / Plural.

Arnold, Denise Y., with Juan de Dios Yapita. 2006. *The Metamorphosis of Heads: Textual Struggles, Education, and Land in the Andes*. Pittsburgh: University of Pittsburgh Press.

Arnove, Robert. 1994. *Education as Contested Terrain: Nicaragua, 1979–1993*. Boulder, Colo.: Westview.

Asamblea del Pueblo Guaraní. 1992. *Tataendí*. Camiri: APG / TEKO-Guarani.

"Aspiran alfabetizar a 1,5 millones de bolivianos." 2006. *El Deber* (Santa Cruz), March 21.

"Una balacera en Warisata terminó con cinco muertos y varios heridos." 2003. *La Razón* (La Paz), September 21.

Barnhardt, Ray, and Angayuq Oscar Kawagley. 2005. "Indigenous Knowledge Systems and Alaskan Ways of Knowing." *Anthropology and Education Quarterly* 36 (1): 8–23.

Bartlett, Lesley. 2003. "World Culture or Transnational Project? Competing Educational Projects in Brazil." In *Local Meanings, Global Schooling: Anthropology and World Culture Theory*, ed. Kathryn Anderson-Levitt, 183–200. New York: Palgrave Macmillan.

Benhabib, Seyla. 2002. *The Claims of Culture: Equality and Diversity in the Global Era.* Princeton: Princeton University Press.

Bernand, C. 1973. "La fin des capitaines." *Bulletin de l'Institut Français d'Études Andines* 2 (1): 72–82.

Blat Gimeno, José. 1981. *La educación en América Latina y el Caribe en el último tercio del siglo XX.* Paris: UNESCO.

"Bolivia tiene más licenciados e ingenieros de los que requiere." 2004. *La Razón* (La Paz), September 12.

Bonfil Batalla, Guillermo. 1991. "Lo propio y lo ajeno: Una aproximación al problema del control cultural." In *Pensar nuestra cultura: Ensayos*, 49–57. Mexico City: Alianza.

Bourdieu, Pierre. 1996. *The Rules of Art: Genesis and Structure of the Literary Field.* Trans. Susan Emanuel. Cambridge: Polity.

Bourdieu, Pierre, and Jean-Claude Passeron. 1990. *Reproduction in Education, Society, and Culture*, trans. Richard Nice. London: Sage.

Bourdieu, Pierre, and Loïc J. D. Wacquant. 1992. *An Invitation to Reflexive Sociology.* Chicago: University of Chicago Press.

Briggs, Charles. 1996. "The Politics of Discursive Authority in Research on the Invention of Tradition." *Cultural Anthropology* 11 (4): 435–69.

Cadogan, Leon. 1992 [1959]. *Ayvu Rapyta: Textos míticos de los Guaraní del Guairá.* Asunción: CEPAG.

Calderón, Magaña, Coral. 2001. "El dama de hierro de la reforma." *Cosas: Una Revista Internacional* (La Paz) (January): 56–58.

Calla, Ricardo. 1999. "Educación intercultural y bilingüe y flexibilización magisterial: Temas de la reforma educativa en Bolivia." *Bulletin de l'Institut Français d'Études Andines* 28 (3): 561–70.

Carneiro da Cunha, Manuela L. and Eduardo Viveiros de Castro. 1985. "Vingança e temporalidade: os Tupinambá." *Journal de a Societé des Americanistes* 51:191–208.

Castro Mantilla, María Dolores. 1997. *La viva voz de las tribus: El trabajo del ILV en Bolivia 1954–1980.* La Paz: Viceministerio de Asuntos Indígenas y Pueblos Originarios.

Centro de Investigación y Promoción del Campesinado (CIPCA). n.d. "Demografía." Unpublished manuscript.

Chatry-Komarek, Marie. 1986. *Libros de lectura para niños de lengua vernácula: A partir de una experiencia interdisciplinaria en el Altiplano peruano.* Rossdorf, Germany: GTZ.

Choque, Celestino. 2005. *La EIB entre los quechuas: Testimonio de parte (1990–1994).* La Paz: PINSEIB/PROEIB/Plural.

Choque Canqui, Roberto. 1992. "La escuela indigenal: La Paz (1905–1938)." In *Educacion indígenal: ¿Ciudadanía o colonización?*, ed. Roberto Choque Canqui et al., 19–40. La Paz: THOA.

——. 1994. "La problematica de la educación indigenal." *DATA: Revista del Instituto de Estudios Andinos y Amazonicos* 5:9–34.

"Las clases se normalizan y un dirigente fue detenido." 2004. *La Razón* (La Paz), June 9.

Chumiray, Mateo. 1992. Text of speech delivered at Kuruyuki. January 28. Mimeo.

Clastres, Hélène. 1995. *The Land without Evil: Tupi-Guaraní Prophetism*. Urbana: University of Illinois Press.

Clastres, Pierre. 1987. *Society against the State: Essays in Political Anthropology*. New York: Zone Books.

Coe, Cati. 2005. *Dilemmas of Culture in African Schools: Youth, Nationalism, and the Transformation of Knowledge*. Chicago: University of Chicago Press.

Cole, Juan R. I. 1998. *Modernity and the Millennium: The Genesis of the Baha'i Faith in the Nineteenth-Century Middle East*. New York: Columbia University Press.

Collins, James, and Richard Blot. 2003. *Literacy and Literacies: Texts, Power, and Identity*. New York: Cambridge University Press.

Combés, Isabelle. 2005. *Etnohistorias de Isoso: Chane y chiriguanos en el Chaco Boliviano*. La Paz: PIEB/IFEA.

Conaghan, Catherine, J. Malloy, and Luis Abugattas. 1990. "Business and the Boys: The Origins of Neoliberalism in the Central Andes." *Latin American Research Review* 25 (2): 3–30.

Confederación Sindical Única de Trabajadores Campesinos de Bolivia (CSUTCB). 1991. *Hacia una educación intercultural bilingüe*. Raymi 15. (La Paz).

Consejo Nacional de Ayllus y Markas del Qullasuyu (CONAMAQ), et al. 2004. *Por una educación indígena originaria: Hacia la autodeterminación ideológica, política, territorial y sociocultural*. Santa Cruz: UNNNIO.

Contreras, Manuel E. 1997. "Formulación, implementación y avance de la reforma educativa en Bolivia." Unpublished manuscript.

——. 2003. "A Comparative Perspective of Education Reforms in Bolivia: 1950–2000." In *Proclaiming Revolution: Bolivia in Comparative Perspective*, ed. Merilee Grindle and Pilar Domingo, 259–86. Cambridge, Mass.: David Rockefeller Center for Latin American Studies, Harvard University.

Contreras, Manuel, and Maria Luisa Talavera Simoni. 2003. *The Bolivian Education Reform, 1992–2002: Case Studies in Large Scale Education Reform*. Washington: World Bank.

Cook, Maria Lorena. 1996. *Organizing Dissent: Unions, the State, and the Democratic Teachers' Movement in Mexico*. University Park: Pennsylvania State University Press.

Corrales, Javier. 1999. *The Politics of Education Reform: Bolstering the Supply Demand; Overcoming Institutional Blocks*. Washington: World Bank.

Crossley, Michael, and Leon Tikly. 2004. "Postcolonial Perspectives and Comparative and International Research in Education: A Critical Introduction." *Comparative Education Review* 40 (2): 147–56.

Dean, Mitchell. 2001. "Demonic Societies: Liberalism, Biopolitics, and Sovereignty." In

States of Imagination: Ethnographic Explorations of the Postcolonial State, ed. Thomas Blom Hansen and Finn Stepputat, 41–64. Durham, N.C.: Duke University Press.

De la Cadena, Marisol. 1991. "Las mujeres son más indias: Etnicidad y género en una comunidad del Cusco." *Revista Andina* 9 (17): 7–47.

———. 2000. *Indigenous Mestizos: The Politics of Race and Culture in Cuzco, Peru, 1919–1991*. Durham, N.C.: Duke University Press.

De Mesa, Jose, et al. 1997. *Historia de Bolivia*. La Paz: Editorial Gisbert.

D'Emilio, Lucia. n.d. "Voces y procesos desde la pluralidad: La educación indígena en Bolivia." Unpublished manuscript.

Dietschy-Scheiterle, Annette. 1989. *Las ciencias naturales en la educación bilingüe: El caso de Puno*. Trans. Susana Carrera. Lima: Proyecto Experimental de Educación Bilingüe-Puno.

Dunkerley, James. 2000. *Warriors and Scribes: Essays in the History and Politics of Latin America*. London: Verso.

Eckstein, Susan. 1983. "Transformation of a 'Revolution from Below'—Bolivia and International Capital." *Comparative Studies in Society and History* 25 (1): 105–35.

Edelman, Marc. 2001. "Social Movements: Changing Paradigms and Forms of Politics." *Annual Review of Anthropology* 30:285–317.

England, Nora. 1995. "Linguistics and Indigenous American Languages: Mayan Examples." *Journal of Latin American Anthropology* 1 (1): 122–49.

Equipo Técnico de Apoyo a la Reforma Educativa (ETARE). 1993a. *Convocatoria concurso de investigación: Identificación de necesidades de aprendizaje (perfil de diseño)*. La Paz: ETARE, Ministerio de Planeamiento y Coordinación. Mimeo.

———. 1993b. *La Educación Intercultural Bilingüe: De la experimentación a la institucionalización y generalización*. La Paz: ETARE/UNICEF.

Erasmus, Charles. 1969. "The Chuquisaca-Tarija Area." In *Land Reform and Social Revolution in Bolivia*, ed. Dwight Heath, Erasmus, and Hans C. Buechler, 63–85. New York: Praeger.

Escobar, Arturo. 1995. *Encountering Development: The Making and Unmaking of the Third World*. Princeton: Princeton University Press.

———. 2001. "Culture Sits in Places: Reflections on Globalism and Subaltern Strategies of Localization." *Political Geography* 20 (2): 139–74.

———. 2005. "El post-desarrollo como concepto y práctica social." In *Políticas de economía, ambiente y sociedad en tiempos de globalización*, ed. Daniel Mato, 17–31. Caracas: Vicerrectorado Académico, Universidad Central de Venezuela.

Fabian, Johannes. 1983. *Time and the Other: How Anthropology Makes Its Object*. New York: Columbia University Press.

Farah, Ivonne H. 2005. "Rasgos de la pobreza en Bolivia y las políticas para reducirla." In *Trabajo y producción de la pobreza en Latinoamérica y el Caribe: Estructuras, discursos y actores*, ed. Silvia Álvarez Leguizamón, 209–38. Buenos Aires: CLACSO.

Ferguson, James. 1990. *The Anti-politics Machine: Development, Depoliticization, and Bureaucratic Power in Lesotho*. Cambridge: Cambridge University Press.

Ferguson, James, and Akhil Gupta. 2002. "Spatializing States: Toward an Ethnography of Neoliberal Governmentality." *American Ethnologist* 29 (4): 981–1002.

Fernández Terán, Roberto. 2004. *FMI, Banco Mundial y estado neocolonial: Poder supranacional en Bolivia*. La Paz: Plural.

Foucault, Michel. 1990. *The History of Sexuality*. Trans. Robert Hurley. New York: Vintage.

———. 1991. "Governmentality." In *The Foucault Effect: Studies in Governmentality*, ed. Colin Gordon, 87–104. Chicago: University of Chicago Press.

Foweraker, Joe. 1993. *Popular Mobilization in Mexico: The Teachers' Movement, 1977–1987*. Cambridge: Cambridge University Press.

Freire, Paulo. 1970. *Pedagogía del oprimido*. Trans. Jorge Mellado. Mexico City: Siglo Veintiuno.

Ganson, Barbara. 2004. *The Guarani under Spanish Rule in the Rio de la Plata*. Stanford, Calif.: Stanford University Press.

Garcés, Fernando, and Soledad Guzmán, eds. 2003. *Educacionqa, kawsayninchikmanta kawsayninchikpaq kanan tiyan: Elementos para diversificar el currículo de la Nación Quechua*. Sucre: CENAQ.

García, María Elena. 2005. *Making Indigenous Citizens: Identities, Education, and Multicultural Development in Peru*. Stanford, Calif.: Stanford University Press.

García Linera, Alvaro. 2003. "Autonomías indígenas: Nación, etnicidad y autogobierno indígena." *Artículo Primero: Revista de Debate Social y Jurídico* 7 (14): 443–64.

Gellner, Ernest. 1983. *Nations and Nationalism*. Ithaca: Cornell University Press.

Gentili, Pablo. 2000. "The Permanent Crisis of the Public University." *NACLA: Report on the Americas* 33 (4): 12–18.

Giannecchini, Doroteo. 1996. *Historia natural, etnografía, geografía, lingüística del Chaco Boliviano 1898*. Ed. Lorenzo Calzavarini. Trans. Leonel Camacho Torres, Pedro de Anasagosti, and Calzavarini. Tarija: Fondo de Inversión Social, Centro Eclesial de Documentación.

Gill, Lesley. 2000. *Teetering on the Rim: Global Restructuring, Daily Life, and the Armed Retreat of the Bolivian State*. New York: Columbia University Press.

Giroux, Henry. 1983. "Theories of Reproduction and Resistance in the New Sociology of Education." *Harvard Educational Review* 53 (3): 257–93.

"El gobierno anunció que será transformada en instituto técnico." 1999. *La Razón* (La Paz), April 6.

"El gobierno clausuró el año en la normal de Warisata." 2003. *La Razón* (La Paz), September 24.

"El gobierno critica y pide procesar a dirigentes." 2004. *La Razón* (La Paz), June 5.

"El gobierno decide desconocer la descentralización educativa." 2007. *El Deber* (Santa Cruz), August 2.

"El gobierno denuncia una emboscada de campesinos." 2003. *La Razón* (La Paz), September 21.

Goldstein, Daniel. 2003. *Spectacular City: Violence and Performance in Urban Bolivia*. Durham, N.C.: Duke University Press.

"Goni acusa a estudiantes y catedráticos de Warisata." 2003. *La Razón* (La Paz), September 22.

Goody, Jack. 1977. *The Domestication of the Savage Mind*. New York: Cambridge University Press.

Gotkowitz, Laura. 2007. *A Revolution for Our Rights: Indigenous Struggles for Land and Justice in Bolivia, 1880–1952*. Durham, N.C.: Duke University Press.

Graham, Laura. 2005. "How Should an Indian Speak? Amazonian Indians and the Symbolic Politics of Language in the Global Public Sphere." In *Indigenous Movements, Self-Representation and the State*, ed. Kay B. Warren and Jean Jackson, 181–228. Austin: University of Texas Press.

Gramsci, Antonio. 1971. *Selections from the Prison Notebooks*. New York: International Publishers.

Grindle, Merilee. 2003. "Shadowing the Past? Policy Reform in Bolivia, 1985–2002." In *Proclaiming Revolution: Bolivia in Comparative Perspective*, ed. Grindle and Pilar Domingo, 318–44. Cambridge: David Rockefeller Center for Latin American Studies, Harvard University.

———. 2004. *Despite the Odds: The Contentious Politics of Education Reform*. Princeton: Princeton University Press.

Grindle, Merilee, and Pilar Domingo, eds. 2003. *Proclaiming Revolution: Bolivia in Comparative Perspective*. Cambridge: David Rockefeller Center for Latin American Studies, Harvard University.

Grünberg, Georg, and Friedl Grünberg. 1975. "Los chiriguanos (guaraní occidentales) del Chaco Central Paraguayo: Fundamentos para una planificación de su desarrollo comunitario." *Suplemento Antropológico* 9 (1–2): 5–109.

"Los guaraníes son adoctrinados para generar la subversion." 1994. *El Deber* (Santa Cruz), January 29.

Gupta, Akhil. 1998. *Postcolonial Developments: Agriculture in the Making of Modern India*. Durham, N.C.: Duke University Press.

Gustafson, Bret. n.d. "Peyeapïsaka Arare: Escuchen al mundo; Apuntes etnográficos para un currículo de ciencia guarani." Unpublished manuscript.

———. 1996. *Ñee: Introducción al estudio lingüístico del idioma guaraní para guaraní hablantes*. La Paz: UNICEF/Secretaría Nacional de Educación/Asamblea del Pueblo Guaraní.

———. 2002. "The Paradoxes of Liberal Indigenism: Indigenous Movements, State Processes, and Intercultural Reforms in Bolivia." In *The Politics of Ethnicity: Indigenous Peoples in Latin American States*, ed. David Maybury-Lewis, 267–306. Cambridge, Mass.: Harvard University Press.

———. 2004. "El concepto de red, los conocimientos indígenas y la educación intercultural bilingüe." *Revista Qinasay* 1 (2): 7–22.

———. 2006. "Spectacles of Autonomy and Crisis; or, What Bulls and Beauty Queens

Have to Do with Regionalism in Eastern Bolivia." *Journal of Latin American Anthropology* 11 (2): 351–79.

——. 2008. "Through Means Legal and Otherwise: The Bolivian Right Regroups." *NACLA: Report on the Americas* 41 (1): 20–25.

Gustafson, Bret, Sabino Manuel, and Lucy Gutiérrez. 1998. *Ñeereñü*. La Paz: UNICEF/APG/Ministerio de Educación Cultura y Deportes.

Hale, Charles R. 2002. "Does Multiculturalism Menace?: Governance, Cultural Rights, and the Politics of Identity in Guatemala." *Journal of Latin American Studies* 34 (2): 485–524.

——. 2006. *Más que un Indio: Racial Ambivalence and Neoliberal Multiculturalism in Guatemala*. Santa Fe: School of American Research Press.

Hall, Gillette, and Harry Patrinos. 2005. *Indigenous Peoples, Poverty, and Human Development in Latin America, 1994–2004*. Washington: World Bank.

Hall, Stuart. 1986. "On Post-Modernism and Articulation: An Interview with Stuart Hall, edited by L. Grossberg." *Journal of Communication Inquiry* 10 (2): 45–60.

"Harvard Helps Celebrate Bolivia's Success." 1997. *Harvard Gazette*, May 8.

Healy, Kevin. 1982. *Caciques y patrones: Una experiencia de desarrollo rural en el sud de Bolivia*. La Paz: CERES.

Herzfeld, Michael. 1993. *The Social Production of Indifference: Exploring the Symbolic Roots of Western Bureaucracy*. Chicago: University of Chicago Press.

Hirsch, Silvia. 1991. "Political Organization among the Izoceño Indians of Bolivia." PhD diss., University of California, Los Angeles.

Hirsch, Silvia, and Angelica Alberico. 1996. "El don de la palabra: Un acercamiento al arte verbal de los guaraní de Bolivia y Argentina." *Anthropos* 91:125–37.

Holston, James, ed. 1999. "Spaces of Insurgent Citizenship." In *Cities and Citizenship*, ed. James Holston, 155–76. Durham, N.C.: Duke University Press.

Hornberger, Nancy. 2000. "Bilingual Education Policy and Practice in the Andes: Ideological Paradox and Intercultural Possibility." *Anthropology and Education Quarterly* 31 (2): 173–201.

Huanca Soto, R. 2005. "La gestión intercultural del conocimiento." *Juguete Rabioso* (La Paz), February 5, 4–5.

Hunter, Ian. 1996. "Assembling the School." In *Foucault and Political Reason: Liberalism, Neo-liberalism, and Rationalities of Government*, ed. Andrew Barry, Thomas Osborne, and Nikolas Rose, 143–66. Chicago: University of Chicago Press.

Hyltenstam, Kenneth, and Birgitte Quick. 1996. "Misión de investigación a Bolivia en el área de educación primaria bilingüe." Education Division Documents no. 2, Sweedish International Development Agency (SIDA), Department of Democracy and Social Conditions (DESO), University of Stockholm Center for Studies of Bilingualism.

Inter-American Development Bank (IADB). 1994. "Education Reform Program" (931/SF-BO; ATN/SF-4718-BO), www.iadb.org/exr/doc98/apr/bo931e.htm.

——. 2004. *Country Program Evaluation (CPE): Bolivia, 1990–2002.* Washington: IADB.

"Intervención a bloqueos deja saldo de seis muertos." 2003. Bolpress, September 20, www.bolpress.com/art.php?Cod=2002072288.

Jackson, Jean. 1995. "Preserving Indian Culture: Shaman Schools and Ethno-Education in the Vaupes, Colombia." *Cultural Anthropology* 10 (3): 302–29.

Kaufman, Robert R., and Joan M. Nelson, eds. 2004. *Crucial Needs, Weak Incentives: Social Sector Reform, Democratization, and Globalization in Latin America.* Washington: Woodrow Wilson Center Press.

Kempff, Manfredo. 2005. "El ádulo a las masas." *La Razón* (La Paz), May 31.

Klein, Herbert S. 1992. *Bolivia: The Evolution of a Multi-ethnic Society.* New York: Oxford University Press.

Langer, Erick D. 1987. "Franciscan Missions and Chiriguano Workers: Colonization, Acculturation, and Indian Labor in Southeastern Bolivia." *Americas* 42 (1): 305–22.

——. 1989. "Mandeponay: Chiriguano Indian Chief on a Franciscan Mission." In *The Human Tradition in Latin America: The Nineteenth Century*, ed. Judith Ewell and William H. Beezley, 280–95. Wilmington, Del.: Scholarly Resources.

——. 1994a. "Caciques y poder en las misiones franciscanas entre los chiriguanos en la crisis de 1892." *Siglo XIX: Revista de Historia* 15:82–103.

——. 1994b. "Mission Land Tenure on the Southeastern Bolivian Frontier, 1845–1949." *Americas* 50 (3): 399–418.

——. 1995. "Missions and the Frontier Economy: The Case of the Franciscan Missions among the Chiriguanos, 1845–1930." In *The New Latin American Mission History*, ed. Erick D. Langer and Robert H. Jackson, 49–76. Lincoln: University of Nebraska Press.

——. 1997. "Foreign Cloth in the Lowland Frontier: Commerce and Consumption of Textiles in Bolivia, 1830–1930." In *The Allure of the Foreign: Imported Goods in Postcolonial Latin America*, ed. Benjamin Orlove, 93–112. Ann Arbor: University of Michigan Press.

Langer, Erick D., and Robert H. Jackson. 1990. "El liberalismo y el problema de la tierra en Bolivia (1825–1920)." *Siglo XIX: Revista de Historia* 5:9–32.

Larson, Brooke. 1999. "Andean Highland Peasants and the Trials of Nation-Making during the Nineteenth Century." In *Cambridge History of the Native Peoples of the Americas*, vol. 3, part 2, *South America*, ed. Frank Salomon and Stuart Schwartz, 558–703. Cambridge: Cambridge University Press.

——. 2003. "Capturing Indian Bodies, Hearths, and Minds: 'El Hogar Campesino' and Rural School Reform in Bolivia, 1920s–1940s." In *Proclaiming Revolution: Bolivia in Comparative Perspective*, ed. Merilee Grindle and Pilar Domingo, 183–212. Cambridge: David Rockefeller Center for Latin American Studies, Harvard University.

Latour, Bruno. 1993. *We Have Never Been Modern.* Trans. Catherine Porter. Cambridge, Mass.: Harvard University Press.

Lave, Jean, and Etienne Wenger. 1991. *Situated Learning: Legitimate Peripheral Participation.* New York: Cambridge University Press.

Layme, Felix. 2002. "The Path to Freedom: Towards Linguistic and Cultural Equity in Bolivia." In *Banners of Belonging: The Politics of Indigenous Identity in Bolivia and Guatemala*, ed. Staffan Löfving and Charlotta Widmark, 25–54. Uppsala: ULRICA.

"Las lenguas en la educación (documento de trabajo)." 1997. Presented at the Conference on EIB in the Chaco, Amazon, and Oriente. Santa Cruz. June 9.

Li, Tania Murray. 2007. *The Will to Improve: Governmentality, Development, and the Practice of Politics*. Durham, N.C.: Duke University Press.

Lienhard, Martín. 1992. *La voz y su huella: Escritura y conflicto étnico-cultural en América Latina, 1492–1988*. 3rd rev. and exp. ed. Lima: Editorial Horizonte.

López, Luis Enrique. 1994. "La educación intercultural bilingüe en Bolivia: Ámbito para el ejercicio de los derechos lingüísticos y culturales indígenas." *DATA: Revista del Instituto de Estudios Andinos y Amazónicos* 5:97–124.

———. 1996. "Reformas al estado y política lingüística en Bolivia." *Boletin Internacional de Lenguas y Culturas Amerindias* 2:3–14.

———. 1997. "To Guaranize: A Verb Actively Conjugated by the Bolivian Guaranis." In *Contributions to the Sociology of Language: Indigenous Literacy in the Americas*, ed. Nancy Hornberger, 321–53. The Hague: Mouton.

———. 2005. *De resquicios a boquerones: La educación intercultural bilingüe en Bolivia*. La Paz: PROEIB-Andes / Plural.

López, Luis Enrique, et al. 1990. "Diagnóstico sociolingüístico de la zona guaraní." Unpublished manuscript.

López, Luis Enrique, and Ingrid Jung. 1998. *Les lenguas en la educación bilingüe: El caso de Puno*. Lima: Sociedad Alemana de Cooperación Técnica (GTZ).

Lowrey, Kathleen. 2006. "Bolivia Multiétnico y Pluricultural, Ten Years Later: White Separatism in the Bolivian Lowlands." *Latin American and Caribbean Ethnic Studies* 1 (1): 63–84.

Luykx, Aurolyn. 1999. *The Citizen Factory: Schooling and Cultural Production in Bolivia*. Albany: State University of New York Press.

Malloy, James M. 1970. *Bolivia: The Uncompleted Revolution*. Pittsburgh: University of Pittsburgh Press.

Mamani Capchiri, Humberto. 1992. "La educación indígena en la visión de la sociedad criolla: 1920–1943." In *Educacion indígenal: ¿Ciudadanía o colonización?*, ed. Roberto Choque Canqui et al., 79–97. La Paz: THOA.

Mamdani, Mahmoud. 1996. *Citizen and Subject: Contemporary Africa and the Legacy of Late Colonialism*. Princeton: Princeton University Press.

Mannheim, Bruce. 1989. "La memoria y el olvido en la política lingüística colonial." *Lexis* 13 (1): 13–45.

Martarelli, Angelico. 1890. *El Colegio Franciscano de Potosí y sus misiones: Noticias históricas*. Potosí: Tipografía Italiana.

———. [1898?] 1918. *El Colegio Franciscano de Potosí y sus misiones y adición a la historia del colegio de propaganda fide de Potosí y sus misiones*. Potosí: Talleres Graficos Marinoni.

Martinez, Françoise. 1999. "¡Que nuestros indios se conviertan en pequeños suecos! La introducción de la gimnasia en las escuelas bolivianas." *Bulletin de l'Institut Français d'Études Andines* 28 (3): 361–86.

Maxwell, Judith M. 1996. "Prescriptive Grammar and Kaqchikel Revitalization." In *Maya Cultural Activism in Guatemala*, ed. Edward F. Fischer and R. McKenna Brown, 195–207. Austin: University of Texas Press.

McCarty, Teresa. 2002. *A Place to Be Navajo: Rough Rock and the Struggle for Self-Determination in Indigenous Schooling*. Mahwah, N.J.: Lawrence Erlbaum.

Meliá, Bartomeu. 1988. *Los Guaraní-Chiriguano: Ñande Reko: Nuestro modo de ser y bibliografía general comentada*. La Paz: CIPCA.

———. 1991. *El guaraní: Experiencia religiosa*. Asunción: CEADUC/Biblioteca Paraguaya de Antropología.

———. 1995. *Elogio de la lengua guaraní*. Asunción: CEPAG.

Melucci, Alberto. 1989. *Nomads of the Present: Social Movements and Individual Needs in Contemporary Society*. Ed. John Keane and Paul Mier. Philadelphia: Temple University Press.

Métraux, Alfred. 1930a. "Études sur la civilisation des indiens Chiriguano." *Revista del Instituto de Etnología de la Universidad Nacional de Tucumán* 1 (2): 295–493.

———. 1930b. "La sécularisation des missions franciscaines du Chaco Bolivien." *Anthropos* 25:315–16.

Mignolo, Walter D. 1995. *The Darker Side of the Renaissance: Literacy, Territoriality, and Colonization*. Ann Arbor: University of Michigan Press.

———. 2005. *The Idea of Latin America*. Malden, Mass.: Blackwell.

Ministerio de Educación y Cultura, Bolivia (MEC). 1970. *Política educativa, cultural y científica del gobierno revolucionario de Bolivia*. La Paz: Ministerio de Educación.

———. 2004. *La educación en Bolivia: Indicadores, cifras y resultados*. Vol 1. La Paz: Ministerio de Educación.

Ministerio de Educación y Culturas, Bolivia (MECs). 2006. "Ante proyecto: Nueva ley de educación 'Avelino Siñani y Elizardo Pérez'; Educación comunitaria descolonizadora." www.constituyentesoberana.org/info/?q=nueva-ley-educacion-avelino-perez.

Moore, Donald. 2005. *Suffering for Territory: Race, Place, and Power in Zimbabwe*. Durham, N.C.: Duke University Press.

Moore, Sally Falk. 1973. "Law and Social Change: The Semi-autonomous Social Field as an Appropriate Subject of Analysis." *Law and Society Review* 7 (4): 719–46.

———. 1987. "Explaining the Present: Theoretical Dilemmas in Processual Ethnography." *American Ethnologist* 14 (4): 737–46.

Muñoz, Hector. 1997. *De proyecto a política del estado: La educación intercultural bilingüe en Bolivia, 1993–1997*. Oaxaca: UNICEF/GTZ/UPN.

Nash, June. 1979. *We Eat the Mines and the Mines Eat Us: Dependency and Exploitation in Bolivian Tin Mines*. New York: Columbia University Press.

———. 1992. "Interpreting Social Movements: Bolivian Resistance to the Economic Conditions Imposed by the International Monetary Fund." *American Ethnologist* 19 (2): 275–93.

Nelson, Diane. 1999. *Finger in the Wound: Body Politics in Quincentennial Guatemala.* Berkeley: University of California Press.

Nelson, Joan M. 1999. *Reforming Health and Education: The World Bank, the IDB, and Complex Institutional Change.* Washington: Overseas Development Council.

Nino, Bernardino de. 1905. *El nene: Para las escuelas de los indios de la raza chiriguana en lengua chiriguana—castellana.* Potosí: Colegio de Propaganda Fide de Potosí.

———. 1912. *Etnografía chiriguana.* La Paz: Ismael Argote.

Nordenskiöld, Erland. [1910] 2002a. *La vida de los indios, el Gran Chaco (Sudamérica).* Trans. Gudrun Birk and Ángel García. Santa Cruz: APCOB.

———. [1924] 2002b. *Exploraciones y aventuras en Sudamérica.* Trans. Gudron Birk and Angel García. Santa Cruz (Bolivia): APCOB.

"Nuestros estudiantes serán trilingües." 2006. *La Prensa* (La Paz), January 31.

Nuñez, Javier. 2005. "Signed with an X: Methodology and Data Sources for Analyzing the Evolution of Literacy in Latin America and the Caribbean, 1900–1950." *Latin American Research Review* 40 (2): 117–36.

O'Connor, Francisco Burdett. [1895] 1977. *Un irlandés con Bolívar.* Caracas: El Cid.

Ong, Aihwa. 2006. *Neoliberalism as Exception: Mutations in Citizenship and Sovereignty.* Durham, N.C.: Duke University Press.

Ong, Walter. 2002. *Orality and Literacy: The Technologizing of the Word.* New York: Routledge.

Paley, Julia. 2001. *Marketing Democracy: Power and Social Movements in Post-dictatorship Chile.* Berkeley: University of California Press.

Patzi, Felix. 1999. "Etnofágia estatal: Modernas formas de violencia simbólica (una aproximación al análisis de la reforma educativa)." *Bulletin de l'Institut Français d'Études Andines* 28 (3): 535–59.

Paulson, Susan, and Pamela Calla. 2000. "Gender and Ethnicity in Bolivian Politics: Transformation or Paternalism?" *Journal of Latin American Anthropology* 5 (2): 112–49.

Pifarré, Francisco. 1989. *Historia de un pueblo.* La Paz: CIPCA.

Popkewitz, Thomas S. 2000. "Globalization/Regionalization, Knowledge, and the Educational Practices: Some Notes on Comparative Strategies for Educational Research." In *Educational Knowledge: Changing Relationships between the State, Civil Society, and the Educational Community,* ed. Popkewitz, 3–30. Albany: State University of New York Press.

Postero, Nancy. 2006. *Now We Are Citizens: Indigenous Politics in Postmulticultural Bolivia.* Stanford, Calif.: Stanford University Press.

Povinelli, Elizabeth. 2002. *The Cunning of Recognition: Indigenous Alterities and the Making of Australian Multiculturalism.* Durham, N.C.: Duke University Press.

Prada, Raul. 2007a. "Articulaciones de la complejidad: Estado plurinacional." Bolpress, March 2, www.bolpress.com/art.php?Cod=2007022803.

———. 2007b. "Encrucijadas de la asamblea constituyente," www.laconstituyente.org/ ?q=node/488, February 4.

Prudencio Lizón, Ramiro. 2004. "El racismo en Bolivia." *La Razón* (La Paz), June 8.

Psacharopoulos, G., and H. Patrinos. 1994. *Indigenous People and Poverty in Latin America: An Empirical Analysis*. Washington: World Bank.

"Los pueblos indígenas muestran el avance de la reforma educativa." 2001. *La Razón* (La Paz), October 13.

Quijano, Aníbal. 2000. "Coloniality of Power, Eurocentrism, and Latin America." *Nepantla: Views from the South* 1 (3): 533–80.

Rama, Ángel. 1996. *The Lettered City*. Ed. and trans. John Charles Chasteen. Durham, N.C.: Duke University Press.

Rappaport, Joanne. 1998. *The Politics of Memory: Native Historical Interpretation in the Colombian Andes*. Durham, N.C.: Duke University Press.

———. 2005. *Intercultural Utopias: Public Intellectuals, Cultural Experimentation, and Ethnic Dialogue in Colombia*. Durham, N.C.: Duke University Press.

Regalsky, Pablo, and Nina Laurie. 2007. "The School, Whose Place Is This? The Deep Structures of the Hidden Curriculum in Indigenous Education in Bolivia." Comparative Education 43 (2): 231–51.

Reimers, Fernando, ed. 2000. *Unequal Schools, Unequal Chances: The Challenges to Equal Opportunity in the Americas*. Cambridge, Mass.: Harvard University Press.

Riester, Jürgen. 1984. *Textos sagrados de los guaraníes en Bolivia: Una cacería en el Izozog*. La Paz: Amigos del Libro.

———. 1985. "CIDOB's Role in the Self-Determination of the Eastern Bolivian Indians." In *Native Peoples and Economic Development: Six Case Studies from Latin America*, ed. Theodore Macdonald Jr., 55–74. Cambridge, Mass.: Cultural Survival.

———, ed. 1995. *Chiriguano*. La Paz: APCOB and Amigos del Libro.

Riester, Jürgen, and Graciela Zolezzi, eds. 1989. *Identidad cultural y lengua: La experiencia guaraní en Bolivia*. La Paz: Ediciones Abya-Yala.

Rivera Cusicanqui, Silvia. 1984. *Oprimidos pero no vencidos: Luchas del campesinado aymara y qhechwa de Bolivia, 1900–1980*. La Paz: HISBOL/CSUTCB.

———. 1993. "La raíz: Colonizadores y colonizados." In *Violencias encubiertas en Bolivia*, vol. 1, *Cultura y política*, ed. X. Albó and R. Barrios, 27–39. La Paz: CIPCA.

Robles, Tomás, Bret Gustafson, and Fernando Rojas. 2002. *Necesidades básicas de aprendizaje: Area guaraní*. La Paz: Ministerio de Educación, Cultura y Deportes.

Rockwell, Elsie. 2005. "Indigenous Accounts of Dealing with Writing." In *Language, Literacy, and Power in Schooling*, ed. Teresa L. McCarty, 5–28. Mahwah, N.J.: L. Erlbaum.

Romano, Santiago, and Herman Cattunar, comps. 1916. *Diccionario Chiriguano-Español y Español-Chiriguano compilado teniendo a la vista diversos manuscitos de los antiguos Misioneros del Apostólico Colegio de Santa Mara de los Angeles de Tarija y partucularmente el Diccionario Chiriguano etimológico del R. P. Doroteo Giannecchini*. Tarija: Colegio Franciscano de Tarija.

Rubin, Jeffrey W. 2004. "Meanings and Mobilizations: A Cultural Politics Approach to Social Movements and States." *Latin American Research Review* 39 (3): 106–42.

Saavedra Weise, Agustín. 2003. "La nueva generación de analfabetos." *El Deber* (Santa Cruz), October 17.

Saignes, Thierry. 1990. *Ava y karai: Ensayos sobre la frontera chiriguano, siglos XVI–XX.* La Paz: HISBOL.

Sanabria Fernández, Hernando. 1972. *Apiaguaiqui Tumpa: Biografía del pueblo chiriguano y de su último caudillo.* La Paz: Amigos del Libro.

Sanjinés, Javier. 2004. *Mestizaje Upside-Down: Aesthetic Politics in Modern Bolivia.* Pittsburgh: University of Pittsburgh Press.

Sawyer, Suzana. 2004. *Crude Chronicles: Indigenous Politics, Multinational Oil, and Neoliberalism in Ecuador.* Durham, N.C.: Duke University Press.

Schaden, Egon. [1962] 1998. *Aspectos fundamentales de la cultura guaraní.* Asunción: Universidad Católica.

Schuchard, Barbara. 1995. "La conquista de la tierra: Relatos guaraníes de Bolivia acerca de experiencias guerreras y pacíficas recientes." In *Chiriguano,* ed. Jürgen Riester, 421–73. La Paz: APCOB and Amigos del Libro.

Scott, James. 1999. *Seeing Like a State: How Certain Schemes to Improve the Human Condition Have Failed.* New Haven: Yale University Press.

Shapiro, Judith. 1987. "From Tupã to the Land without Evil: The Christianization of Tupi-Guarani Cosmology." *American Ethnologist* 14 (1):126–39.

Shore, Cris, and Susan Wright. 1999. "Audit Culture and Anthropology: Neoliberalism in British Higher Education." *Journal of the Royal Anthropological Institute* 5 (4): 557–75.

Sikkink, Kathryn. 1997. "Development Ideas in Latin America: Paradigm Shift and the Economic Commission for Latin America." In *International Development and the Social Sciences: Essays on the History and Politics of Knowledge,* ed. Frederick Cooper and Randall Packard, 228–58. Berkeley: University of California Press.

Sillitoe, Paul. 1993. "The Development of Indigenous Knowledge: A New Applied Anthropology." *Current Anthropology* 39 (2): 223–52.

Silverstein, Michael. 1998. "Contemporary Transformations of Local Linguistic Communities." *Annual Review of Anthropology* 27:401–26.

Simón, Brigitte, et al. 1980. *I Sold Myself, I Was Bought: A Socio-economic Analysis Based on Interviews with Sugar-Cane Harvesters in Santa Cruz de la Sierra, Bolivia.* Copenhagen: IWGIA.

Slater, David. 1995. "Democracy, Decentralization, and State Power: The Politics of the Regional in Chile and Bolivia." *Yearbook, Conference of Latin Americanist Geographers* 21:49–65.

Soares, Sergei, et al. 2005. "Impact Evaluation of Intercultural Bilingual Education in Bolivia." Unpublished manuscript.

Solíz Rada, Andrés. 2007. "A contra ruta." *Bolpress,* September 7, www.bolpress.com/art.php?Cod=2007070901.

Stephen, Lynn. 1997. "Redefined Nationalism in Building a Movement for Indigenous Autonomy in Southern Mexico." *Journal of Latin American Anthropology* 3 (1): 72–101.

Stephenson, Marcia. 1999. *Gender and Modernity in Andean Bolivia.* Austin: University of Texas Press.

——. 2002. "Forging an Indigenous Counterpublic Sphere: The Taller de Historia Andina in Bolivia." *Latin American Research Review* 37 (2): 99–118.

Stepputat, Finn. 2005. "Violence, Sovereignty, and Citizenship in Postcolonial Peru." In *Sovereign Bodies: Citizens, Migrants, and States in the Postcolonial World,* ed. Thomas Blom Hansen and Stepputat, 61–81. Princeton: Princeton University Press.

Stoll, David. 1983. *Fishers of Men or Founders of Empire? The Wycliffe Bible Translators in Latin America.* London: Zed.

Strathern, Marilyn. 1996. "Cutting the Network." *Journal of the Royal Anthropological Institute* 2 (3): 517–35.

Stromquist, Nelly. 2002. *Education in a Globalized World: The Connectivity of Economic Power, Technology, and Knowledge.* Lanham, Md.: Rowman and Littlefield.

Swedish International Development Agency (SIDA). 2000. *Education for All—a Human Right.* Stockholm: SIDA.

Taussig, Michael. 1980. *The Devil and Commodity Fetishism in Latin America.* Chapel Hill: University of North Carolina Press.

——. 1992. *Mimesis and Alterity: A Particular History of the Senses.* New York: Routledge.

Torres, Carlos Alberto. 1991. "A Critical Review of the Education for All (EFA) Background Documents." In *Perspectives on Education for All,* 1–20. Ottawa: International Development Research Centre.

——. 1995. "Fictional Dialogues on Teachers, Politics, and Power in Latin America." In *The Politics of Educators' Work and Lives,* ed. Mark B. Ginsburg, 133–68. New York: Garland.

——. 2000. "Public Education, Teachers' Organizations, and the State in Latin America." In *Educational Knowledge: Changing Relationships between the State, Civil Society, and the Educational Community,* ed. Thomas S. Popkewitz, 83–110. Albany: State University of New York Press.

Trapnell, Lucy. 2003. "Some Key Issues in Intercultural Bilingual Education Teacher Training Programmes—as Seen from a Teacher Training Programme in the Peruvian Amazon Basin." *Comparative Education Review* 39 (2): 165–83.

Tsing, Anna Lowenhaupt. 2005. *Friction: An Ethnography of Global Connection.* Princeton: Princeton University Press.

Turner, Terence. 1991. "Representing, Resisting, Rethinking: Historical Transformations of Kayapo Culture and Anthropological Consciousness." In *Colonial Situations: Essays on the Contextualization of Ethnographic Knowledge,* ed. George Stocking, 285–313. Madison: University of Wisconsin Press.

United Nations Development Program (UNDP). 2005. *La economía más allá del gas.* La Paz: UNDP.

Unzueta, Fernando. 2000. "Periódicos y formación nacional: Bolivia en sus primeros años." *Latin American Research Review* 35 (2): 35–72.

Urioste, Miguel. 1982. "Educación popular en el altiplano boliviano: El programa ECORA." *América Indígena* 42 (2): 253–68.

Van Cott, Donna Lee. 2000. *The Friendly Liquidation of the Past: The Politics of Diversity in Latin America*. Pittsburgh: University of Pittsburgh Press.

———. 2005. *From Movements to Parties in Latin America: The Evolution of Ethnic Politics*. Cambridge: Cambridge University Press.

Véliz, José Domingo. 1999. *Ñeemoesakaa*. La Paz: UNICEF/Ministerio de Educación, Cultura y Deportes.

Ventiades, Nancy, and Augusto Jauregui, eds. 1994. *Tataendi: El fuego que nunca se apaga; Campaña de alfabetización en Guaraní*. Santa Cruz: UNICEF/PROCESO/TEKO/APG.

Viveiros de Castro, Eduardo. 1992. *From the Enemy's Point of View: Humanity and Divinity in an Amazonian Society*. Chicago: University of Chicago Press.

Walsh, Catherine. 2005. "(Re)pansamiento crítico y (de)colonialidad." In *Pensamento crítico y matriz (de)colonial*, ed. Catherine Walsh, 13–35. Quito: Abya-Yala.

Warren, Kay. 1998. *Indigenous Movements and Their Critics: Pan-Maya Activism in Guatemala*. Princeton: Princeton University Press.

Warren, Kay, and Jean Jackson, eds. 2002. *Indigenous Movements, Self-Representation, and the State in Latin America*. Austin: University of Texas Press.

Weber, Max. 1978. *Economy and Society*. Ed. Guenter Roth and Claus Wittich. Berkeley: University of California Press.

Whitman, Gordon. 2004. *Red Pen, Blue Pen: The Impact of Internationally-Financed Education Reform on Classroom Practice in Ecuador*. Quito: FLACSO.

Willis, Paul. 1977. *Learning to Labor: How Working Class Kids Get Working Class Jobs*. New York: Columbia University Press.

Wilson, Fiona. 2001. "In the Name of the State: Schools and Teachers in an Andean Province." In *States of Imagination: Ethnographic Explorations of the Postcolonial State*, ed. Thomas Blom Hansen and Finn Stepputat, 313–44. Durham, N.C.: Duke University Press.

World Bank. 1995. *Priorities and Strategies in Education: A World Bank Review*. Washington: World Bank.

———. 1998a. "Report No. 17912-BO: Project Appraisal Document on a Proposed Credit to Bolivia for an Education Quality and Equity Strengthening Project." Human and Social Development Group (LCSHD), Country Managing Unit—LCC6C, Latin America and the Caribbean Region. Mimeo.

———. 1998b. "Report of Evaluation Mission—Bolivian Educational Reform." Mimeo.

World Conference on Education for All (WCEFA). 1992. *Catalogue of Documents*. Paris: UNESCO.

Yandura, Ángel, ed. 1996. *Iyambae: Persona sin dueño; Testimonios de la alfabetización con los guaraní de Chuquisaca*. La Paz: UNICEF.

Yashar, Deborah J. 2005. *Contesting Citizenship in Latin America: The Rise of Indigenous Movements and the Postliberal Challenge.* Cambridge: Cambridge University Press.

Zulawski, Ann. 2007. *Unequal Cures: Public Health and Political Change in Bolivia, 1900–1950.* Durham, N.C.: Duke University Press.

Index

Guarani terms and phrases appear in italics.
Italicized page references refer to
illustrations.

Arnold, Denise, 201, 299n.2 (Shifting States)
articulation: of complexity, 279; contingent, 161; Hall on, 286n.18; indigenous knowledge and, 128–30; indigenous movements and, 113; networked, 24–25, 151–65, 167–69, 286n.18; props for, 186, 296n.9
asamblea, 191
Asamblea del Pueblo Guarani (Assembly of the Guarani People). *See* APG
assimilation, 17, 163–64
authenticity, 150, 197–98, 297n.6
authority: in education, 198–99; indigenous knowledge and, 199, 297n.6; of scribes, 89–90, 92–93
autonomy: of APG, 282, 290n.13; vs. decolonization, 269–78; regionalism and, 273, 282
Ava (Bolivia), xix
Avelino Siñani and Elizardo Pérez Law, 252, 269–73, 300n.6
Ayemotï, Juan, 34–37, 47, 50
Aymara: literacy demanded by, 44; political mobilizations by, 44, 186–88; population of, 12; poverty/racism/marginality suffered by, 7, 16 (table); role in indigenous movements, 6–8, 9; Spanish-speaking abilities of, 277; urban vs. rural, 9–10. *See also* Warisata Bilingual Intercultural Teacher Training Institute

Baha'i, 245, 299n.16
Bánzer, Hugo, 55, 81, 162, 179–81, 209, 235
Barrientos, José, 69–70
Barrientos, René, 78, 290n.11
Bartlett, Lesley, 151
"Basic Education Needs" social science research, 138–41, 168
beauty pageants, 298n.12

Bedregal, Guillermo, 173–74, 176
Benhabib, Seyla, 286n.9
bilingual education: early projects/demands for, 154, 157–58, 183; expansion of, 92, 136–38; indigenous rights to, 15, 295n.16; vs. monolingual, 1; neoliberal interculturalism and, 165–69; in schools, 121–25, *123*. *See also* education reform; EIB
bilingualism: and indigeneity/poverty/literacy, 16 (table) (*see also under* poverty); language maintenance and, 173; levels of, 57; textbooks and, 84–89, 178, 196–205, 209, 220, 261, 297n.1 (Interlude). *See also* code switching; EIB; language
blockades, 234–35, 245, 249, 264
"bloody September" (La Paz, 2000), 186
Blot, Richard, 177
Bolívar, Simón, 101
Bolivia: civil conflict as intensifying in, 282; as a colonial state, 33, 286n.2; colonial vision for, modern, 260; constitution of, 255, 267, *267*, 269, 272, 281–82; decentralization of, 185–86, 294n.11; GDPs (gross domestic products) of, 6; independence wars with Spain, 40; indigenous population of, 7, 285n.7; map of, *2*; skilled vs. unskilled workers in, 279
Bonfil Batalla, Guillermo, 154
Bono, 294n.12
Bourdieu, Pierre, 296n.14
Brazil, 114, 229
Bruno, Petrona, 266–67

Cadogan, León, 114
Cajías, Magdalena, 273
Camargo, Enrique (Guarani scribe), 69–70, 87–88, 199–202, 204, 222–25, 232, 237, 257, 289n.4

liberalism in, 3–4, 138, 146, 148, 150, 243; opposition to, 3–4; public vs. private schools, 52–53; reformists vs. teachers, 189–96; research on, 3–4; rural vs. urban schools, 52–53; secularization, 270, 300n.6; statistical culture of, 149, 294n.4; structural adjustment and, 1, 3, 147, 168; Swedish curriculum, 43; teacher opposition to, 138, 141, 146, 168, 189–96; World Bank support of, 136–39, 149, 166, 295n.15

EIB (Bilingual Intercultural Education), 27, 143–45, 149–162, 164–65, 169; activist networks for, 14, 16–17, 163; Andean support of, 58; anthropological engagement and, 129–30; APG support of, 11, 13, 231; assessment of, 256–58; as decolonization, 271–72; defense of, 264–65, 269; definition of, 1, 14–17; dismantling of, 261–64; as disruptive containment, 177–78, 203–4; donor aid for, 14, 65–66, 112, 138, 146, 148, 166–67, 261; evaluations of, 256–58; modules (schoolbooks), 197–202, 209, 220, 297n.1 (Interlude); NGOs and, 128, 293n.14; vs. North American counterparts, 14–15; officialization of, 14, 150–51, 168, 201, 263; opposition to, 1–3, 14–15, 90–91, 126, 146–47, 168, 209, 259–60, 291nn.18–19; orality-literacy transition via, 76; origins/goals of, 1–3, 64–66, 146–47; poverty and, 15–16, 279; Spanish textbooks and, 209, 297n.1 (Interlude); transformative effects of, 125–27, 293n.13; World Bank on, 167, 203. See also scribes
epistemic contemporaries, 286n.9
epistemic normalization/insurgence, 272
epistemic rights, 285n.5
Espinal, Luis, 59, 179
ETARE (Technical Support Team for Educational Reform), 136–38, 168, 174, 178, 180–81
ethnography: articulations and, 1–29; of coloniality/inequality/schooling, 4–5, 17–19; engagement and, 28–29; indigenous knowledge and, 116–17, 292–93n.10; of indigenous movements and reformist networks, 3, 12–17; methods of, 11, 19–28; of schools, 19–25. See also anthropology
Eurocentrism, 43–44, 183

Fabian, Johannes, 286n.9
Farah, Ivonne, 280
Ferguson, James, 92
Foucault, Michel, 20, 190, 297n.17
Franciscans. See education, mission; missions
Fraser, Nancy, 86
free-market economics, 162. See also neoliberalism
Freire, Paulo, 10, 55, 154, 290n.8; on generative words, 155–56; Pedagogy of the Oppressed, 75
Friedman, Milton, 162

Ganson, Barbara, 46
García, María Elena, 112–13
García Linera, Alvaro, 299–300n.4
gas industry, 264, 281
Gas War (2003), 249, 252
Gates, Bill, 195–96
Gellner, Ernest, 151, 202–3
generative words, 155–56
Gentili, Pablo, 299n.15
German Technical Aid Agency. See GTZ
Giannecchini, Doroteo, 49, 225; Chiriguano-Spanish Dictionary, 72
Gill, Lesley, 161
Goni. See Sánchez de Lozada, Gonzalo
governmentality, 20–24, 27
Gramsci, Antonio, 67, 91

indigenous movements, 1–2, 4; Andean, 12; APG involvement in, 65; articulations and, 113; Aymara, 6–8, 9; communitarian identities/politics and, 112–13; EIB as resurgence, 65–69, 128, 157 (see also EIB); Guarani, 7–8; lowland, 182, 186, 234, 296n.6; national mobilization, 264–66; press coverage of, 65, 289n.1; Quechua, 6–8; reformist networks and, 3, 12–17 (see also education reform); scribes' role in, 67–77; unions and, 188–89. See also APG

indigenous resurgence, 215–45; classroom changes due to reform and, 216–21; fears of, 212–13, 215, 227, 229; hunger strike, 216, 230–45, *238*; Kuruyukɨ commemoration and, 216, 221–29, *228*, 243; overview of, 215–16

individualization, 203–4, 297n.17

inequality: epistemic, 5, 285n.5; ethnographic articulations and, 4–5, 17–19; ethnographic vs. quantitative study of, 285n.3; legitimation of, 4; linguistic, 5

Inkawasi range, 61

INS (Institutos Normales Superiores), 244

INSPOC (Pluriethnic Superior Teachers' Institute of the Bolivian East and Chaco; Camiri), 244–45, 248, 262–63

intellectuals: indigenous, 53, 67–68, 86, 146–47, 152–53, 157, 204, 248 (see also scribes); technocratic, 152

Inter-American Development Bank. See IADB

interculturalism: vs. assimilation, 163–64; bilingual (see EIB); decolonization and, 27–28, 271; governmentality and, 22–24, 27; grassroots, 22–23; history of, 7; intraculturalism and, 270–71; meanings of, 7, 22, 80, 163; vs. multiculturalism, 163; neoliberalism and, 6–8, 11, 22, 27, 163–69, 176–77, 278,

281; official/managerial, 22–23, 27; political practice and, 205

International Labor Organization Convention (ILO) 169 (indigenous rights), 15, 159

ipayes (curers or shamans), 34, 70, 74, 287n.5

Ipiña, Enrique, 157, 159, 165, 168

Isoso (Bolivia), xix, 12–13, 49, 127, 155, 217–18, 232, 301

Itavera (Bolivia): Camiri–Itavera travel, 95–100; community structure/ties in, 110; corn in, 121–22, 262; EIB in, 105–7, 111–12, 262; geography/history of, 115–19; Guarani language's importance to sociality in, 114–18; Guarani school in, 121–25, *123*; houses/layout of, 108–9; masculinity in, 120; NGO aid for, 262; visiting/knowing in, 127–31

Itɨka Guasu (Simba region), 102, 104–5

Ivo (Bolivia), 33

Jackson, Jean, 68

Jolibert, Josette, 290n.8

Jomtien World Conference on Education for All (Thailand, 1990), 135–36, 138–39, 159, 166–68, 180

juvicha (leader), 110

karai ipɨte rupi (Guarani karai their-midst through), 78–79

Katari, Tupak (Julián Apaza), 40, 188, 196, 247, 270

Katarista movement, 146, 155, 168, 172, 301–2

kereɨmba (Guarani warriors), 66

knowledge: bureaucratization of, 20–21; new geopolitics of, 258–66; state control of, 202–4; state sovereignty over, 151–52; universal, 162. See also *arakuaa*; indigenous knowledge; *yemboe*

kolla (Andean Bolivians), xx

165–66, 171, 179–82, 186, 293n.14, 296n.6

missions: bilingualism and, 153; education by, 45–51; evangelizing by, 45–46; Franciscan, 45–51; Guarani dependence on, 45–46; Jesuit, 45; labor control via, 47; literacy and, 49–50, 153, 287nn.11–12; Protestant, 153; secularization and, 51, 287n.13

mística (mystique), 184, 243, 296n.7, 298–99n.14

mita (forced Indian labor), 101

MNR (Nationalist Revolutionary Movement): decline of, 186; on education, 165, 173; the Kataristas and, 172; reform, 162; reformism of, 183; revolution led by, 51–53; rightward shift by, 180

Moore, Sally, 240

Morales, Evo: on education, 258, 267, 270; educational background of, 299n.4; election of, 5, 14, 252–54; at Kuruyukɨ commemorations, 227; rise of, 27; support for, 268. *See also* MAS

movements: "camba," 292n.2; as democratizing, 281; Katarista, 146, 155, 168, 172, 301–2; middle-class, radical (1940s), 182–83; mid-twentieth-century, 182–83; NGOs' role in, 105, 111–12; state transformation as a goal of, 278–79; Tüpaist, 34. *See also* EIB; indigenous movements

Movimiento al Socialismo (Movement to Socialism). *See* MAS

multiculturalism, 168, 176. *See also* interculturalism

ñande ru (our father; male ancestors), 80, 290n.12

ñande vae (our kind), 125

Nash, June, 291n.3

National Education Congress (2006), 269, 271–72

nationalism, 122–24, 255–56, 268, 274. *See also* nation building

Nationalist Democratic Action. *See* ADN

Nationalist Revolutionary Movement. *See* MNR

nation building, 33–60; democracy and, 19, 279; histories and, overview of, 39–40; the Kuruyukɨ massacre and, 33–34, 36–39, 59–60, 286n.4; military discipline in schools, 54–58, 288n.18; mission schooling and, 44–51; overview of, 33–39; race and nation in the Andes, 40–44; redistribution and, 255–56; revolution's effects on, 26, 51–54

Native American languages, 15

Nebrija, Antonio, 261

Nelson, Diane, 164

Nelson, Joan, 295n.17

neoliberalism: centralization of education and, 151–52, 294n.7; collapse of, 27, 279; in education reform, 3–4, 138, 146, 148, 150, 243; effects of, 5–6, 285n.6; elite rule and, 176–77; interculturalism and, 6–8, 11, 22, 27, 163–69, 176–77, 278, 281; as a rationality of power, 22; rise of, 161–62; structural adjustment and, 5–6, 158, 285n.6; technocratic elites and, 161–62, 294n.11; vs. unions, 196; violence of, 162, 294n.13; welfare/foreign aid's support of, 6, 285n.6

networks: EIB and, 14, 16–17, 163; NGO, 105, 111; props, 186, 296n.9; reformist, 3, 12–17; submerged, 249, 299n.2 (Interlude). *See also* articulation, networked

NGOs (nongovernmental organizations): APG dependence on, 282, 290n.13; development agendas of, 137; vs. EIB, 128, 293n.14; interculturalism embraced by, 6; networks, 105, 111. *See also specific organizations*

Bret Gustafson is an assistant professor of anthropology at Washington University, Saint Louis.

Library of Congress Cataloging-in-Publication Data
Gustafson, Bret Darin, 1968–
New languages of the state : indigenous resurgence and the politics of knowledge in Bolivia / Bret Gustafson.
p. cm. — (Narrating native histories)
Includes bibliographical references and index.
ISBN 978-0-8223-4529-9 (cloth : alk. paper)
ISBN 978-0-8223-4546-6 (pbk. : alk. paper)
1. Education, Bilingual—Bolivia. 2. Indigenous peoples—Education—Bolivia.
3. Guarani Indians—Education—Bolivia. 4. Education—Social aspects—Bolivia.
5. Ethnology—Bolivia. 6. Indigenous peoples—Bolivia—Social conditions. I. Title.
II. Series: Narrating native histories.
LC3735.B5G87 2009
370.117'50984—dc22   2009005701